PUBLIC SCIENCE POLICY AND ADMINISTRATION

Edited by ALBERT H. ROSENTHAL

Q
127
U6
R62

UNIVERSITY OF NEW MEXICO PRESS
Albuquerque

© 1973 by the University of New Mexico Press. All rights reserved.
Manufactured in the United States of America.

Library of Congress Catalog Card No. 73-129809.
International Standard Book Number 0-8263-0272-6.

First Edition

PUBLIC SCIENCE POLICY AND ADMINISTRATION

Foreword

The publication of this book as part of the activity of the Program for Advanced Study in Public Science Policy and Administration is of personal as well as institutional gratification to me. Having served for twenty years on the staff of the Institute of Public Administration at the University of Michigan before coming to the University of New Mexico, I recognize the importance of and need for a significant university contribution to the improvement of the public service. In my inaugural address, I set this as a major goal during my tenure as President of the University of New Mexico. The development of competence and the publication of a study in science policy and administration by the University of New Mexico are particularly appropriate because of the large number of major public and private science agencies located in this area.

Two purposes were stated in establishing the Program for Advanced Study in Public Science Policy and Administration, as part of the Division of Public Administration at the University of New Mexico: (1) "To provide graduate-level interdisciplinary course work and research in Public Administration-Science leading to an advanced degree," and (2) "To add to, and make readily available, the body of knowledge concerned with the formulation and administration of public policy in the field of science." The program is now entering its fifth year of academic work, seeking to improve the effectiveness of science-administrators. The publication of this book significantly contributes toward the accomplishment of the second of our stated objectives.

I extend my congratulations and appreciation to the editor, to the authors who contributed chapters, and to the National Aeronautics and Space Administration, which provided financial support for the establishment of the University of New Mexico program and for the publication of this book.

I am pleased that this important work was conceived, developed, and edited by a faculty member at our University and published by the University of New Mexico Press.

Ferrel Heady, President
The University of New Mexico

Preface

A great many people and large amounts of money are involved in the development of public policy in science and technology and the administration of programs in this field. During the past two decades, growth has been so rapid that the practice has far outstripped education and research concerning the process itself. For some time the need has existed for an introductory study providing an overview of the field. In this book we seek to provide approaches to study and research in this area, as well as to emphasize important subareas that have been frequently overlooked in the literature.

I am greatly indebted to the authors of the following chapters. Despite busy schedules, they undertook to prepare statements in the areas of their special competence. It is a truism in public administration that many of the people who know the most about particular facets of this field are, because of the responsible posts they hold, usually too busy to write. But wisdom based on the actual experiences of top-level practitioners is required to give substance to theoretical and philosophic study. The contributors to this volume represent both practice and theory.

We look at this study as a beginning and hope that it will stimulate other efforts in the same direction. The topic of each chapter deserves a complete study of its own.

Sincere thanks are expressed to Dr. Reuben Gustavson, who provided encouragement and wise counsel in the establishment of the University of New Mexico Public Science Program and the undertaking of this book. A great deal of assistance in developing the program was provided by the Regional Advisory Committee in Public Science Policy and Administration, composed of the directors and deputy directors of the major science agencies in the region. Particular thanks are due Ray Powell, Vice President, Sandia Laboratories and Chairman, New Mexico State Personnel Board and James McCraw, recently retired as Deputy Manager, Albuquerque Operations, Atomic Energy Commission. I would like to thank the officials of the National Aeronautics and Space Administration, particularly James Webb, Frank Smith, and Rich Stephens, who during their tenure in key posts in NASA sponsored programs that helped to establish the Public Science Policy and Administration

Program at the University of New Mexico and at other universities. Interest in improving the competence of science-administrators has been carried forward by Dee Wyatt, Frank Hansing, and Jerry Morris, presently with NASA, and by Clarence Ohlke and Frank Hersman of the National Science Foundation. Special appreciation is due N. J. Oganovic, previously Executive Director of the U.S. Civil Service Commission, and his successor, Bernard Rosen. Jack Young, now with the Office of Management and Budget, has kept interest in his field alive.

To Betty Wollerman, who typed sections of the manuscript, my thanks.

Albert H. Rosenthal

Contents

Foreword   v

Preface   vii

Figures and Tables   xiii

1 Approaches to Public Science Policy and Administration   1
    Albert H. Rosenthal
- History   2
- Organization   5
- Law and Politics   10
- Personnel   12
- Finance   14
- Policy Formulation   18
- Science Leadership for Tomorrow   27
- New Frontiers   29

2 Human Resources For Science Management: Identification and Development of Administrative Talent   32
    Lynton K. Caldwell
- Public Goals and Administrative Roles   33
- Context of the Technological Society   37
- Tasks of Technoscientific Administrators   41
- Methods of Developing Administrative Talent   46
- Administrative Development—An Integrated and Continuing Process   52
- Essence of Administrative Development—Enlargement of Opportunity for Self-Development   52
- Environment of Administrative Development   53

Information Content of Administrative Development Programs   55
Policy Basis for Administrative Development   56
Model Curriculum   60

3 Human Resources for Science Administration: Can Quality Be Enhanced?   64
Nicholas J. Oganovic and Harold H. Leich

Introduction   64
Importance of Managerial Skill   65
Duties of the Technical Manager   66
Characteristics of the Science Manager   69
Should the Technical Manager Have a Technical Background?   72
Intake of Juniors with Management Potential   77
The Dual Ladder System   78
First Rungs Up the Managerial Ladder   82
Preparing an Employee for His First Managerial Duties   83
How Can the Technological Manager Increase His Effectiveness?   85
Rotational Assignments   87
Should the Technological Manager Continue His Own Research?   88
The Environment for Creativity   89
Report of a Special Study of Scientists and Engineers   91
Need for Better Personnel Data on Science Manpower   95
Conclusion   97
Appendix: Results of Questionnaire   99

4 Guiding Work Relationships among Scientific, Engineering, and Administrative Professionals   109
Wesley L. Hjornevik

Nature of the Problem   109
Institutional Background   110
Approach to Problem   115
MSC Special Problems   118
Basic Organizational Development   120
Other Developmental Approaches   126
Current Investigations   140

5 Organizational Dynamics: Building Effective R & D Departments   143
Rensis Likert

Creative Tensions   144
Other Demands on R & D Administration   147
Requirements which R & D Administration Should Meet   148
A More Effective Management System   149
Potential Value of System 4 for R & D Administration   154
System 4 Permits Two Bosses   156
Effective Lateral Coordination   159

6 Basic Concepts of Operational Control   160
C. West Churchman

Summary and Purpose   160
Meaning of Control   160
Control in Science   161
Sociotechnical Systems   162
Bounded versus Open Control   170
Techniques of Bounded Control   170
A Method of Open Control: Dialectics   172
Control and Progress   174
Control: A Dirty Word   175

7 Fiscal and Management Dilemmas in Science Administration   177
Elmer B. Staats and William D. Carey

Analytic Methodology   178
Research and/or Development?   184
Budget Expectations   186
The Policy Process   187
The Problem of "Hot Pursuit"   189
Government, Research, and Campus   190
Social Costs   193
Evaluation in Research   194
Conclusion   199

8 Task Setting and Goal Achievement in Technoscientific Missions 200
C. West Churchman
Introduction 200
Structural Considerations 204
Dynamic Considerations 204
Top Management's Goals 205
Definition of the Task Area 207
Inventing New Tasks 207
Evaluating Projects 208
Designing the Research Task 209
Assessing the Environment 211
Providing Top Management with Budgetary Guides 212
Detecting Changes in the Organizational Goals and Objectives 213
Control 214
Supports of the Division Manager 218
The View from the Bottom 223

9 Developments in Government Policies toward Science and Technology 227
Harold Orlans
Academic Science 228
Civilian Technology 237

10 Reflections on Public Science Policy and Administration in a Troubled Milieu 254
Dwight Waldo
An Environment of Critical Problems, Quickening Change, and Increasing Turbulence 255
An Environment of Intellectual-Social Change 258
Predictions and Speculations 262
Policy Making and Administration 269
The Technoscience Administrator 271

References and Notes 273

Bibliography 295

Index 315

Figures and Tables

Figures

1. NASA Organizational Chart (May 1968)	111
2. MSC Organizational Chart (January 1969)	122
3. Example of Subordinate Serving as Linking Pin for Horizontal Coordination	157

Tables

1. Federal R & D Expenditures under the Alternative Functional Classification System ($ million)	16
2. Duties Listed in 209 Position Descriptions of Federal Science and Engineering Managers (Grades GS 16-18 and Equivalent)	68
3. Educational Backgrounds of Science Administrators	71
4. Educational Backgrounds of Science Directors	72
5. Questionnaire Results Regarding Salary Differences	99
6. Questionnaire Results Regarding Highest Degree Attained	99
7. Questionnaire Results Regarding Year Highest Degree Attained	100
8. Questionnaire Results Regarding Professional Field of Highest Degree	100
9. Questionnaire Results Regarding Plan for Selecting and Training Technological Administrators	101
10. Questionnaire Results Regarding Plan for Advancing Individual Workers to Higher Levels without Administrative Duties	101
11. Questionnaire Results Regarding Importance of "Two-Track" System	102
12. Questionnaire Results Regarding Extent to Which Organization Provides for a Two-Track System	102

13. Questionnaire Results Regarding Ways of Selecting and Training Technological Administrators — 103
14. Questionnaire Results Regarding Desirability of Manager Performing Research — 104
15. Questionnaire Results Regarding Research Time Available (Administrators Only) — 104
16. Questionnaire Results Regarding Kinds of Professional Employees Supervised (Administrators Only) — 105
17. Questionnaire Results Regarding First Administrative Assignment (Administrators Only) — 105
18. Questionnaire Results Regarding Advancement to Present Level (Administrators Only) — 106
19. Questionnaire Results Regarding Training Received (Administrators Only) — 106
20. Questionnaire Results Regarding Courses of Value (Administrators Only) — 107
21. Questionnaire Results Regarding Preference for Administrative versus Individual Professional Work (Individuals Only) — 108
22. MSC Manpower Profile — 112
23. Characteristics of MSC Professionals — 112
24. ALSEP Roles — 134
25. Eight Creative Tensions — 146
26. Profile of Organizational Characteristics — 152–53

ABOUT THE AUTHORS

Albert H. Rosenthal. University of Denver, B.A.; University of Minnesota, M.A.; Harvard University, Littauer Fellow, PhD. He has served as Professor and Director, Graduate School of Public Administration, University of Denver; Regional Director, DHEW, Denver, 1951-64; Professor of Public Administration, University of Minnesota; and, since 1967, Director of the Program for Advanced Study in Public Science Policy and Administration and Professor and Director of the Division of Public Administration, University of New Mexico. He was selected by the United Nations to advise in setting up a School of Public Administration in Dublin, Ireland and served also as Visiting Professor at Trinity College, Dublin. He served as Head, Office of the Public Understanding of Science, the National Science Foundation, 1970-71. He is a recipient of The Rockefeller Public Service Award; the Denver Federal Civic Award; the HEW Superior Service Award, and the New Mexico Distinguished Public Service Award (1971). He is the author of *Administrative Problems in the Establishment of UNESCO, The Social Programs of Sweden,* and numerous articles. He serves as a consultant to several federal and state agencies.

Lynton K. Caldwell. Arthur F. Bentley Professor of Political Science at Indiana University. Holding graduate degrees from Harvard University and the University of Chicago, he has served on the faculties of Syracuse University, the University of Chicago, and the University of California, Berkeley. He was appointed by President Nixon to the National Commission on Materials Policy; is a Fellow of the American Association for the Advancement of Sciences; is a Guest Scholar at the Smithsonian Institution Woodrow Wilson International Center for Scholars; is a member of the National Academy of Public Administration; is a trustee of the Institution of Ecology and a member of the Committee on International Environmental Programs of the National Academy of Sciences. He serves on a number of scientific and governmental boards, including the Environmental Advisory Board to the U.S. Corps Atmospheric Administration. He has published five books and numerous articles and monographs.

Nicholas J. Oganovic. St. Cloud State Teachers' College, B.E.; University of Minnesota, M.A. During a thirty-year career in the federal government, he held positions as Regional Director of the U.S. Civil Service Commission in St. Paul and Denver. From 1960 to 1971, he served as Deputy Director and Executive Director of the Civil Service Commission in Washington, D.C. Upon his retirement from government, he was appointed Professor of Administration, Minnesota Metropolitan State College, St. Paul. He currently serves as Consultant to the President, Minnesota Metropolitan State College, and Professor of Administration at Mankato State College. Through the years, he initiated innovations in intergovernmental affairs, equal opportunity, labor-management relations, and rehabilitation. He has been a consultant on education programs to the U.S. Office of Education, the Veterans Administration, and the Bureau of Indian Affairs. He received the President's Award for Distinguished Service in 1962, as well as the Civil Service Commission's Award for Distinguished Service, the St. Cloud State College Alumni Award, and the AMVET's Silver Helmet Award. He is a member of the President's Committee on the Employment of the Handicapped and is active in numerous federal, state, education, and community councils.

Harold H. Leich. Dartmouth College, A.B., American University, M.A. He served in the U.S. Civil Service Commission as Chief of the Standards Division and Chief of the Policy Development Division; he retired in 1972. He represented the Commission on the Board of Examiners for the Foreign Service and the Committee on Federal Laboratories, and served on the task force that established the new Environmental Protection Agency. In 1963, he received the Commissioners' Award for Distinguished Service. He has written many articles on personnel management and outdoor and conservation topics. At the Environment Forum in Stockholm, June 1972, he was elected Chairman of the Workshop on Protection of Ground Waters, Rivers, Lakes, Estuaries, and Oceans.

Wesley L. Hjornevik. North Dakota State University, B.S. in Economics. He has served as Budget Examiner, Bureau of the Budget, Washington, D.C.; Assistant to the Under Secretary, Department of Health, Education and Welfare, Washington, D.C.; Assistant to the Administrator, National Aeronautics and Space Administration, Washington, D.C.; Deputy Director of Business Administration, NASA, Washington, D.C.; Director of Administration, NASA Manned Spacecraft Center, Houston, Texas; Associate Director, NASA Manned Spacecraft Center, Houston, Texas. Since 1969, he has been Deputy Director, Office of Economic Opportunity, Washington, D.C. He is the recipient of the NASA Distinguished Service Medal and the Arthur S. Flemming Award.

Rensis Likert. University of Michigan, A.B.; Columbia University, Ph.D. He served as Director of the Institute for Social Research at the University of Michigan from 1948 to 1970. His personal research interests have focused in recent years on a study of organizational theory and management practice. His book *New Patterns of Management* received the 1962 Publications Award of the Organization Development Council, the James A. Hamilton Hospital Administrator's Award for the outstanding book on administration published in 1961, and the American Academy of Management's McKinsey Foundation 1962 Book Award. *The Human Organization* was published in 1967. He is a past president of the American Statistical Association. He is a recipient of the Distinguished Faculty Achievement Award of the University of Michigan, the Stockberger Award for achievement in the field of personnel administration, the degree of Doctor Honoris Causa by the University of Tilburg, Holland, and the 1968 Human Relations Award of the Society for Advancement of Management. In December 1970, Dr. Likert established Rensis Likert Associates.

C. West Churchman. University of Pennsylvania, B.A., M.A., Ph.D. in Philosophy. He has served as Head of Philosophy Department at the University of Pennsylvania and Head of the Mathematics Division of the Frankford Arsenal Ordnance Laboratory in Pennsylvania; he taught philosophy at Wayne State University and Case Institute of Technology. Since 1957, he has been Professor of Business Administration at the University of California, Berkeley and has served as Associate Director for the Social Sciences Research Group at the Space Sciences Laboratory. He has been editor-in-chief of *Philosophy of Science and Management Science.* He serves as consultant to federal agencies and private industry. Among his numerous writings are *Introduction to Operations Research* (with R. L. Ackoff and L. E. Arnoff); *Prediction and Optimal Decision, Challenge to Reason* (selected as one of the best books on management, 1968); and *The Systems Approach,* which received the McKinsey Book Award for one of the best books on management. His latest book is *The Design of Inquiring Systems;* his article "On The Facility, Felicity, and Morality of Measuring Social Change," *The Accounting Review,* January 1971, was selected as one of the notable contributions to accounting literature in 1971.

Elmer B. Staats. McPherson College, McPherson, Kansas, B.A.; University of Kansas, M.A.; University of Minnesota, Ph.D.; Fellow, The Brookings Institution. He has served as Research Assistant, Kansas Legislative Council, 1936; teaching assistant, University of Minnesota, 1936-38; staff member, U.S. Bureau of the Budget, Washington, D.C., 1937-47; Assistant to the Director, 1947-49; Assistant Director, 1949-50, 1958-59; Deputy Director, 1950-53, 1959-66; Research Director, Marshall Field & Co., Chicago, 1953; Executive Officer, Operations Coordinating Board, National Security Council, 1954-58. He is a member of Phi Beta Kappa and an honorary member of Alpha Kappa Psi, and received the Rockefeller Public Service Award in 1961. He has also received distinguished service awards from the University of Kansas (1966) and the University of Minnesota (1964) and the honorary degrees of Doctor of Public Service from The George Washington University in 1971 and Doctor of Laws from McPherson College in 1966. He has been Comptroller General of the United States since 1966.

William D. Carey. Columbia University, A.B., M.A.; Harvard University, M.P.A., Littauer Fellow. He has served in the Bureau of the Budget, Executive Office of the President, 1942-69, and as Assistant Director, 1966-69. He was Professor, Salzburg Seminar in American Studies, 1965. He was recipient of the Rockefeller Public Service Award, 1964, the Exceptional Service Award of the Bureau of the Budget, 1968, and the Career Service Award of the National Civil Service League, 1958. He is a member of the Committee on Public Engineering Policy of the National Academy of Engineering, and the Board on Human Resources of the National Academy of Science. He was a member of the Commerce Technical Advisory Board from 1969 to 1972, and currently is a Presidential appointee to the National Committee on the Oceans and Atmosphere. He is Vice President of Arthur D. Little, Inc., and Director of its Public Affairs Center.

Harold Orlans. City College of New York, B.S.S., journalism; Yale University, Ph.D., anthropology. He received scholarships or fellowships from New York Regents, Yale University, Social Science Research Council, and Fulbright Commission. He served on the staff of the *San Francisco Call-Bulletin*; the Social Survey, London; the National Science Foundation, 1954-59. He was director of Studies, 1960 White House Conference on Children and Youth; consultant to House Subcommittee on Government Research and Russell Sage Foundation; visiting associate at Harvard Program on Technology and Society. He is the editor of fours books, and the author of some forty papers and five books, including *The Effects of Federal Programs on Higher Education*, Brookings Institution, 1962; *The Nonprofit Research Institute*, McGraw-Hill, 1972; and *Contracting For Knowledge*, Jossey-Bass, 1973. He has been a senior fellow of the Brookings Institution since 1960.

Dwight Waldo. University of Nebraska, M.A.; Yale University, Ph.D. He held various positions in Office of Price Administration and U.S. Bureau of the Budget, 1942-46. From 1947 to 1967, he was successively Assistant Professor, Associate Professor, and Professor, University of California, Berkeley; from 1958 to 1967, Director, Institute of Governmental Studies, Berkeley. He has lectured abroad extensively, and was engaged in technical assistance in Italy in 1956-57 and 1961-62. He is the author or editor of eight books and author of two score essays in political science and public administration. Since 1967, he has been Albert Schweitzer Professor in the Humanities, Maxwell School, Syracuse University.

Approaches to Public Science Policy and Administration

ALBERT H. ROSENTHAL
Professor and Director
Program for Advanced Study in
 Public Science Policy and
 Administration
University of New Mexico
Albuquerque

Public science policy and administration comprises those activities of government, at all levels, that are primarily concerned with the use of science and technology to meet recognized public needs. It includes: (1) the laws that govern the establishment and operation of public agencies responsible for administering science and technology programs; (2) the political processes by which laws, and regulations issued under the laws, are established and modified in this field; (3) the network of public agencies, and their organizational structures, established to administer the programs adopted by legislation; (4) the policies, regulations, and procedures developed and administered by the public science agencies in the conduct of their programs; (5) the impact of public and private organizations and interest groups in the field of science and technology on legislation, policies, programs, priorities, and finances; and (6) the effect of science and technology upon the quality of life and the public's evaluation of policies and programs as enhancing or degrading the national well-being.

The field of public science policy and administration is many-faceted. Each of the elements affect the others. Public views expressed to representatives in Congress or state legislatures may have a deciding effect on legislation and appropriations. Legislation affects administrative patterns and, in normal course, governs policy formulation. Public and private interest groups have a significant impact on legislation, on policy formulation, and on the impression the general public receives of the effectiveness of programs.

This book attempts to provide an overview of the field of public science policy and administration and to explore several of its aspects in some depth. While other approaches to this subject are available, the limitations of space and the importance of the areas selected require us to confine our examination of this field to these basic approaches: history, organization, law and politics, personnel, finance, policy, and trends for the future.

HISTORY

Public interest and activity in science go back to the founding documents of the government of the United States. The framers of the Constitution specifically empowered the Congress "to promote the progress of science."[1] Every schoolchild is familiar with Benjamin Franklin's interest in science. Many leaders of the emerging American government were, like the early Greeks, "whole men," combining interests in science and technology, architecture, land use, music and the arts, and government and society.

Public funds have long been expended for agricultural research and military research and development. The country's leadership has given great impetus to science and technology in each period of war. During the Civil War, the National Academy of Sciences was established as a quasi-governmental agency.[2] World War I brought significant support to research and development (the National Research Council was established then), and World War II even more dramatic growth in this field. Before World War II, federal scientific activities were conducted primarily by the Coast and Geodetic Survey, the departments of Army and Navy, the Weather Bureau, the Census Bureau, the National Bureau of Standards, and the Bureau of Chemistry in the Department of Agriculture.

Several excellent studies outline in some detail the early developments in science and technology in the United States. Daniel S. Greenberg (in a chapter titled "When Science Was an Orphan") pointed out that at first "government was not inclined to reach to the assistance of the scientific community,"[3] and that scientists were not anxious to seek government support on the grounds that it might influence scientific objectivity.

A fundamental study initiated during World War II by Franklin D. Roosevelt and issued as a Report to the President in July 1945 formed the basis for the establishment of the National Science Foundation and provided recommendations and goals that have, to a large extent, stimulated and guided the expansion of government efforts in science and technology in the United States.[4] In a letter to Vannevar Bush dated November 17, 1944, President Roosevelt commended Dr. Bush for the significant contribution the Office of Scientific Research and Development (of which Bush was then head) had made in applying scientific knowledge to the solution of problems during the war. The President added, "There is, however, no reason the lessons to be found in this experiment cannot be profitably employed in times of peace." He gave as his major goals "the improvement of the national health, the creation of new enterprises bringing new jobs, and the betterment of the national standard of living." He outlined four specific goals:

1. To make known to the world, as soon as possible, the contributions made during the war effort to scientific knowledge, and to diffuse and use such knowledge to stimulate new enterprises providing jobs and making possible the improvement of the national well-being
2. To organize a scientific program as a "war against disease"
3. To address the question, "What can the government do now and in the future to aid research activities by public and private organizations?" and to consider the respective roles of public and private research efforts and their interrelations
4. To establish an effective program for developing scientific talent in American youth to maintain a future level of scientific research in the United States comparable to that of the war years

President Roosevelt closed the letter with an exciting statement of policy:

> New frontiers of the mind are before us, and if they are pioneered with the same vision, fullness and drive with which we have waged this War, we can create a fuller and more fruitful employment and a fuller and more fruitful life.[5]

In his Report to the President, Dr. Bush addressed major issues that are relevant to current discussions of public activity in science. Emphasizing the fact that scientific progress is essential in many phases of the national welfare, he pointed out that "without scientific progress no amount of achievement in other directions can insure our health, prosperity and security as a nation in the modern world." Regarding the question of science as a proper concern of government, he said, "for reasons presented in this report, we are entering a period when science needs and deserves increased support from public funds." And on the need to remove rigid classification and security requirements imposed during the war, he observed, "many of the lessons learned in the wartime application of science under government may be profitably applied in peace"— an issue highly current in the minds of many scientists.

A major, specific result of Dr. Bush's recommendations came five years after the publication of his report, when Congress passed the National Science Foundation Act of 1950, bringing the new agency into being.[6]

A number of amendments to the act have since expanded the activities of the National Science Foundation (NSF). The NSF received additional authority through the passage of the National Sea Grant College and Program Act of 1966 and the National Defense Education Act of 1958, establishing the Science Information Service.[7] In 1959 Congress authorized the National Science Board to delegate authority to the director and the executive committee to approve grants and contracts and to assume additional functions and responsibilities. The 1968 amendments to the National Science Foundation Act, based upon extensive hearings (particularly by the Subcommittee on Science, Research and Development) during the mid-1960s, greatly strengthened and extended the responsibilities of the NSF.

The trend to expand the activities of the NSF continues. The Senate, toward the close of the 92d Congress, by an overwhelming vote of 70-8 passed the National Science Priorities Act, which would give additional authority to the NSF and more than $1 billion over a three-year period to carry out the purposes of the act:[8] "to authorize the National Science Foundation to conduct research, education and assistance programs to prepare the Country for conversion from defense to civilian, socially oriented research and development activities and for other purposes."[9]

Another milestone in the history of public science in the United States was the President's Message to Congress of March 16, 1972. In this message, which has become known as the Presidential Message on Science and Technology, President Nixon said, "The ability of the American people to harness the discoveries of science in the service of man has always been an important element in our national progress."[10] He called for cooperative endeavor:

> Finally, we must appreciate that the progress we seek requires a new partnership in science and technology—one

APPROACHES TO PUBLIC SCIENCE POLICY 5

> which brings together the Federal Government, private enterprise, State and local governments, and our universities and research centers in a coordinated, cooperative effort to serve the national interest. Each member of that partnership must play the role it can play best; each must respect and reinforce the unique capacities of the other members. Only if this happens, only if our new partnership thrives, can we be sure that our scientific and technological resources will be used as effectively as possible in meeting our priority national needs.[11]

The President also stressed the importance of wisdom in public policy decisions in science:

> The years ahead will require a new sense of purpose and a new sense of partnership in science and technology. We must define our goals clearly, so that we know where we are going. And then we must develop careful strategies for pursuing those goals. . . . The investment we make today in science and technology and in the development of our future scientific and technical talent is an investment in tomorrow—an investment which can have a tremendous impact on the basic quality of our lives. We must be sure that we invest wisely and well.[12]

ORGANIZATION

A network has evolved of public agencies and organizations that are responsible for the administration of scientific activities, including those in research and development (R & D). Although almost every federal department and agency conducts at least one program that could be included in a listing of federal R & D activities, only those agencies that were established primarily to work in this field and the major coordinating agencies are discussed here.

For approximately a decade, at the top of the federal hierarchy was the Office of Science and Technology (OST), established in the Executive Office of the President by Reorganization Plan 2 of 1962, effective June 8, 1962.[13] The director and deputy director were appointed by the President with the advice and consent of the Senate. The director served as the President's Advisor in Science and also chaired the eighteen-member President's Science Advisory Council (PSAC), composed of the heads of major departments and science agencies. It is interesting to note that as the head of the OST the director could be called on for questioning by congressional committees, but as presidential advisor he might be restricted from testifying by the President on the grounds of executive privilege.

Dr. Edward D. David, most recent head of the OST and science advisor to President Nixon, was the subject of a recent *Saturday Review* article.[14] A major difficulty in the job, wrote Daniel S. Greenberg,

> is that Dr. David is politically chaste and Mr. Nixon is scientifically illiterate, par for high achievers in serious science and serious politics. . . . While David is the most outside man of Nixon's official inner circle (he usually speaks to the President only two or three times a month), his place on the periphery is not unusual in the fifteen-year record of efforts to institutionalize scientific advice at the presidential level.

However, several advances are at least partly credited to the influence of the OST and PSAC: "Budgets have started to rise again, following the damaging decline that set in under Johnson. . . . Henceforth, reversing a budget-cutting trend that traditionally puts long-range science first in line for the ax, all government departments are authorized to support fundamental research."

Dr. David's own position, quoted in the Greenberg article, is of some interest: "I look on science and scientists as the antidote to politics. Science is the technique for establishing reality. In all these arguments about pollution, energy, drugs, product safety, some group has to stand up for reality. That's what science is all about."

A second, related federal coordinative body has been the Federal Council for Science and Technology (FCST). The FCST was established by the President by executive order in 1959. The major purpose stated in the executive order is a coordinative one, providing that "the Council shall consider problems and developments in the fields of science and technology and related activities affecting more than one Federal agency or concerning the overall advancement of the Nation's science and technology."

Recently, President Nixon, as part of his plan to streamline the top level of federal government and reduce the White House staff, has transferred the responsibilities of OST and FCST to the National Science Foundation.

Other coordinating bodies include the President's Science Advisory Council established in 1951, the National Aeronautics Space Council (1958), the National Council on Marine Resources and Engineering Development (1966), and the Council on Environmental Quality (1969).

As indicated above, almost every federal agency engages in some scientific or technological activity or provides funds for such work. The *Government Organization Manual* published each year by the Office of the Federal Register of the General Services Administration provides ready reference. Most reviewers are surprised by the extent and wide variety of federal scientific and research activities.

Agencies that have as their primary purpose scientific or technological work include the National Bureau of Standards (NBS), established in 1901; the Atomic Energy Commission (AEC), established in 1946; the NSF, established in 1950; and the National Aeronautics and Space Administration (NASA), established in 1958. A large part of the work of the National Institutes of Health of the Department of Health, Education, and Welfare (HEW), and the Health Services, Mental Health Administration, Consumer Protection, and Environmental Health Service of that department may also be included. The same is true of the Environmental Protection Agency, the Department of Transportation, and several branches of the Department of the Interior.

The list of Federal R & D installations includes more that 735 laboratories. More than 300 are under the jurisdiction of the Department of Agriculture. The Forest Service alone operates 77. The Commerce Department, the Department of Interior, and even the Office of the Attorney General of the Justice Department maintain research laboratories. The Department of Defense, by far the largest financial supporter and user of science and technology, includes a large number of laboratories, proving grounds, or test ranges under the departments of the Air Force, Army, and Navy.

The Tennessee Valley Authority, among government corporations, engages in extensive research, as do quasi-official agencies such as the National Academy of Sciences, the National Academy of Engineering, and the National Research Council. The Smithsonian Institution, which was established by public statute, may also be included under this heading, although it conducts extensive activities through nongovernment funds and programs.

The Smithsonian Institution sponsors four major laboratories or research institutes; the Tennessee Valley Authority, nine laboratories; NASA, ten laboratories or research centers; and the Environmental Services Administration, a large number of laboratories. A number of small research laboratories, test facilities, and manufacturing plants are operated for NASA by industrial and university contractors.

Of special interest is the network of laboratories and research centers sponsored by the AEC, because some of them have been proposed for conversion to "national scientific laboratories" to be used by a number of agencies and universities with common interests in scientific research. The AEC-related organizations include:

Ames Laboratory	Mound Laboratory
Argonne National Laboratory	National Accelerator Laboratory
Atomic Bomb Casualty Commission	National Reactor Testing Station
Bettis Atomic Power Laboratory	Nuclear Rocket Development Station
Brookhaven National Laboratory	Oak Ridge Associated Universities
Cambridge Electron Accelerator	Oak Ridge National Laboratory
Health and Safety Laboratory	Pacific Northwest Laboratory
Knolls Atomic Power Laboratory	Plasma Physics Laboratory
Lawrence Berkeley Laboratory	Sandia Laboratories
Lawrence Livermore Laboratory	Savannah River Laboratory
Los Alamos Scientific Laboratory	Stanford Linear Accelerator Center

Not to be overlooked in sketching the intricate pattern of organization for public science policy and administration is the emergence of science agencies at state and local levels. Every state conducts some laboratory research activity in its health department, policy laboratories, road and water departments, food and drug departments or laboratories, and to differing degrees in the various states, in other state agencies and departments.

A recent study by the Committee on Intergovernmental Science Relations of the Federal Council for Science and Technology, *Public Technology: A Tool for Solving National Problems*, points out the need to develop capacities in state and local governments for developing and testing science applications.[15] The Office of Interstudies of state government capacities and needs in the field of science and technology.[16] A number of states have established scientific advisory boards, in most cases serving as an advisory body to the governor. In California, a separate advisory group provides advice to the legislature.

The report of the Committee on Intergovernmental Science Relations recommends that additional funds be provided to support joint federal-state-local public technology research projects and proposes that "new institutional arrangements be created by the academic institutions and state and local governments to deal with the application of science and technology to state and local problems."[17] The report also recommends that federal laboratories be made available for use by state and local agencies wherever possible.

The committee structure in Congress in the fields of science and technology is an important facet of the organizational approach. Treated briefly here, it is relevant also to the next section, "Law and Politics" (pp. 10-12).

Most committees and subcommittees of Congress, both House and Senate, deal with the parent department or agency in which a scientific agency or branch is located. For example, the Senate

Commerce Committee treats legislation concerning the Weather Bureau and the NBS. The House Merchant Marine and Fisheries Committee deals with the Coast and Geodetic Survey. The Joint Committee on Atomic Energy, established in 1946, was the first congressional committee created for the sole purpose of dealing with an aspect of science and technology. The joint committee has played a powerful role in the development of the AEC and its programs and is the only joint committee dealing exclusively with science.

Since the creation of NASA, several new committees and subcommittees responsible for aspects of science and technology have arisen. The Senate Committee on Aeronautical and Space Sciences and the House Committee on Science and Astronautics were established with primary responsibility for the space program. No full Senate committee has been created with jurisdiction over science generally. However, the House Committee on Science and Astronautics is responsible for the programs of the NFS, the NBS, and related scientific and technological programs.

Much of the work of the full committees is done by subcommittees. For example, the House Science Committee's Subcommittee on Science, Research and Development holds hearings periodically on scientific and technological programs. The reports of this subcommittee provide valuable texts for advanced students in this field. The House Government Operations Committee has established a Subcommittee on Research and Technical Programs and a Subcommittee on Intergovernmental Relations, both of which have assumed some jurisdiction over the HEW National Institute of Health Programs. The Senate Government Operations Committee, a subcommittee on government research, has been replaced by the Ad Hoc Subcommittee on the National Science Foundation of the Senate Committee on Labor and Public Welfare.

While these committees have major responsibility for particular aspects of federal programs in science and technology, other Senate and House committees and subcommittees from time to time exercise significant jurisdiction in these fields. The House Appropriations Subcommittee on Independent Offices withheld further funds for an NSF project entitled "Project Mohole" in 1966, eliminating the program. Some scientific programs are supervised by other House and Senate committees and subcommittees. The OST came under the jurisdiction of the House Government Operations Committee rather than the House Science Committee. This lack of a logical pattern in congressional organization leads Michael D. Reagan to write, "Unlike the Executive Branch, the Congress has no single hierarchy, formally or factually, but only a series of little hierarchies [committees and subcommittees]. ...If the Executive Branch can be characterized as pluralistic, the appropriate term for the legislature is chaotic. . . ."[18]

LAW AND POLITICS

Three closely related but distinct elements—the law, the legislative process, and interest-group practices—constitute the political approach.

In 1954 Don Price defined the dimension of this approach.[19] Daniel S. Greenberg in 1967 and William R. Nelson in 1968 brought attention in an organized and sophisticated way to the politics of formulating federal science policy and programs.[20] Nelson defined the political approach as "an application of the decision-making process, but an application requiring the quantification of variables on a scale far broader than is normally associated with the formulation of government policy."[21] He went on to state a basic, although somewhat idealistic, model for such decision making:

> In order to reduce the range of potential error in these decisions to the realm of acceptable risk, it is necessary that every possible effort be devoted to an examination of the conflicting values involved and the most effective ways of making decisions in which these values will be given due consideration. The relative merits of proposed programs must be balanced with the apparent likelihood of successfully achieving the identifiable objectives of the programs.[22]

That government activities in science and technology are deeply political in nature is clear to any observer of the legislative process or even of significant parts of the administrative process. All public decision making and policy formulation have their roots in the political process. In political decision making with respect to science,

> Difficult political decisions are involved at every turn. The question of how much money should be appropriated for science, what priorities will be given to various programs, what individuals, institutions or corporations will be entrusted to the development of the programs, and what degree of administrative control and management should be maintained are absolutely critical.[23]

A recent analysis pointed out that scientists and engineers have become increasingly active in political matters:

> ....within academic science, now so profoundly politicized, there is considerable dissent on all manner of political and professional issues. Some of these divisions unquestionably are highly functional, in the sense of contributing to stimulating, even creative, exchanges. But others suggest that scientists, like their colleagues in other divisions of the multiversity, have entered an era of often trying disputation that extends far beyond the boundaries of their scholarly concerns.[24]

The term "political approach" has several meanings. It can denote the total legislative process, including subcommittee hearings and deliberations, Senate and House committee recommendations, and legislative action. It includes presidential orders and White House recommendations. Since many of the votes and recommendations are made along political party lines, it also includes what is frequently termed "political influence"—political party activities or the influence of special-interest groups.

Because of the last definition of the term, for many years scientists have sought to insulate themselves from the political process. The very structure of the Smithsonian Institution, although established by statute, illustrates the effort on the part of scientists to maintain an independent posture with respect to government and political process. At the same time, scientists have sought to obtain substantial support from public funds. During and following World War II, with the tremendous impetus added by the development of the National Institutes of Health (NIH) programs and by the space effort, the substantial funds that were made available somewhat obscured the basic issue. The decline of large military, health, and space budgets for R & D has brought into sharp focus again the desire of many scientists to do pure research without government interference of any kind and, at the same time, to receive large amounts of public funds to support this research. Harvey Brooks, a spokesman for the scientists' point of view, provides a rationale in his definition of basic research as a purpose of our society and a goal in itself:

> Basic research is recognized as one of the characteristic expressions of the highest aspirations of modern man. It bears much the same relation to contemporary civilization that the great artistic and philosophical civilizations of the Greeks did to theirs or the great cathedrals did to medieval Europe. In a certain sense it not only serves the purposes of our society, but is one of the purposes of our society.[25]

The agreement of senators and congressmen with this position clearly waned, as shown by sharp reductions in specific programs of basic research. The Mansfield Amendment reveals congressional intent that funds appropriated to a particular agency, in this case the Department of Defense, be spent only for purposes clearly demonstrated to be closely related to the purposes of the programs of that agency. This issue remains a current one. A recent response to Congress's desire to tie appropriations for science to solving high-priority problems was the establishment by the NSF of a multi-million-dollar program, "Research Applied to National Needs."[26]

A classic example of the interplay involved in the political approach, involving the pressures of both public and private interests, occurs in the area of energy needs. Public needs for increased energy have been demonstrated. At the same time, environmental groups have been critical and active in bringing court and other actions against the expansion of coal-burning energy producers. New developments such as the breeder reactor in using atomic sources for energy are still questionable. Private power companies are expending vast sums in advertising and unknown amounts of money to influence legislation. Several governors in the United States have established special energy committees to provide advice in this highly sensitive area. And the energy problem, of course, is only one of many involving science and technology.

PERSONNEL

Only recently has attention been focused on the people involved in administering science agencies. Because of the relative lack of attention given to this important aspect of the subject, four chapters in this book are devoted specifically to this topic and two chapters touch on it peripherally.

A study recently published by NASA used questionnaires to determine the functions and the skills used by science administrators in NASA and the NIH.[27] The U.S. Civil Service Commission also has published a number of studies that indicate the significance of the science administrator in the overall picture of federal employment, particularly at the higher levels.

Some scientists have said that administration can be learned "by the seat of the pants." Outstanding scientists like Robert Oppenheimer and Norris Bradbury, who have had no formal training in management or administration, have made remarkable contributions as science administrators. James Webb, who holds a law degree, provided brilliant leadership as the administrator of NASA. Most thoughtful observers, however, have concluded that there is a value, for most people and over the longer range, in identifying and developing administrative talent in the field of science and technology, as in many other specialties. In Chapter 2, Dr. Lynton K. Caldwell addresses the question of "how American society can match its administrative capabilities to its public needs." Indicating that his objective is to outline a useful program that would contribute to the nation's science management capabilities, he provides a list of the attributes an effective administrator needs, particularly in what he calls "technoscientific administration."

In Chapter 3, former Executive Director of the U. S. Civil Service Commission Nicholas J. Oganovic and Harold H. Leich, also of the Civil Service Commission, report on an analysis of the duties listed in more than two hundred position descriptions of federal science and engineering managers at the "supergrade" level, GS 16-18, in the federal service. In cooperation with the Program for Advanced Study in Public Science Policy and Administration at the University of New Mexico, the U.S. Civil Service Commission sponsored a questionnaire to approximately two hundred federal scientists and engineers who rated themselves as administrators, and to the same number who rated themselves as individual scientists and engineers in several federal laboratories and in Sandia Laboratories, a private corporation supported by the AEC.

In many large agencies, professional people are at odds with administrators. For example, no one has yet been able to define clearly the respective responsibilities of HEW regional directors in relation to the heads of the regional professional staffs.[23] This kind of conflict is examined in an article by philosophy professor Thomas A. Cohan, "Paradoxes of Science Administration."[29] Reminding us of Hegel's "Lordship and Bondage"[30]—the paradox in which the supervisor becomes the slave and the worker is ennobled by his tasks—Cohan says, "Time and again, the boss begins to deteriorate as a human being, and the worker gains in moral stature." He delineates the problem as it exists peculiarly in science administration:

> Granted that science administration raises all the problems that administration in general does, and that the work of science is not exempt from the universal paradoxes [that the supervisor becomes the slave], in what way does the paradox get its special coloration so far as science is concerned? Is there anything special about the nature of science that makes this kind of work different from other types of human

activity? . . . I think much of what an administrator must do for a scientist is to treat him as a unique human being in sore need of a multitude of services to enable him to practice his art. . . . his role is to create an environment that nourishes scientific creativity.

Wesley J. Hjornevik, former Associate Director of the NASA Manned Spacecraft Center in Houston, takes up this significant topic in Chapter 4.

Closely related but so significant as to require separate treatment is the subject of organizational dynamics as it provides a more useful environment to the practicing science administrator. In Chapter 5 Rensis Likert, former Director of the Institute for Social Research at the University of Michigan, relates the pattern of organization to the effective administration of complex, large-scale programs, particularly in creative and technical areas. Likert's analysis draws on the work of Donald Pelz.[31] In a number of other publications, and in consultation with a number of public and private organizations, Dr. Likert has developed the concept of "beehive" organization patterns as opposed to hierarchical organization patterns. He has concluded that, particularly in scientific and technological research agencies, lateral organization may be the more useful.

In Chapter 6, C. West Churchman discusses personnel from the viewpoint of top-level management. He suggests a systems approach, useful in almost all organizations but especially necessary in what he calls "the development of sociotechnical systems." In Chapter 8 Churchman discusses the role of the division chief in research organizations, or dean in universities—the position at least one step down from top management and two above actual operations—in an attempt to portray what the research director should be trying to do and the resources he should use to do it.

FINANCE

Understanding the financing of public science policy and administration is essential to understanding the field itself and some of its most critical issues. The financial approach yields insights into the economic importance of public science and technology, provides measures of the results of decision making, gives indications of trends, and is an essential tool for analyzing problems of long- and short-range funding.

Economic importance. A glance at some of the total annual expenditures for science and technology shows that public science administration is big business in the United States. Although exact and comparable figures on expenditures in public science administration are difficult to obtain, it is clear that such expenditures represent significant amounts in overall public spending.

The results of decision making. The financial approach also provides measures of the results of the political decision-making processes. The relative amounts made available to agencies and programs reveal what policy decisions have been made. Assigned or changed priorities are reflected in increases or decreases in funding to particular programs.

Determining trends. Perhaps the only accurate method of determining trends in public expenditure for science and technology is through application of the financial approach. For example, charges that public and private support of R & D is waning are not substantiated by the statistics.

In 1961 the federal government spent $9 billion for R & D. A continuing rise in government R & D spending from $11.3 billion in 1963 to $16.6 billion in 1973 (estimated) represents a 47-percent increase over that ten-year period (Table 1). National defense and the space program, which represented 90 percent of the federal R & D cost until 1966, are expected to account for 77 percent in 1973; other programs have grown steadily, gaining more than 5 percent between 1970 and 1973.[32]

In 1971, total public and private expenditures for R & D in the United States were approximately $27.8 billion,[33] or about 2.7 percent of the gross national product for that year. Of funding from all sources (industry, colleges and universities, federal agencies, and private nonprofit institutions), basic research accounted for $3.9 billion, applied research $6 billion, and development $17.9 billion. The federal government spent about $15 billion, or 53 percent of the total. Private R & D spending was up 30 percent from its 1968 level; universities and colleges, spending $2.7 billion, were up 5 percent from their 1968 level.

The total R & D expenditure for 1971 represented a gain of about 4 percent over the 1970 level of $26.8 billion.

A significant increase was authorized in funding for the NSF for fiscal year 1973-74. Congress approved a $704-million authorization (of which $650.2 million was actually appropriated) to NSF, or approximately $50 million more than the amount recommended by the White House. This congressional authorization was the largest in the twenty-two-year history of the NSF. The authorization included a number of specific budget floors in various categories, an effort by Congress to ensure that certain major programs are emphasized. The chief items in the bill included: $274.3 million for

TABLE 1

Federal R & D Expenditures under the Alternative Functional Classification System
($ million)

Function	1963	1968	1971	1972 (est.)	1973 (est.)
Defense	7,273.3	8,592.8	8,161.7	8,702.7	8,860.6
Space	2,429.7	4,576.7	3,207.5	2,960.1	2,929.7
Health	593.8	1,125.3	1,217.3	1,386.8	1,607.2
Advancement of science and technology	296.4	544.5	619.3	704.6	777.6
Environment	171.9	304.1	419.6	509.2	572.2
Transportation	112.0	365.9	684.1	607.3	563.2
Energy conversion and development	265.3	344.7	336.9	405.2	452.1
Agriculture	138.8	225.9	261.8	288.1	300.7
Economic security	22.1	97.5	149.1	153.9	170.9
Education	9.6	86.8	115.0	125.5	151.5
Government operations	7.6	14.9	35.9	42.8	69.1
Housing	0.2	6.3	39.3	55.9	53.2
International cooperation and development	9.7	20.1	25.1	24.8	27.0
Crime control and prevention	--	0.6	8.1	17.6	23.3
Communications	6.8	12.6	12.8	14.1	16.6
Commerce and industry	1.5	14.4	6.6	9.0	9.6
Total	11,338.7	16,333.1	15,300.1	16,007.6	16,584.5

Source: National Science Foundation, *National Patterns of R & D Resources, Funds and Manpower in the U.S., 1953-1972*, NSF 72-300, December 1971, p. 2.

scientific research support; $108.6 million for a series of special programs such as biological and atmospheric studies; and $87.5 million for programs to apply technology to environmental, urban, energy, and similar problems.

Thus many observers are puzzled to see growth figures that reflect increased expenditures for science, including R & D, and at the same time read public statements by leading scientists proclaiming a "crisis in science" because of reductions in funding. A headline in the *Washington Post* of December 3, 1970, read "Research Fund Losses Decried by Scientists." In the article Dr. Philip Handler, then President of the National Academy of Science, urged increased federal funds as he announced a report from committee of the National Academy of Science. The committee report indicated that reduced research budgets "are now restricting research activities, morale among life scientists is falling and apprehensions are rising." The Committee urged steady increases in recent "on-again, off-again" Federal funds for research and training.[34]

According to an article in the *National Journal*, "A sharp slowdown in the growth rate in Federal research spending has given rise to concern that the United States may be in danger of losing its scientific and technological eminence. Scientists in universities are turning an increasingly critical eye at the organization of Federal support and at the scientists-administrators who lead the Federal efforts."[35]

The plight of scientists whose budgets have been reduced or eliminated is explained by the fact that priorities have changed. Sharp reductions have occurred in the space program and in some health programs. Priorities for research in the massive defense area have changed. Large-scale support for basic, undirected research has been reduced and the large amounts previously made available to universities, particularly for advanced education in science and technology, have been cut back. Testifying before Congress in 1971, Dr. Handler expressed dismay concerning the budget proposed for fiscal year 1972. He pointed out that, while an increase of $116 million to the NSF was planned, $74 million of that was for activities previously funded by other federal agencies, largely the Department of Defense, so that for the federal government as a whole, this is not an increase in activity; it is merely a change in bookkeeping."[36] Dr. Handler urged continued support for educational institutions and for individuals in training rather than the transfer of funds previously used for these purposes to the new NSF program, "Research Affecting the Nation's Needs."

Problems in range of funding. The financial approach is fundamental to many management or administrative problems in public science. As Elmer Staats and William Carey explain in Chapter 7:

> A natural tension exists between the doers of research and the managers who must find reasons for supporting them. The researcher expects independence to be creative, along with stable flow of funds. The public manager also wants scientific creativity but is bound by rubrics that were devised for practical pursuits.

A number of leading scientists, including the director of the NSF, have called for longer range financial support rather than the on-again, off-again funding that results from rapidly changing appropriations. Sorely needed for sound administration of science agencies and university science programs, long-range support is nonetheless very difficult to obtain. The Office of Management and Budget reflects the views of the White House concerning priorities and programs. Congressional decisions are often based on pressures from public and private interest groups as well as the legislators' own assessments of public interest and concern. For these reasons many thoughtful people are urging an extensive program aimed at building "public understanding of science." Thus we see a move away from support of what in the past was called "basic research" to research directed toward current social problems.

POLICY FORMULATION

The aspect of public science that attracts the widest attention and is touched on frequently in newspapers and magazines is policy— public decisions made in the field. Even relatively minor policy decisions attract widespread public attention as they are seen to affect the well-being of the people. While these considerations cut across other elements in this field, the significance of policy debate and decision making requires that this approach be given special treatment.

Public science policy and administration is highly dynamic. While all government processes reflect frequent change, the opportunity for new discoveries and the need for dramatic reshaping of policies, organizations, and programs to take into account new findings are especially noticeable here.

Atomic developments during and following World War II, for instance, radically reshaped public activity in science and technology. Similarly, the policy decision made by the President and supported by Congress to pour an all-out effort into the space program resulted in the establishment of a major independent federal agency and related branches in other departments, the expenditure of huge amounts of public monies, and the development of a new technology. A vaccine has practically eliminated infantile paralytic poliomyelitis, and a new drug has had the same result for tuberculosis as a public health threat. Such developments have dramatically modified public organization, financial expenditures, and programs.

In Chapter 9 Harold Orlans defines "policy" as "the illusion that intelligence can reduce the confusion of events and guide us toward desirable, timely, and orderly objectives," pointing out that government policy is frequently the result of self-interest pressures and may be simply a cover of purely political decisions.

The formulation of public policy in science is little different from that of public policy in many other areas. It combines some efforts to create programs in the public interest with initiating or continuing programs directed toward and supported by special interests. The agricultural subsidy programs and the oil depletion allowances are examples of the impact of special-interest groups on policy.

Even idealistically motivated groups differ widely on the "facts" upon which decisions can be made. For example, some leading scientists charge that the atomic reactor is dangerous to health and the environment; others "demonstrate" that it is not. In an effort to introduce some order in this situation, Congress in 1972 enacted a technology assessment bill that would create a board, responsible to Congress, to set up standards and methods of evaluating past and new technological developments.[37]

Objectivity

One of the foremost issues involved in public decision making and policy formulation involves the question, How can objectivity be assured in the development of factual information essential to this process? (In a recent article Daniel Greenberg, treating the subject of technology assessment, makes this point plainly in his title: "Don't Ask the Barber Whether You Need a Haircut.") For many years, the federal government has used committees of the National Academy of Science and the National Academy of Engineering in conjunction with the National Research Council for this purpose. Lower level issues have often been assigned by contract to university or private research groups. Naturally, when public funds are expended and the positions of key officials may be known, objectivity of research findings can be a matter for concern. No one likes to think that leading scientists or heads of research programs would subvert their integrity because projects are supported at the instance of particular leaders. Nonetheless, public confidence in the findings may be reduced because of the approach taken. Here is an area where large private foundations, presently undergoing some congressional questioning, may find a public-interest use of funds and support.

It is not likely that unanimity can be obtained. The views and backgrounds of scientists differ. The difficulty lies in distinguishing honest differences, based on information achieved by sound research and study, from points of view developed to support preconceived ideas or special interests.

Grant decisions

A second area of controversy in the decision-making process involves the use of peers in allocating grant funds. The NIH have established many committees made up of experts and specialists who review grant proposals. Nicholas Wade in a recent *Science* article, "Peer Review System: How To Hand Out Money Fairly," describes the present system in some detail. (See also Barbara Culliton's article in the January 26, 1973 issue of *Science*, "NIH Training Grants: Going, Going, Gone?") The NSF uses reports of individual specialists. Many scientists consider this process a "lottery," since much depends on having someone on the grants committee who is knowledgeable and interested in one's special area.

While the use of specialists and peer group committees in grant allocation has its drawbacks, it may be better than having decisions made by scientists employed full time by public agencies, who could be subject to political and other pressures. Possibly, also, innovative methods of reviewing grant proposals are needed.

Grant duration

A third aspect of policy making that concerns scientists and other research managers is the relatively rapid change of programs and priorities by Congress and by program agencies. The problem is clear enough. A university or other research group recruits a highly qualified group of scientists and spends large sums of public and university funds for equipment. It may have to offer tenure to a qualified research manager. If a few years later the sponsoring agency discontinues support, the contractor is in trouble. The faculty member with tenure must be kept on even though his chief qualification was for the defunct project. No easy solution is in sight. Some proposals have suggested longer range programs, say, five to seven years. Some universities are refusing to accept grants unless they are guaranteed over a substantial time period. NASA developed the "step-funding" grant program, in which a non-renewable five-year grant would be reduced by one-third during each of its last three years. Thus the university or research group had the opportunity to develop other funds if it wished to continue the program.

Level of organization

A fourth policy issue, widely treated in the literature and proposed in several congressional committee hearings, is that of the establishment of a Department of Science. In 1960, Senator Hubert Humphrey advocated the establishment of such a department to provide coordination and eliminate duplication.[38] A number of scientists and nonscientists have opposed the idea:

> ....whatever case may once have existed for a Department of Science to coordinate programs and develop overall policy (and it was a weak case to begin with) has been effectively answered for the foreseeable future by the Executive Office structure that has developed since 1957. ... Such inadequacies as may now exist in this area are more likely to require extension and further development of existing apparatus than to call for supplantation by a Department of Science.[39]

> Only a power near the summit of the Federal structure can hope for success.[40]

> Another choice involves the recommendation for a unified department of science and technology. ... But the proposal encounters today, as it has since John Wesley Powell advocated it before the Allison Commission in the 1880's, the stubborn pluralism of the scientists themselves, the uncertainties of the scientists about the boundaries of their interests, and the opposition of government scientists more willing to endure their existing, familiar organizational environment than to risk the unknowns of a new and untested arrangement.[41]

Currently, attention is being focused on strengthening the coordinative function of the OST and on expanding the responsibilities of the NSF rather than on creating a new department. The decision to locate OST within NSF was probably based on this premise. (These changes are discussed in "David, PSAC Exit Predicted," *Science*, January 12, 1973, and a *Science* editorial, "Departure of the President's Science Adviser," January 19, 1973.)

This has been difficult to accept for advocates of existing departments and agencies who feel that their R&D activities need to be closely tied to their organizations' functions. In addition, pressures continue for the establishment of other departments, such as education and natural resources, raising the question of extending the President's span of control over a larger number of federal departments.

Public understanding of science

A fifth area, possibly the most significant aspect of policy formulation or decision making in science administration, is what we have called "public understanding of science."

In the past, the general public seems to have been intrigued by a hazy notion of science, represented by a dedicated researcher in a white coat working amid test tubes and other mysterious equipment in search of a cure for a dread human disease. On the other hand, the strong and informed support of legislators like Senator Lister Hill and Congressman James Fogerty also had much to do with the unlimited support given to the development of the NIH. It is difficult to say whether increased appropriations for health resulted from personal interest on the part of congressional leaders or from public desire to see high priorities given to research in medicine. Both probably played a part.

Because of the interest of leading scientists, and with the encouragement of Congressman Emilio Daddario (at that time Chairman of the House Subcommittee on Science, Research and Development of the House Committee on Science and Astronautics), the NSF in 1970 sought to revitalize its program in public understanding of science. Dr. William D. McElroy, then NSF director, testified before Congress:

> Scientists, science policy, and the very value of science to society are under sharp emotional and intellectual attack. Large numbers of our citizens are said to be disenchanted with science and, by and large, I believe this is true. Although some reasons for this attitude are understandable and we scientists must accept a share of the blame, the net result of this viewpoint is a deplorable and dangerous situation. At the very time science is experiencing this low esteem, man's need for its beneficial products is at its highest level. Simply put, civilized man cannot survive many generations on this planet without the increased creation of new knowledge and its enlightened use.[42]

McElroy pointed out that to the average citizen, American science policy is a complex and frustrating subject: "Few public policy issues have such shades of critical subtlety, few are less understood—much less debated—by informed citizens." He urged two things: (1) science policy must be considered as a system (effects upon one part have ramifications upon others), and (2) science policy must be distinguished from the mechanism for arriving at those policies. "Because science is absolutely crucial to the future of our society, the mechanism for developing national science policy is a matter of importance to all of us. In the final analysis, science policies exist to serve society and the Nation, and are but one aspect of national policy. Science policies, then, should be developed through the widest possible participation by well informed citizens."[43]

A leading environmentalist, Barry Commoner, concurred: "The age of innocent faith in science and technology may be over,"[44] and "Science can now serve society by exposing the crisis of modern technology to the judgment of all mankind."[45]

The participation of large numbers of people in the development of science policy requires the use of the network of established groups. The task of involving people in this process will not be easy, however. Most citizens prefer to sit back and criticize retrospectively, explains Peter Schrag, "For most citizens are unable or unwilling to penetrate the legal and political jungle in which public issues are often lost. Indeed, in their confusion, they are only too glad to let someone else—a bureaucrat or an 'expert'—do all the thinking and assume all the responsibility."[46]

Systematic advice in the development of science policy must be obtained from at least five sources, according to McElroy: (1) mission-oriented agencies of the federal government; (2) industry; (3) colleges and universities; (4) state and local governments; and (5) national organizations.[47] In addition to calling for means to involve large numbers of people and groups in formulating public science policy, McElroy set out five guidelines for policy making:

1. Federal mission agencies should support fundamental as well as applied research in areas determined to be pertinent to their mission.
2. Administrative procedures should be maintained so that individual science projects, so-called "little science," do not directly compete with large-scale or "big science" programs, such as the National Research Centers.
3. Federal funds must be of an adequate level and sustained over a predictable period of time.
4. Problem-oriented research, often of a multi-disciplinary nature, should be funded in its own right and not at the expense of certain fundamental investigations which, for a variety of reasons, seem more productive when nurtured through disciplined orientation.
5. Priorities, with adequate safeguards to hedge against imprudent judgments, can and should be established among fields of scientific research.[48]

In *Science, the Endless Frontier*, Vannevar Bush quoted James B. Conant, former president of Harvard University: "in every section of the entire area where the word *science* may properly be applied, the limiting factor is a human one. We shall have rapid or slow advance in this direction or in that depending on the number of really first-class men who are engaged in the work in question. . . . So in the last analysis the future of science in this country will be determined by our basic educational policy."

McElroy's testimony embraced this point as well:

> Highly trained scientific manpower is essential for performing scientific research, meeting the requirements of industry and government, and educating future generations. Because this training underpins our national science effort, the Federal Government has a particular responsibility to maintain the stability and general health of graduate education, and here I include the humanities as well as the sciences. At the graduate level, research and education are too closely related to be separated, and the process itself is too expensive to be borne solely by the institutions.

McElroy closed his testimony to the subcommittee (referring to a draft of Chapter 10 of this volume by Dwight Waldo concerning the "New Romanticism" in science) with the following statement:

> Because of this new spirit, I don't think we scientists can look at science in the future as we have in the past. The science community, I believe, must make its accommodation with this new spirit. We really have little choice, for changes will come whether we like them or not when today's young scientists reach positions of power and influence.

Thus at this time a great deal more information concerning science must be provided to the public, through the formal education system as well as on a continuing basis. The statement "science is no longer popular" is not true. Science and technology are being increasingly used and highly supported by government subsidies and grants. This does not mean that in particular instances there are no serious questions or strong reactions: the effort to develop breeder reactors in the use of atomic energy to meet increasing energy needs is a prime example of controversy; effective research in prolonging human life has made it possible for people to live longer, but the quality of that longer life has been neglected. In his Message on Science and Technology, President Nixon stated:

In all these efforts it will be essential that the American people be better equipped to make wise judgments concerning public issues which involve science and technology. As our national life is increasingly permeated by science and technology, it is important that public understanding grow apace.[49]

Dilemmas in public understanding of science

The following sections explore some of the dilemmas we face in developing a program of public understanding of science.

Public opinion. Critics say that science and technology have been oversold, and stress the many unmet needs of our society. Young student activists, cynical and disillusioned with the results of science and technology, attack the concept of computers and picket computer centers. Yet the computer combined with scientific method offers the major hope for coping with the complex needs of our society—protection of the environment, urban renewal, minority opportunities, fuller employment, and the like. Many of the positions of the activists are based on what has been called "New Romanticism" and start with rejecting rational or logical approaches. "When the irrational guides human conduct it becomes rational," wrote Freud; that is, the irrational must be taken into account in any effort to deal with such situations.

Competing disciplines. Faced with the same kinds of problems and theoretically directed toward achieving the same or parallel objectives, science and engineering groups still have become rivals and even antagonists. How can conflicts between specialized fields be resolved in favor of the use of knowledge for common objectives? In particular, how can knowledge in the social and physical sciences be combined to solve "people problems"? There are high degrees of specialization within the social sciences—political science, economics, sociology, psychology—as well as within the physical sciences. Most so-called interdisciplinary programs are not effective. Better progress has been made in training people who themselves have capabilities in several fields. Does this not offer a challenge to revise educational programs, particularly at the advanced graduate levels? Dr. Willard Libby at the University of California, Los Angeles, is developing an advanced program on this premise. Syracuse University and the University of New Mexico have developed advanced programs in "public science policy and administration" to build specially designed courses of an interdisciplinary nature into the graduate curriculum.

Basic versus applied research. In the training of most scientists, a fundamental premise stressed early in their careers is the importance of unrestricted research directed solely toward the "search for truth." In the chemistry or physics laboratory, the negative finding, properly recorded, is as significant as a positive result. Few question the value of basic research:

> We have repeatedly encountered instances in which a rather esoteric piece of research finds application in a manner which the original observer would never have supposed. A most recent instance is the history of a drug called cytosine arabinoside.
>
> This drug is by all odds the most promising drug we have for the treatment of two major forms of leukemia. For one form of leukemia it has been achieving a 75% cure rate. Cytosine arabinoside was found originally by a zoologist who was investigating the biochemical properties of Caribbean sponges; this compound had never before been seen.[50]

But another approach to research is needed, one that falls between "pure" and "applied" research. Using the methodology of basic research, the scientist would attack a problem recognized as significant to meeting current needs. Although this practice is not new—it has been used for many years in health, environmental, and other research areas—the development of an expanded concept may be useful in interpreting its value in solving social problems, particularly those involving the quality of life.

Coordination of public agency efforts. Many major federal agencies are deeply involved in scientific and technological efforts. In his Science and Technology Message, President Nixon requested that all federal agencies try to support research in program activities and other ways. Large sums are spent by individual agencies without particular regard to common goals or established priorities. There appears to be no discernible overall public science policy, a lack that has been noted at the international level:

> As did the OECD report just described, the UNESCO report also finds that the United States does not have a single science policy, but rather a constellation of science policies that have evolved, largely in an *ad hoc* fashion. Consequently, much of the development of U. S. science policies has taken place in the context of the utilization of science for a variety of purposes by a plurality of public agencies and private institutions. The resulting plurality of our science policies, said the UNESCO report, provides the opportunity for ex-

tensive discussion of major issues that tends to insure against mistakes caused by undue dominance of a single point of view. However, this same plurality "often increases the difficulty of coordination and of the achievement of a coherent national perspective on the development and utilization of scientific and technological resources."[51]

As the scientific capacities of state and local governments are developed, more mutual cooperation and coordination will be needed.

Modernization of the grant system. Closely related to the need for improved organization of public science agencies is the need for coordination of the federal grant process. Most procedures for requesting grants call for elaborate proposal statements and involve long delays. In addition, investigators find a morass of complicated instructions and different forms and procedures among closely related programs. "Grantsmanship" has become a profession. How can public grant systems be organized so that the ablest investigators are assisted, with their time preserved for the investigations in which they are trained rather than in the drafting of grant proposals?

Constituency. Many people, both as individuals and as members of large and powerful organizations, are deeply interested in the future of science and technology. They come from industry, large institutions, general education, and civic groups. How can their informed support be enlisted? Are new organizations needed?

Interpretation by scientists. A few scientists are interested and able when it comes to interpreting their research to the public. Scientists are trained, of course, to be conservative about their goals and findings.[52] The dilemma is this: How can progress in scientific and technological research be promptly reported and interpreted to the general public, particularly when the findings seem to be important breakthroughs, without violating sound scientific discipline—so that the claims are not later discovered to be unfounded or to have unanticipated consequences? There is no easy answer to this question, but a need does exist to encourage scientists to develop skills in communicating their findings to the public. Most people, including legislators, do not want to hear from public relations staffs about scientific research; they want to hear from the scientists themselves.

SCIENCE LEADERSHIP FOR TOMORROW

Most graduate programs in science, engineering, and the social sciences have a very narrow focus. How can a specific program be developed to answer the need for future leadership in science and technology?

The University of New Mexico was among several universities asked to design a program toward this objective.[53] During 1968, extensive consultation was undertaken by a small staff at the University of New Mexico and advice was sought from the heads of some eighteen science agencies in the Albuquerque area. The Regional Advisory Committee on Public Science Policy and Administration, composed of the heads and deputy heads of these agencies, was formally constituted.

The University of New Mexico program was established with two objectives:

1. On the basis of graduate research to add to, and make readily available, an additional body of knowledge concerned with the formulation and administration of public policy in the field of science

2. To develop and provide a graduate-level interdisciplinary curriculum and research program in public administration–science, leading to the Master of Arts degree, designed to supplement the scientific and technological background of advanced students and practitioners preparing for responsible positions as science-administrators

Guidance in developing a meaningful curriculum was also obtained from a questionnaire (see pp. 62-63 and Chapter 3) concerning the areas of academic work that have helped science administrators perform effectively in their present jobs or study. An interdisciplinary curriculum was set up. Faculty members are drawn from the Department of Economics and the Medical School as well as the Division of Public Administration, which administers the program. In the first three years of program operation, thirty-nine Fellows were assigned by their agencies to undertake the academic year course. Seven federal agencies as well as state and local agencies have participated, including the city of Albuquerque, NASA, the state of New Mexico, the U. S. Bureau of Mines, the U. S. Air Force, the U. S. Army, the AEC, the U. S. Navy, the U. S. Office of Economic Opportunity, and, in 1972, the U. S. Bureau of Sport Fisheries and Wildlife.

A few other universities are developing or operating programs seeking to bridge the gap between the scientific and technological preparation afforded most researchers and the administrative and social science skills required to meet overall administrative responsibilities. Further programs are needed.

NEW FRONTIERS

A forecast of major issues and programs in science policy and administration could cover a wide range of topics. We will here review briefly just a few areas in which significant trends seem to be emerging.

First, as discussed previously, is a move away from the dual concepts of basic research and applied research. The development of programs in the National Science Foundation "directed toward the nation's needs" and the ripple effect of the Mansfield Amendment have focused research within specific areas and toward stated goals. If the independence and approach of the researchers are carefully insulated from preconceived findings and goals, this may maintain the environment of "pure research" with the difference that parts of the research program are directed to specific social problems. We might call this new approach "focused basic research." It may both stimulate congressional support and awaken public interest in scientific problems.

Second, the last few years have seen some attention to specific training for science administrators. While many federal agencies call for the performance of science management in their programs, the elimination of NASA support in this area means that there is no longer a support program for this purpose. Some interest has been indicated by the NSF and it is hoped that a specific program of university and other organization support will grow up.

Third, recent attention is being given to new patterns of organization in science administration. The work of Rensis Likert (Chapter 5) and the outstanding results of the NASA Apollo program in using "beehive" organization have aroused the interest of numerous major agencies.

In addition to changes in the organization of the science agencies themselves, there is a trend away from continued support of some agencies established during World War II. Some large federal organizations have encouraged the establishment of "captive" agencies, or private corporations entirely supported by public funds, such as Sandia Laboratories, contractor for the AEC, and the RAND Corporation.

The National Center for Atmospheric Research (NCAR) in Boulder, Colorado, a branch of the University Corporation for Atmospheric Research (UCAR), illustrates another emerging pattern. A number of universities have formed a corporation, with subsidiaries designed for special purposes. NCAR receives its total budget from the NSF and is responsive to priorities established by Congress and NSF[54] but is relatively insulated from political or special-interest pressures. The success of NCAR may result in part from the exceptional quality of its leadership, but may also result in part from its innovative type of organization.

A fourth trend is toward widespread support for building public understanding of science programs and their relationship to human and social problems. For example, in a recent publication, Senator John V. Tunney and M. E. Levine pointed out the urgent need for public interest, participation, and debate in the controversial field of "genetic engineering":

> The cry has been raised by many that the impact of science has been too fruitful. It has been raised by some with regard to the nuclear sciences. It might well be reiterated in the near future with regard to the biomedical sciences. . . . All segments of society should be involved in the debate these new technologies demand. The techniques must be discussed and debated among lawyers, doctors, theologians, legislators, scientists, journalists, and all other segments of society. The issues raised require interdisciplinary attention. We cannot begin too soon to consider them.[55]

The same position has been held regarding other areas of research and development; that is, "Science is too important to be left to the scientists."

A fifth trend is toward designing grant mechanisms to provide effective control in the expenditure of public funds but minimal control over activities, so that research managers have the greatest possible freedom in pursuing objectives. The aim is to achieve more research for the dollar, and to reduce the use of scarce research funds for other purposes. The pattern of overhead charges in research administration should be reviewed.

In Chapter 10, Dwight Waldo presents evidence of concern about the "social relevance" of science and technology in meeting human problems. He sees turbulence developing in a number of areas of science policy and administration and concludes that science will not be allowed to remain a self-directing enterprise. But many scientists are already interested in using the findings of science and technology to solve social problems, in directing their lifework toward humanistic ends. As this movement grows and significant advances demonstrate the value of science and technology in meeting society's problems, it is hoped that increased and sophisticated public interest, understanding, and support will develop for research.

Only through the methods and knowledge of science and technology *can* society solve the massive problems it is confronting. As

Peter Drucker points out, "Consider, for example, the widespread illusion that a clean environment can be obtained by reducing or even abolishing our dependence on technology. . . . The truth is that most environmental problems require technological solutions—and dozens of them."[56]

Human Resources for Science Administration: Identification and Development of Administrative Talent

LYNTON K. CALDWELL
Arthur F. Bentley Professor of
 Political Science and Professor of
 Public and Environmental Affairs
Indiana University
Bloomington

The general objective of this chapter is a set of reasoned propositions as to how American society can match its administrative capabilities to its public needs. The specific objective is an outline of a university program that would contribute to the nation's science management capabilities. A model curriculum in the administration of science and technology is included in an appendix.

Identifying public needs and relating means to ends intended to satisfy needs are an integral part of the administrative process. Scientific information and technology have, however, enlarged the task. Through science, the known needs of man are better understood, and unknown needs are identified. The range of social action that may answer these needs has been increased by science and technology. The range of policy choice in modern technoscientific society is enormously greater than that available at any previous stage of human social development. Modern man finds himself as beneficiary of the legendary three wishes. His choices become critical, because now he may receive what he requests. Responsibility, therefore, rests heavily on those who are chosen to articulate the goals of society and to direct programs of action for attaining them.

Applying technical means to social ends requires the mediation of public administrators. The amount of administrative skill available to any society at a given time is relatively fixed, but the ultimate capabilities of society for administrative effectiveness are indeterminate. More administrative talent almost certainly inheres in all societies than is actually developed and used. However, for technological societies at the beginning of the last third of the twentieth century, public needs for administrative skills have outrun the supply of expertise. The deficiency is partly due to greater demands of the technoscientific society upon public decision makers. But it is also partly attributable to the failure of our methods of selecting and developing public administrators. Our society has not produced, in sufficient numbers, men with the combinations of information, skill, and personality that are required for wise management of the resources created by science and technology.

Consequences of this deficiency in public administration are already evident in the growth of alienation and disorder in society. Failure to obtain the public leadership that the technoscientific society requires could result in disaster. Matching social needs with administrative talent now calls for a major cooperative effort among governments, universities, professional societies, and industrial organizations. Without this cooperation, current challenges to administrative competence cannot be met, because the political, technical, economic, and educational affairs of modern technological society are complexly interrelated and interdependent. Competence in the administration of only one or even several of the major sectors of society is not sufficient to compensate for failure in a major sector—for example, in the administration of higher education or of local government. Moreover, cooperative action is needed to obtain the policy and financial support that major, national administrative development would require.

PUBLIC GOALS AND ADMINISTRATIVE ROLES

Especially at higher levels of public affairs, an administrator must play several roles, but he is primarily a leader in policy making and a director of operations. Unlike a judge or a legislator, the administrator is an activator who translates intentions into actualities. To do this, he must interpret the intentions that he is called upon to actualize. He may adopt the interpretations of courts, legislators, his administrative associates, or clients. Yet he may still be creative. Laws and public policies are seldom so accurate and comprehensive as to absolutely mandate his decisions. The greater the complexity or ambiguity of the policy area, the greater his leeway in policy shaping.[1]

This latitude available to the public administrative decision maker is the reason why his goals are of greatest social importance. Administrative goals tend to become public goals. The individual public official, sensitive to legal restraints, bureaucracy, politics, and public opinion, may object that this imputation of latitude is unduly exaggerated. There are occasions when administrative action has little freedom for maneuver.[2] But the primacy of administrators in the policy process is widely accepted and supported by evidence.[3]

The power of decision is seldom exercised by the public administrator as an isolated individual. His decisions almost invariably take in the views of others, not only those in his immediate agency but also his peers in related offices, program specialists and technicians, and auxiliary administrators of personnel, budgetary, and fiscal policy. The goals of the administrator tend therefore to be those accepted, although sometimes only tacitly, by the functional groups through which his work is done. His accomplishments as administrator are dependent upon his playing a role within this operational context that facilitates the achievement of goals which he and his associates may have significantly influenced.

The training and development of the public administrator, if they are to be effective, must therefore assist him in trying to achieve goals in a manner consistent with his own success and the public welfare. To do this, they must help him understand the context in which his activities are carried on. Within this context the operational goals of public administration are shaped, and the administrator's understanding of his operational environment is essential to his effectiveness in goal selection and attainment.

A meaningful discussion of the development of administrative talent requires establishment of "parameters of administrative action." In everyman's language, these parameters could be stated as the conditions and necessities that cause administrative behavior to occur in the way it does. It is hardly feasible to consider the identification and development of administrative talent without some reference to the interaction of factors that determine what administration is and what it can do.

Two sets of factors govern the performance of administrative roles. The first is *functional;* the second is contextual or *environmental.* Functional aspects of administration are largely inherent in the ways in which human beings work together. These ways are conditioned by environmental factors and influenced by interactions among the individuals involved. The properties and limitations of human physiology and psychology, and of the existing technologies of organization, communication, and information handling, make some roles and tasks of administrators inevitable, regardless of cultural milieu.

Technology presents a special difficulty in defining the parameters of administrative behavior. It is not only an environmental or cultural influence; it also may become a psycho-physical extension of the individual personality. The complex interrelationship between human behavior and technology has become the subject of a large and growing literature. For example, students of automation, biotechnology, cybernation, information science, and human engineering evidence a growing concern with the interrelations between man and mechanized technologies and the effect of these interrelationships upon organizational and administrative behavior.[4]

There is greater certainty that administrative behavior *is* significantly affected by these interrelationships than there is about precisely *how* it is affected. The typewriter, the telephone, the computer, statistical techniques, and systems theory have influenced administration in numerous ways. The synergizing effects of these technologies on the people involved with them may be more significant than the identifiable effects of specific techniques. But the relevant sciences are not yet sufficiently advanced to yield understanding of the man-technology interface that would enable its complex relationships to be brought under intelligent, purposeful control. Therefore, the technological problems of administrative behavior must be met with an honest recognition that their significance is not fully understood.

The psycho-physiological and technological aspects of administration occur in a cultural milieu that determines what the administrator is trying to accomplish. Environmental parameters of administration include the goals of organizations and societies involved in the administrative process. Also included among these parameters are assumptions, laws, and procedures that influence priorities among goals and that determine permissible routes toward goal attainment. The environment of administration may be as complex as its technology. Since the environment sets fixed conditions to which society and its administrators must respond, many tasks of administration are mainly adaptive. But environment is made up of multiple elements, social and physical, some of which are highly variable.

The individual administrator may affect the immediate social or physical environment of his organization. But the larger environment within which his organization functions is beyond his immediate personal control. The individual administrator performs his roles in an environment that is rarely subject to direct personal or organizational variation. It channels and constrains the performance of his tasks, and within its context are the goals which his organization pursues. This context and the goals that have been established within it are sometimes referred to as "the task environment."[5]

An ability to deal perceptively and creatively with organizational goals within the task environment is an attribute of administrative effectiveness. This dictum is not intended to suggest that environment is always the critical factor in administration or that, because environments differ, every administrative role or function is unique. On the contrary, the scientific approach to the study of administration is based upon the assumption that its functional aspects constitute a generic social process.[6] Scientific management, management science, and organization theory are predicted on the premise that there are forms of behavior and interaction that are common to collective human effort. The student of administration is concerned with the operation of certain basic processes (delegation or reporting, for example) in a changing and varied environment. The study of interactions between functional and environmental parameters is now frequently designated as the "ecology of administration."[7]

The first major proposition of this chapter is that the identification and development of administrative talent can be explored with meaning only in relation to the roles that administrators play. The nature of these roles, which are shaped by environmental forces as well as by basic human necessities, determines the tasks that administrators perform to meet role expectations. These roles and their performance are in themselves goal-shaping operations. The relationship between administrative action and its consequences for society is therefore of major concern to anyone responsible for the training and development of administrators. The influence of the roles played by administrators in the formulation and attainment of public goals is fundamental to any general, educational effort toward effective public administration of science and technology.

CONTEXT OF THE TECHNOLOGICAL SOCIETY

To interpret the roles of the administrator, certain pertinent characteristics of the modern technological society must be reviewed, for this is the environment in which his tasks are shaped and take on significance. The United States and the administration of its public policies for science and technology are of chief concern; although the social context of American public administration is basically the same as that of other contemporary technological societies, some of its characteristics are significantly more accentuated. The characteristics of concern here are largely the results of the relatively uncontrolled thrust into American life of science-based technology during America's peculiar historical development.

In brief, those aspects of greatest concern are

1. Specialization
2. Complex diversity
3. Interdependent movement
4. High level of information demand

Following is an analysis of how these characteristics of the American technological society affect the environment in which the roles and tasks of the technoscientific administrator are performed.

Specialization is an inevitable concomitant of the growth of knowledge and technique. The capacities of human individuals to learn and do are limited. Only through a division of knowledge and skill among its members can the capabilities of society be expanded. But this expansion through specialization creates new problems. Communication and cooperation require more attention. Responsibility tends to be fractionalized. Generally accepted goals are more difficult to set and common values more difficult to define. Goal interpretation and the coordination of diverse skills become increasingly important among the tasks of administration as the trend toward specialization continues. In a society of specialists, the phrase "government by the people" becomes anomalous. The concept can no longer hold the same meaning that it had in an era of town meetings and courthouse politics.

In America today technical specialization has accentuated a second aspect of social development—complex diversity. Societies may be complex, but homogeneous rather than diverse. They may be diverse—culturally heterogeneous—but uncomplicated in structure. American technological society is both complex and diverse, and the two traits interact to create a society which defies generalizing description. Valid generalization is possible, but exceptions are numerous and often of critical importance in the processes of government and public administration. For example, generalizations regarding the political attitudes of industrial workers, college professors, ethnic minorities, and corporate leaders are invariably subject to exception.

There is a counter-generalization to the proposition that American society is complexly diverse—Americans in mass are alleged to be a people of stereotyped conformity and routinized behavior. The effects of public education and mass communications do tend to produce uniformities in American life that are further extended by mass production technology. It is apparent that American society tends toward uniformity in some respects and diversity in others. Which of these tendencies is the more significant in public policy and administration depends upon the issue in question. The diversity of the social context is probably the more significant factor in the decision-making process because it is the accommodation of differences, in decisions sufficiently coherent to be operational, that poses one of the greatest challenges to the administrator's special role and skill. The uniformities of American life are preponderant. They are never absolute. The mass goals of American society as expressed through government are very general and diffuse, with ample latitude for dissent in the formulation of a goal or in its practical implementation.

The American economy is highly interdependent, a moving and changing system in both space and time. Highly pluralistic and physically dispersed, it lacks monolithic cohesion. The economy works when all of its constituent parts are functioning, but it is vulnerable to disruption at many points. The November 1965 electric power failure in the northeastern states and parts of Canada illustrates the possibility of major ramifications of otherwise minor technical obstructions.[8] Added to technological interdependence is the human frailty of the federal form of government and the federated organizations of unions, trade associations, and professions. The techno-economic system or its subdivisions can be blocked by human failure or intent as well as by technological breakdown. A very small number of strategically placed persons can obstruct the operations of interdependent systems in the United States in ways vastly disproportionate to their numbers, status, or knowledge.

This society of interdependent variables moves and changes with more coherence than its complex structure would seem to permit. In recent decades change within the "system" has occurred at an accelerating pace. But the rate of mobility of change varies greatly among the components of the system. These differentials give rise to stresses within the system—as for example, when the economic structures of communities change, but the political structures remain static. The dynamism of the system, added to its complex diversity, makes it unstable and its behavior difficult to predict. Yet, because the interdependent system *is* vulnerable to disruption and to unforeseen effects of change, prediction becomes a major preoccupation.

A consequence of accelerated rates of change is obsolescence. Things, systems, and people become dysfunctional before they are worn out. Numerous complications in all aspects of administration are introduced by obsolescence. In large part, obsolescence occurs because knowledge increases more rapidly than adjustment to its implications. The more extensive and rapid the increase, the more obsolescence. And demand for more knowledge and for its rapid transmission and dissemination is another major aspect of the technological society. It is truly a society of built-in obsolescence.[9]

The quantities of information required to administer public affairs in a technoscientific industrial economy have been growing at unprecedented rates. The growth of knowledge appears to create the necessity for its use. Technological societies tend to do what they can do, with feasibility becoming a criterion of policy. For example, in response to the congressional query, "Why supersonic transport?" representatives of the aerospace industry replied that it was the logical next step.[11] The test of technological feasibility as a criterion for what society should do has been sharply criticized.[11] To say that society should do a thing because it can is, in effect, to say that technicians should determine priorities and the direction of public policy. The relationship of technical information and feasibility to the process of policy determination is problematic and widely disputed. The growth of science and technology has created a "high-information-level culture," emphasizing the production and management of knowledge.[12] Since repositories of effective knowledge are the minds of men, the specialization of modern learning and technique makes the administrator's task of coordination more important and more difficult.

This knowledge is used to formulate, shape, or implement policy most often in the process of administration. This not only means that more knowledge is now required for administrative performance, but also that the individuals who are placed at the critical points of policy decision—the administrators—become more and more the interpreters, mediators, and synthesizers of the work of specialists. In principle, these have always been administrative tasks, but they become more difficult as the administrator becomes less able to apply informed critical judgment to the recommendations of highly specialized associates and subordinates. For this reason the education of the technoscience administrator should help him to cope more wisely with the criteria of policy choice. The essence of this choice is evaluation of the possible uses of knowledge, surely the single most important responsibility of technoscience administration and one which is shared with other branches of society. Its importance is concealed by its latent or implicit character. Our society and its educational institutions have not understood, or at least have not made explicit, this responsibility of the administrator. Prevailing images of "the administrator" as a man of action are often inconsistent with the administrative capabilities for farsighted judgment that society needs.

To be an integrative force in his organization, an administrator must unite his role as director of operations with his role as leader of policy making. Technological society, however, presents a major hazard to accomplishing this task of synthesis. The danger lies in the tendency, which has been noted, for techniques to displace other factors in policy choice. To discover the ends that society might most wisely pursue to meet its needs, policy leaders must avoid accepting technical feasibility as a governing criterion. To properly relate means to ends, the administrator must assert the primacy of social goals over operational techniques.[13]

Control of administrative policy and political action through technology is as old as government itself. The Greeks had techniques for it.[14] To be effective as policy leader or as operations director, the administrator must work through the system in which he performs. He must live with the system to survive, and the system in American government and industry is strongly influenced by technical concepts and procedures. He must master the technology of administration, or it will most assuredly control him.

The technical infrastructure of administration is most evident in the organization of functions of finance, personnel, and planning. These aspects of administration are controlled through rules and specified procedures that can as easily retard goals as advance them. Technical procedures are often reliable and impersonal means for protecting the primary goals of organizations from diversion of administrative efforts toward socially illegitimate ends. The "automation of honesty" (exemplified by electric voting machines and computerized accounting systems) is not inconsistent with the attainment of primary social goals. But as procedures are elaborated, refined, and amended, they may become so compendious and complex that only a technical expert can really comprehend them, and even the technicians may disagree over their interpretation.

At some vague point of elaboration, technical controls begin to lose their efficacy. Their very complexity enlarges opportunity for conflicting interpretations. Administrators, aided by their own staff technicians, can learn to manipulate the rules and techniques to reduce their utility as control devices. But manipulating the techniques of administrative control absorbs personnel, time, and attention. Administrative efficiency in attaining primary goals, the ostensible purpose of the organization, is diminished in the process. One of the purposes of "systems management" is to rationalize, streamline, and monitor technical procedures to prevent their interference with primary goals.

Can a society in which technical achievement is widely accepted as an end in itself fully realize the benefits or even the full power of its technology? The primacy of technical goals has clearly induced remarkable technical achievements. But goals are usually complex. The larger the goal, the more likely it is to be ambiguous. The values in postulated goals are difficult to analyze. Critics of the technological society contend that its technological achievements too often attain goals of relatively minor social utility. It is plausible that only through a scientific analysis of social needs and values, and through the development of criteria for wise choices among alternative courses of action, can the beneficial possibilities of the technoscientific society approach realization. This proposition would be well worth considerable cost in testing, could it be formulated so as to be verifiable.

Beginnings of a systematic analysis of the decision process and of the assessment of advantages among alternatives have been made by Herbert A. Simon and his associates.[15] A new science of management decision is beginning to provide the information and the indicators that can bring more rationality and predictability into an environment of uncertainty and change (see Chapter 6). Science, as well as ethics, is now capable of joining technique to policy and making it easier for the administrator to play his directive role more consistently with his role of policy leadership. The technological society increases the administrator's burden of responsibility, but it also provides tools and understanding that make the burden easier to bear. Sophistication in the uses of technology, and awareness of its social implications, are clearly major objectives in the development of administrators.

TASKS OF TECHNOSCIENTIFIC ADMINISTRATORS

The functions of the administrator, as they tend to be understood in contemporary American society, may be classified as direct and latent. Those classifications correspond generally to the roles of manager and of leader in policy development described earlier in this paper. The direct or managerial functions of administration are commonly specified as the tasks of administration. They are made explicit in a job description, a contract, a letter of appointment, a legislative act, an executive order, or verbal instructions. Latent functions are inherent in the nature of administrative action and are not often explicitly identified as administrative tasks or duties. Nevertheless, ability to perform the latent functions of administration is generally sought in prospective administrators. This ability is commonly and vaguely identified as "capacity for leadership."[16] In the more stable and less dynamic decades of the nineteenth century, latent functions of the administrator tended to be subsumed under the word "character." Leadership, however, is a preferred value during change and uncertainty when future conditions are not expected to be like those of the past or present. Conversely, character is valued where traditional standards and relationships can be sustained and where the challenge of change can be faced with norms and methods that have proved reliable in the past.

The displacement of character by leadership as an essential attribute of administrative capability is more a consequence of the changing environment of administration than of administrative functions. When the conditions affecting public policy tend to favor a firm exemplification and defense of status quo values, the latent functions of public administration indicate a need for men of "character" in administrative positions. Persuasiveness, innovativeness, drive, and rapport with organizational rank and file are less significant attributes during relative environmental stability. Under conditions increasingly prevalent in the United States since 1930, the policy functions of public administration have required innovative leadership. To the extent that it has not been forthcoming, public administration has failed to achieve its full potential and the quality of public life has suffered.

Administrators commonly perform certain specific tasks. Among them are handling of superordinate-subordinate interpersonal relationships (especially through communications), planning (especially regarding future policy and financial commitments), appraisal of current progress toward specified goals, and reporting. The operational aspects of these tasks may be facilitated by techniques which can be taught and learned. When tasks can be reduced to commensurate techniques, it becomes possible to develop objective criteria for measuring operational performance. Competence in performing the technical tasks of administration is an important attribute of success in many administrative situations. But excellence in performing these techniques (as distinguished from the tasks themselves) indicates no more than competence as an administrative technician. It does not imply total effectiveness as administrator.

With the growth of organizational size and complexity, coincident with the growth of technical implementation of administrative action, the number and importance of administrative technicians have increased. These workers differ from those that we have called "administrators" primarily in that their functions are direct and specific—not indirect and latent. They perform the so-called staff management, personnel, fiscal, and logistical functions. These technical areas may afford avenues to the more generalized levels of higher administration. But proficiency in administrative technology does not necessarily indicate promise in fulfilling the latent functions of administration. And it follows that training in the technical aspects of administration does not in itself provide an adequate apprenticeship for higher levels of administration.

To distinguish administrative technicianship from administration in the broader sense is in no way derogatory to technical tasks or to the need for proficiency in their accomplishment. The distinction is drawn to indicate that reliable criteria for identifying and developing administrative talent must take account of all the tasks that the administrator must perform. It is easier to be concrete, specific, and even quantitative about the jobs that the technician must do. Of course, more than technique is involved in successfully accomplishing tasks in the technical aspects of administrative operations. Administration is a human relations process, and its most technical procedures are (or should be) intended to provide for some nontechnical human need. Efforts toward identifying and developing technical proficiency should not fail, therefore, to find ways of obtaining in prospective administrative technicians a sufficient level of human relations skills for effective participation in cooperative enterprise. A common cause of failure in applying technical knowledge to administrative problems is the inability or unwillingness of people to accept technical solutions because of human relations reasons.[17]

The latent tasks and functions of administration belong chiefly to its higher echelons and are performed primarily to fulfill an administrator's role as policy leader. The term "latent" is used, because this aspect of administration is more often tacit than explicit in descriptions of administrative duties. The policy leadership function is also latent in that its overt manifestations are often delayed until occasion for public action arises. The policy leadership function is further obscured by the variety of ways in which it can be performed. Much of it may occur in day-to-day decisions regarding the operative functions of an organization. Some of it occurs in decisions regarding personnel, budget, and finance. It is often difficult for anyone, including the administrator himself, to tell the extent to which his role as director of operations is simultaneously a role of policy leadership.

No informed person doubts the importance of these latent functions of administration in shaping and executing public policy for science and technology. When students of administration or government gather to worry collectively about the role of the administrator in society, it is this leadership function, its absence, or the manner in which it is performed that is the ultimate object of concern. The primary objective of executive development, mid-career management training, and advanced graduate education in business or public administration is to induce and develop organizational leadership capability in prospective administrators. Policy leadership is a major ingredient of the leadership function. Much of the superficially technical or analytic training now provided in advanced management education is, in fact, intended to enable the future top administrator to be an effective policy leader, communicator, and decision maker in a task environment populated by specialist technicians.

The tasks of technoscience administrators in fulfilling policy leadership do not differ, in principle, from those of other administrators. Although the focus of this paper is upon the administrators of predominantly technical or scientific programs, its relevance is not confined to this specific sector of higher administration. Nevertheless, the administration of technoscientific programs, industrial and governmental, tends to differ in degree from other areas of administration—primarily in two particulars. Although the purposes of the programs may appear to be clear to average citizens, corporate stockholders, or their elected representatives, the means by which the specified purposes are realized are beyond the understanding of anyone untrained in the relevant technoscientific specialities. An obvious corollary is that technoscientific programs tend to be administered by highly educated specialists, who are seldom "common men."

The specialized nature of the work and of the men who direct it tends to remove the administration of technoscientific programs from the degree of popular scrutiny or control that democratic theory in America has historically assumed necessary for self-government. The advent of advanced technology and science-based public policies has increased the complexity of the decision process. Specialized knowledge and concepts not possessed by many people or their elected representatives are growing factors in major public policy decisions. Paradoxically, in an age of science, the citizen must accept more and more policy decisions on faith. He must defer to the judgment of specialists and of those public officials whose knowledge of technoscientific capabilities and public needs equips them for dealing with matters beyond the experience of most people.

The latent functions of higher technoscience administrators require mediation between technical and scientific subordinates and associates and the nontechnoscientific public and its representatives. The top administrator who must play this mediating or interpretative role is himself, characteristically, a product of advanced technical and scientific training. His formal education and professional experience seldom contribute to his ability to play this role. He may do well in it—one can identify scientists and engineers who have become administrators with great political and social effectiveness. But these notable successes are seldom attributable to prior education or experience in their professional specialty.

The overarching influence of science and technology in contemporary society now makes the adequate performance of this policy leadership role of highest importance. Growing recognition of the necessity to ensure that this role is adequately performed explains the recent emergence of science policy and administration as a field of study in American universities. Today, there is widespread concern at the highest levels of government, industry, and education, that the nation's human resources for science policy administration be more readily identified and more fully developed. When the need is recognized, why have we been so slow to implement the concern? In part, the explanation may be that it is easier to sense the need than to define its dimensions. Without a clear view of what the welfare of men in a technoscientific society requires of its administrative leadership, there is no visible goal for this aspect of training and development. The technical functions of administration and their associated tasks are more readily visible and definable. But universities and training programs have not been notably successful in combining education for the direct and latent functions of administration in the way that these functions combine in the actual lives of administrators. Technical education tends to find its purpose in technique itself. Too often it proceeds on a pedestrian level of mere proficiency, unelevated by a view of its relationship to higher purpose. This is why the earlier portions of this chapter have dealt with the context of the technoscientific society and the rules, functions, and tasks of its administrators. These discussions have established the premises and foundations for considering methods of developing the kind of administrative capabilities that our future welfare and security require.[18]

METHODS OF DEVELOPING ADMINISTRATIVE TALENT

In the development of administrative talent, opportunities are more important than techniques. Administrative development necessarily must be, in large degree, self-development. The function of formalized development programs is, therefore, less that of applying training techniques than of opening the way of the growth of personal capabilities. But opportunities and techniques should not be thought of as dichotomies. Techniques are often employed to enlarge opportunities, but they should be subordinate to the process of internalized personal development that occurs only within the individual personality.

Because most administrative development is and has always been self-development, the effective "self-made" administrator tends to be skeptical of the usefulness of formal administrative development programs. If innate administrative capability develops only in response to the challenges of life in organizations, then learning in seminars, libraries, and conferences can hardly be expected to contribute to on-the-job effectiveness. It may be argued that those individuals who have the required capabilities find the opportunities to demonstrate and develop them. Certainly some administrators have done so—many of them with great success. But two questions remain to be answered. First, does all of the talent that society possesses for administrative leadership identify itself in this voluntary and unassisted manner? And, second, would our known capability be more rapidly developed and more effectively used if thoughtful attention were given to its development?

There is really no way to determine how much talent for administration exists in society. There is no reason to believe that all that is activated is all that is there, or that the talent that is employed is either quantitatively or qualitatively all that is needed. Estimates of high-level administrative manpower needs are highly conditional. That is, they are based on a definition of "need" that can hardly escape some element of the subjective and the arbitrary. If highly technical qualities were required of high-level administrators, such as the specialized training required of electrical engineers or surgeons, needs would be easier to estimate. But the qualities sought at higher levels of administration are not so specialized as to limit their application to specialized opportunities. There is a point of saturation in the ability of society to absorb technical and professional specialists. But administrative capability, although often combined with technical or professional specialization, is not inherently confined to a narrow field of application.

Because of the indeterminate scope of administrative opportunity, estimates of administrative manpower needs are of limited value in planning educational programs for administrative development. Such estimates are obviously important in the internal planning activities of particular industrial or governmental organizations but would have direct relevance to educational programs insofar as a determination of an agency's future quantitative and qualitative needs in administrative manpower were joined to explicit plans for administrative development in which formalized educational programs were employed. For the United States, now and for the decade ahead, no estimate of the supply of administrative manpower talent in relation to the needs of a technoscientific age seems better than the pragmatic "not enough."

There seems to be little likelihood that our society will obtain enough of the high-level administrative leadership required to resolve its difficulties. The practical task for those persons and agencies concerned with meeting the need is to do their best to narrow the "talent gap." No comprehensive national effort to identify and develop administrative talent has been publicized, nor does one seem probable. The task is fractionalized among many institutions; yet collaboration is needed among the principal types of institutions that are trying to develop administrators. These institutions are universities, government, industry (in the broad sense), and the professions. Their interrelating functions in creating administrators should be acknowledged here, although discussion of the means for effecting their collaboration will be reserved for later.

Any practical effort to narrow the administrative talent gap must identify its objectives. In relation to the individuals for whom development opportunities are to be provided, answers must be found to the questions: Who? When? How? and Where? Who are the most promising recipients of administrative development opportunities, and how can they be identified? When, in the life histories of these individuals, can their promise be most accurately assessed and special development opportunity most profitably offered? How can development opportunity most effectively be provided—do different phases of development require different methods? And, where can formalized development efforts best be undertaken—on the job, at short-term agency-sponsored training courses, in professional associations, or on university campuses? None of these questions have unequivocally "right" answers. Circumstances determine which answers may be best in a given instance.

Identifying the persons capable of growth in the qualities required for high-level administration is basic to all other aspects of the development effort. Unfortunately our diagnostic and predictive methods for ascertaining administrative capability are not very reliable. Self-selection and the judgment of peers and administrative superiors appear to be as reliable as any means yet discovered, provided the judgment of the persons concerned is thoughtful and informed. Psychological tests have been employed to identify administrative aptitude. But the variety of methods and measurements that have been reported from corporate enterprise and from government suggest that no generally reliable psychological tests for administrative aptitude has yet become available.[19] These are obvious weaknesses in the subjective and empirical methods most commonly employed. Successful executives tend to be unduly confident regarding their ability to pick their successors. In all cases, the efficacy of the method is dependent upon a correct appraisal of the need.

The question Who? leads directly to the question When? At what stage in the life of an individual can his aptitude for administration be assessed? Individuals, as well as organizations and their task environments, change with time. Some estimate of trends in each of these factors is required, to identify the type of individual most likely to meet the administrative needs of the foreseeable future. Because of limited ability to see very far into the future, and because of the relatively short time between the maturation of personality in early adulthood and the attainment of high-level administrative responsibility, the most practical method of identifying talent is to look for indications of promise among persons on the job. This method is something better than mere trial and error if those making the selection are guided by appropriate criteria.

To find the "right" criteria for identifying promising talent, consideration must be given to the two major roles of the administrator. In his role as director of operations, technical qualifications are pertinent. The criterion of technical proficiency is seldom neglected in the selection of administrators, but it is often misapplied. The man who knows the most about the technical operations of an enterprise is not necessarily the person best qualified to relate those operations to the broader needs and activities of the organization. The appropriate criterion for technical competence in the administrator is an understanding of the essential processes of the organization, their human and material resource requirements, and their relationship to organization goals and objectives and to the task environment. The ability to see relationships must be joined to a basic understanding of technical processes.

Of importance equal to the perception of relationships is the ability to synthesize these relationships into a plan of action. Skill in perceptual analysis may qualify a man for scholarship or operations research. But the administrator who fulfills the requirements of the technoscientific age must be capable of performing the creative act of synthesis. Traits of intellectual curiosity, breadth of interest, and ability to imagine are indicators of the quality of mind that the policy aspects of administration require. Added to these traits, however, must be intellectual discipline. Evidence of this quality is thoroughness in marshalling the evidence relevant to a decision, ability to rationally order priorities among organizational tasks, and demonstrated capacity to see a task through to termination.[20]

These characteristics of administrative capability are not likely to be demonstrated in combination in an individual until he has had some significant organizational responsibility. The "performance test" is still the most reliable method of identifying administrative talent. If this is true, then formalized programs for administrative development should be planned primarily for an early career or mid-career clientele. Further, the most effective contribution of universities to administrative development will be at the graduate and postgraduate school level. It is possible to learn about administration at the undergraduate level, but this learning would be most usefully directed toward understanding administration as a social phenomenon rather than toward developing personal capabilities for administrative responsibility.

If the premises developed in this chapter are correct, the undergraduate years should broaden the intellectual foundations of the prospective administrator. The breadth of view and the intellectual flexibility gained through an adequate liberal arts education will be of greatest value in helping the future administrator develop the insight and perspective that his responsibilities require, and it will prepare him better to cope with the inevitable threat of personal obsolescence.[21]

Administrators of scientific and advanced technological programs may need graduate training in science, medicine, or engineering. Too, not all graduate students in the sciences or professions will wish to follow careers of research, teaching, or professional practice. Some of them, including some very able students, will become sufficiently concerned with the social implications of their discipline to alter their career expectations. Today, many young physicists, chemists, biologists, and engineers elect a social or behavioral science as a minor field in a doctoral program. The combination of policy studies with science has not been easy in most universities. But recognition of the need for such combinations is growing, although the existing arrangements for graduate and postdoctoral fellowships discourage deviations from single-track specialization.

The graduate school is a change-over point at which the specialist in a scientific or technical field can move toward an administrative career. At this stage in his life, the prospective administrator may not have been tested in action. But he may possess sufficient personal maturity and understanding to enable him to accurately appraise his own capabilities and to permit others to make a preliminary estimate of his potential. Post-doctoral study in public policy and administration for science and technology would ideally prepare the prospective administrator to conceptually relate his technoscientific knowledge to social needs and purposes pertinent to his future policy decisions (see Chapter 1).

Postdoctoral study in science and public policy would extend the duration and increase the cost of education for prospective technoscience administrators whose prospects for administrative careers would be uncertain. But this graduate education would equally prepare them for alternative careers. Science policy research has become an employment field in the federal government and may be a small but growing field in state government. There are also limited opportunities for this type of work in research and development organizations and in policy-oriented technoscience journalism. In addition, research and teaching in public policy for science and technology are growing in American universities; the graduate student who has not established himself in governmental or industrial technoscience incurs no great risk by enlarging his educational experience through science policy studies.

A second cross-over point from science or technical specialization to administration is during early or mid-career when the individual's aptitude for administration has been demonstrated and his professional knowledge and experience have added greatly to his value. To make the transition at this point may require a considerably heavier investment than would be required at the graduate or postdoctoral level, before earnings and financial obligations have risen. A man who has been immersed for a number of years in scientific or technical work, but has shown an aptitude and a desire for a new career in administration, may need a break in his work experience to reorient himself for new responsibilities. One means of providing for this reorientation is a leave of absence, usually for a year, for study in a university. The Career Education Awards Program sponsored by the U.S. Civil Service Commission illustrates the administrative "sabbatical experience," in which promising junior officials in government are given an opportunity for a year of study in one of several universities that have established special programs to assist their development as public executives.[22]

Not all scientific or technical people who aspire to managerial positions have aptitude for administrative work, and fewer yet could effectively play the roles required of top-level administrators. Pay and prestige attract some persons toward administration, but many of them have no great inclination toward administrative roles or responsibilities.[23] For lower levels of management, the educational development may not be the same kind that is needed to prepare top administrators. Yet the development of supervisory personnel should not be slighted. Sabbatical leaves may not be indicated at this level of responsibility, but proficiency at the supervisory level is essential to the functioning of the entire agency and to the full effectiveness of top-level administration. Moreover, it is at this level that positive indications of aptitude for higher administrative responsibilities can be observed.

Turning from the Who and When to the How and Where of administrative development, the following propositions are basic to the discussion of specific efforts.

Regardless of the level or magnitude of the development effort, the environment of an organization will greatly influence whatever benefit the organization receives. Payoff to the organization implies retention of its administrative talent. Organizational investment in administrative development does not pay off if too many of its individual beneficiaries move out into other organizations. Some outward movement of talented administrators may indirectly benefit the organization. In government, departmental officials often move into central control agencies but retain sympathy for their former employer. But an organization that discourages self-development, fails to encourage it, or tolerates indifferent performance will not obtain good results from the best conceived development effort.

Organizations heavily populated by scientists, engineers, or other professional workers often have accentuated value conflicts among their personnel. The assumptions of scientists and managers concerning the nature of work and the nature of authority are often widely variant. As scientists and technicians become more numerous and more influential in governmental agencies and industrial corporations, this area of potential value conflict requires increasing attention.[24] Robert Best suggests counseling within the organization to reconcile, so far as feasible, the individual aims of scientists and engineers with those of their corporate employer. This communicative process could be more readily achieved if scientists and engineers better understood the necessities of organizational life and the administrative process. Best believes that "new emphasis is needed in the college curriculum on the role scientists and engineers will play as employees in a corporation."[25]

The tasks of administrative development are divided between what governmental and industrial organizations can do best and what educational institutions can do best. Interaction and cooperation between the schools and the employing organizations are gradually evolving a widely applicable pattern for administrative development. Our examination of this pattern in this chapter will be confined to those parts relating to the development of capabilities for highest administrative levels. The methods of development are largely implicit in the pattern and will be described within that context. For convenience, the principal elements of this pattern are described under appropriate subheadings.

ADMINISTRATIVE DEVELOPMENT—AN INTEGRATED AND CONTINUING PROCESS

Because of the forces of change and obsolescence in our society, education cannot be a one-time, terminal affair. Personnel planning in a present-day organization must anticipate a continuing flow of human resources through the organization and must act to offset obsolescence and to mobilize capabilities for future contingencies. *Ad hoc* and "single shot" training programs will not adequately assist this effort. To be effective, the organization's development program must be woven into its pattern of operation. University programs for administrative development can maximize their contributions only if a long-term and continuous relationship to governmental or industrial programs can be established. The reasons why this continuity is important appear under other elements of the development pattern.

ESSENCE OF ADMINISTRATIVE DEVELOPMENT—ENLARGEMENT OF OPPORTUNITY FOR SELF-DEVELOPMENT

Self-development is not peculiar to administration, but to a greater degree than in more clearly programmed professions, the administrator is a product of his own experience. His direct managerial functions can be described only in part, and his implementing technique inculcated only partially through training. Because high-level administrators reach their assignments from a variety of backgrounds and over diverse routes, formal development education is best adapted to their need when it combines common intellectual experience concerning the basic tasks of the administrator with great flexibility for individual development. Much self-development of administrators will occur in interaction with other administrators under the perceptive guidance of mature scholars, experienced in both the world of public and business affairs and the world of research and academia.

Formalized administrative development programs gain force and effectiveness if they can channel the "lessons of experience" of the prospective or mid-career administrator into his growth in perception and skill. Shared experiences among a peer group of administrators may be a valuable learning experience when validly interpreted. Experience can be a false teacher and in an age of galloping change and obsolescence, must be carefully appraised for present and future relevance. In no case, however, should experience be discounted prior to a critical review.

ENVIRONMENT OF ADMINISTRATIVE DEVELOPMENT

Development for higher administrative responsibilities entails a reintegration of the individual's previous knowledge and experience. New knowledge may be required, but often its most useful function is to catalyze the reorganization of knowledge already possessed. Although we have no reliable explanation of how this process occurs in the individual, we have empirical evidence that certain types of experience or interaction are favorable to its occurrence. As suggested, exchange of ideas and evaluation of prior events among persons of comparable, but varied, experience is one such type of interaction. Joint efforts among developing administrators to solve complex organizational problems is another. In addition, action research (directed toward some specific decision or course of action) has emerged as a method especially well adapted to modern management training.[26] In all of these alternatives, the guiding presence of a perceptive and thoughtful academic mentor or adviser would be highly desirable. His presence is needed to draw significance from exchanges that might otherwise fail to get beyond the "swapping of yarns" as in a firehouse or country store.

The development process seems to require variety in interpersonal association. The administrative learner makes most apparent headway when vigorously interacting with a peer group large enough for variation in viewpoint and background, but not so large as to prevent meaningful and sustained intellectual interchange. The "critical mass" for such associative learning does not appear to have been established. Personalities, as well as mere numbers, are factors in the equation, suggesting that a range rather than a specific number would be the most reliable estimate of a catalytic group of learners. I would place the range between ten and fifteen individuals with a twenty percent margin upward or downward for exceptional aggregations of personalities. This collegial relationship is possible only where its participants share common facilities for study and informal association. Major high-level administrative development programs, such as that of the Administrative Staff College at Henley-on-Thames,[27] provide a physical setting that facilitates this interaction. Similar physical arrangements have been generally sought in other high-level administrative development programs, including those sponsored by the United States Civil Service Commission and, to some extent, by the armed services. Because special buildings, common rooms, seminar rooms, or reference libraries are elements in these arrangements, the cost of providing this type of development opportunity is high compared to many other forms of graduate education. And yet, if the facilities for interaction learning are viewed as comparable to the laboratories and instruments required for graduate education in science, medicine, and engineering, the relative costliness of the facilities diminishes.

The learning process seems to require isolated reflection as well as intellectual interaction. Overstructuring the formal development program should be especially avoided to provide uncommitted time in an amount reasonable to the needs of the learners. But there is also something to be learned by exposure to strongly contrasting attitudes and values. One of the great advantages of mid-career development programs on college campuses is the academic contrast to the normal environment of bureaucracy or professionalism. The utility of this exposure to the intellectual and cultural diversity of academia is that it affords a kind of shock therapy for the complacent or narrow technician who aspires to responsibilities requiring broader perspectives and more refined perceptions.

Because self-development is the essence of the process, well-planned development programs should provide for self-teaching. Materials facilitating individual study include special collections of books, magazines, and reports that pertain especially to the administrative process, the politics and sociology of the policy process, and public policy for science and technology. Ideally, publications in these areas, and in a broader range of scientific and humanistic fields, should be brought together in a common room used exclusively or primarily by the administrative development group. In addition to encouraging self-instruction, this library and tools for its use (such as bibliographies) help to economize the use of the learner's time, which by any scale of measurement is expensive. Carefully prepared syllabi and well-planned special libraries could free the learner from the wasted time and effort of trying to locate his own study materials. Learning to search libraries may have some value to the incipient researcher but its value to the prospective administrator appears minimal.

INFORMATION CONTENT OF ADMINISTRATIVE DEVELOPMENT PROGRAMS

A model curriculum that would seem to optimize the academic contribution to administrative development is included in this chapter (pp. 60-63). Eric Ashby declares that the education of the administrator must equip him to do four things: ". . . to know how to code his requests to experts; to teach experts how to code their requests to him; to know how to integrate the replies he gets into a simple decision; and how to transform this decision into action."[28] Ashby is right, of course, in asserting that "there is no cut-and-dried curriculum which provides this equipment." But it is possible to identify, as Ashby does, "certain ingredients in the higher education of administrators." Various curricula may be devised to provide these ingredients, but there is no stereotype for them to follow. The model suggested here merely illustrates one way of organizing a curriculum. Yet, because there are a limited number of ways to provide the information and experience that high-level administrators need, some similarities can be expected among the various curricula that may be devised. The purpose of the model curriculum would be to assist the administrator in seeing relationships between ends and means and in learning how to bring them together. The purely technical content of such a curriculum would be low, although some techniques must be understood to be used or controlled by the administrator.

The information content of administrative education should not be separated from its practical significance. I suggest that the things that the administrator needs to know may be organized in a curriculum to correspond to the major roles that he plays. Ashby's four elements related principally to the role of director of operations, although, of course, the latent function of policy leadership may be played simultaneously with the more direct and overt functions. The substance of a formal development program for high-level administrators in a technoscientific age should include the following major categories:

1. Structure and Operation of the Techno-economic System of Modern Industrial Society
2. Strategy of Scientific Inquiry and Its Relationship to Technological Innovation and the Advancement of Learning
3. Synergistic Effects of Scientific and Technological Innovations and their Implications for Society
4. Tools and Techniques of Administrative Analysis and Decision Making
5. Legal and Ethical Responsibilities of the Administrator
6. Art and Science of Communication with Professional Associates at all Organizational Levels and with "the Public"

The specific content of these categories is obviously subject to variation. Whatever the mixture, melding the topics into a coherent body of experience must be attempted. This objective may be sought in several ways, but most of them are forms of problem solving or, as Ashby puts it, "exercises in the art of making viable decisions in areas of ignorance." But these problem-solving exercises should be undertaken with the best possible understanding of the context of the decision and its implication for the future. This integrative phase of development has been sought through case studies, action research, management games, and policy analysis. No one of these methods or combination of them can be intelligently prescribed for an administrative development program without knowing how it will be used. Each should be realistic enough to allow for the constraints of time, knowledge, and social acceptance that limit all administrative action.

POLICY BASIS FOR ADMINISTRATIVE DEVELOPMENT

How can the development experience for high-level administration that has been outlined in this chapter be provided? Although the broad range of development experience has been acknowledged, our focus has been on that experience provided in universities for the higher levels of administration. In formal education, programs for high-level administration appear to belong to the graduate or postgraduate phases. Formalized development programs may or may not carry certification by diploma or academic degrees. Degree requirements, as conventionally prescribed, have tended to compromise flexibility. The growth of knowledge continually outpaces the adjustive responses of academia. Agreement in the academic community as to what its degrees should represent is more apparent than real. Even the most liberal-minded members of university faculties often become arch-conservatives when changes in degree requirements or the authorization of new degrees is discussed. Although formalized programs may be highly flexible and individualized, their relative costliness and the need to specify their intended outcomes suggest that some form of appropriate certification that will satisfy the sponsoring agencies is desirable.

Certifying successful completion of a program gives the funding agencies some tangible indication of participant accomplishment. The time, attention, and facilities to meet the needs of high-level administrative development programs can be obtained, but only if someone is willing to finance them. At present, the most probable sources of financial support are the governmental and industrial organizations that need the kind of high-level administrative talent described in this chapter. Programs for high-level administrative development require time to plan and implement. The necessary investment to make them effective is relatively great, and universities could not justify allocating resources to such education without reasonable prospects of long-term continuity. This continuity and the necessary funding can be provided only through common-purpose collaboration between the universities and the government agencies and industrial corporations that employ the administrators, provide the leaves of absence, and pay the principal costs of the advanced education.

Collaboration among government agencies, industries, universities, and professional societies is essential to matching the nation's administrative capabilities to its varied needs. But we have not yet developed systems for obtaining administrative capabilities that are comparable to those devised for procuring technological hardware and services. We do not hesitate to budget funds for maintaining computers, accelerators, reactors, or other physical components of our technoscientific system. But we are reluctant to spend money to protect or upgrade the utility of the most valuable component of the system—man himself.

In developing systems and hardware, the combined contributions of the four principal sectors of our technoscientific society—

government, industry, universities, and professional societies—have been accepted as normal and indispensable to the attainment of national goals. Innovative arrangements have been worked out for developing space technology and weapons systems. The nation pioneered government-industry-university-professional collaboration in agricultural science and is beginning to explore its utility for biomedicine and health care. But we have no adequate system as yet for developing the most important component of these, or any other, major national systems—the administrative capability that guides the system and without which it would not work or would not work well.

The Civil Service Commission is attempting to remedy this deficiency for the government of the United States. But the resources which it and various other administrative agencies have been able to muster are not yet adequate. The commission should be assisted to enlarge its commitment to mid-career development education. The prejudice against assistance for self-development should be combated insofar as it prevents government sponsorship of programs in which self-development must occur if the public interest is to be served.

Attention should also be given to the effects of Internal Revenue Service policies on self-development or on education for transfer to a new occupation. In an age of epidemic obsolescence, the efforts of individuals to upgrade their own capabilities, or to move into new fields of endeavor, should be accorded at least as much consideration as tax write-offs on the depreciation of plant or equipment. Why not accord a comparable benefit to the individual who must spend money to forestall or overcome the effects of technological change?

The nongovernmental industrial sector may be less favorably situated than government in developing administrative capabilities needed in the future. Theoretically, so-called private enterprise has a freer hand than government in developing its human resources, and competition is alleged to spur self-improvement. But in fact, the competitive environment of business may reduce the ability of talented individuals to develop their potential, if it requires absence from their jobs. If government cultivates its administrative resources and industry does not, or does not do so adequately, an eventual preponderance of techno-economic power in government seems probable.

In the technoscientific society "knowledge becomes a tool of power, and the effective mobilization of talent becomes an important way of acquiring power."[29] In this society, the university becomes intensely involved in innovating ideas and technology. But its role in mobilizing the administrative talent of the future is still largely unperceived and unappreciated. Our prevailing thought patterns are old-fashioned, overvaluing the once-scarce machine and undervaluing the abundant and expendable man. Now, in an age of enormous productive potential, the material object is expendable—only man is unique.[30]

Do we need a special institution—for example, a National Foundation for Administrative Development—to give us greater assurance that the power of knowledge, dramatically increased through science, will be freely applied in a socially responsible manner? Has managing the scientific superculture become as important as expanding its parameters through research and development? In principle, I would answer "yes" to both questions. A continuing and well-funded agency for assisting the development of the nation's administrative resources seems to me as valid as appropriating public money to educate scientists, engineers, and other professionals whose contributions are heavily dependent upon the wise management of science and technology.

A National Foundation for Administrative Development could help provide a mix of industrial and governmental administrators in university-based development programs. The foundation could also assist universities to establish effective programs and could stimulate state and local governments to upgrade their administrative personnel through training. (The idea may seem utopian, but the need is very practical.) The world is becoming a dangerous and endangered place, largely as a consequence of our failure to bring adequate social guidance to science and technology. Few, if any, more practical measures could be taken in this technoscientific society than the installation of a system for ensuring—so far as feasible—adequate administrative leadership.

In 1968 the National Academy of Public Administration[31] began a study of the conversion of professional specialists to managerial and executive roles. Phase I of this research is concerned with the transition of scientists and engineers to administrators. The results of this study, when available, should add materially to our ability to design training and development programs to meet the needs outlined in this chapter. The following section outlines the substance of a curriculum for the development of administrators with special reference to technoscientific programs.[32] Obviously this model could not be applied without modifications to fit the resources and organization of particular training centers or universities. In view of the thesis developed in this chapter, it should not be surprising that emphasis in the curriculum is on guided self-development rather than on formal classroom courses.

MODEL CURRICULUM

General considerations

In the design of any curriculum, certain assumptions regarding purpose and clientele are essential. This model assumes study at, or equivalent to, the graduate level of the university. It assumes students who have a significant background of understanding in science or technology, many of whom will also have had practical work experience in a scientific, technical, or professional field. The curriculum could be offered as a "field" toward the Ph.D. (for example, science, in engineering or public health), or it could be the area of major concentration for the degree of Master of Public Administration. But the curriculum could also be pursued by advanced or postdoctoral students without reference to academic degrees.

Important to converting scientific and technological specialists to administrators are the personal interactions of a peer group among its own members and with skilled faculty leadership. In addition, periodic interaction, seminar style, with articulate, competent administrators would be highly desirable. These administrators would, ideally, spend two or three days with the study group. Because variations in the experience of mature students are greater than would normally be expected in undergraduates, special attention is needed to develop a foundation for the group interaction aspect of the curriculum. The perceptiveness, experience, and human relations skills of the university faculty are of particular importance.

Although peer group interchange is valuable to the educational experience, the curriculum for developing the technoscientific administrator at early or mid-career must also provide for highly individualized development. Attention to common and basic understanding is important but it is equally important to allow each individual opportunity to optimize his aptitudes and to minimize his inadequacies. A really good curriculum will permit the adaptation of the program of study to the needs and capabilities of each individual student. The counseling and advisory "costs" of such flexibility would probably be higher than those normally expected in graduate education. But there is no evidence to suggest that routine academic course offerings can provide the experience needed for the development of administrative skills.

The purpose of the curriculum is to assist the development of administrative capabilities with special reference to scientific and technological programs and issues. To pursue this purpose, special facilities for study are needed. These include a "common room" for seminars and informal meetings, a reference collection of pertinent literature, and direct accessibility to at least one or two key faculty members knowledgeable in the needs of the specialist-in-transition and in the organization and "folkways" of the university. These arrangements should not isolate the student from the university, nor should they tie him by lead-strings to a faculty adviser. They should maximize the usefulness of his academic experience, whatever its duration.

What attributes of an effective administrator would a program and curriculum for technoscientific administration be designed to develop? The following listing of qualities has been suggested by the Albuquerque Operations Office of the Atomic Energy Commission.

> Ability to seek and obtain *cooperation* from his peers, so that his decisions almost invariably are taken in concert with others.
>
> *Leadership*, or the ability to persuade and inspire people to perform at or near the potential of their abilities.
>
> *Sensitivity* to the restraints of law, bureaucracy, politics, and public opinion.
>
> Ability to identify *priorities* of the various activities and goals of his organization and to recognize changes in priorities over a period of time.
>
> *Perception* of the effects that an operational decision or policy change can have on the organizational environment.
>
> Ability to effectively *communicate* organizational goals to those who execute them and to obtain appropriate feedback on performance.
>
> Ability to *synthesize* diverse views of both peers and experts, to comprehend basic differences in view, and to narrow down the number of choices to arrive at a decision.
>
> Ability to *interpret* the views and activities of scientific/technical personnel and *mediate* these with organizational requirements and needs of the non-scientific/technical segment of the organization and the general public.

The attributes of administrative effectiveness may be formulated in various ways but this list is consistent with the needs emphasized in this chapter. For it is not only knowledge and technical skill that the wise administration of our technoscientific society requires. Administrative effectiveness also implies the ability to translate knowledge and technical skill into action through people. So cultivation of these personal attributes is essential to the development process.

An actual curriculum can be constructed only at the university or training institution for which it is intended. Without knowledge of the particular organization, procedures, and resources of an institution, it is hardly feasible to design a program of education for it to administer. Moreover, university faculty cannot be counted upon to cooperate in implementing a curriculum they did not help to develop. Consultants from outside an institution can play a useful catalytic and informational role in curriculum building. But the basic work and definitive decisions must be undertaken by those who are responsible for the program.

Substantive content

The following four categories are suggested as basic elements of a one-year graduate curriculum. The categories are not necessarily integral courses. They could be organized as academic courses, provided a university could accommodate their multi-disciplinary character. Each of the categories could be organized as a one-semester course, two offered each semester. The four courses would account for approximately one-half of the required program time. The other half could be divided between individual instruction and work on a common action research or decision problem. Faculty leadership of extraordinary intellectual breadth would be required, even though participation of scholars from several disciplines were obtained.

Structure and Operation of the Techno-Economic System of Modern Industrial Society

The content of this category would be derived from history, economics, political science, sociology, and law, as well as business and public administration. Possibly the closest approximation to its substance is represented by John Kenneth Galbraith's *The New Industrial State*.[33] Its objective would be an integrative view of the complexity and dynamism of modern society. The outcome should not be an anthology of social science perspectives, but a genuine synthesis of knowledge concerning the task environment of contemporary public and industrial administration.

*Strategy of Scientific Inquiry and Its Relationship to
Technological Innovation and Advancement
of Learning*

This category draws upon the history, philosophy, and sociology of science and technology. Understanding of its substance is needed by scientists and nonscientist alike. Advanced graduate study in science, engineering, or medicine does not necessarily include consideration of science as an intellectual or social force. The prospective high-level administrator needs to understand the nature of scientific work and its effect upon the attitudes, habits, and values of scientists. An academic course in this category might usefully employ case studies of scientific inquiry. Representative of the substance of this category would be Kuhn's book, *The Structure of Scientific Revolutions*.[34]

*Synergistic Effects of Scientific and Technological Innovations
and Their Implications for Society*

No discipline corresponds to this category, which includes the new fields of science and public policy and the political science of science. This is the broadest of the four categories and, more than the others, involves the actual substance of scientific knowledge. Among the topics germane to this category would be the impact of science and technology on man's behavior and self-image and on his relationship to his environment. Other areas of concern would be the reciprocal effects of science and technology on social structure, aesthetics, ethics, cosmology, and religion. No single book adequately represents this category, but a growing number of journals encompass its substance. Among them are the *Bulletin of the Atomic Scientists*, *Scientist and Citizen*, and *Impact of Science on Society*.

*Tools and Techniques of Administrative Analysis and
Decision Making*

The objectives of this category are the ability to understand the significance and limitations of technology and proficiency in using that ability. Computer programming would not be a relevant skill under this category, but understanding how to communicate with computer technicians would be. For the higher levels of administration, technique is relevant primarily in its broadest sense. No single book summarizes the content of the category, but two books suggesting its essence are those of Simon, *The New Science of Management Decision* and Johnson, Kast, and Rosenzweig, *The Theory and Management of Systems*.

3

Human Resources for Science Administration: Can Quality Be Enhanced?

NICHOLAS J. OGANOVIC
Professor of Administration
Minnesota Metropolitan College[1]

and

HAROLD H. LEICH
Retired Chief
Policy Development Division
Bureau of Policy and Standards
U.S. Civil Service Commission
Washington, D.C.

INTRODUCTION

This chapter considers some personnel questions about the manager in scientific and engineering organizations: Where does he come from? How does he differ from the individual contributor? What does he typically do? How can he be developed to a high degree of effectiveness? The chapter combines three approaches to this subject:

1. A review of numerous books and articles in this field, although no comprehensive sweep of the literature is claimed. (The well-known exponential curve describes the increasing output on this subject, as in so many other aspects of modern society; a bibliography published by the U.S. Civil Service Commission lists 93 pages of references on scientists and engineers)[2]

2. A consideration of some aspects of personnel programs for scientists and engineers in the federal government, the nation's largest multilaboratory enterprise
3. Reports of several recent studies of federal scientists and engineers

IMPORTANCE OF MANAGERIAL SKILL

The critical importance of managerial skill in conducting technical enterprises in today's world is stressed by many writers. Several authors state that this element is largely responsible for the present technological gap between the United States and Europe.[3] In the American electronics industry, a drastic future shortage of competent managers of scientists and engineers has been forecast, and a major effort to develop the managers of tomorrow has been urged.[4]

The shortage of able managers may be common to all companies:

> The demand for able and highly trained managerial personnel far exceeds the supply of this limited human resource, and few firms appear to have an adequate supply of managerial talent for any level of management responsibility.[5]

The federal government, too, suffers from similar shortages. A deputy director of the Department of Defense for Research and Technology has said of its 79 defense in-house laboratories, "there is stagnation resulting from an inadequate flow of new blood for key R & D management positions."[6]

A statement on the importance of technology to our society comes from a former Special Assistant to the President for Science and Technology:

> In the course of supporting science and its applications, the Government and the people have come to realize how many of the problems of the modern world are affected by scientific and technical considerations and how vital scientific and technical progress is to many of the goals we set for ourselves. As a result, scientific and technical people play an important part in the Government; they comprise 40% of the top three Civil Service grades, for example.[7]

Although authorities claim that the need for technological managers is increasing (and no author was found who disagreed), little precise information is available on the numbers actually needed in the United States in the years ahead. The National Science Foundation, for example, estimates the number of U.S. scientists (excluding engineers) to be roughly one-half million, of whom 298,000 are included on the National Register of Scientific and Technical Personnel. Of the latter group, some 63,000 or 21 percent are primarily administrators or managers.[8] But no future projections of managerial needs are made.

Science and engineering, of course, will feel the same pinch as other fields during the immediate future from the smaller total number of persons who will be entering the 35-45 age bracket. The low birth rates of the Depression of the 1930s and early 1940s will pose a problem in managerial talent for all fields and will place a premium on the identification and development of competent young administrators in the years ahead.

DUTIES OF THE TECHNICAL MANAGER

To do a systematic job of selecting, training, and motivating technical managers, it would seem elementary to start with an analysis of duties or a statement of typical tasks that they perform. Only by understanding the job to be done can one intelligently map out recruitment and development plans for a particular occupation.

Two statements of such tasks throw such light on this important subject. The first lists the following typical duties in fairly general terms:

- Setting organizational objectives
- Evaluating risks
- Discovering problems inside and outside the organization before they lead to crises
- Establishing priorities
- Appraising results of programs
- Planning future courses of action
- Making decisions in complex areas involving subtle and elusive problems[9]

The second statement was developed for a preliminary study of research administrators by the Space Sciences Laboratory, University of California. The study listed the following specific functions of R & D administrators:

1. Budgeting
2. Assessing and evaluating personnel—hiring and firing
3. Long-range planning of important areas of R & D; developing new R & D programs

4. Short-range planning—selecting and approving specific projects and work assignments, reviewing ongoing work
5. Coordinating plans and projects with objectives and policies of the organization and funding sources
6. Creating and maintaining good morale and human relations
7. Criticizing scientific and technical ideas; encouraging development of good ideas
8. Maintaining adequate work levels on projects and adherence to schedules
9. Disseminating the R & D activities and accomplishments of the organization
10. Keeping up with scientific and technical events in the field
11. Conducting research or development work—personal projects[10]

To explore this subject further for this chapter, the University of New Mexico in November 1968 undertook a special study of the duties of science and engineering managers in the federal civil service, prepared by Isadore Risen. A representative sample was drawn from the job description files of the Bureau of Executive Manpower of the U.S. Civil Service Commission.

These files include all top-level positions in the three highest career grades (GS 16, 17, and 18 and certain other equivalent levels) in every federal department and agency in the competitive civil service. Approximately 2800 position descriptions were found in the fields of natural science, medicine, and research engineering. A random sample, approximately 8 percent, deemed representative of distribution among agencies, fields of work, and grade levels, yielded 209 position descriptions of managerial or related staff jobs. In considering the following tabulation of duties (Table 2), one must keep in mind that the data come from written *job descriptions,* indicating what management had in mind when each job was established, and that actual *job performance* may vary. Also it should be emphasized that the sample represents only the highest levels of the career service. First- and second-level managers and even some third-level managers are normally in lower grades.

Immediately after the tabulation was completed, Risen prepared the following statement of duties for a typical federal science manager. It represents an impressionistic composite of what the top science manager does in government.

1. He is a *line manager* in about 75 percent of the cases checked, with the same problems of staffing, organizing, budgeting, laying out work, and reviewing performance that any other line supervisor has. He may be the head of a giant laboratory

TABLE 2

Duties Listed in 209 Position Descriptions of Federal Science and Engineering Managers (Grades GS 16-18 and Equivalent)

Duty	Times Listed in 209 Position Descriptions	
	Number	Percent
Technical liaison. Service on many committees, intra- and inter-agency; speaking engagements before many organizations—other agencies, local and state governments, foreign governments, and contractors; affiliation with professional organizations to help stay abreast of changes in the field.	171	81
Program planning. Long- and short-range planning of research activities; in most cases, joint planning with other agencies, universities, and contractors, including the development of policies and procedures	168	80
Line management. Management of large organizations and small organizations, and management limited to *technical* direction as opposed to general administration	160	76
Technical advising. In an age of specialists, being a specialist who advises his boss, other agencies, college laboratories, and private contractors	136	65
Program coordination. Coordinating research with work being done by outside organizations	102	49
Program evaluation. Evaluating research being done in different places, different research organizations	88	42
Individual research. In addition to some line or staff management function, performing individual research	51	24
Staff management work. Performing usual management functions—personnel, budget, space, equipment, supplies, etc.	45	21
Preparation and presentation of scientific papers. Self-explanatory	44	21
Contract administration. Negotiation, checking of contractor capacity, and managing the contract	18	9
Contract evaluation. Monitoring contractor performance to see whether the contract has been fulfilled	16	8
Systems development. Systems development, operations research, and management "games."	12	6
Management analysis. The usual organization and procedural study made by management specialists	10	5
Technical direction of contract work. On-site technical supervision of the contractor's performance	5	2
Public information. Preparation and dissemination of reports and articles	4	2
Congressional committee presentations. Self-explanatory	3	1

or the supervisor of a small group, or he may direct only the technical or scientific effort of the group.
2. He is a *program planner, coordinator, and evaluator*. The "program" is a research activity. This research effort must be related to similar activities being undertaken in other agencies by private contractors, other governments (including foreign governments), and college laboratories. Integration of all these research efforts is crucial to the success of the total research program. The growing use of contracts as part of a unified research program is a unique feature of federal science management today.
3. He is a *technical adviser*. A scientist and research engineer is generally an expert in a narrow specialty, and others are constantly looking to him for advice—his boss, contractors, his associates, other agencies, universities, and other governments. He may be the only person *in the entire world* with the answer to their problem.
4. He is usually up to his ears in *technical liaison activity*. He is constantly representing his agency before other agencies, contractors, governments, professional societies, university laboratories, and sometimes congressional committees. He is on many special committees both within his agency or on an inter-agency basis. Because of his specialized knowledge, he is in great demand by organizations outside his agency that have a particular interest or stake in his research activity.
5. He is engaged in *individual research* in about 25 percent of the cases checked. This is very hard to measure because he undoubtedly contributes very substantially to the research success of fellow scientists that he supervises. It should be remembered that many scientist supervisors are like deans of a college in that the supervision they exercise can be described as "leadership among equals." Yet the leadership they do exercise is probably more technical than administrative, and they do contribute scientific ideas that go far to solve research problems.
6. He is engaged in *preparing and presenting scientific papers* in about 20 percent of the cases checked. This is one of the hallmarks of success for a scientist—an invitation to read his paper before his peers.

CHARACTERISTICS OF THE SCIENCE MANAGER

Several authors stress the personality differences between the typical individual worker in science and engineering and the typical manager of a technical operation.[11] One study traced these differences back to high school activities.[12]

The individual scientist or engineer is often described as introverted, absorbed by detail, possibly somewhat brusque in personal relationships, and seeking neat solutions to problems. These characteristics, often associated with successful achievement as an individual, become handicaps when the person attempts to make the transition to managerial work.[13] The science manager is dealing in areas of human relationships where black-or-white solutions may not be possible; he must have a tolerance for ambiguity. Leadership ability requires interest in people rather than introversion, as well as the capacity to take some risks in areas where results cannot be predicted.[14]

On the other hand, the able individual technical worker has some traits that are useful if he aspires to the managerial role: objectivity in solving problems, planning ability, motivation toward high productivity, intellectual curiosity, and perseverance.[15]

The following is an excellent statement of the need for managers to be aware of human relationships.

> What is the heart of the broad managerial process? I might put it in these words: management requires a humanist outlook on life rather than mere mastery of technique. It is based on the capacity for understanding of individuals and their motivation, their fears, their hopes, what they love and what they hate, and understanding the ugly and the good side of human nature. It is an ability to move these individuals to help them define their wants, to help them discover, step by step, how to achieve them.[16]

As to the educational backgrounds of science administrators, a wealth of information is buried in files of the U.S. Civil Service Commission (with respect to those on the federal rolls) and is slowly coming to light as scholars have an opportunity to delve into the data. Two studies are pertinent to this chapter, both prepared as background papers for a conference of representatives from universities and federal agencies at Bloomington, jointly sponsored by Indiana and Purdue universities and the Civil Service Commission in November 1965.

The author of the first study identified 377 federal science and engineering administrators in the three top career grades (GS 16-18) who were R & D managers.[17] His analysis showed that 73.4 percent of these had been educated in seven principal fields (Table 3). The absence of business administration, the social sciences, and the humanities from the top seven fields indicates that education in

TABLE 3

Educational Backgrounds of Science Administrators

Field of Study	Persons
Physics	64
Mathematics and statistical mathematics	58
Electrical engineering	49
Chemistry	46
Aeronautical engineering	24
Mechanical engineering	24
Chemical engineering	10
Total	275

technology is the primary background of federal science administrators.

The author of the second study analyzed the educational records of a somewhat more restricted group from the same source. He identified 161 federal civilian laboratory, scientific, or technical directors. Their fields of study appear in Table 4. The study concluded with a profile of the typical federal laboratory director:

> In common with his university or industrial counterpart, the federal laboratory director has had long service in his present laboratory environment and with his present employer.* He is somewhat older and better educated than the average industrial facility director, and younger and less well educated than university counterparts. (Education in this context applies to terminal degree by field of specialty, thus comparing engineering laboratory directors with other engineering directors, and biologists with biologists.) He has had somewhat more "bench" experience than his industrial and much less than his university counterparts. He has "come up through the ranks" in his own laboratory environment, and in all probability will remain in his present position until retirement if the laboratory or facility is in the engineering or physical sciences. If it is in the biological sciences, he may go on to a university or to industry after several years additional experience in his present position. He has probably come from one of the latter environments, for most

---

*Interpreted in the case of industrial or university directors as industry or universities in the generic sense.

TABLE 4

Educational Backgrounds of Science Directors

Major field (only one field indicated)	Persons
Engineering	41
Physical sciences and mathematics	47
Biological sciences and medicine (MD/DVM)	43
Behavioral science	5
Social sciences	3
Subtotal	139
Major fields (two fields indicated)	**Persons**
Engineering and physical sciences/mathematics	8
Engineering and biological sciences/Medicine	2
Physical sciences/mathematics and biological sciences	9
Biological sciences/medicine and social sciences	3
Subtotal	22
Total	161

biomedical laboratory directors have had lengthy experience in other occupational categories prior to Federal service. The Federal laboratory director has had little technical training, offered either by universities or Government, since completing his terminal degree. The probability that he will have more training before retirement is quite small.[18]

SHOULD THE TECHNICAL MANAGER HAVE A TECHNICAL BACKGROUND?

Granted that human relations awareness and leadership ability are essential to the science manager's success, should he come from a technical field or can he be a capable all-around administrator who is not qualified in technology?

An overwhelming number of commentators on this subject affirm the importance of having a technical staff under the management of technically qualified persons.[19] In addition to his knowledge of the the work itself and of the unique characteristics of the scientists and engineers who perform it, a technically qualified manager is more acceptable to the group supervised:

> Scientists and research engineers want the decisions which intimately affect their environment to be in the hands of first-class scientific or technical leadership. There is no

substitute for having in the top post of a research installation a technical man whose individual scientific contribution has been indisputably accepted by his peers over a period of years.[20]

An attitude survey of a broad sample of federal science administrators and engineers in 1965 tended to confirm this statement. The study was undertaken by a committee under Dr. Allen V. Astin, then director of the National Bureau of Standards, for the Federal Council for Science and Technology. The survey form, completed by 1025 persons in many departments and agencies, presented 51 statements which the respondents were asked to rate by showing the five they considered the *most important* and the five they considered the *least important*. Two of the 51 statements are pertinent here:

> Management should know enough about scientific work to provide conditions which permit productive work.

Statistically this ranked *fifth* in importance among all 51 statements. Note that it does not directly require that management be *technically qualified*, as the second pertinent statement does:

> Intermediate laboratory managers and supervisors should be competent in technical skills.

This statement ranked *twenty-first* in frequency of identification as one of the most important among the 51 statements. So, although not one of the top-ranking items, it was singled out for special emphasis by a fairly large number of respondents.[21]

The position of a principal advocate of the nontechnically qualified manager of technical functions is as follows:

> One reason for the separation of science from policy is the wide assumption that only scientists can administer scientific enterprises. This one can be changed with ease. Executives should choose the administrators of all enterprises, whether scientific or not, according to their ability as administrators and not according to their field of specialized knowledge.[22]

Another opinion is that scientists should be supervised directly by scientists, but that the next level should be composed of nontechnical persons specially trained for such assignments,[23] and a similar one (voiced during a symposium conducted jointly by the Federal Council for Science and Technology and the Civil Service Commission in 1964) is that the *third* level of supervision does not require a technical background. (for example, the manager over several laboratories), although the speaker acknowledged the difficulty of training a nontechnical person for this role. The discussion group in which he participated, however, did not agree fully:

> In the long run, there is no solution but . . . real competence in both the technical and administrative areas. . . .
>
> Because the profession of research management is so new, the method of finding people, selecting them, advancing them, and keeping them alive technically is not well understood. Over the next decade or so, we will have to learn more about it, and we can only find this out by trial and error.[24]

An intermediate position argues for an appropriate mixture of scientists and administrators:

> But if science, as such, cannot give us automatic answers to our great issues of public policy, that does not mean that scientists cannot play an important role in answering them. The administrator and the scientists are not two quite different categories of people. Indeed, it seems to me that the whole history of American government shows that the scientist and the engineer have often moved successfully into many of the most responsible and difficult administrative positions. In this respect American government has had an experience similar to that of American private business. . . .
>
> These considerations argue, it seems to me, for having a few men with quite general administrative background in the top ranks of even those agencies with heavily scientific programs. On the other hand, I would argue with equal emphasis that the administrative personnel of almost all agencies ought to have a fair proportion of men with some training and experience in science and engineering. If administration is to serve as a useful layer in the pyramid of policy between the peak of political power and the base of science and technology, it needs in its composition an appropriate mixture of general competence and special knowledge.[25]

It may be that the argument is more apparent than real; few would dispute that first-line supervisors should be qualified in the specialized work they supervise, but at some step near the top of the hierarchy, management must cease to be expert in every profession practiced near the base of the pyramid:

> Can a commanding general be expert in medicine, religion, supply, construction, road-building, railways, retail stores,

show business, and all the branches of fighting that work under his command? Can the head of any federal department be an expert in all the work that he directs? Or the head of a bureau?[26]

The following statement summarizes the situation with respect to the federal civil service:

> Similarly, American administrative reformers gave up as their goal an administrative class of the civil service based on an education in the humanities; instead they see that general administration, in many fields, must usually be built on a foundation of scientific or professional competence.[27]

And it is not only American reformers who have come to this conclusion. The administrative class in the British Civil Service, long regarded as a model by Americans and others, has come under attack in Britain itself. The Committee on Civil Service, under Lord Fulton's chairmanship, reported the findings of a two-year study in 1968. The British civil service has enjoyed a high reputation for efficiency and integrity, based largely on a tradition of recruiting young persons of liberal rather than technical education. Yet the committee recommended a basic change in this long-established system:

> [1.] First, the Service is still essentially based on the philosophy of the amateur (or "generalist" or "all-rounder"). This is most evident in the Administrative Class which holds the dominant position in the Service. The ideal administrator is still too often seen as the gifted layman who, moving frequently from job to job within the Service, can take a practical view of any problem, irrespective of its subject-matter, in the light of his knowledge and experience of the government machine. Today, as the report of our Management Consultancy Group illustrates, this concept has most damaging consequences. It cannot make for the efficient despatch of public business when key men rarely stay in one job longer than two or three years before being moved to some other post, often in a very different area of government activity. A similar cult of the generalist is found in that part of the Executive Class that works in support of the Administrative Class and also even in some of the specialist classes. The cult is obsolete at all levels and in all parts of the Service....
>
> [2.] Thirdly, many scientists, engineers and members of other specialist classes get neither the full responsibilities and

corresponding authority, nor the opportunities they ought to have. Too often they are organized in a separate hierarchy, while the policy and financial aspects of the work are reserved to a parallel group of "generalist" administrators; and their access to higher management and policy-making is restricted. Partly this is because many of them are equipped only to practice their own specialism; a body of men with the qualities of the French *polytechnicien*—skilled in his craft, but skilled, too, as an administrator—has so far not been developed in Britian. In the new Civil Service a wider and more important role must be opened up for specialists trained and equipped for it. . . .

[3.] Scientists and other specialists are also open to criticism here: not enough have been trained in management, particularly in personnel management, project management, accounting and control.[28]

In carrying out the managerial function over technical work, the British have sometimes split the assignment between two people—one from the administrative hierarchy (that is, a nontechnical administrator) and one from the technical hierarchy (for instance, an engineer). This is what they call a *joint* hierarchy, and a variation is called a *parallel* hierarchy. (Note that this is different from what we describe on p. 79 as *parallel ladder*.) But in practice the technical hierarchy is subordinate to the administrative one. The management consultants who studied this form of organization for the Fulton Committee recommended that it be superseded by *one* hierarchy:

> . . . In our view, therefore, there is no case for joint or parallel hierarchies . . . we consider the best organizational form to be a single integrated structure under a single head. Where the administrative content is preponderant, it may be that a non-specialist with the right background may be most suitable to head the group. However, in all the situations we examined, it would have been more appropriate had the head of the group spent most of his career as a specialist and been given the necessary training and experience in the administrative procedures of government. It is essential, in our view, that such posts as these, and higher ones, should be open to specialists with the appropriate qualifications and that personnel and management procedures should be devised to assist and encourage them to fit themselves for top posts. . . .

... We saw that this principle had already been accepted in the research establishment we visited. Not only did the Head of the Establishment—a scientist—have a significant autonomy in respect of financial expenditure but he was also the single head of an organization which included scientists, other specialists and administrators.[29]

To summarize this much-discussed issue, there is general agreement that the immediate supervisor of scientists and engineers should be technically qualified, and that the person at the very top in a large organization (for example, a large corporation or a government department) need not be, although the trend seems to favor the technically trained top manager. The area of disagreement lies in the intervening echelons; here the preponderance of opinion argues for requiring technical competence in addition to administrative skill at levels considerably above the first-line supervisor (see Chapter 1).

INTAKE OF JUNIORS WITH MANAGEMENT POTENTIAL

If the need for technical managers is critical, and if, ideally, they should emerge from technical fields, it would seem desirable to pay considerable attention to management potential in recruiting young scientists and engineers. But comparatively little comment on this important subject was found in the books and articles reviewed for this chapter. Apparently recruiters are primarily looking for high technical competence, and university students, as well, are concentrating on preparation for technical assignments. One observer believes that recent engineering graduates are not likely to be attracted to the administrative aspects of engineering work, since they are more interested in professional and technical development.[30] On the other hand, those engineers who are becoming aware of the need for courses in the behavioral sciences to date must go outside schools of engineering to find such offerings, for example, to schools of business administration.[31]

That a high proportion of engineering students will eventually find themselves in managerial roles seems indicated by a study published by the University of California at Los Angeles. Fourteen years after graduation, 60 percent were in clearly managerial positions while only 8 percent had no supervisory responsibilities at all.[32]

The Bloomington conference of universities and federal agencies included the following statement in the summary of its proceedings:

> It was recognized that universities have a part in the general broadening of the interests and knowledge of persons employed in Government. It was thought to be particularly important that scientists and engineers (especially those who will later be managers) achieve breadth in undergraduate education. With a basic education including sophistication in the social sciences they should be better able to interpret and learn from their experiences.[33]

The strongest statement on the need for a technical organization to assess managerial potential in its junior intake comes from the vice president of a research and engineering company:

> When we interview people in colleges, we look first for a strong technical background and then we look for indications of leadership potential. When new people start with the company, we make a very concerted effort to spot as early as possible the ones who have some interests and some leaning and some ability for administrative matters.[34]

Two suggestions seem to come naturally out of this discussion: (1) that engineering and science faculties encourage interested students to take optional courses in the behavioral and management sciences, wherever they may be offered on the campus; and (2) that recruiters assess leadership potential as well as technical competence, so that intake will not be restricted to highly competent but introverted graduates.

THE DUAL LADDER SYSTEM

Traditionally, in the old-style industrial or federal laboratory, advancement in grade and status came chiefly by promotion into supervisory and managerial posts. The poor changes of advancement as an individual worker created a strong incentive for the ambitious to compete for administrative assignments, even if they considered them distasteful. In many cases this situation led excellent technical people to leave the field of their competence in order to flounder unhappily in their new management jobs. "Spoil a good plant pathologist to make a poor supervisor" is the way one of the authors first heard this cliché, from Dr. W. W. Stockberger, pioneer director of personnel of the U.S. Department of Agriculture in the 1930s.

As a distinguished federal science administrator has noted:

> The administration of scientists requires that some scientists of high professional reputation be moved into administrative

positions. For those few who also have administrative talent this is proper. But when excessive administrative responsibility is a necessary concomitant to promotion, scientific productivity is lost . . .[35]

In recent years many technical organizations have attempted to solve this problem by deliberately setting up a channel for advancement of qualified scientists and engineers outside of the supervisory line. This plan is variously known as the "dual ladder" or "parallel ladder" or "two-track" system. Numerous references to it are found in the literature.[36]

The general idea of the dual ladder system is to allow technical people to seek advancement to high salaries and prestige by continuing their creative role as individual contributors. In this way the productive output of the organization is maintained or even stimulated, and persons who have no liking or aptitude for management are not tempted into such a role. A study of a number of technically oriented companies indicated that most of the high-quality companies had established dual ladders, while the lower quality companies seldom had done so.[37]

Related to the dual ladder plan is a principle known as the "impact of the man on his job" or the "man-in-job" concept. Traditionally in a personnel system based on job evaluation, primary attention became centered on the characteristics of the job, and the special qualifications of the person in the job were sometimes overlooked. Under the newer emphasis, it is recognized that in professional work the impact of the person's qualifications and performance is crucial. That is, the person can make or break his grade-level in the personnel structure.

This principle is fully provided for in the federal personnel system as it affects professional workers. The following statement is taken from the Civil Service Commission's guide for evaluating research positions:

> The duties and responsibilities of a research position are especially dependent upon the interplay between the research situation or assignment (within an appropriate job environment) and the individual qualities of the incumbent. Creativity and originality are inherently of central importance in a research situation, because the purpose of research is to extend man's knowledge and understanding. Yet, while the job situation may call for creativity and originality, the extent to which these qualities are actually brought into play is dependent in large part on the incumbent. Furthermore, while nonresearch situations are typically structured as to breadth

(necessarily so, in order to fix responsibility and prevent functional overlapping), the research situation is typically expandable in breadth in accordance with the incumbent's capabilities. Hence, it is recognized that where the nature of the research situation involves a high potential for original and creative work, the work of the position may be performed at any one of several levels, depending in part upon the level at which the incumbent is capable of working and his motivation. This leads to what may be termed a "man-in-job" concept, based on the interaction of the assignment and the incumbent. . . .

In recognition of the fact that the incumbent's personal qualifications do, in a research situation, have a profound impact on the dimensions of the job which results, this guide provides for considering both the research situation or assignment, and the qualifications of the scientists who occupies the situation or assignment. These factors together constitute the position actually being performed and form the basis for determining grade level.[38]

How this plan actually works in a federal research organization is illustrated by the following statement in the Agricultural Research Service's evaluation guide:

The Plan provides for consideration of the researcher as an individual professional scientist. It provides an opportunity for him to exercise his individuality and initiative and provides for his advancement on the basis of an evaluation of his specific scientific contributions. This evaluation is made by a committee of his "peers" who are familiar with the area of work involved. The Plan offers a challenge to each of our research scientists. His advancement depends primarily upon his own accomplishments. There is nothing automatic or periodic about these promotions. They are contingent upon the scientist's own efforts.

On the matter of grade relationship with the administrative supervisor, ARS takes the position that an outstanding scientist can very well be placed in the same grade or, in some instances, in a higher grade than his supervisor. This is predicated on the fact that the basic concept of the Evaluation Plan involves the recognition of the importance and value of the individual's contributions derived from his personal originality and creativeness. These factors are unique to the individual and cannot be supervised in the normal sense. In essence, the scientist involved in the conduct of research has been removed from the normal administrative grade ladder.[39]

Some evidence points to the preference of technical workers to advance up the professional rather than the administrative ladder. According to one study, 62 percent of the scientists and engineers queried in industry preferred the professional route and only 38 percent preferred the administrative one.[40] Another investigator found that scientists rate the opportunity to be promoted within the research field as more important than advancing to supervisory positions.[41]

On the other hand, a professional ladder based on the individual's high qualifications does not necessarily solve all of management's problems. The literature reflects some disillusionment with the dual ladder system.[42] Individuals often cannot rise as high on the professional as on the management ladder; persons on the professional ladder tend to become isolated from the organization, and they may become difficult to supervise and coordinate.[43] A study of the operation of a dual ladder in a large electronics manufacturing firm found that advancement to senior levels was possible only by the managerial route.[44] Another study also found that the managerial ladder is the one that gets true recognition,[45] and a third, of a research company,[46] ended similarly.

Likewise in federal laboratories, it appears that the top three career grades are attained by science and engineering managers and related consulting, staff, and contract-supervision types. The University of New Mexico study summarized by Risen (pp. 67-69) identified only 2 individual "bench" scientists, in contrast to 209 line managers and individual workers in consulting or staff roles. Although the Civil Service Commission's instructions to federal agencies on how to grade professional positions encourage the use of dual ladders and set no artificial limits on the advancement of individual creative workers, that survey indicated that in practice the "bench" scientist rarely attains the topmost grades. This may reflect the belief of agency administrators that senior science administrators and consultants properly belong in higher grades than even the most productive individual scientists.

A recent study by the Civil Service Commission's Bureau of Executive Manpower verified the University of New Mexico sample survey. In making a functional classification of all federal scientists and engineers in the three top career grades, the bureau found that only 4 percent of the group served as individual workers, the same percentage as for those in other occupations.[47]

To the extent that top positions can be filled only via the management ladder, we return to the original problem of forcing highly qualified technical people to become managers to advance, sometimes against their own preferences.

Another problem of the professional ladder, if not carefully handled, is the danger that its occupants will be looked on as misfits who could not make it in the administrative field.[48] To avoid such a stigma, some laboratories transfer scientists from one ladder to another.[49] An executive of Bell Telephone Laboratories would go even further and eliminate any artificial boundaries between the two ladders, which he feels tend to fence people in; instead he would establish a broad classification system that would reward creative effort wherever found.[50]

A glimpse into the future may reveal an even greater use of dual ladders in years to come: *American Labor* reports that white-collar unions in Canada are beginning to make such ladders a collective bargaining objective, so that individual scientists and engineers can advance to higher levels.[51]

FIRST RUNGS UP THE MANAGERIAL LADDER

The prediction of managerial potential in any one individual is still uncertain despite the efforts of numerous psychometricians.[52] Further comments on this subject are made by Dr. Lynton K. Caldwell in Chapter 2 of this volume.

Without going through psychometric procedures it may still be possible to identify those who show aptitude for the management ladder by their interest in people or their seeking additional responsibility.[53] These are the ones who might be given trial assignments as science interns, project leaders, junior members of management committees, arrangers of symposia, and similar duties.

As a guide to federal agencies in identifying kinds of experience that show supervisory aptitude, the Civil Service Commission recently published the following list as part of its new qualification standard for white-collar positions:

1. Assignments which involved providing guidance and training to new employees
2. "Project leader" assignments which involved coordinating and integrating the work of others into a completed work product
3. Assignments which required the candidate to work closely

with others to resolve problems, coordinate activities, or gain acceptance of a product or procedure
4. Assignment as a "troubleshooter" or source of advice to others regarding the work of the unit or organization
5. Assignments which involved devising new work methods and procedures or improvements in existing work practices, and getting the cooperation of employees in applying the new methods and practices[54]

At this early stage in a young person's career the choice of ladders should not be irrevocable.[55] Rather this should be an experimental career phase to see if the candidate performs acceptably in his new administrative role and if he enjoys the experience. If the trial does not work out as hoped, he could return gracefully to full-time professional work without stigma or what government terms an "adverse personnel action."

If the first trial run is successful, two or three similar experiences might help to confirm managerial ability, coupled with training in human relations skills and the business of the organization. If success continues, the next rung might be formal assignment as a section head.[56]

Regardless of the details, some systematic plan for identifying and training promising juniors for future administrative assignments is of major importance to all technical organizations. The report of a special committee of the National Academy of Sciences, under the chairmanship of James R. Killian, Jr., made the following comments on this subject in 1964:

> The early identification, development, and assignment of men capable of playing key roles in the technical direction of big projects is one of the most important responsibilities of top management in companies engaged in large-scale research and development. . . .
>
> Industry, government, and the universities all share a responsibility to train and develop more managers and project engineers who combine thorough understanding of the technology they manage with mastery of the art of leadership.[57]

PREPARING AN EMPLOYEE FOR HIS FIRST MANAGERIAL DUTIES

When a technical employee receives his first supervisory assignment, whether on a trial or a regular basis, in all fairness he should be given suitable training or coaching in the human relations aspects of his new role, rather than be left to flounder on his own. One of the authors remembers the day when a fellow worker, after four years on a first-name basis, was elevated to his first leadership position and let it be known that "Mister" should be used on both sides.

Many industrial research organizations have established formal training programs for this purpose.[58] A good management development program for engineers might include the following training techniques: classes, seminars, evening courses, conferences, outside reading, job rotation, service on committees, coaching, understudying executives, advanced management courses, and membership in professional societies.[59]

As reported later in this chapter (pp. 91-95, 99-108), a questionnaire completed by managers in some federal science and engineering organizations showed that the majority had not been given training on assuming their first management responsibilities. This situation is now being corrected; in 1968 the commission established a new standard for promotion to supervisory jobs at lower and middle grades that *requires* all agencies under the program to give appropriate training to employees who are being promoted into their first supervisory assignments. This applies to professional as well as other white-collar positions.[60]

In the federal service the greatest amount of in-service training is and should be done by the employing agencies. The Civil Service Commission, as the central personnel agency, conducts a wide variety of courses that can best be done centrally for the whole government or introduces new courses on a demonstration basis. For example, the commission conducts a course for inexperienced first-line supervisors on nomination and reimbursement from any federal agency. The prospectus includes the following paragraph:

> The first-line supervisor is often selected from among the most capable employees. In most instances he brings knowledge of his technical area to his new responsibility, but very little supervisory experience. The transition is a challenge and is made difficult when there has been a lack of training. This course provides timely and concentrated assistance to the employee making this frequently difficult transition. It introduces him to the basic legal requirements affecting the management of Federal employees and to selected managerial techniques and concepts which may be studied in greater depth in subsequent courses developed for experienced supervisors.[61]

Clearly the Civil Service Commission could never conduct all the supervisory and management courses needed to serve a government of nearly three million civilians. In a recent twelve-month period, 4509 scientists and engineers participated in commission-conducted courses, ranging in length from two or three days to two weeks. These participants were at all grade levels and therefore were by no means all novice supervisors.

The commission's role is rather to stimulate each agency to conduct its own training programs, to develop model or demonstration courses and a few central courses where indicated, to improve the competence of agency trainers, and to coordinate training among all agencies so that courses in one agency can be opened up to employees of other agencies. The latest trend is to include state and local government employees, as well, in federal training programs where appropriate arrangements can be made.

HOW CAN THE TECHNOLOGICAL MANAGER INCREASE HIS EFFECTIVENESS?

As the technological manager climbs the ladder above his first supervisory assignment, his need for training continues but becomes considerably broader.

One list of the qualifications of a good manager includes such elements as decision making, willingness to take risks, planning for the future, working knowledge of all phases of the organization, organizing and leading a team, and delegating authority.[62] Systematic training at middle management and higher levels by such methods as seminars and case studies would therefore seem appropriate to enhance the manager's capacity to meet his responsibilities.

An organization that gears special training programs to each rung of the management ladder is Esso Research and Engineering Company, as described by McNab.[63] Similarly, the U.S. Civil Service Commission offers central training programs for technological managers of federal agencies at middle and higher levels. These concentrate on the principles of good management and issues of science policy in a public service setting rather than on scientific subject matter as such. They are designed to complement existing agency programs by filling in the gaps.

One such course for middle-level professionals, entitled *Supervisory Scientists and Engineers,* offers the following content:

> The program will examine the special nature of the managerial job in R & D organizations by identifying the unique motivational characteristics of scientific personnel, by discussing the impact of organizational structure on the productivity of scientific groups, and by exploring the leadership

patterns best designed to release and accelerate scientific creativity. The program will also take up such topics as the flexibilities of the Federal personnel system in managing scientific groups, career development concepts applicable to scientific personnel, and the administrative and financial practices which permit the most effective direction and control of scientific groups.[64]

A management course conducted by the Civil Service Commission for top professional employees of federal agencies is titled "Management of Scientific and Engineering Organizations" and covers the following topics:

> Management planning for science and engineering programs
> Formulating and administering science and engineering budgets
> Direction and development of human resources
> Communications requirements of modern science and technology
> Management of in-house resources and contract programs
> Behavioral science research and its implications for managers of research, development, and other technical programs[65]

A special advanced seminar on science policy for top federal career officials takes the form of meetings with noted authors to discuss their works:

> The Ideas and Authors program in Science and Government is designed to afford senior Federal science and engineering executives an opportunity to meet with individuals outside the Government community who have made extremely significant contributions to the operational and philosophical base which directly, or indirectly, influences Federal policies and their application in practice. In addition, the program is constructed in such a fashion as to afford the senior executive with responsibilities for direction of major government projects, an opportunity to interact directly with guest authors, thus conveying the executive's critical and/or constructive commentary to the author himself.[66]

In addition, many agencies conduct their own management courses, and to an increasing extent individual federal laboratories are making arrangements with universities nearby to conduct courses, some for academic credit and some not, at the actual work site after hours. In 1971, twelve federal agencies sponsored 125 such off-campus study centers in cooperation with 91 schools and colleges, and more than 26,000 employees participated. (These

HUMAN RESOURCES: CAN QUALITY BE ENHANCED?

figures cover many fields in addition to science and engineering.) A typical off-campus center at a federal laboratory is the one at the Naval Weapons Center, China Lake, California, run in cooperation with the University of Southern California. The following courses are offered:

> Administrative Systems Analysis
> Research in Complex Organizations
> Organization and Management Theory
> Fundamentals of Public Administration
> Public Administration Problems
> Problems in the Administration of Financial Resources[67]

As another example, Florida State University offers a graduate program at the Kennedy Space Center, Cocoa Beach, Florida, for NASA employees. This leads to the degree of Master of Science in Management.[68]

ROTATIONAL ASSIGNMENTS

In addition to training courses of various types, a planned program to rotate promising technical people among a variety of assignments may be useful in intensifying their preparation for a managerial role. Two current examples may be of interest in the federal service, one depending on selection of highly qualified candidates from outside the service and the second one relying on internal selection:

Grants associates program in NIH

To select and develop managers for the burgeoning field of medical research, the National Institute of Health (NIH), with the cooperation of the Civil Service Commission, appoints scientists with doctorate degrees in health-related sciences to become "grants associates." Typically the new appointees have had from two to five years of post-doctoral experience. They undertake a year's program of seven to ten actual work assignments in a research management situation. Carefully planned training conferences and seminars are combined with this work experience under the guidance of a senior scientist who serves as preceptor to the grants associate. Since its beginning in 1963, about fifty scientists have completed the program and some have already advanced to positions of broad responsibility.[69]

Science and technology fellowships in Commerce Department

In recent years the Department of Commerce has run a program designed to enhance the abilities of highly selected scientists and engineers in its technically oriented components, such as the Environmental Science Services Administration, National Bureau of Standards, and Patent Office. About fifteen participants are chosen each year. They undertake first a four-week orientation in federal science activities, conducted by the Brookings Institution, and then a one-week orientation in the Department of Commerce. The purpose of this introductory period is:

> .... to expose the participants to such broad issues as the criteria for choice among scientific and technical programs, the economics of fiscal policy and the budget for science in Government, technological innovation as an element in the Nation's economic growth, scientific man-power as a problem of national policy, the role of higher management in decisions on technical programs, science and technology in world affairs, and the organization of scientific activities in the Federal Government.[70]

The participants are then given work assignments of eight to nine months in bureaus other than their own, designed to provide challenging work experience in fields related to their specialties. These assignments involve decision-making activities and offer good opportunities for career development. On completion of the program, the participants return to their original organizations. Success of the new program is indicated by the later selection of many participants for key leadership positions.

SHOULD THE TECHNOLOGICAL MANAGER CONTINUE HIS OWN RESEARCH?

Once successfully launched on a managerial career, the scientist or engineer may be faced by a difficult personal problem: should he continue to leave some free time for his own technological work—creative work that built his reputation and gave him deep personal satisfaction—or should he devote himself fully to his new management duties? Can he find equal personal satisfaction through technological achievements at second hand, that is, by "getting results through people" rather than by conducting his own "dirty hands" experiments?

Here again authorities disagree. Substantial numbers conclude that the manager must spend full time as a manager and delegate the actual performance of technological work.[71] Pertinent here is a preliminary study of research administrators in which self-administered rankings of certain functions were tabulated. The great majority of respondents gave low rankings to the importance of doing their own research and to the time actually spent on research. On the other hand, a majority rated their personal satisfaction in performing research as high or medium, thus hinting at the frustration a research administrator must experience.[72]

Other authorities advocate that the technological manager should continue his own research activities if possible.[73] The following statement was made at a 1964 symposium by a deputy director in the office of the Secretary of Defense:

> One of the troubles of a technical administrator is that everything is all worked out slickly on charts. Except for dividing by two or three, once in a while, or maybe for using a slide rule to get some percentages—one never is forced to think quantitatively at all, and this is very bad indeed. The technical administrator *must* participate—either in research, himself (which is hard to do on a part-time basis and not get lost and fall behind)—or he must have extensive personal contact with the technical people.[74]

The amount of time a technological manager can devote to his own projects will vary, of course, depending on his particular rung on the management ladder. So, one would expect a project leader, on the bottom rung, to spend a considerable amount of time performing the same work as others in his group. This was borne out in studies of companies in which the typical project leader spent about 30 percent of his time on engineering duties and about 70 percent on administration.[75] In the upper echelons such a high proportion of technical work would be rare.

THE ENVIRONMENT FOR CREATIVITY

A large subdivision of the growing literature of scientists and engineers deals with this topic. There is general agreement that a light touch is needed in the management of technological workers.[76] Traditional methods of discipline and giving order from the industrial or military past are clearly inappropriate for professionals. Instead, an academic environment of colleagues working together is sought, and the term "lead" seems more appropriate than "manage," "direct," or "control." R & D laboratories often use "project leader" or "group leader" rather than hierarchical titles.[77]

Elements needed to build a creative environment can be summarized as follows:

> Make challenging assignments and set mutually agreed upon goals
> Give the professional sufficient latitude to operate in achieving these goals
> Provide adequate technical tools, as well as clerical and technician assistance
> Provide fair and equitable salary and benefits and adequate work places
> Promote a professional-level environment[78]

The matter can also be expressed in the following terms:

> Management is also responsible for creating an environment which is receptive to innovation and professionally stimulating but which does not foster individualism to the point of organizational anarchy. It must recognize the problems, needs, motivations, and idiosyncrasies of the professional and draw him into a participating role in the organization so that he can see an association between his personal objective and the group objectives.[79]

Excessive paperwork, punching a time clock, spending time on subprofessional work, and restrictive delegations of authority for such things as minor purchases are well calculated to drive out the creative spirit. Sometimes in large organizations these administrative annoyances slowly accumulate without awareness by management of their stifling effect. In the Department of Defense a systematic effort was made to sweep such accumulations out of military laboratories. The program resulted in many improvements:

> Better communication between professionals and management echelons
> Greater delegations of authority to laboratory management, for example, for security review of scientific papers
> Relaxation of restrictions on purchase of scientific periodicals and instruments
> More favorable interpretation of restrictions regarding employee training[80]

In an organization as vast as the federal service, there is an understandable lag in communicating changes down through the echelons. The Civil Service Commission has made many changes in personnel policies designed to enhance the quality of the staffing and the environment in federal laboratories, but sometimes the intervening echelons add restrictions so that the intended flexibility is lost by the time it reaches the laboratories. To counteract this tendency, the commission seeks to communicate directly with federal scientists and engineers through training conferences, journal articles, and a special pamphlet designed to inform the technological worker about the personnel system as it affects him.[81]

A report on joint efforts of the commission and the Department of Defense to improve personnel practices in defense laboratories stated that 89 percent of the problems could be solved within existing federal personnel policies and were caused by internal procedures and controls:

> The key to laboratory effectiveness is flexibility. It is possible to tailor a system of controls within the Federal Personnel System which is compatible with the need for a creative environment within technical organizations. This can be different from those applied to other organizations . . .
>
> There is no reason why we cannot achieve a tailored management system for technical organizations, which is comparable to that of progressive industrial technical organizations and compatible with the Federal Personnel System. . . .[82]

On a government-wide scale, the Federal Council for Science and Technology urged agencies to take the following steps:

[1.] To sustain a challenging scientific environment capable of keeping and attracting good people, the mission of laboratories should be broad enough to present a set of scientifically challenging tasks, and redefined wherever necessary to give them continuing vitality;

[2.] Research directors should have more authority;

[3.] Layers of management over laboratories should be reduced;

[4.] Full advantage should be taken of the flexibility existing in Civil Service regulations, and these regulations should be less often used as a rationalization for ineffective personnel management.[83]

REPORT OF A SPECIAL STUDY OF SCIENTISTS AND ENGINEERS

To throw additional light on many of the points discussed in this chapter, the authors conducted an informal questionnaire survey, with the cooperation of Professor Albert H. Rosenthal,

Director of the Program for Advanced Study in Public Science and Administration of the University of New Mexico, during the winter of 1968-69. The questionnaires were circulated in several federal laboratories and in Sandia Laboratories, a major public-private agency established under a contract with the Western Electric Company for public purposes and financed by public funds. The results are reported in Tables 5-21, which appear in the appendix to this chapter (pp. 99-108; see also pp. 13 and 28).

Usable responses were received from 193 federal scientists and engineers who rated themselves as administrators and from 195 who rated themselves as individual professional workers. The survey should not be taken as representative of all federal scientists and engineers, since it was heavily weighted in favor of engineers and physical scientists, omitting the life sciences, and in favor of a few developmental laboratories rather than research laboratories. (More than half of the responses came from the Army Department's White Sands Missile Range, New Mexico.) As to levels of responsibility, the respondents represented lower and middle rather than top levels.

From Sandia Laboratories, 161 usable responses were received from scientists and engineers who rated themselves as administrators and 144 from those who rated themselves as individual professional workers.

The results are reported separately for federal administrators and individual workers, and Sandia administrators and individual workers. The small number of cases precludes any definitive conclusions, but within the limitations mentioned, the study may throw some light on the characteristics and attitudes of administrators as opposed to individual professionals.

Salary Differences (Table 5). As might be expected, the administrators as a group were clearly ahead of the individual workers in salaries. Sandia respondents were substantially ahead of the federal respondents in both groupings.

Highest Degree Attained (Table 6). The Sandia respondents in both groupings showed a marked edge in level of educational attainment over the federal groupings. This may explain, in part, the salary advantages shown in Table 5.

Year Highest Degree Attained (Table 7). The administrators are definitely the older group, judging by the year of attaining highest degree. This may, in part, explain the salary advantage of administrators over individual workers noted in Table 5. No marked differences are apparent between the federal and the Sandia respondents.

Professional Field of Highest Degree (Table 8). This study agrees with many predecessors in indicating how few technological administrators come from nontechnical disciplines. The four groups are all heavily weighted toward engineering, with the individual federal workers showing a high proportion in physics and mathematics as well.

Plan for Selecting and Training Technological Administrators (Table 9). The question regarding this item was put to the sample groups in different ways: The administrators were asked about the situation *when they made the initial move into* administration, while the individual workers were asked about the situation *in their present organization.* The responses are therefore not directly comparable, although the results are very close. It seems clear that the great majority of respondents were skeptical about the existence of a systematic plan.

Plan for Advancing Individual Workers to Higher Levels without Taking Administrative Duties (Table 10). The question regarding this item was asked in the same way as the question in Table 9. Again, the great majority reported the absence of a systematic plan. The Sandia administrators felt somewhat more strongly than the individual workers that there was no such plan.

Importance of a "Two-Track" System (Table 11). The questionnaire briefly defined the two-track system in the same terms as this chapter (pp. 78-82) and asked respondents to rate its importance. No great difference is shown among the four groups of respondents; the majority affirmed the desirability of having such a system.

Extent to Which Organization Provides for a Two-Track System (Table 12). The responses to this item indicate that despite numerous articles in the literature recommending a two-track system, most respondents in several federal laboratories and in a major industrial laboratory did not think such a system existed in their organization. These responses, compared with those in Table 11, hint at potential dissatisfaction among the individual workers. That is, most of them rated the importance of a two-track system as being high, yet a majority reported that their present organization does not provide for one. The responses of the individual workers to this item can be compared to their responses in Table 10, which asked the question in a different way. This internal test of consistency of responses seems to yield satisfactory results.

Ways of Selecting and Training Technological Administrators (Table 13). The four groups of respondents were in very close agreement on two methods of selecting and training administrators: more than half of each group favored an internal tryout by assigning candidates to minor administrative duties, and a quarter of each group favored periodic screening of candidates by a committee of senior professionals. Regarding the other three choices offered to respondents, no pattern was detected in the answers of the four groups.

Desirability of Manager Performing Research (Table 14). A large majority of all four groups voted yes on this question, with the individual workers showing a somewhat larger affirmative response than the administrators. Some respondents wrote in qualifications to their answers. The general tenor of these comments was to the effect that the administrator must keep up with his field, if not by doing research then in other ways.

Research Time Available, Administrators Only (Table 15). Almost half of the administrators reported no research time available, although a majority rated individual research as highly desirable on Table 14. Here again is a hint of potential frustration.

Kinds of Professional Employees Supervised, Administrators Only (Table 16). An attempt was made to have respondents assess the extent to which their employees were in the same field as themselves, in related fields, or in different fields.

Entrance into First Administrative Assignment, Administrators Only (Table 17). The leading method by which the responding administrators first came into administrative work was through suggestions by supervisors or other officials, followed by their taking the initiative themselves.

Advancement to Present Level, Administrators Only (Table 18). Administrators were asked whether they could have advanced to their present levels as individual workers. A majority replied that they could not have done so, in a sense verifying their responses on Tables 10 and 12.

Training Received, Administrators Only (Table 19). A majority of administrators replied that they had received no special training or coaching on beginning their first administrative assignments. This points to the need for management action to ensure that new supervisors are properly prepared for their changed responsibilities.

Courses of Value, Administrators Only (Table 20). The administrators were queried about the courses that had assisted them in preparing for administrative roles and about the university graduate-level courses they would recommend to prepare people for such roles. The replies were by free answers rather than by check-lists and related courses have been grouped in the summary in Table 20. As to recommended courses, the responses of the federal and the Sandia administrators were surprisingly similar. Judging from this study, an ideal curriculum to train new administrators would concentrate on such subjects as organization and management (preferably in the context of technological organizations), supervision, leadership, personnel management, psychology, communications skills, and possibly finance.

Preference for Administrative versus Individual Professional Work, Individuals Only (Table 21). Finally, the individual workers were asked whether they had ever made a definite choice between administrative and individual work and were asked to amplify their responses. The great majority replied that they had not made such a decision, and nearly half (exactly the same percentage of federal and Sandia respondents) said they would welcome an opportunity to move into administration. This result differs from the findings of other studies reported earlier in this chapter.

NEED FOR BETTER PERSONNEL DATA ON SCIENCE MANPOWER

Despite the many statistics and studies cited in this chapter, there is still a serious lack of current information on science manpower in the United States. The problem was delineated several years ago in the Killian report of the National Academy of Sciences, which listed the following item among its seven major themes:

> The pressing national need for meaningful, reliable data, expertly analyzed and coordinated, on the allocation and utilization of scientists and engineers. Because of the inadequacy of such data, decisions affecting utilization have so far been based largely on hunches, intuition, and fragmentary information.[84]

The report was supported by an accompanying article, which included the following statement:

> Reports and monographs about scientists and engineers are accumulating, it is true, but since the study of the subject is still in its early stages, having begun on any scale only during the past decade, relatively little "hard" information has been established. Definitions and classifications are not yet standardized, so that to the query of how many scientists and engineers were working in 1960, several answers over a range of about 20 per cent or more can be obtained. It is ironical that the Bureau of Labor Statistics knows much more about the wages of streetcar motormen than about the salaries of research scientists.[85]

A second article with the report gave as one of its conclusions:

> The time is now ripe to give serious attention to developing more adequate, timely, and decision-oriented information concerning one of the nation's most valuable resources—its scientists and engineers—and their work, objectives, supporting personnel, and other factors closely related to their utilization and development.[86]

As one step in the effort to standardize the reporting of data on science and technical manpower, the National Science Foundation requested the Civil Service Commission to develop a functional classification scheme. The resulting study, published in 1966, covered professional personnel in engineering and the physical, biological, mathematical, social, and health sciences and listed standard codes and categories.

Functional Classification for Scientists and Engineers

Code	Category
11	Research
12	Research Contract and Grant Administration
13	Development
14	Test and Evaluation
21	Design
22	Construction
23	Production
24	Installation, Operations, and Maintenance
31	Data Collection, Processing, and Analysis
32	Scientific and Technical Information
41	Standards and Specifications
42	Regulatory Enforcement and Licensing
51	Natural Resource Operations
81	Clinical Practice, Counseling, and Ancillary Medical Services
91	Planning
92	Management
93	Teaching and Training
94	Technical Assistance and Consulting
99	Other—Not Elsewhere Classified[87]

If the science community can agree on such a standardized classification, as well as on standard occupational definitions, it may be possible in the future to visualize a national reporting system that will continuously yield trends on intake, mobility, career development, turnover, and functional patterns of technological manpower in this country on a real-time basis. Within the Civil Service Commission, plans are under way toward such a system for the federal work force, and we hope that it can become part of a larger system for the whole economy. Such a plan would allow meaningful comparisons among universities, nonprofit organizations, private industry, and federal laboratories.

CONCLUSION

To answer the question in the title of this chapter, it seems clear that the quality of science administration *can* be enhanced by systematic planning and follow-through. The literature in this fairly recent but fast-growing field gives many case studies and examples in industry and government of planned programs that appear to give better results than hit-or-miss efforts.

Details must necessarily vary according to the history, environment, and mission of each organization, but several guidelines seem to be emerging that can be applied in the selection and development of competent science administrators. The answers are still suggestive rather than definitive, and much additional thought and effort need to be applied to this important problem. With these qualifications, the following suggestions for improving the quality of science management are offered by way of summary:

1. Undergraduate and graduate students of science and engineering who are interested in managerial careers should be encouraged to take such courses as psychology, organization, and management as optional subjects.
2. Selection programs for entrance-level scientists and engineers should seek a due proportion of candidates who show evidence of administrative interests and ability as well as those with high academic records in technical subjects. (Note: These two groups are not mutually exclusive.)
3. A planned effort should be made to assess the administrative interests and potential of junior scientists and engineers so that, early in their careers, those who show promise can be exposed to administrative opportunities. Methods for such exposure might include formal administrative internships,

less formal rotation among a variety of technical and administrative assignments, or committee work. The key element here is the tryout concept. If the candidate is successful and wishes to pursue the opportunity, he can be formally placed on the first rung of the administrative ladder. If the tryout does not work, he can be returned to full-time technical assignments with a minimum of embarrassment.

4. R & D organizations should consider the possibility of some appropriate "dual-ladder" system for professionals. By providing opportunities for advancement in individual technical assignments, management will decrease the motivation for professionals without administrative potential to seek advancement by the supervisory route. At the same time, the system should not rigidly type all professionals as being permanently on one ladder or the other. Interests and abilities may change and the way should be open for movement between the ladders.

5. Professionals who are selected for their first supervisory assignments should be given formal training or coaching in supervision, management, human relations skills, or related subjects if they have not recently had such training.

6. Middle-level professionals who are selected for higher managerial or policy assignments should be given graduate university training, or the equivalent, in such fields as advanced management and public policy implications of science and technology. Here again rotational assignments may be valuable in broadening the knowledge and background of such persons.

7. Once started up the managerial line, the science manager should earn further advancement on the basis of his demonstrated effectiveness and his potential for further development, rather than automatically by length of service.

8. Definite efforts should be made to ensure that science administrators keep up with pertinent developments in science and technology through such means as science symposia, refresher courses, or actual participation in research.

9. Every effort should be made to develop and encourage a stimulating environment for creative work by providing a challenging and worthwhile scientific mission for the organization, by eliminating administrative annoyances, and by building a professional spirit in colleague relationships.

APPENDIX

Results of Questionnaire to Federal and Sandia
Laboratories Administrators and
Individual Professionals

TABLE 5
Questionnaire Results Regarding Salary Differences

	Administrators		Individual Workers	
	193 Federal	161 Sandia	195 Federal	144 Sandia
Median salary	$18,760	$22,720	$13,280	$16,400

TABLE 6
Questionnaire Results Regarding Highest Degree Attained

Highest Degree	ADMINISTRATORS				INDIVIDUAL WORKERS			
	193 Federal		161 Sandia		195 Federal		144 Sandia	
	No.	%	No.	%	No.	%	No.	%
Bachelor's	129	66	74	47	152	78	58	40
Master's	37	19	43	27	30	15	51	35
Ph.d.	13	7	44	27	3	2	35	24
None	10	5	0	0	6	3	0	0
No response[a]	4	2[b]	0	0	4	2	0	0

[a] Respondents were told to omit answers to any questions they regarded as inappropriate.
[b] Percentage columns may not add to 100 because of rounding of figures.

The tables in this appendix are from N. J. Oganovic and H. H. Leich, Questionnaire to Federal and Sandia Laboratories Administrators and Individual Professionals, U.S. Civil Service Commission in cooperation with the University of New Mexico, Program for advanced study in Public Science Policy and Administration (1968-69).

TABLE 7

Questionnaire Regarding Year Highest Degree Attained

Year of Highest Degree	ADMINISTRATORS				INDIVIDUAL WORKERS			
	193 Federal		161 Sandia		195 Federal		144 Sandia	
	No.	%	No.	%	No.	%	No.	%
1930-39	15	8	3	2	5	2	4	3
1940-49	45	23	45	27	12	6	20	14
1950-59	90	47	74	47	62	31	42	29
1960-68	31	16	39	24	104	53	77	53
No response	12	6	0	0	12	6	1	1

TABLE 8

Questionnaire Results Regarding Professional Field of Highest Degree

Field of Highest Degree	ADMINISTRATORS				INDIVIDUAL WORKERS			
	193 Federal		161 Sandia		195 Federal		144 Sandia	
	No.	%	No.	%	No.	%	No.	%
Engineering	118	60	107	66	88	45	100	69
Physics	24	12	32	20	46	24	23	16
Mathematics and Statistics	23	12	8	5	45	23	5	3
Other Natural Sciences	11	6	13	8	7	3	15	10
Social Sciences, Humanities	6	3	1	0	3	2	1	1
No response	11	6	0	0	4	2	0	0

TABLE 9

Questionnaire Results Regarding Plan for Selecting and Training Technological Administrators

Did/does your organization have a systematic plan for selecting and training administrators in science and technology?	ADMINISTRATORS				INDIVIDUAL WORKERS			
	193 Federal		161 Sandia		195 Federal		144 Sandia	
	No.	%	No.	%	No.	%	No.	%
Yes, a systematic plan	11	6	5	3	17	9	7	5
Some plan, less than systematic	76	39	43	27	75	39	43	30
No such plan	103	53	111	69	94	48	86	60
No response	3	2	2	1	9	5	8	6

TABLE 10

Questionnaire Results Regarding Plan for Advancing Individual Workers to Higher Levels without Administrative Duties

Did/does your organization have a systematic plan for advancing individual professionals contributors to higher levels without taking on administrative duties?	ADMINISTRATORS				INDIVIDUAL WORKERS			
	193 Federal		161 Sandia		195 Federal		144 Sandia	
	No.	%	No.	%	No.	%	No.	%
Yes, a systematic plan	9	3	5	3	23	12	19	13
Some plan, less than systematic	75	39	39	24	58	30	37	26
No such plan	104	54	114	71	106	55	82	57
No response	5	2	3	2	8	4	6	4

TABLE 11

Questionnaire Results Regarding Importance of a "Two-Track" System

In your opinion, should a scientific or technological organization provide a systematic two-track system of advancement for its professionals?	ADMINISTRATORS				INDIVIDUAL WORKERS			
	193 Federal		161 Sandia		195 Federal		144 Sandia	
	No.	%	No.	%	No.	%	No.	%
Yes, an important feature of a good place to work.	159	82	122	75	170	87	119	83
Not too important	13	7	19	12	14	7	20	14
Undesirable	7	4	7	4	5	2	2	1
No response	14	7	13	8	6	3	3	2

TABLE 12

Questionnaire Results Regarding Extent to Which Organization Provides for a Two-Track System

Does the personnel system in your organization adequately provide for the two-track system? (Can check more than one.)	ADMINISTRATORS				INDIVIDUAL WORKERS			
	193 Federal		161 Sandia		195 Federal		144 Sandia	
	No.	%	No.	%	No.	%	No.	%
Yes, fully provided for	33	17	15	9	12	6	13	9
Personnel office should make greater effort to publicize the program	50	26	19	12	43	22	26	18
Not provided for	87	45	105	65	115	59	88	61
Can't get top grades as individual worker[a]	14	7	4	2	10	5	0	0

[a] These responses were write-ins.

TABLE 13

Questionnaire Results Regarding Ways of Selecting and Training Technological Administrators

What are the soundest ways in which a scientific or technological organization can select and train current professional employees to become administrators? (Can check more than one.)	ADMINISTRATORS				INDIVIDUAL WORKERS			
	193 Federal		161 Sandia		195 Federal		144 Sandia	
	No.	%	No.	%	No.	%	No.	%
Let the employee's aptitude and preference for administrative duties show themselves in the normal course of his employment, without a special program	80	41	95	59	56	29	48	33
Temporary assignment to minor administrative duties (acting as unit chief, coordinator, committee member, etc.) on an informal "tryout" basis	112	58	91	56	112	58	77	53
Periodic screening of possible candidates for administrative work by a committee of senior professionals	52	26	40	25	45	23	35	24
Periodic announcement of opportunities to enter a selection and training program for administrative work	78	40	22	14	96	50	51	35
Special training or coaching for administrative duties, prior to or following first administrative assignment	108	56	61	38	91	47	61	42

TABLE 14
Questionnaire Results Regarding Desirability of Manager Performing Research

In general, is it desirable for the science or technological administrator to be able to spend some time on his own individual investigations or research?	ADMINISTRATORS				INDIVIDUAL WORKERS			
	193 Federal		161 Sandia		195 Federal		144 Sandia	
	No.	%	No.	%	No.	%	No.	%
Yes, highly desirable	125	64	105	65	143	74	99	69
Doesn't matter too much	30	15	31	19	17	9	17	12
Undesirable	11	6	5	3	13	7	10	7
Depends on level of job[a]	8	4	9	6	9	5	3	2
Other ways to keep up (reading, etc.)[a]	6	3	3	2	2	1	1	1
No response	13	7	8	5	11	6	14	10

[a]These responses were write-ins.

TABLE 15
Questionnaire Results Regarding Research Time Available (Administrators Only)

Time Available	ADMINISTRATORS[a]			
	193 Federal		161 Sandia	
	No.	%	No.	%
No research time available	92	47	68	42
10% or less	23	12	9	6
11–20%	33	17	31	19
21–30%	19	10	21	13
31–40%	3	2	9	6
41–50%	6	3	6	4
More than 50%	13	7	17	10
No response	4	2	0	0

[a]Tables 15-20 show responses to questions asked of administrators only.

TABLE 16

Questionnaire Results Regarding Kinds of Professional Employees Supervised (Administrators Only)

Professional Fields Supervised	ADMINISTRATORS			
	193 Federal		161 Sandia	
	No.	%	No.	%
All employees supervised in same professional field as the administrator	52	27	27	17
In same and related fields	75	39	77	48
In same, related, and different fields	30	15	40	25
All in related or different fields	20	10	14	9
No response	16	8	3	2

TABLE 17

Questionnaire Results Regarding First Administrative Assignment (Administrators Only)

How did you happen to enter upon your first administrative assignment in science or technology?	ADMINISTRATORS			
	193 Federal		161 Sandia	
	No.	%	No.	%
Suggested by supervisor or other official	82	43	105	65
Took initiative in seeking such assignment	71	37	41	26
"Happenstance"	23	12	8	5
Other	13	7	7	4
No response	4	2	0	0

TABLE 18

Questionnaire Results Regarding Advancement to Present Level (Administration Only)

In your opinion, could you have advanced as an individual worker to your present level?	ADMINISTRATORS			
	193 Federal		161 Sandia	
	No.	%	No.	%
Yes	72	37	45	27
No	111	58	97	60
No response	10	5	19	12

TABLE 19

Questionnaire Results Regarding Training Received (Administrators Only)

When you began your first administrative assignment in science or technology, did you receive any special training or coaching in your new responsibilities?	ADMINISTRATORS			
	193 Federal		161 Sandia	
	No.	%	No.	%
Yes	60	31	59	37
No	110	58	101	63
No response	23	12	1	0

TABLE 20

Questionnaire Results Regarding Courses of Value (Administrators Only)

Name of Course	What university courses or programs have you participated in that have assisted you in preparing for administrative, management, or administrative policy posts in the field of science administration?				What courses at graduate level would you recommend be made available to prepare people of scientific backgrounds for more responsible positions in science administration or management policy formulation?			
	193 Federal		161 Sandia		193 Federal		161 Sandia	
	No.	%	No.	%	No.	%	No.	%
Organization, management, business administration	56	29	14	9	52	27	31	19
Management of technical organizations	-	-	5	3	18	9	13	8
Systems/industrial engineering	4	2	3	2	2	1	6	4
Technical courses in science and engineering	2	1	11	7	5	2	7	4
Supervision, leadership, human relations, personnel	14	7	5	3	41	21	33	20
Psychology	16	8	4	2	19	10	28	16
Operations research	3	2	0	0	12	6	3	2
Computer	2	1	3	2	1	0	3	2
Economics	8	4	5	3	8	4	11	7
Law	4	2	0	0	1	0	3	2
Speech	6	3	1	0	5	2	10	6
Writing	2	1	2	1	7	4	9	6
Accounting/finance	3	2	2	1	5	2	13	8
Mathematics/statistics	3	2	0	0	2	1	0	0
Philosophy	-	-	1	0	2	1	4	2
Other liberal arts and social sciences	1	-	2	1	2	1	10	6

TABLE 21

Questionnaire Results Regarding Preference for Administrative versus Individual Professional Work (Individuals Only)

Have you at any time made a deliberate decision to continue in individual productive work in your profession rather than go into the administrative channel?	INDIVIDUAL WORKERS[a]			
	195 Federal		144 Sandia	
	No.	%	No.	%
No (without further amplification)	39	20	23	16
No—would probably not be interested in administrative work if an opportunity opened up	31	16	34	24
No—would welcome opportunity to move into administration	91	47	68	47
Yes—primary aptitudes and interests are focused on making individual contributions rather than on administration	27	14	13	9
Yes—better opportunities in individual productive work	5	2	1	1
Other	2	1	5	3

[a]Responses to a question asked of individual professionals only.

Guiding Work Relationships among Scientific, Engineering and Administrative Professionals

WESLEY L. HJORNEVIK
Deputy Director
Office of Economic Opportunity
Washington, D.C.

NATURE OF THE PROBLEM

The administration of science and technology as we know it today, institutionalized in large organizations, presents a number of problems, not the least of which is the task of guiding working relationships among scientific, engineering, and administrative professionals. Regardless of the nature of the institution, the multidisciplinary requirements of complex technological goals necessitate interaction between professionals of varying value systems, expectations and satisfactions, and work habits. Although such institutions are becoming more and more commonplace, NASA's Manned Spacecraft Center (MSC) at Houston, Texas, is a unique example of this particular phenomenon. Since its creation in 1961, those of us responsible for guiding the development and operation of MSC have been concerned with this problem on a continuing basis. In fact, since both our space programs and the mission of MSC are becoming more varied, we are more concerned now than ever. This is the result of the expansion of the scientific content of the flight programs, accompanied by a proportionate increase in the importance of the scientist as a member of the team.

In this chapter I have attempted to deal with the practical tasks of the administrator in inducing teamwork among scientific, engineering, and administrative professionals. Such aspects of the problem as the influence of professional attitudes on work relationships, the interpretation of goals, communications, and operational techniques for facilitating goal-directed coordination are discussed. I have relied heavily on specific situations and experience at MSC since I am a directly involved practitioner rather than an academician. Frequent references are made to the applicable literature, much of which is based on studies of many situations. The experiences and techniques described, based on the MSC situation, are a very limited sample and should be assessed with the knowledge of their limitations. Before proceeding directly to these topics, however, a brief account of the assumptions underlying the decision to create MSC will be presented to provide a more penetrating understanding of why the organization has its present design.

INSTITUTIONAL BACKGROUND

Early history

The National Aeronautics and Space Administration (NASA) was founded in 1958. During its early stages of development, NASA had to organize swiftly and carry out an operational space program simultaneously. At its birth, NASA absorbed the National Advisory Committee for Aeronautics (NACA), a 43-year-old aeronautical research agency which had also pioneered in space research. In addition to NACA, several other smaller groups from the Navy and Army helped form the initial staffing of NASA. In fact, about one-half of NASA's 34,000 employees came from other agencies.

About 50 percent of NASA's employees work under the Office of Manned Space Flight (OMSF). OMSF includes three field centers and a headquarters staff in Washington. The organizational location of OMSF and its supporting centers in NASA Headquarters is shown in Fig. 1. The Manned Spacecraft Center (MSC), Houston, is responsible for flight crews and spacecraft; Marshall Space Flight Center (MSFC), Huntsville, Alabama, is responsible for the launch vehicles; and Kennedy Space Center (KSC), Florida, is responsible for launch operations.

GUIDING WORK RELATIONSHIPS AMONG PROFESSIONALS 111

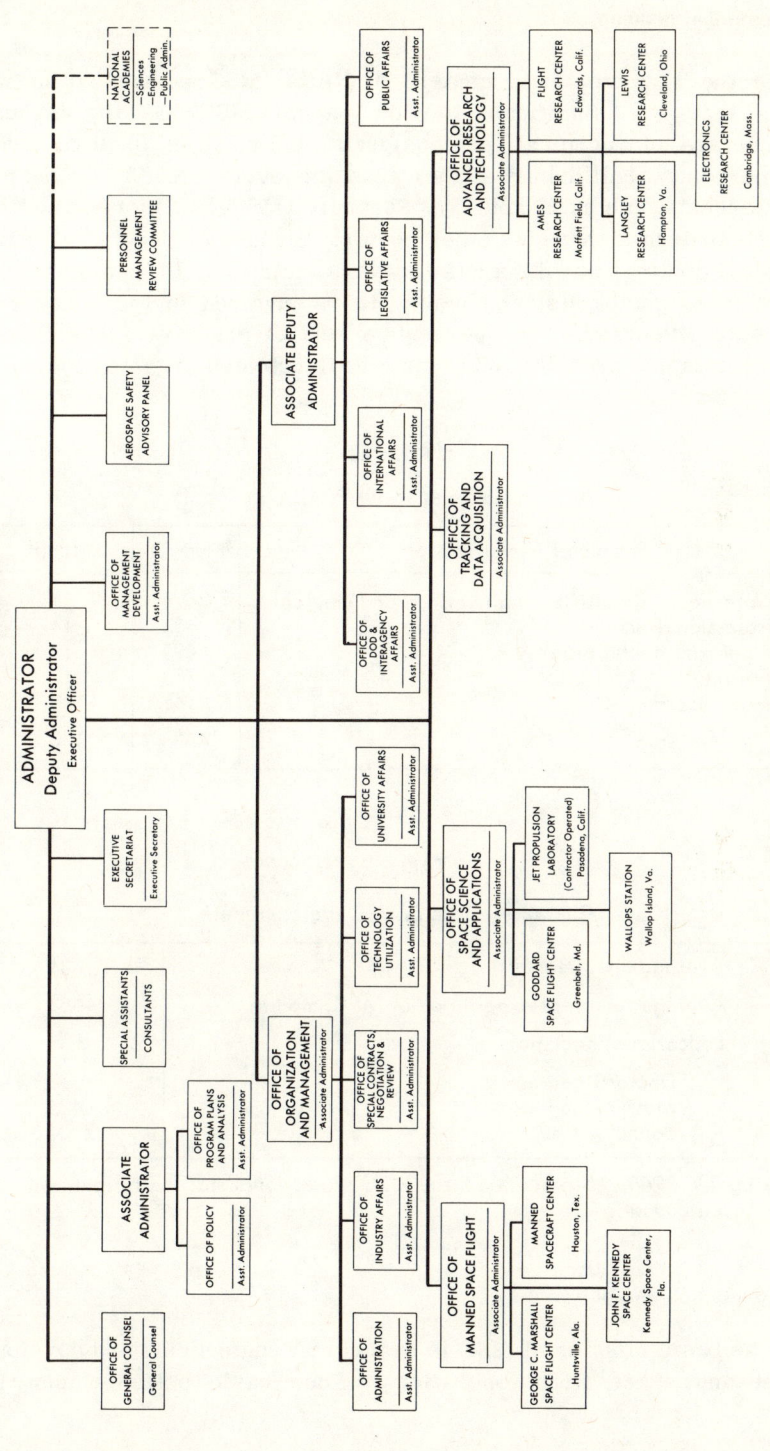

Fig. 1. NASA Organizational Chart (May 1968)

Professional makeup

Of the 11 major field centers of NASA, MSC is unusual in two ways that are significant to this paper. MSC has the highest percentage of technical professionals in relation to total staff (55 percent), significantly higher than the overall NASA percentage (38 percent) (Tables 22 and 23). Secondly, MSC has more varieties of professionals than any other center. Besides engineers, we have medical doctors, physiologists, lawyers, nutritionists, optometrists, physicists, geologists, and many others involved in the conduct of the Apollo Program. The percentage and diversity of our technical specialists are probably unique in a goal-oriented organization.

TABLE 22

MSC Manpower Profile

Personnel Classification	Number	Percent
Professional scientific, engineering, and medical	2494	55
Professional administrative	653	14
Supporting technician	495	11
Clerical	753	17
Wage Board	141	3
Total	4536	100

TABLE 23

Characteristics of MSC Professionals

Average age, years	35
Average length of experience at MSC, months	53
Educational background[a]:	
Doctor's degrees	90
Master's degrees	424
Bachelor's degrees	2304

[a] During FY 1968, 15 percent of the MSC professional staff participated in the Advanced Education Program.

Basic mission and policies

The basic mission of MSC is spacecraft engineering and development and space flight operations. Four basic policies must be explained at this point to understand why the MSC mission is what it is and to begin to explain what we have done in guiding work relationships at MSC.

A fundamental NASA policy that had considerable effect upon MSC was the decision to keep space and aeronautical research as divorced from development activities as possible. It was the judgment of Deputy Administrator Hugh L. Dryden that the glamour and dollars associated with development programs could overwhelm research effort, and thus that the two types of activities should be conducted in separate organizations and centers.[2] As a result of this policy, the former NACA aeronautical research centers, Langley, Ames, and Lewis (Fig. 1), have been largely preserved as research laboratories, and the major hardware development programs have been assigned to the other centers either created by NASA or transferred from other agencies.

The second policy concerns how the development programs would be executed, that is, how the responsibilities would be divided between government and industry. In evaluating this problem, NASA management thoroughly reviewed the experience of the other government agencies—the Departments of Army, Navy, and Air Force and the Atomic Energy Commission—that had previously been charged with managing large development efforts. Various methods had been used by each of these agencies, and each was considered. After weighing the matter carefully, it was decided that NASA would perform technical management of its programs, including the conduct of flight tests, and rely upon industry for the design, development, and manufacture of the component systems. With the existing base of strong technical staffs at the various NACA centers to build upon, the most effective utilization of available national resources strongly suggested that NASA manage its programs with civil service personnel.[3] Relying upon NASA's experienced research personnel for management and industry's combination of personnel and facilities for design and manufacturing appeared to be the most effective means of employing the nation's resources.

Not overlooked, however, was the necessity for NASA's development managers to maintain their own technical competence if they were to be effective managers. In view of this requirement, it was determined that the task of technical management would also include conducting certain systems and subsystems tests in NASA facilities under NASA direction. As a consequence, the new development centers, Manned Spacecraft Center (MSC), George C. Marshall Space Flight Center (MSFC), and John F. Kennedy Space Center (KSC), became conceptual design and test and evaluation laboratories instead of merely management office complexes. So the staffs of these centers would then be able to maintain their competence, certain test and evaluation functions were assigned to the centers.

It should be pointed out here that you can clearly run a research and development (R & D) program from an office; laboratory environment is not a prerequisite. For example, the development of the nuclear submarine was managed from a program office in Washington. Without question, a project manager can go wherever the laboratory capability exists to buy his technical and research competence. However, the intent of those who envisioned space flight was not simply to pursue and complete a project; rather, it was to build a solid baseline of advanced technological competence in the United States.

The fourth policy concerned the conduct of space science research. It was decided that NASA would rely upon the universities for much of the scientific research—recognizing that many of the most competent scientists were conducting space research at universities, and basic research facilities were already available.

Organizational framework

Essentially, then, the following four basic policies and their consequences established the operational framework for MSC:

1. Separation of research and development
2. In-house technical management and contracted design, development, and manufacturing
3. Technical competence maintained by providing laboratory facilities at development centers to perform in-house testing
4. Reliance upon universities for much of the scientific research

Within this framework, MSC management has developed the organization, facilities, and management practices that have enabled it to progress in 10 years from a small cadre of 35 people to a major government installation whose programs at peak periods involve as many as 200,000 people from government and industry.[4]

With these policies established, it was time to establish the organizational framework for the development programs of NASA. MSC was created around a nucleus of highly creative and competent scientist-engineers from the Langley Research Center. This group, known as the Space Task Group, had been working together on a manned satellite program for some time before they were officially established as an entity November 5, 1958. Langley Research

Center was world-renowned as an applied science center. The Space Task Group members, among them the design engineers who conceived Project Mercury, reflected the applied research and development environment of Langley.

President Kennedy's decision in 1961 to land a man on the moon and bring him safely back to earth by 1970 focused NASA's attention on the enormity and complexity of the challenge it was nurturing in Project Mercury. His decision laid to rest the attitude some had held toward the Space Task Group—that their activity was more or less a stunt, a premature overreaction to the Russian Sputnik, and would go away. It was obviously not going away, and it was also obvious that the immense resources they would need to develop manned flight would dwarf and bury the efforts assigned any other center. Consequently, in 1962, the Space Task Group moved to Houston, Texas. Men who had been primarily producers of research services would now have to learn to be buyers of both services and products on a very grand scale. It should also be clear from the preceding discussion that the basic goal of the organization had been clearly and unmistakably set by the highest level of government, that it was immense, that it was a development job and not a basic research mission.

APPROACH TO PROBLEM

Definition of professional

We have chosen to approach the subject of this paper, guiding work relationships among managers, scientists, and engineers, from the standpoint of the professional and the organization. Understanding professionalism is basic to understanding what we have tried to do at MSC as managers. I use the term "professionalism" to include engineers, life and physical scientists, medical doctors, and people from fields such as personnel, law, resources management, and procurement. The subject of professionalism, as it applies to scientists, has been treated very thoroughly by William Kornhauser in *Scientists in Industry: Conflict and Accommodation*.[5] In it, he states that the following four criteria are essential if a person is to be considered a professional:

1. Specialized competence that has a considerable intellectual content
2. Extensive autonomy in exercising the special competence

3. Strong commitment to a career based on the special competence
4. Influence and responsibility in the use of the special competence

Nature of negative factors

A manager should clearly understand professionalism because of its importance to the organization. Because professionals must necessarily work in organizations in our society, the manager must do all he can to achieve a balance between professionalism and the organization. "Professionalism has as its primary function the protection of standards for creative activities; organization has as its primary function the efficient coordination of diverse activities."[6]

How does this dichotomy of function manifest itself in an organization? "The scientific enterprise seeks understanding rather than utility, technical excellence rather than operating ease, creativity rather than routine. Specialized organization, on the other hand, is an instrument designed for utilitarian ends; it places a premium on orderly and predictable action."[7] In other words, the organization's goals are in conflict with such professional goals as autonomy, the search for new ideas, and making contributions to the scientific community.

If professionals need, and are needed by, organization, is there any chance that such an arrangement will work out, given the respective goals of the professional and his organization? Kornhauser suggests that "the tension between the autonomy and integration of professional groups, production groups, and other participants tends to summon a more effective structure than is attained where they are isolated from one another or where one absorbs the others."[8]

Basic differences of approach exist among the professional subgroups. The scientist wants to know everything about his particular interest and wants a perfect answer if scientifically possible, and the resulting requirements may well exceed budgetary and manpower limitations. The engineer is more used to practical limitations, but may well ask for more stringent quality controls than are necessary for the purpose, or for heavier or more expensively produced materials or devices, all of which render solutions more difficult and more costly. The administrative professional is more used to dealing with hard numbers of dollars, man-hours, production rates, interest, and overhead, and has a tendency to think in terms of numerical identities or rates for all aspects of a task, whereas the other professionals recognize that many aspects are subject to a judgmental range of values and can never be given a firm number. To assure understanding of these points in administering NASA's programs, the Civil Service announcements recruiting for NASA administrative positions require that these professionals have had close prior working relationships with R & D organizations, or a certain number of scientific or engineering educational credits, or both.

Methods of handling

The literature also gives us some clues as to what the organization can do to facilitate the professional's adjustment to the organization. "Organizations that use professionals can usually create for them specialized roles in partially segregated substructures of the organization so that the professionals may carry on their own activities as they require. This differentiation of roles in a variety of specialized substructures of the organization as a whole helps to preserve professional needs for autonomy."[9]

Further, there are certain specific things that can be done, as this listing from Pelz and Andrews[10] shows:

1. Distribute authority and decision-making functions as widely as possible.
2. Recognize that risk-taking is a necessary component of innovation.
3. Establish an effective and comprehensive communications system.
4. Minimize the burden of formal structure as much as possible.
5. Reward innovative behavior.

All of the literature seems to come around eventually to one key point—the organization relies on the professional, cast in the role of manager, to bridge the gap between the organization and the professional.

> The role of scientist-administrator seeks to accommodate the professional demand that only professionally trained persons are capable of judging professional work, and simultaneously to accommodate the organizational need for administrative controls. It also seeks to accommodate professional autonomy by relying on advice rather than orders in matters directly relating to professional judgment, notably in the formulation

of specific research problems and procedures. At the same time, it seeks to meet the needs of efficient organization by operating unilaterally on administrative matters, such as the scheduling and coordination of work.[11]

MSC SPECIAL PROBLEMS

In light of the considerations of professionalism, the four basic policies underlying MSC discussed earlier take on new meaning because they each harbor potential problems that must be reckoned with by management. Additionally, three other dilemmas are inherent in the MSC environment which require further amplification: (1) the multiplicity of professional values, (2) the complexity of the management job, and (3) the long lead time of the Apollo Program. First, the nature of MSC's work requires that we have a highly competent technical staff capable of advancing current technology simultaneously. And, to support this very heterogeneous effort, we need a broad complement of administrative professionals who can perform the support activities, which are neither science nor engineering. Clearly, we have a large organization of what Peter F. Drucker[12] refers to as "knowledge workers," and especially of people of different knowledges and skills working together.

Multiplicity of values

It is probably an understatement to suggest that our objective, lunar landing and return, is very clearly viewed with different emphasis by all these people, depending upon their professional bias. Our medical doctors would capitalize "Man." In a sense, they are a constraining influence. They are concerned with "How much can a man take? What is his limit? Why?" The engineer would undoubtedly underline the word "landing." His overriding concern is the technology of flight, the spacecraft, and its performance as a dynamic, complex machine. The scientist would probably emphasize "moon" and the almost breathtaking opportunity it offers to advance man's knowledge. "Where did it come from? What was its evolution; what forces have been active?" The astronaut test-pilot would view the goal from a different polarity: the challenge, adventure, and opportunity to test and ride man's most advanced vehicle. The manager would look at all these things and worry about finding the proper balance.

Complex managerial environment

The second dilemma for management results from the complex managerial environment, and it manifests itself in two ways. First, almost all the technical staff at MSC are managers in a sense, because all of the design development and manufacture of the hardware is done by industry. MSC's job is one of defining the mission, selecting the approach, giving the contractor requirements, monitoring his progress, and approving his product. This management responsibility includes control of costs and schedules as well as technical matters.

The environment is further complicated by the controls, as reasonable as they are, held by NASA Headquarters and the fact that at least 50 percent of the work is performed by subcontractors, who take their direction from the prime contractor and not from MSC. In other words, every action must go through a maze of channels and approvals. An independent-minded, action-oriented engineer can find such an involved managerial environment very frustrating.

The second aspect of this particular dilemma is the problem for those within the MSC environment who are managers of this contract-monitoring function. They are, in effect, managers of managers, and so are three steps removed from the actual work, the technical details with which they enjoy working. These men have even less time for technical involvement since they must administer the monitoring organizations which they head and, consequently, spend much time on personnel, budget, space, equipment, and other administrative matters. Obviously, people adjust to the circumstances to varying degrees, but the basic situation does contain some inherent incompatibilities.

Long lead time

The final dilemma, and perhaps the most unsolvable, is the time factor. The original feasibility studies conducted by NASA were performed in 1960 and 1961. Although spacecraft design continued for several years, I feel safe in stating that the basic technological approaches had been selected relatively early, and that there was little opportunity as the program matured to incorporate new technology into the Apollo Program. From then on, it was essentially the hard, detailed, demanding job of making it work. It is only natural that the more creative engineers would at some point begin losing interest and start looking for a new design problem to solve. In fact, in many industrial situations, the analytical team does move on to new projects within the company. However, in MSC we do not have that kind of flexibility. We had to manage the Gemini and Apollo Programs simultaneously and have no new large program yet to follow Apollo. Therefore, our people are more or less glued to seeing Apollo through to its finish. The engineer in this case finds himself deeply involved in technology that is becoming more and more obsolete each day that he works on it. Consequently, there is the managerial task of keeping engineers diligently devoted to the task through the flight test program when their deepest interests are really in some new advance taking place elsewhere.

Obviously, the task of guiding professional relationships does not lend itself to easy solution. The problem has been well defined by Kornhauser, Abrahamson, Pelz and Andrews, Marcson, and others.[13]

Nevertheless, every institution has its own peculiarities and must seek its own solutions as we tried to do at MSC. When my friends from other organizations ask, "How can you have any problems when your organization has the clear-cut objective of landing on the moon before the end of the decade?" I can only patiently respond that the outward simplicity of the goal belies the very difficult organizational and managerial task involved.

At the same time I must admit we enjoyed several important advantages, including the *esprit de corps* engendered by the space program, an excellent recruiting position, the reception we received when we moved to Texas, and the opportunity to build from scratch, rather than having to modify an existing organization. The purpose of the original technical professionals who came here was very specific—to advance space flight technology. It was their project. They had been a part of the design phase, and they were able to see themselves in the context of the master plan. They, in fact, had immense *esprit de corps*. The related capabilities they would develop included crew training, mission planning, and mission control.

BASIC ORGANIZATIONAL DEVELOPMENT

The organization was created around the idea of projects. There were three major programs to conduct simultaneously—Mercury, then Gemini, then Apollo, in an overlapping sequence. From an organizational standpoint, this is quite different from a situation where you try to superimpose a project organization on one that has been traditionally functional. At MSC, we, in effect, grew a functional organization to support our programs. The climate created was such that everyone recognized the superiority of the program manager. The other administrators, such as I, saw our roles primarily as assistants to the main effort.

Matrix organization

The concept of the matrix organization—the overlay of programs across functions—is one of the basic management principles of MSC (Fig. 2). Program management is necessary so we can coordinate and manage the spacecraft programs. Functional management is necessary to provide the skilled functional specialists (professionals) who furnish technical inputs used in managing the programs and to provide the reservoir of talent necessary to conceive and design new programs.

The program organization is one established for, and tailored to, a specific program such as Apollo, as a general management activity responsible for the planning, control, supervision, engineering, test, and manufacturing activities involved in producing the hardware end item. It is similar to the functional organization in that it is basically getting work done through people. It differs, however, in ways which have far-reaching effect. The program organization has very specific objectives which, when achieved, mean the end of the organization, which is anathema to professionals because they do not want their careers tied to the life or death of an organization. The program manager has no line authority over the functional specialists who are so important to the program's objectives, which is good from the professional's standpoint but a potential source of trouble for the program manager.

Each of these organizational concepts has obvious advantages and disadvantages, and, in almost every case, the advantage of one coincides with a disadvantage of the other. For example, a program organization provides full-time attention of its personnel to accomplishing the program's objectives; a functional organization does not. A functional organization provides a reservoir of personnel skilled in a particular functional area; a program organization does not. A program organization provides program visibility and a focal point for all program matters; a functional organization does not. A functional organization provides relatively free interchange of ideas and problem solutions in a given functional area; a program organization does not.

At MSC we have attempted to organize functionally when possible, to provide the best climate for professional development. When the program demands it, however, we have had to subordinate professionalism to the mission goals. It has been said that program

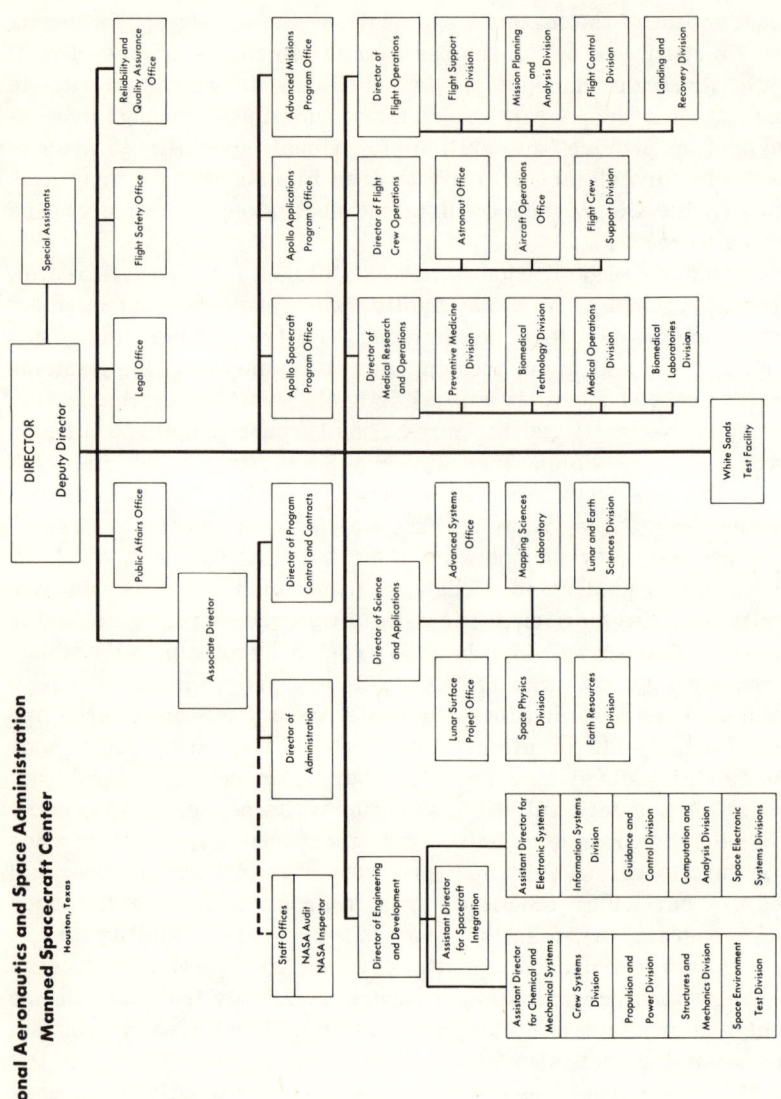

Fig. 2. MSC Organizational Chart (January 1969)

organization has something in common with weaving: it involves the interlacing of the traditional vertical "strands" of organization with the horizontal "fibers" of program organization into a fabric-like matrix. Thus, two complementary management organizations exist: the vertical functional organization and the horizontal program organization, with a resulting matrix structure extending across such functions as engineering, budgeting, contract management, and procurement. A series, or hierarchy, of matrices evolves because program management at MSC involves intracenter and intercenter functions and often one or more other government agencies.

Since 1961, MSC has operated with this joint program/functional organizational matrix which attempts to capitalize on the advantages of each concept and minimize the disadvantages. We believe that an organization of this type, with proper balance of responsibility and authority between the program and functional organizations, is the optimum one to take advantage of the positive aspects of professionalism and to minimize the negative aspects. At the same time, we believe it is the best way to organize so that the professional can best use the organization's resources and feel the least conflict with his professional values.

Decentralized responsibility

The second basic principle of MSC's management of its diverse staff is the concept of decentralized responsibility. With the talent drawn from the parent Langley Research Center and the advantageous position of MSC when it began staffing for Apollo, we could carefully select key people in whom we would have the greatest confidence. For all practical purposes, once a key leader was selected in any given functional area, he was essentially given a free hand to recruit and create the type of organization he felt was necessary to do his job. As a result, an individual achieved personal self-confidence and a sense of responsibility for his own organization that perhaps could not have existed if we had done more hand-holding.

I believe this concept of decentralized responsibility has been basic to the Center's activities. There is always a great deal of concern among top-level managers with the idea of management visibility throughout the organization. But in an operation as complex and as technical as the conquest of space, the key administrators simply cannot understand every detail about the spacecraft or understand every aspect of the flight plan. A highly professional and diverse organization cannot be run on the basis of all decisions coming to the top for solution. One must have people who are competent, in whom he has confidence, and to whom he can then give a good deal of latitude to go ahead and assume the initiative and attack the problems.

Laboratory environment

The third significant management principle practiced at MSC is the concept of supporting the laboratory environment. Of course, this is an extension of the early basic decision that NASA would manage its contractors from a laboratory environment in which the staff could maintain its technical competence. This concept is implemented at MSC both in terms of the facilities and the resources required. In spite of the overwhelming importance of the Apollo Spacecraft Program at MSC, management has provided manpower and funds so that the functional organizations could pursue their interests on a modest scale. This might be described as an in-house parallel to the Independent Research and Development Agreements that the Department of Defense (DOD) and NASA have with their contractors. This practice has been applied to our engineering organizations as well as our life and physical sciences groups. Many small, well-equipped research areas have developed throughout our functional organization. Several conditions favorable to the environment of a good research laboratory are the following:

1. Strong personal emphases are placed on science-oriented values using one's ability rather than institutional values, having freedom to pursue ideas, and making contributions to basic scientific knowledge.
2. There is frequent contact with colleagues in settings, with values, and in fields different from one's own.
3. The chief neither gives complete autonomy nor excessive direction.
4. Laboratory chiefs are themselves highly competent and motivated. Motivation and a sense of progress toward scientific goals are strong.
5. Chiefs employ participative leadership rather than directive or *laissez faire* policies.[14]

Without the opportunity to pursue the kind of research effort compatible with his professional values, the professional becomes extremely dissatisfied. The opportunity for independent research is necessary for both morale and motivation; and the acceptance and funding of these relatively small projects by top management represents their concession to and understanding of the potential this research can have for providing the germ for new missions.

In MSC's Space Physics Division, we have five highly specialized branches with personnel pursuing a large number and variety of research projects. Only about one-third of these support the Apollo Spacecraft Program Office. The chief was carefully selected for his recognized competence and motivation as a research scientist and has written numerous articles and papers. The scientists within the division have had considerable freedom in the definition of their own research. Academic relationships are strongly encouraged. Scientific colloquies and biweekly seminars are utilized, not only for their broadening effects on the scientists, but also to include the engineers and technicians, so necessary to the research teams, in the information flow. These factors are helping to produce some extremely promising research efforts.

For example, our very outstanding cosmic ray group has taken the lead in proposing a manned orbiting physics laboratory as part of NASA's long-range program. As a result, NASA Headquarters has established an *ad hoc* study group for high-energy cosmic rays which has nationwide membership and interest. The instrument development for such a mission has already begun at MSC and is providing a current research program through use of high-altitude balloons. One such project, the Cosmic Ray Ionization Spectrograph Program (CRISP) will launch a balloon to the top of the atmosphere next summer. The 37-million-cubic-feet balloon will be the largest ever constructed, and the more than 4-ton payload will be the heaviest ever launched. This program is closely related to the High Altitude Particle Physics Experiment (HAPPE), a collaboration by the group with the 1968 Nobel laureate in physics.

Application to operations

These principles, then, constitute the basis for our day-to-day operations. We try to recognize the professional values and outlooks of the varied members of the team: the design and test engineers; the medical doctors; the scientists; the contract, budget, and legal specialists. It is the job of the program managers to persuade, coerce, direct, and, finally, order all of the professional functions to do what is necessary to meet the objectives and milestones placed upon MSC by NASA Headquarters.

This is our normal mode of operation for conducting the majority of our business. Right now, in the management of the Apollo Spacecraft Program, this decision-making process is crystallized in the Apollo Spacecraft Configuration Control Board. Comprised of each functional director and the manager of the program office, it controls both the configuration of the spacecraft and the mission and approves all significant changes. This board provides each functional director ample opportunity to present and defend his position on any matter before the board. However, the buck has to stop somewhere, and in this case it is with the program manager. It is up to him to hear all sides of the case, weigh the trade-offs, and decide what alternative best serves the overall objectives of the program. These meetings are held regularly every Friday. Because of the large attendance, the meetings also serve as an excellent means of communication, since all of the interested parties can observe the decision-making process in action and better understand the reasons for the decisions. Periodic concern with the size of meetings has usually given way to this critical communication need.

OTHER DEVELOPMENTAL APPROACHES

Through these basic principles and their application, we have tried to operate in a manner conducive to both professionalism and the attainment of mission objectives. In addition, however, we have experimented with various other means of facilitating goal-directed coordination between multidisciplinary professionals. These operational practices fall into a graduated order in which the degree of formalized organizational change is the distinguishing characteristic. The six practices that I wish to discuss here may be described as follows:

1. A multidisciplined effort achieved by assigning the required professionals to a project office for the duration of the project
2. A multidisciplined effort achieved by creating a small, coordinating project office but leaving the professionals in their respective organizations
3. A multidisciplined effort achieved through informal working groups and panels without any organizational change
4. A multidisciplined effort achieved by physical colocation of personnel without any formal or informal organization changes
5. A multidisciplined effort achieved by assigning specific missions to an organization or individual
6. A multidisciplined effort achieved through a flexible personnel

classification system that permits a diversified staff within any given functional organization.

Each of these degrees of adaptation has been used in varying situations with varying degrees of success.

Development of lunar receiving laboratory

As an example of the first practice, I might tell how we went about designing and building the very unique laboratory for receiving and analyzing the rock samples brought back from the moon. Although only a small part of the relatively massive manned lunar landing program, it is a good example of how many disciplines had to work together to do a job and how we successfully accomplished it. This is a unique and outstanding facility, since it must first be a quarantine facility and then fulfill its role as a scientific laboratory. Consequently, its design and completion required the inputs of many different scientists, construction engineers, and administrative specialists.

About three years after the inauguration of the Apollo Program, serious thought was given to the kind of laboratory facility which would be needed to handle the lunar samples which the astronauts would bring back from the moon. Careful handling of the samples under controlled conditions would be required to preserve the unique information contained in them.

The scientific implications of our first opportunity to study extraterrestrial material are obviously tremendous, and the interest of the scientific community in the project was, and still is, worldwide. In fact, the proposed experiments of approximately 110 principal investigators from universities and research institutions around the world were approved by NASA to be performed on these samples as they became available. And, I doubt seriously that any of these scientists consider their particular project as second-rate. However, they were not to be our only consideration in constructing these facilities.

A committee of the National Academy of Science pointed out to NASA that an imperative potential problem was that of back contamination. Put simply, this meant that we must protect the earth from the potential hazard of harmful lunar organisms brought here on the return trip.

In addition to NASA and the scientific community, three other government agencies—Public Health Service, Department of Agriculture, and Department of Interior—were directly interested, because of their specific statutory responsibilities for possible contaminants entering the United States. It was obvious to us that we would be dealing with some very delicate professional interfaces. We would be trying to satisfy not only some very outstanding scientists but three distinctly independent agencies.

As we looked at the job which faced us, several things were clear. We were about to build a facility which would be unique in the world. Its design and construction would distinctly be an R & D effort, and the time factor was very severe. Assuming that we would be able to make a lunar landing on schedule, there was absolutely no cushion in the schedule for completing the Lunar Receiving Laboratory. Also, financial resources were marginal. We had very strict budgetary orders from Congress on the construction costs, and we had to adhere.

These constraints were coupled with the multiplicity of disciplines involved: the biosciences, medicine, geology, engineering (design, systems, construction, and so on), the administrative functions (particularly procurement and resources management), the astronauts, and many more. All in all, I think we harbored the fear that we might have all the ingredients for a disaster:

1. An impossible schedule
2. A marginal budget
3. An internal multiplicity of disciplines
4. Specific external interest, also multidisciplinary
5. Other government agencies involved by law

The commitment to build the Lunar Receiving Laboratory (LRL) was actually the first attempt MSC had made to create a facility or hardware to serve basic science. As I mentioned earlier, our charter was to advance flight technology, and, at this time, we had not developed an in-house scientific capability for pure research. So, in effect, this was about to be our first, full-scale experience in guiding relationships among managers, scientists, and engineers.

To accomplish the job, management established an LRL Project Office. This usually has a very positive effect on inducing teamwork. Aside from the resources, authority, and maneuverability it provides the manager, it has a beneficial psychological effect on the group selected to work with him. By top management's specific recognition of the importance of the job to be done, the team members share in a sense of recognition and prestige. It is very important to team spirit to be able to say "we are a special group." Although this is less important as a motivating factor to the individual research scientists, who is notoriously independent, it still does exercise some influence simply because he is human.

The project manager wants to build something that works, on time, and within the financial constraints of the project. He is responsible for the integration of the project, for seeing that the pieces fit. On the other hand, the groups which he is being asked to integrate—the scientists, engineers, and technicians of various specialties—all will be working to optimize the returns on their particular piece of the project—without regard to the optimization of the project as a whole. Each discipline is being paid to do its best, and each will try to do precisely that. What we have then is not so much a conflict between the manager and the specialist but an interdisciplinary conflict. In this situation, it becomes extremely important to have a neutral leader. The leader must not be viewed as being in competition with any of the disciplines involved.

This differs from the attitudes held by the professional concerning the type of leadership he expects in his smaller, more homogenous functional unit. Here, he expects the leader to be a highly competent and motivated member of his discipline. It is very important to him that the judgments which intimately affect the nature of his work—its professional nature—be made by a leader in whom he has professional respect. It is also important that he see the leader as a "fighter," willing to defend—and aggressively, if necessary—the integrity of the discipline within the organization.

However, when the professional leaves his functional base to participate in a multidisciplined team effort, it becomes important to him that the leader be fair, impartial, and neutralized as an arbitrator.

As the literature points out, when the number of disciplines cooperating in one organization increases, the balance and process of goal implementation becomes considerably more difficult, especially if there is no clearly defined or understood pecking order. The greater the number and higher the tensions among the various professions, the greater is the need for a neutral administrator as final authority.[15]

A manager placed in such a situation obviously is going to perform the task of balancing the conflicting requirements of the participating disciplines. But even more important, he acts as an interpreter, always attempting to broaden the baseline of understanding of the professionals with whom he works. The disadvantage of professionalism from a manager's viewpoint comes when its members cannot, or will not, see themselves in the broad perspective. The creation of a program office offers a kind of alleviation to this dilemma. Through colocation and common leadership, the ability to understand each other is increased. The LRL Project Office was kept intentionally small and its leader was able to get involved with his people's work—assist them when necessary—and know their names. As we had expected, he was able to develop a genuine rapport with both his people and his many outside interfaces.

The professionals in the physical and the life sciences were the prime consideration in the facility's design, from the quarantine aspects to the equipment needs of the research areas. Because of the requirements and specifications of the scientists, the engineers were needed. To serve them both, administrative specialists in program control, contracts, and so forth were essential to the team. Although all were working toward the same clear objective, their motivations were somewhat different.

To the scientists, the motivation was very definitely the opportunity to extend knowledge in their respective fields, and because of the excitement of this opportunity they were very active participants. The motivation of the engineers was the opportunity to advance the current technology. The project posed some very challenging technical problems. Also, the project was an important front-line Apollo task, which added considerably to its attractiveness. But the mission-relatedness had decidedly more motivational value to the engineers than to the scientists, and it was a prime motivating factor to the administrative personnel.

These motivations were utilized effectively by the project leader, and he was able to show a balanced interest and concern in the different groups. Their image of him was that of a man who would assist them to do their job, rather than that of a unilateral manager. This was appropriate, because they were the professionals in their areas; he was not.

For this project, as for many which NASA has undertaken, the idea of advisory groups or committees was extremely important. The scientific community had been asked to establish an advisory group with appropriately representative membership. They assembled a well-balanced panel which represented the disciplines in their broadest sense. Although purely advisory, the group was highly useful. When conflict arose outside NASA or when there were internal scientific questions, the group was available for expert consultation.

Within MSC, a Lunar Receiving Laboratory Policy Board was established in addition to the LRL Project Office, "to make any necessary (MSC) policy decisions required to implement the design and construction of the Lunar Receiving Laboratory and to periodically review LRL program plans and status." The board was composed of representative MSC professionals, as well as the project manager and the MSC associate director. The board, then, was responsible for policy, and the project office was responsible "for the schedules, costs, and technical aspects of the LRL" (MSC Announcement 66-57, May 9, 1966).

As the man who actually had to effect the coordination of the different groups, the project manager found that the scientists were least organizable—not, however, in terms of their own particular part of the project. Rather, their difficulty in appreciating their integration into the overall plan. This, again, was the optimization factor and was to be expected. He found that the factors necessary to an interrelated plan—to the business of scheduling the tasks in some logical order—such as contracts, budget, and operational procedures, were considerations with which the scientists were not particularly familiar. Therefore, his role was not only to coordinate, but to educate and aid understanding of what and why things were being done. He kept up with the project and, as milestones and schedules were met or missed, he pointed them out, explained the consequences, and so forth. If the scientists were having trouble, he would assist them in establishing controls. In effect, he explained the red tape and made every effort to assist them through it.

He also found that as early as possible it is good to draw a circle around an effort and make sure that everyone knows where the boundaries lie. Without this, equipment wanted and changes to be made can be endless. In this case, the major constraints were easily understood; they were time and money.

Development of ALSEP

An example of the second practice involves the method used for developing the array of scientific instruments to be placed upon the moon's surface on one of our early lunar landing missions. We call this instrumentation the Apollo Lunar Surface Experiments Package, or ALSEP.

In 1965, the NASA Summer Conference on Lunar Exploration and Science was held in Massachusetts to recommend scientific programs covering a 10-year period to begin with the first Apollo flight. The conference was held under the auspices of the Manned Space Science Coordinating Committee, a broadly representative body established to advise the NASA Headquarters Director for Space Science and Applications. Seven working groups developed a report which represented the current thinking of some of the outstanding lunar scientists in the United States, and, as was NASA's intention at the time, we have made every effort to implement those parts of the recommendations which are feasible within the constraints of available resources.

Although the collection of lunar samples was given highest scientific priority for the first landing, this did not exclude the possibility that it might be feasible to obtain other valuable data for use by physicists, astronomers, geodesists, and so on. Following inputs from the conference, from the National Academy of Science, and from other agency and center elements, it was determined that the concept which best fit these additional objectives would be that which later became known as the ALSEP.

ALSEP developed as a self-contained package of scientific instruments and supporting subsystems which would be deployed on the lunar surface by the two astronauts scheduled to leave the spacecraft. For a one-year period, it would transmit data to earth receiving stations to aid us in understanding the composition and structure of the moon, the magnetic field, the atmosphere, and the solar wind. The data would be a great advance in our ability to decipher the evolution of the moon, the state and composition of its interior, and other mysteries. About nineteen principal investigators were selected from universities and institutions across the country and awarded research contracts by NASA.

In the initial planning, ALSEP was given constraints by the Apollo Program Office. It must fit a given area in the lunar module, the craft which descends to the surface of the moon. It could weigh 300 pounds, and 90 minutes would be allotted for its deployment. It was thought that the flexibility of the space suit would allow the astronaut to bend over and reach to about 12 inches from the surface. The intention was to fly the package on the first four lunar landing missions.

The overall responsibility for the development and integration of this or any other mission-related activity or hardware rests with the Apollo program manager. In scale, the ALSEP is roughly comparable to the larger of the unmanned satellites. However, the specific job of overseeing and coordinating ALSEP was assigned to a project office created within the Science and Applications Directorate, the functional home of the scientists. This Lunar Surface Project Office (LSPO), then, provides the interface with the scientific community on the one hand and the Apollo Spacecraft Program Office on the other, and is aided in doing so by participation in many formal and informal meetings and reviews.

Because ALSEP represented only one part of the Apollo Program, its manager, of course, could not optimize his project or its schedule independently, but rather was dependent on the optimization of the larger Apollo Program. The scientific project was to be particularly impacted by those designing the pressure suit and the portable life support system, the medical group responsible for the consideration of human factors, those responsible for crew training, and the astronauts themselves. And, usually, each of these groups would need information from one of the others before it became available.

In programs as highly interdependent as those which NASA has undertaken, it is essential that everyone understand the basic program plan into which they must be integrated. Each discipline must be made to feel a part of the program and given control milestones which they, in fact, have helped to set. Some of these goals will be more artificially established than others—these can be relaxed later, if needed—but the key is to extract commitments and then develop an overall plan which will allow for controlled changes. This must be done by continually reviewing not only schedule and cost but also performance goals.

The Lunar Surface Project Office, then, was the body designated to develop the ALSEP. This necessitated developing a set of relationships with all of the MSC and outside elements involved in the project. Table 24 lists the groups and their roles in the project. To integrate the efforts of these elements, a series of informal mechanisms evolved to bring together the many disciplines and conflicting priorities that needed to be resolved. These may be summarized as follows:

Monthly conferences with the principal investigators were established so that all MSC elements could be aware of the scientific objectives and requirements.

Specific individuals were named as subsystem managers by the Engineering and Development Directorate to support the project manager.

The Lunar Surface Operations Panel was permanently established as a subgroup to the Flight Operations Planning Meetings to plan the specific activities that the crew would perform. This panel included representatives of all the involved elements.

The LSPO representatives attended all meetings between MSC and the lunar module spacecraft contractor to keep abreast of the vehicle's status.

Regular meetings were established between LSPO representatives and Bendix, the ALSEP contractor, for reviewing progress.

Representatives of the Apollo Spacecraft Program Office responsible for the status of equipment furnished by the government (GFE) to the spacecraft prime contractor met regularly with LSPO management to review progress.

All decisions affecting the interface of ALSEP with the lunar

TABLE 24
ALSEP Roles

Organization	Role
Lunar Surface Project Office, MSC Science and Applications Directorate	Project management
Bendix	Contractor selected to develop the ALSEP
Office of Space Science and Applications, NASA Headquarters	Selection of principal investigators from universities, institutes, government and industry laboratories
Apollo Spacecraft Program Office (MSC)	Mission objectives, systems engineering (weights and mass properties)
Apollo Spacecraft Configuration Control Board	Configuration control
Engineering and Development Directorate (MSC)	Subsystems (power, environmental control, communications) management support
Flight Operations Directorate (Lunar Surface Operations Panel)	Mission planning
Flight Crew Operations Directorate	Crew procedures and training

module were brought before the Apollo Spacecraft Configuration Control Board (CCB) which approved all hardware or mission design baselines and changes. The CCB is composed of the Apollo Spacecraft Program manager and each of the directorate heads, including the director of Science and Applications, and serves as the principal decision-making body in the program.

Recent developments in the ALSEP project, which I would like to relate, testify to the complexity of the interrelationships involved in executing what may appear to be, on the surface, a very simple thing. I also believe that these developments indicate the effectiveness of the working relationships that I have described, because they helped to avoid what might have been a very embarrassing and disappointing failure.

As ALSEP progressed, it met all the constraints imposed originally. But, as more knowledge was gained, more constraints were added. Also, the very specific, overriding concern for crew safety would be a basic factor in any decisions affecting the optimization of the total mission. As time passed, the space-suit people concerned themselves with developing the best pressure vessel possible for the safety of the astronauts. In doing so, they developed a space garment less flexible than anticipated earlier. The life-support people wanted more emergency oxygen. This added weight to the back pack and shifted the center of gravity of the suit. It was moved upward on the shoulders from the earlier waist position. This limited the mobility of the astronaut. He could now reach only to about 22 inches from the surface, which affected the deployment of ALSEP. Also, it affected the stability the astronaut has when he attempts to maneuver in gravity one-sixth that of earth.

This last point—what can the crew actually do in $\frac{1}{6}$ g—is still very subjective, based on our present knowledge. The data points available to extrapolate from are very limited. In fact, no really good simulation is possible. For instance, an aircraft can execute a parabolic trajectory, a controlled dive, but the simulation lasts for only about 30 seconds. Also, at MSC we have what is called the "Peter Pan rig," which is, in unsophisticated terms, a harness attached to ropes and weights and designed to support five-sixths of a man's weight. This is a very good training device, but it is certainly not a perfect simulation.

The uncertainty caused by this lack of adequate testing had a conservative effect on those responsible for refining the mission plans for the first lunar landing. The crew was not fully confident of what they could do in their suit, and the process of deploying the ALSEP is an involved one, requiring two special tools. Since it is one package, the experiments must be detached by releasing about $3\frac{1}{2}$ dozen bolts. Although in theory this task should not be difficult, it and the alignment of the instruments do require considerable concentration and time, and would effectively require all the time available to one man for extravehicular activity (EVA) before the need to retreat to the craft. In other words, to perform both ALSEP and the lunar sampling exercise, two EVA periods would be required.

The lunar module which ferries the astronauts to the lunar surface is a complicated vehicle. And, the attention and effort required for the crew to land and return to the orbiting spacecraft mean two very active days. To reduce the fatigue factor before the extremely crucial ascent from the moon, it was decided to perform only one EVA on the first mission using a less demanding derivative of the ALSEP hardware. This automatically removed ALSEP from the first lunar landing mission although, of course, not from the next three.

A great deal of discussion and debate preceded this decision, carried on through the various panels and meetings described. As a result of the close working relationships, the constraints were recognized and understood. Eventually the problem came to the attention of the Apollo CCB for a decision. Because of the participation of all MSC elements in the total process, with the managers themselves all participating in the final decision, the solution as well as the problem was understood across the organization.

Throughout the development process, the Lunar Surface Project Office served as the focal point for all of the activities. In the following example of the third technique, a similar array of working relationships evolved; however, the resulting products were produced by the formal organizations without a project office to direct the effort.

Specific flight mission planning

As in the development of the spacecraft, the planning of any particular mission is an involved process of finding a way within certain constraints of achieving predetermined objectives. The design of the mission is basically determined by these objectives, but the design must also consider spacecraft capability, fuel and electrical supplies, radiation hazards, ground tracking, communication, control limitations, crew considerations, and a multitude of other factors that affect manned space operations.

Because of the breadth of considerations involved in mission planning, virtually all MSC elements are involved in the process. The interrelatedness of all aspects of the mission and the requirement for compatibility between all parts have been the impetus for the development of another group of organizations. This is a semiformal organization to achieve across-the-board coordination of the mission-planning activities. This organization consists of boards, panels, and working groups established for specific purposes and, almost always, containing membership from numerous organizations. These organizations are both working-level groups brought together for the purpose of doing their work, and management groups brought together for the purposes of review and decision making. Essentially, the mission-planning process is a matter of taking a set of objectives, a set of operational constraints, and a spacecraft with given capabilities, and developing an optimal trajectory and flight plan that achieve as many of the objectives as the constraints and limitations will allow.

As the subsequent documents are developed—trajectories, constraints, flight plans—more and more is learned about what can and cannot be done. Consequently, as planning proceeds, there is a continual feedback of pressures for changes in all of the preceding planning. Trajectory development is a continuous iterative process as analysts seek to determine an optimum design that satisfies the objectives while recognizing the appropriate constraints. Since it is not always possible to have everything, many trade-off decisions, must be made.

The semiformal organization that has been created within the formal does much to break down artificial organization barriers, increase personal contacts, and increase horizontal information flow. These matters are the concern of much of the management research being done today on large-scale organization (Chapter 5).

Perhaps the primary element that assures cohesiveness among the various informal panels, boards, and working groups is the Apollo Program. The complexities involved in planning an Apollo mission are of such a high order that teamwork both inside and outside the formal organizational structure is recognized as necessary.

As a consequence of this phenomenon, people seem to be very open-minded in their attitude toward the work of others. They feel a responsibility to seek out the other person's problems and take the initiative to do so. This attitude is extremely important, because it fosters the communication of data. As previously mentioned, a large amount of specific information is in flux during the mission-planning period. All participants must be made aware of how changes impact their own particular planning activity. There is also the responsibility for resolving problems through participation in the informal groups. On the whole, the people involved in the mission-planning process tend to be imaginative, expansive, and action-oriented.

Although this situation in general is very desirable, it does contain the potential for management losing the control and visibility that it perhaps should have. But this is an extremely subjective matter, and specific answers are not easily forthcoming on the degree of visibility and control necessary. In a highly professionalized, highly specialized organization such as MSC, many decisions must be made at lower levels, and it is most desirable to have a management system that permits this. Higher management is concerned that all of the decisions fit together. To date, the informal organization has been very satisfactory, providing communication links between professional personnel involved in the mission-planning and decision-making process.

Geographical collocation

In situations where the involvement is less complex but closer day-to-day relationships are required, a technique we have tried is geographical collocation. We have collocated professionals without changing their line reporting relationships. For example, our financial people sit right with the engineers or scientists who spend the money; however, they still report to the Financial Officer. The reason for collocation is to break down the barriers caused by professionalism and to attempt to get an identification of teamwork and common leadership, even though not necessarily line leadership in the normal sense of the term. Along with this comes effective communication, which is more than the flow of paperwork and similar formal communication. It includes getting to know each other, developing rapport, and truly understanding each other.

An example which illustrates how this works is our mission-planning interface with the Apollo Spacecraft Program Office. The program office has the basic responsibility for mission design. The mission-planning people have responsibility for the detailed implementation of the design. To make certain that what is designed is implementable, the operations manager has located a small staff of mission planners with the mission designers in the program office. Working together, these two groups of people essentially become one group and follow the design and detailed planning for the mission from start, through all the changes, to finish.

Of course, I am not belittling professionalism. I have already discussed the rationale of operating in a laboratory environment. The professional and his professional value system are also needed to balance the program manager's "go-go" tendency. At the same time, the professional's tendency to make perfect, rather than workable, solutions has to be balanced by the schedule and budget constraints of the program. Simple geographical collocation has been useful in helping achieve this balance in certain situations.

Specific role assignments

In still other situations, we have found it better not to collocate and have left the professional in his home organization, assigned him a special role, and, in effect, created a "two-boss" situation. In this case, the general technical responsibilities of the functional organizations were buttressed by the designation of specific individuals as subsystem managers who had a special personal responsibility to the program manager.

There are approximately 50 subsystem managers. Each is responsible through normal supervisory lines to the manager of the program office for the development of his subsystem to given or developed specifications within the cost and schedule constraints of the program. The subsystem manager has responsibility for all technical and administrative aspects of the management of his subsystem, short of official authority to direct the contractor, which must be accomplished through the program manager.

We developed the subsystem management role because the traditional horizontal program office and vertical functional organizations were not meshing properly. By superimposing a special role on individuals in the functional organization we changed the way the professional operated, even though he stayed in his professional environment.

The purpose of role assignment is to get the professional to see his role as directly related to the goals of the organization, instead of seeing himself just as a specialist or as a member of a professional organization. The concept has been employed successfully at MSC. In fact, within a short time of the implementation of the concept, each of the functional organizations had reexamined and changed its organizational structure to be better able to accomplish the program goals.

Flexible personnel system

Finally, one of the problems frequently mentioned in discussing work relationships among professionals in a government laboratory is the restrictions inherent in a bureaucratic, government-wide personnel system. However, I think the system is overrated as a source of problems. I believe that the regulations themselves are fairly flexible; it is during their implementation down through the hierarchy that restrictions are imposed.[16] Thus, in NASA we have encouraged our personnel professionals to go to the source of the regulations, the Federal Personnel Manual, rather than write agency implementing documents.

We have also used the collocation technique to break down the personnel professional's natural inclination to hide behind regulations and paperwork. By making it clear through the rewards system that they are to identify with, and share responsibility for, the goals of the technical organization, we have made it more difficult for them to hide behind a comfortable bureaucratic system.

Another thing which the agency has done is develop its own tailormade civil service examination. This system, the Aerospace Technologist (AST) Examination, is used to fill all technical positions in NASA. Applicants submit a standard government application form, a transcript of college course work, and certain pertinent papers to be evaluated by NASA professionals. The applicant is given a rating score and placed on the register of eligibles for the particular specialty for which he is best suited.

The system has four significant features: (1) it is work centered; (2) it uses an interdisciplinary approach; (3) it emphasizes demonstrated ability in contrast with experience only; and (5) it is scored by NASA's own professionals who are experts in the specialties they evaluate.

Among the benefits that we have received from having the AST examination system are that it gives the agency the hiring flexibility to keep pace with the fast-changing technology upon which our programs are based, it gives NASA much better control over those we hire, and it gives us the ability to move professionals within specialty groups.

Because the major hiring effort for MSC was completed several years ago, I will not dwell on the advantages of the system related to hiring. The flexibility the system provides in assigning and reassigning personnel within MSC allows us to reflect the interdisciplinary character of the job to be done. In other words, we are able to assign engineers, mathematicians, and physicists to the same organization. We do actually have 20- or 30-man branches with three or four breeds of engineer (such as, electrical, mechanical, chemical, nuclear, aeronautical), mathematicians, and physicists all working together to accomplish their particular mission. Obviously, this is an embodiment of the collocation concept at the individual level and is another example of efforts to facilitate goal-directed coordination among our managers, scientists, and engineers.

CURRENT INVESTIGATIONS

Seminar series

These then, are six techniques by which we have attempted to solve the problems of getting professional scientists, engineers, and administrative professionals to work toward common goals in an effective, harmonious, and satisfying manner. We have also tried other techniques, on a lesser scale. I hope that our imaginations are not yet exhausted and that we will continue to seek new means. As a matter of fact, the director of administration at MSC is now conducting a seminar series that I hope other MSC elements will copy. He has been having high-level MSC managers, as well as outsiders, come in to talk to selected groups from the administrative organization about the goals, objectives, and problems in their particular areas. Although this program was intended for development and motivational purposes, I have no doubt that hearing the problems of the technical organizations, such as the Apollo Spacecraft Program Office, directly from the boss himself does much to enhance the administrative professional's understanding of his relationship to the technical organization he supports, and thereby improves the relationship.

Management evaluation

We are also attempting to evaluate these techniques as we proceed, to determine their degree of success or failure and to make improvements as we go. In a development center, such as MSC, performance is not too difficult to measure. Our job is to build hardware, flight test it, and achieve a specified set of objectives. We either meet, surpass, or fail to meet those objectives. It is all too tempting, particularly when successful, to equate successful performance with successful management. The two, however, do not correlate so easily. In an R & D environment, technical failures do occur in well-managed enterprises, and technical brilliance can overcome in a poorly managed effort. Therefore, it is necessary to continually evaluate our managerial performance independently of MSC's technical achievements to find out where we stand. One method of doing this is through our management research program where we have university faculty and doctoral- and masters-level researchers evaluate elements of our managerial practices. Recently we have had completed a doctoral dissertation[17] which was basically a study of the relationships among job ambiguity, job tension, and job satisfaction. His results proved that there is a direct relationship between job ambiguity and job tension and an inverse relationship between job ambiguity and job satisfaction. The results also showed that ambiguity and tension are low among professionals and that job satisfaction is high. In fact, using a scale ranging from a low of 7 to a high of 35, more than 75 percent of all the respondents to Hamilton's study scored above the actual median of 23.5.

Although Mr. Hamilton's study aimed specifically at the relationship among ambiguity, tension, and satisfaction, it also included an evaluation of the managerial styles at MSC. This evaluation was made to determine the professional's attitudes toward and perceptions of his organization as well as his particular position. The findings of this part of the study indicated that a consultative, and in some cases participative, management style exists across the four organizations included in the sampling. Mr. Hamilton used the following definition of "consultative": "relatively sensitive and concerned for the human element in the organization; people are not viewed as materials and tools, but with motives, desires, and productive potentialities; members are generally consulted; however, many decisions are made at the top unless they can be made more appropriately at lower organizational levels."

Since MSC is a field center of a large government agency and is assigned specific development missions to execute on given schedules, we are pleased that our management is able, within these constraints, to create an atmosphere in which professional employees feel involved and not merely pawns in an exploitatively or benevolently authoritative environment. No doubt, this is partly because the technological complexity of the task and the high degree of specialization required forces a great deal of decentralized decision making and the participation and consultation of members of the organization. Nevertheless, in view of the importance placed upon participative-consultative management by the research conducted so far, we are pleased with the findings. These attitudes toward the organization must contribute in some way to the high degree of satisfaction that the professionals found with their positions.

Now, these findings, assuming that they are the results of valid research, do not necessarily mean that everything we have done is correct. However, the low degree of ambiguity and tension would appear to indicate that we are managing to keep our professional employees reasonably well directed toward well-identified goals. Certainly the various means we have employed must have made some contribution toward the creation of these attitudes in the professionals' minds. In the near future, we should conduct research projects, as a continuation of Mr. Hamilton's efforts, that would enable us to investigate more specifically the relationship between job satisfaction and the particular organizational arrangements employed.

In summary, the limited but penetrating literature on the management of professionals provides considerable insight into the nature of the problem and points the way toward potential solutions. Each institution facing the problem is going to have to experiment within the limitations of its own constraints and seek its own answers.

Organizational Dynamics: Building Effective R & D Departments

RENSIS LIKERT
Director Emeritus
Institute for Social Research
University of Michigan
Ann Arbor

Donald Pelz, after a decade of research on the administration of research and development organizations,[1] wrote a provocative paper, "Creative Tensions in the Research and Development Climate."[2] In this paper he pointed to a number of conditions associated with high performance by scientists and engineers. These conditions state important specifications which a system of management of R & D personnel should meet to enable scientists and engineers to achieve high performance levels of creative and technical accomplishment.

Pelz and his associate, F. M. Andrews, measured "each man's scientific performance, including his scientific or technical contribution to his field of knowledge in the past 5 years, as judged by panels of his colleagues; his overall usefulness to the organization, through either research or administration, also as judged by his colleagues; the number of professional papers he had published in the past 5 years (or, in the case of an engineer, the number of his patents or patent applications); and the number of his unpublished reports in the same period."

CREATIVE TENSIONS

Based on extensive analyses of data from 1300 scientists and engineers in eleven R & D laboratories, Pelz concluded that "creative tensions" between sources of stability or security on the one hand and sources of disruption or challenge on the other contributed to effective performance. Pelz's "creative tensions" are summarized in Table 25, which is Table 1 in his paper on that topic.

One tension concerns independence in contrast with interaction. Pelz points out that scientists and engineers require freedom:

> Scientists place high priority on freedom. To measure this need, an index of "motivation from own ideas" was constructed from self-reported (i) stimulus by one's previous work, (ii) stimulus by one's own curiosity, and (iii) desire for freedom to follow one's own ideas. This score—the index might also be labeled intellectual independence—was analyzed in relation to the four performance measures within each category of scientific personnel. A series of positive correlations appeared. Among the 36 correlation coefficients, 25 were positive ($r = +.10$ or larger) and none were negative; this was one of the most stable trends in the analysis, and was consistent with other research.

But Pelz adds that complete freedom is disastrous:

> In these loosely coordinated settings, the most autonomous individuals were able to isolate themselves from challenge. A nondemanding organization permitted them to withdraw into an ivory tower of maximum security and minimum challenge. There they atrophied (Table [25], tension 4a).
>
> What about the more demanding organizations—those of moderately tight coordination? Why was autonomy an asset here and not a handicap? We found that autonomous persons here had more diversity in their work, not less. One can speculate that in these departments the technical man had to face problems important to the organization; personal freedom enabled him to find the best solutions.

Pelz illustrates the need for interaction combined with freedom by examining the influence of the individual in establishing goals:

> The "decision-making sources" were grouped into four categories: the individual, his immediate supervisor, his colleagues or subordinates, and higher executives or clients. We scored for each scientist how many of the four sources

were said to have had at least some weight (10 percent or more) in selecting his technical goals.

The results were clear: both Ph.D.'s and engineers performed well when all four sources had some voice in shaping their goals but when, at the same time, the individual could influence the main decision-makers. From this arose creative tension 5 (Table [25]): influence received from several others (challenge) combined with influence exerted on others (security).

Another tension which the administration of R & D should provide concerns differences and disagreements. In discussing disagreements, Pelz draws upon a label which Weaver (1959)[4] borrowed from British colleagues who built into anti-aircraft computing devices a "small eccentric or vibrating member which kept the whole mechanism in a constant state of minor but rapid vibration. This they called the 'dither.' . . . We need a certain amount of dither in our mental mechanisms. We need to have our ideas jostled about a bit so that we do not become intellectually sluggish."

Pelz asks:

> How much dither or disagreement is healthy? In our data the answer depended on the kind of dither. One objective measure concerned the source of motivation—whether one's superior, the technical literature, or some other source. Scientists who responded to the same sources were somewhat more effective—perhaps because they had similar interests.
>
> On three other measures we found the opposite to be true. Scientists and engineers did somewhat better when they saw themselves as different from colleagues in technical strategy, and when, as scored objectively, they differed from colleagues in style of approach (when, for example, the individual stressed the abstract, his colleagues the concrete) or differed in career orientation.
>
> How to reconcile this paradox? In some preliminary data obtained by Evan[5] for industrial R & D groups, the teams he found most effective reported personal harmony or liking among members, but intellectual conflict. Colleagues who report the same sources of motivation as the scientist's own probably provide personal harmony and support—a form of security. When they argue about technical strategy or approach, they provide dither or challenge.
>
> As R & D teams get older they can remain productive if they stay cohesive . . . yet have their technical strategies differ and remain intellectually combative (tension 8).

TABLE 25 Eight Creative Tensions[a]

Security	Challenge
Tension 1	
	Effective scientists and engineers in both research and development laboratories did not limit their activities either to pure science or to application but spent some time on several kinds of R & D activities, ranging from basic research to technical services
Tension 2	
Effective scientists were intellectually independent or self-reliant; they pursued their own ideas and valued freedom . . .	. . . But they did not avoid other people; they and their colleagues interacted vigorously
Tension 3	
a) In the first decade of work, young scientists and engineers did well if they spent a few years on one main project . . .	. . . But young non-Ph.D.'s also achieved if they had several skills, and young Ph.D.'s did better when they avoided narrow specialization
b) Among mature scientists, high performers had greater self-confidence and an interest in probing	. . . At the same time, effective older scientists wanted to pioneer in broad new areas
Tension 4	
a) In loosest departments with minimum coordination, the most autonomous individuals, with maximum security and minimum challenge, were ineffective . . .	. . . More effective were those persons who experienced stimulation from a variety of external or internal sources
b) In departments having moderate coordination, it seems likely that individual autonomy permitted a search for the best solution . . .	. . . to important problems faced by the organization
Tension 5	
Both Ph.D.'s and engineers contributed most when they strongly influenced key decision-makers . . .	. . . but also when persons in several other positions had a voice in selecting their goals
Tension 6	
High performers named colleagues with whom they shared similar sources of stimulation (personal support) . . .	. . . but they differed from colleagues in technical style and strategy (dither or intellectual conflict)
Tension 7	
R & D teams were of greatest use to their organization at that "group age" when interest in narrow specialization had increased to a medium level . . .	. . . but interest in broad pioneering had not yet disappeared
Tension 8	
In older groups which retained vitality the members preferred each other as collaborators . . .	. . . yet their technical strategies differed and they remained intellectually combative

[a] From Donald C. Pelz, "Creative Tensions in the Research and Development Climate", Science, vol. 157, no. 3785 (July 14, 1967), pp. 160-165. Copyright by the American Association for the Advancement of Science. (Used by permission.)

Another form of dither is the diversity which comes from multiple assignments. Pelz reports that

—Ph.D.'s in both research-oriented and development-oriented laboratories were judged most effective, on the basis of several criteria, when they devoted only half their technical time to research as such and the rest to activities described as development or technical services. Similarly, Ph.D.'s in development-oriented laboratories were most effective when they spent only one-quarter or one-third of their time on activities labeled "development."
—Effective scientists, in short, did not limit their efforts either to the world of pure science or to the world of application but were active in both (see Table [25], tension 1).
—Other findings reinforced the importance of diversity. Individuals performed better when they had two or three "areas of specialization" within their scientific discipline, rather than one. The Ph.D.'s did their best work not when they devoted full time to technical activities but when they spent about one-quarter of their time in either teaching or administration.

OTHER DEMANDS ON R & D ADMINISTRATION

Other research reveals additional requirements which an effective R & D administration must meet. For example, development engineers on large-scale projects have been found to have relatively low levels of motivation and job satisfaction.[6] In contrast to the high levels of motivation and job satisfactions which professionals usually have, the development engineers were the lowest of all classes of employees except production workers. These engineers reported that their work was highly specialized and that they lacked career mobility. They were especially dissatisfied with the extent to which their professional competence was utilized. More than two-thirds of them reported that they were given assignments which any competent technical assistant could perform equally well. They indicated that they spent about one-third of their time on these nonprofessional tasks. The frustrations they felt from this underutilization of their professional training and experience were heightened by their feeling of impotence concerning their ability to correct the situation. They reported that they have little capacity to exert influence upward. More than one-fourth said that they could not communicate technical facts upward; two-fifths reported they were unable to influence their own manager or to suggest upward better ways of doing a job; and over three-fifths felt that they had no chance to have any voice in the solution of larger development problems. They revealed a situation in which they had little opportunity to be heard and to communicate and exert influence upward even though they recognized from their own experience that they had observations, ideas, and insights which could significantly improve the results achieved.

Other studies of R & D administration, and of how to manage a firm so as to make the best use of investments in R & D point to the importance of efficient lateral coordination,[7] if the results of R & D work are to flow rapidly and smoothly into production and successful marketing. Good vertical coordination is no substitute for effective lateral coordination in these circumstances.

REQUIREMENTS WHICH R & D ADMINISTRATION SHOULD MEET

Pelz's creative tensions and the results of other studies indicate that the success of R & D administration will be influenced appreciably by the extent to which the following conditions are met. That is, the more that the R & D administration of an enterprise uses a management system and structure which provide the following, the greater will be the probability of an effective R & D effort:

1. Adequate and accurate communication in all directions, especially *upward*
2. Capacity to exert effective influence in all directions on matters which the individual is convinced are important or which he feels need to be acted upon if the organization is to achieve its objectives, that is, the ability to exert influence where there is no direct traditional authority
3. Supportive superiors
4. Superiors and peers, even though differing vigorously on scientific and technical matters, supportive and personally warm
5. Capacity for individuals to have two or more bosses without threat or jeopardy to the individual subordinates

These conditions, which an R & D administration should meet if the R & D effort is to be most effective, are demanding. The management systems most widely used in business and government today do not meet them. The view that a person can have only one superior and should be given orders by him and no one else is based on "hire-and-fire" authority.[8] This is a central concept of current, formal, organization theory.[9] Product or project manager concepts are recognized as deviating from accepted management principles. B. C. Ames[10] has pointed out that "the concept (product manager) is an organizational anomaly in that it violates a proven management precept—i.e., that responsibility should always be matched by equivalent authority—and yet it works, if properly applied."

Although the management theories most widely used today do not meet the above conditions, a management system based on the principles used by the highest producing managers in American business and government comes, as we shall see, much closer to doing so.

A MORE EFFECTIVE MANAGEMENT SYSTEM

Over the past two decades the University of Michigan's Institute for Social Research has conducted studies in more than 200 United States firms, involving thousands of managers and tens of thousands of employees. These studies have revealed that the highest producing managers in American firms, irrespective of the kind of work being done, are using, on the average, the same *basic principles* of managing the human organization. These principles differ in fundamental respects from the principles being used by managers who are achieving only average or poor productivity, performance, and earnings.[11]

It is possible to integrate these findings into a general organizational theory which can be applied to the structure and management of any enterprise.[12] This organizational theory recognizes that high levels of *cooperative motivation* are required among the members of an organization. The theory states that to achieve the highest levels of cooperative motivation among the members of an organization, both managerial and nonsupervisory, it is necessary to fully harness their noneconomic motives so that they reinforce, rather than conflict with, the motivational forces stemming from the economic motives. The theory accepts the view of the highest producing managers that the best results are not obtained by merely buying a man's time and issuing orders—that it is necessary to harness the noneconomic motives with the economic motives.

Extensive use of research and development, which is characteristic of highly industrialized nations, increases appreciably the necessity for cooperative motivation and behavior within an enterprise. Complex technologies are needed to effectively use the results of R & D. To be successful, firms which use these complex technologies must achieve high levels of cooperative behavior among the highly specialized persons and departments in the enterprise. As increasing use is made of R & D, the extent of cooperative behavior among the members of an enterprise will become increasingly important in determining the success of the firm.

To apply the theory to a particular company or department, it is necessary to develop operating procedures (for example, for supervision, communication, compensation, and decision making) which are applications of the theory appropriate to the unique conditions and traditions of that company. A fundamental principle, *the principle of supportive relationships* can be used as a guide to derive the operating procedures most suitable for a particular company in the light of its history and current situation. This principle can be stated as follows:

> The leadership and other processes of the organization must be such as to ensure a maximum probability that in all interactions and all relationships within the organization each member will, in the light of his background, values, and expectations, view the experience as supportive and one which builds and maintains his sense of personal worth and importance.[13]

Consistent with this principle, the highest producing managers create an organization which approaches the following model:

> This social system is made up of interlocking work groups with a high degree of group loyalty among the members and favorable attitudes and trust between superiors and subordinates. Sensitivity to others and relatively high levels of skill in personal interaction and the functioning of groups are also present. These skills permit effective participation in decisions on common problems. Participation is used, for example, to establish organizational objectives which are a satisfactory integration of the needs and desires of all members of the organization and of persons functionally related to it. High levels of reciprocal influence occur, and high levels of total coordinated influence are achieved in the organization. Responsibility for the organization's success is felt individually by the members and each initiates action, when necessary, to assure that the organization accomplishes its objectives. Communication is efficient and effective. There is a flow from one part of the organization to another of all the relevant information important for each decision and action. The leadership in the organization has developed what might well be called a highly effective social system for interaction and mutual influence.[14]

The system of management based on this theory has been labeled System 4 for convenient reference. An indication of the leadership style and operating characteristics of this management system is illustrated by the items in Table 26. These items compare System 4 with prevailing management systems based upon traditional theories or organization. The items in Table 26 are from a much longer table.[15]

A steadily growing body of data from an increasing number of studies reveals that firms (plants, departments, and so on) whose management systems are toward the System 4 end of the continuum, in comparison with firms whose management systems are more toward the System 1 end, achieve higher productivity and earnings, lower costs and less waste, less absence, better labor relations and employee satisfaction, and better physical and mental health among their employees.[16] Moreover, as firms shift their management system toward System 4, they experience a favorable shift in these variables, provided the shift is not so rapid or great that it exceeds the expectations and skills of the members of the organization to successfully adapt to it. That is, the shift, if it is to yield beneficial results, has to be within the interactional capabilities of the members of the organization as determined by their cultural heritage. When a firm shifts toward System 1 in its management system, the *long-range consequences* are unfavorable just as a shift toward System 4 is favorable. The short-range results from a shift toward System 1 usually appear to be favorable, but this is due to serious inaccuracies and inadequacies in the accounting reports of firms. When all the assets of a firm are considered, a shift toward System 1 decreases the actual earnings of a firm even though there may be an increase in cash flow from the liquidation of human assets.[17]

It is significant that the experience of R & D administrators is consistent with these findings. Thus, for example, when Table 26 is used with the instructions below, R & D administrators report that the management systems used by the most productive laboratories fall at the border between the System 3 and System 4 range while those of the least productive are in the middle of System 2.

> Instructions: Please think of the *most* productive research department, laboratory, or organization you have known well. Then place the letter *h* on the line under each organizational variable in Table 2 to show where this organization would fall. Treat each item as a continuous variable from the left extreme of System 1 to the right extreme of System 4.
>
> After you have completed the form to describe the most productive research department or unit you know well, please

TABLE 26[a]
Profile of Organizational Characteristics

	System 1	System 2	System 3	System 4
Leadership				
1. How much confidence is shown in subordinates?	None	Condescending	Substantial	Complete
2. How free do they feel to talk to superior about job?	Not at all	Not very	Rather free	Fully free
3. Are subordinates' ideas sought and used, if worthy?	Seldom	Sometimes	Usually	Always
Motivation				
4. Is predominant use made of (1) fear, (2) threats, (3) punishment, (4) rewards, (5) involvement?	1, 2, 3, occasionally 4	4, some 3	4, some 3 and 5	5, 4, based on group set goals
5. Where is responsibility felt for achieving organizational goals?	Mostly at top	Top and middle	Fairly general	At all levels
Communication				
6. What is the direction of information flow?	Downward	Mostly downward	Down and up	Down, up, and sideways
7. How is downward communication accepted?	With suspicion	Possibly with suspicion	With caution	With open mind
8. How accurate is upward communication?	Often wrong	Censored for boss	Limited accuracy	Accurate
9. How well do superiors know problems faced by subordinates?	Know little	Some knowledge	Quite well	Very well

ORGANIZATIONAL DYNAMICS FOR R & D DEPARTMENTS

Interaction				
10. What is character of interaction?	Little, always with fear and distrust	Little, usually with some condescension	Moderate, often fair amount of confidence and trust	Extensive, high degree of confidence and trust
11. How much cooperative teamwork is present?	None	Relatively little	Moderate amount	Very substantial amount throughout organization
Decisions				
12. At what level are decisions formally made?	Mostly at top	Policy at top, some delegation	Broad policy at top, more delegation	Throughout but well integrated
13. What is the origin of technical and professional knowledge used in decision making?	Top management	Upper and middle	To certain extent throughout	To a great extent throughout
14. Are subordinates involved in decisions related to their work?	Not at all	Occasionally consulted	Generally consulted	Fully involved
15. What does decision-making process contribute to motivation?	Nothing, often weakens it	Relatively little	Some contribution	Substantial
Goals				
16. How are organizational goals established?	Orders issued	Orders, some communication invited	After discussion, by orders	Group action (except in crisis)
17. How much covert resistance to goals is present?	Strong resistance	Moderate resistance	Some resistance at times	Little or none
Control				
18. How concentrated are review and control functions?	Highly at top	Relatively high at top	Moderate delegation to lower levels	Quite widely shared
19. Is there an informal organization resisting the formal one?	Yes	Usually	Sometimes	No—same goals as formal
20. What are cost, productivity, and other control data used for?	Policing, punishment	Reward and punishment	Reward, some self-guidance	Self-guidance, problem solving

[a] Adapted from *The Human Organization* by Rensis Likert, pp. 196–211. Copyright (c) 1967 by McGraw-Hill, Inc. (Used by permission of McGraw-Hill Book Company.)

think of the *least* productive department, laboratory, or organization you know well. Preferably it should be about the same size as your most productive unit and engaged in the same general kind of work. Then put the letter *p* on the line under each organizational variable to show where, in the light of your observations, you feel this least productive organization falls on that item. As before, treat each item as a continuous variable from the left extreme of System 1 to the right extreme of System 4.

The reports from R & D administration indicate that the management system, System 4, which has been derived from the principles used by the highest producing managers, appears to resemble the management system which R & D administrators observe is most effective in achieving high levels of R & D performance. Since this is the case, System 4 should be a management system which would more adequately meet the requirements for effective R & D administration than do the management systems used by most firms today, which fall almost entirely in the range from the middle of System 1 to the middle of System 3.

POTENTIAL VALUE OF SYSTEM 4 FOR R & D ADMINISTRATION

The extent to which System 4 more adequately provides the kind of management system required for R & D administration can be tested readily by examining available research findings. As will be recalled, R & D administration is likely to be more effective when the five conditions listed on page 148 are met well rather than poorly.

A form similar to Table 26 but containing many more items and with each item stated more fully[18] has been used in more than twenty firms to measure the management system being used. Each manager or supervisor in the firm or department was asked to describe the management system which, in his experience, is being used by his firm. The findings obtained were related also to such end-result measurements as productivity, costs, and earnings of the firm.

The data obtained using the longer form reveals that System 4 organizations to a greater extent than System 3 firms and to a much greater extent than System 2 or 1, display the following characteristics:

1. Communication
    a. Communication in all directions, including upward, is more adequate and accurate.

ORGANIZATIONAL DYNAMICS FOR R & D DEPARTMENTS   155

    b. There is greater willingness to accept communication as being accurate.
    c. Subordinates feel more responsibility for communicating accurate information upward and for taking the initiative to see that information, which for effective organizational performance should flow upward, does so.
    d. Superiors, as a consequence, better understand the problems faced by subordinates and by the organization generally.
    e. The perceptions of each other by superiors and subordinates are more accurate.

2. Influence, Cooperation, and Coordination
    a. All hierarchical levels in the organization, including nonsupervisory, can exert more influence on the objectives, procedures, activities, and so on, of the total organization and of subunits. The total amount of influence is greater; superiors have more and subordinates have more.
    b. This increase in the total amount of influence does not rely on punitive power or authority but is created instead by the interaction processes which are used.
    c. The motivation for cooperative behavior is greater.
    d. The greater amount of influence from nonpunitive sources and the greater degree of cooperative motivation enable influence to be exerted laterally as well as vertically. Lateral coordination is as effective as vertical.

3. Supportive Behavior
    a. Superiors have more confidence and trust in subordinates.
    b. Subordinates are more supportive in their interactions with colleagues and others in the organization.
    c. Superiors, and in turn subordinates, listen well to each other and are genuinely interested in understanding the ideas and contributions of the other even though they may disagree.
    d. Superiors seek to involve subordinates in decisions related to their work. They generally use group problem solving in the process.

4. Responsibility
    a. The members of the organization at all hierarchical levels, not just at the top, feel responsible for the organization attaining its objectives.

b. The prevailing atmosphere in the organization is one of "no nonsense." Objectives are set and work is done in an efficient, highly motivated manner.

Research findings from many other studies using other measuring instruments also have yielded data consistent with the above result. These have been reported or summarized in several publications.[19]

SYSTEM 4 PERMITS TWO BOSSES

As stated above there is a fifth requirement which a management system should meet; namely, the system must enable an individual to have two or more bosses without threat or jeopardy to him. The manner in which System 4 does this has been stated elsewhere:

> How would the operation work as a formal system if he (the individual) were a member of both a functional work group and a product, or cross-function, work group? These two work groups each consist of a superior to whom he and the other subordinates under that particular superior report. Figure [3] shows these two work groups and the overlapping member, M-1c, who reports to two superiors. One work group is the functional-line (e.g., marketing) work group and its superior is M-1. The other work group is the product cross-function work group with its superior, A-1.
>
> If both of these work groups have high group loyalty and are using group decision making well (Bradford et al., 1963; Maier, 1963; Marrow, 1964a; Schein & Bennis, 1956), subordinates in each work group would be able to exercise significant amounts of upward and lateral influence (Likert, 1961, Chaps. 8, 9, 11, 12). (If these groups are not performing in this way, the superiors of these work groups and, in turn, their own superiors, as we shall see, have some training and organization building to do.) This would mean, of course, that the individual we are considering (M-1c), who is the subordinate under two superiors, can exert upward influence via group decision-making processes in both work groups. As a consequence, when one superior (e.g., product, cross-function superior, A-1) and the work group reporting to him approach decisions which are incompatible or in conflict with the points of view held or decisions being arrived at by the other superior (marketing department superior, M-1) and his work group, the individual who is in both work groups is obligated

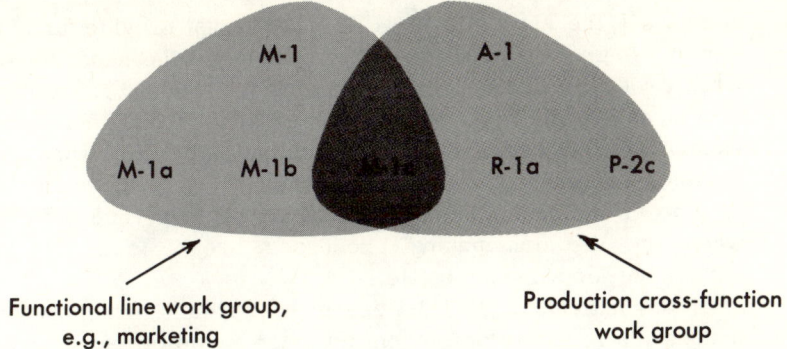

Fig. 3. Example of subordinate serving as linking pin for horizontal coordination.

to bring such information to the attention of both work groups. This information is relevant data to be used by each work group in its decision making. Even though the chief of one or the other groups may be reluctant to consider such information, the group members are likely to want to do so. They, themselves, are likely to be members of other cross-function work groups and recognize that they, too, sooner or later may find themselves caught in a developing conflict between the two or more work groups of which they are subordinate members. They will wish, consequently, to resolve this conflict constructively and thereby help to create a well-established process and precedent for handling such differences.

Under System 4, both work groups shown in Figure [3] will be expected to engage in group decision making in order to resolve the differences. The decision-making processes should strive to create an innovative solution which satisfactorily meets the requirements and opportunities presented by the situations faced by both groups. The focus should not be, as is often the case with System 2 man-to-man decision making, on obtaining a decision favorable to a particular work group or its department, irrespective of how costly it is for the rest of the organization. The primary objective of the decision making of the two work groups should be to discover a solution which will serve the best interests of the entire organization.

Whenever the members of one or both of the two groups display inability to use group decision making sufficiently well to achieve consensus in terms of the best interests of all concerned, the higher-level work groups must provide further training in group progresses. This training of the subordinate work groups in group problem solving and related processes should enable all work groups to recognize from their own experience that everyone in the organization benefits when the decision making is focused on discovering the best solutions for the entire organization and that almost everyone suffers when the decision-making processes break down into a bargaining, or win-lose battle.

If the individual (M-1c) were in a System 2 organization and caught in a developing conflict between his two superiors, the situation could be resolved only by getting one or both of his superiors to change their decisions and their expectations regarding his behavior. The individual's only recourse in his attempt to change the conflicting demands on him would be man-to-man interaction separately with each superior. He would have to try to persuade one or both of his superiors to change their decisions in a subordinate-superior discussion with each. Often the requested change would be seen by the particular superior as implying a criticism of him, or as taking sides with the other superior against him. Neither criticism nor taking sides is warmly received. In this System 2 situation, the subordinate's attempts to change the decisions of one or both of his two superiors would not be likely to succeed, and he would be left in jeopardy, unable to satisfy the conflicting demands. It is for this reason that a cardinal principle of System 2 is that a man can have only one boss.

As we have seen, System 4 handles this problem by providing the resource of group rather than man-to-man interaction. With System 4, the individual caught between conflicting demands initiates discussion of the problem in the relevant work groups. Discussion of it takes place there in a much more impersonal way than is possible when the subordinate raises the question personally with each one of his two superiors.

There is impressive evidence to show that, in comparison to man-to-man interaction, a work group which uses effective group decision making with its superior can give him substantially more information which is valuable to him but which may involve criticism of him. It can also present a strong case for a course of action other than the one the superior initially prefers. In group decision making, individual members of the group can "toss the ball" back and forth among themselves and through such group processes communicate safely to the chief information which is important to him, but which no single individual dares communicate in a man-to-man session. This kind of group decision making requires two broadly different kinds of skills. Group members need skill in leadership and in membership interaction processes in order to build and maintain a group efficient both in solving problems and in coping with conflict and differences. Skill is also required in the intellectual processes of problem solving (Kepner & Tregoe, 1965) (Majer, 1963).

When an individual has two superiors, one must be designated to take the initiative on personnel functions, such as salary review and recommendations. In the System 4 model, decisions are reached through consensus, and recommendations or action reflect the combined judgment of the superiors involved. Therefore, it is immaterial which superior is given the responsibility for initiating any necessary actions and for seeing that the decisions or recommendations are implemented. It is merely necessary that one superior be given this assignment.[20]

EFFECTIVE LATERAL COORDINATION

System 4 with its multiple overlapping group structure and group problem solving, in addition to its capacity to enable an individual to have two or more bosses, provides unique resources for achieving effective lateral, as well as vertical, coordination. Since the successful use of R & D usually requires effective lateral coordination, a shift to System 4 can increase appreciably the benefits an organization derives from its R & D expenditures.

An adequate discussion of the use of System 4 for the effective lateral coordination required for the successful use of R & D is another chapter in itself.[21]

The general trends in American society are likely to make a shift to System 4 management even more necessary by any firm or governmental agency which seeks to derive profitable returns from R & D expenditures. Young scientists and engineers expect to a greater degree than their predecessors to be involved in decisions related to their work. Events on college and university campuses indicate that the next student generation entering R & D employment is likely to insist on having even more influence upon decisions affecting itself. If Systems 1, 2, and 3 are unable at present to meet the requirements for effective R & D administration, they will become appreciably more obsolete in each future decade.

Basic Concepts of Operational Control

C. WEST CHURCHMAN
Professor and Research Philosopher
Space Sciences Laboratory
University of California
Berkeley

SUMMARY AND PURPOSE

This chapter is concerned with the concept of control in sociotechnical systems development. It reviews briefly some of the techniques of control, but its major emphasis is on the meaning of control. A ship destined for the wrong port may be admirably controlled in the narrow sense that it travels the best pathway to the wrong place, but in a broader sense we would have to say that it was not well controlled at all. The increased capability of employing control techniques which we have witnessed in the last two decades has often led to the neglect of the very pertinent question: Control for what purpose?

MEANING OF CONTROL

Control is derived from a French word which meant "to make a copy of a record (or scroll)." Hence its historical meaning suggests the capability of reexamining what has occurred. Its modern meaning adds the idea of modifying one's plan of action as a result of this examination.

Norbert Wiener, whose book *Cybernetics* inspired many engineers to work on control theory, suggests in the title the illuminating idea that control is well illustrated by the steering of a ship (in Greek *kybernetes* means "steersman").[1] Imagine you are steering a motorboat across a choppy lake. As you observe the waves deflect the bow from the target, you react to bring the boat back on course. Note the theme of (1) recording what has happened and (2) modifying behavior to accomplish the goal. Wiener referred to the transmittal and recording of what has happened as "feedback." The illustration of the steersman helps illuminate one important aspect of feedback control, namely the timeliness of the recorded message. Imagine your plight if it took ten seconds to learn where the boat is headed; by the time you had reacted after a ten-second delay you would probably do exactly the wrong thing.

Control and consciousness are closely related concepts, for consciousness means an awareness or reaction to what has been happening. Thus the conscious mind plays one critical role in the control of human behavior. When you lose consciousness you lose control of yourself; you can no longer react to what has been happening.

CONTROL IN SCIENCE

The concept of control is pervasive in science, for science is not merely inquiry based on observation and reason. Even if every witness of an Unidentified Flying Object agrees that there was a large white saucer with green men in it, the scientist remains skeptical, simply because he has learned that general agreement of witnesses by itself is not a very sound control procedure.

The concept of a controlled observation in measurement can be described as follows. A concept like length is defined by a series of steps to be taken in an idealized environment. This is called the "standard" of length. When someone makes an observation of length in a real environment, he must be able to argue on the basis of the known laws of nature that such-and-such a reading, termed an "adjusted reading," would be obtained in an ideal environment. Finally, a number of adjusted readings must be independently obtained and tested for statistical consistency. One sees that the process of establishing so-called facts in science is rather complicated, but the important point to be drawn from the example is that *control cannot operate without a theory of natural events*. The measurer of length needs to assume with some confidence the laws of nature which enable him to adjust his observation to the standard.

That theory plays a very critical role in all control processes in sociotechnical systems will be seen.

SOCIOTECHNICAL SYSTEMS

Control of sociotechnical systems is a label that may give rise to a certain amount of repulsion on the part of the humanist. It need not do so; and it is very essential that we try to understand the concept of a social system, for a sociotechnical system is simply a social system some of whose goals or resources can be understood in technological terms.

A social system, of course, is a system with people in it. But the major question is: What makes a group of persons into a system? The word "system" derives from a Greek word meaning "a whole, compounded of parts." Modern systems theory has supplied many meanings for "compounded," so that the student is apt to be overwhelmed by the profusion of authoritative but conflicting definitions of the word "system" he finds in textbooks. Rather than add to this confusion by yet another definition, it will serve us better to list the questions about social systems which are relevant to the concept of control. All we need accept by way of meaning is that social systems have a set of goals which are desirable for some group of people, and that for purposes of development each system can be broken down into subsystems or components, each with its own set of goals which presumably serve the goals of the whole system. In other words, control can best operate when it can look at specific sectors of a whole and help us decide whether the sector or component is behaving properly. (If it still seems that control is anti-humanistic, a judgment on this matter should be postponed until the details are filled in.)

From this very general account of a social system, the following questions fall into a rather obvious sequence: (1) *What are the goals of the system?* and correlatively, (2) *Whose interests does the system serve?* At the outset we should recognize that since we are discussing the *development* of sociotechnical systems, all our questions are normative rather than descriptive. That is, we are asking what the goals ought to be and whose interests should be served, in order that the system be developed properly.

For example, a hospital is a sociotechnical system, since it is a social system and some of its goals and resources can be described in technical terms. Its goal might be defined as overcoming physiological detriments of people with diseases or wounds. The people whose interests it serves can be called the "clients." These might be all the people in a certain area, with a given income, who request aid from the hospital and pay the prescribed fee.

It is to be noted that hospitals may have other goals, i.e., biomedical research, or income of doctors, administrators, and nurses. These goals very often conflict and pose a very difficult problem for control. The more or less obvious way out of the difficulty is to weight the goals in terms of their relative importance. This might be done, for example, by enlarging the client into a community (e.g., the citizens of a city), and asking how the specific goals of some people serve the interests of that community, e.g., in economic terms. Thus qualitative goals like health, or research, or income become transformed into the more quantitative goal of economic benefit.

From the point of view of the use of control in development with respect to goals, the attempt to encompass diverse goals under one overriding social purpose can be expressed by the following question: *What is the measure of performance of the system?* It is easy to see why such a measure provides a basis for control and planning. In looking ahead, one can scan alternatives and estimate which one will maximize the imputed measure of performance. Indeed, the use of mathematical models and simulation provides a very rich way of scanning alternatives. In mathematical programming, for example, the measure of performance, z, is expressed as a function of the level of activity (e.g., manpower) in each component of the system, and the solution is an estimate of that set of activity levels which maximizes z, subject to certain constraints. Control consists of examining the system after the solution is implemented to see whether the measure of performance is satisfactorily near the estimated measure. One can also control the solution by running the plan parallel with the old plan, e.g., in a computer simulation.

Finding a suitable measure of performance is no easy matter, even in firms in a free market. It seems natural to say that the measure of performance of a firm should be its net profit, but net profit is usually calculated annually whereas the worth of a firm for its owners spans numbers of years. Furthermore, the method of calculating net profit, e.g., for income tax purposes, may fail to measure the real performance of the firm.

In the case of governmental agencies and other public institutions, the task of finding a suitable measure of performance becomes even more difficult. There is a strong tendency to use the amount of activity as a measure (number of students graduating, number of patients serviced, and so forth), although clearly activity by itself is not the real value to the client. As previously indicated, it may sometimes be possible to translate the objectives of the system into economic measures, e.g., income streams. Thus a new school building provides jobs and upgrades education, both of which can be translated into economic gains to the community. When this is done, we say that a cost-benefit analysis has been made.

It is important to note that any budgeting process which allocates resources to programs implicitly assumes a measure of performance, because the allocation in effect weights certain objectives more heavily than others. But it does not follow that the implicit weighting ought to be made explicit. For example, publication of the measure of performance may set off political battles that damage the organization. Thus the answer to the question, What is the measure of performance? may be, "There is no such measure." If so, then the problem of control becomes difficult but not necessarily impossible. One may be able to generate surrogate measures, which, while they do not represent the real values of the organization to the clients, nevertheless provide managers with information about the stability of the organization. In large contracts, for example, "slippage days" is such an indicator; the client is only indirectly concerned with delays in various sub-programs of the contract, but the number of such delays may be a good control measure, i.e., may tell the manager when he should respond by changing the system.

The next set of questions are concerned with the manner in which the system is run: (1) *What is the decision maker of the system?* (2) *What are the components of the system?* (3) *What are system boundaries?*

The neuter form "What" rather than "Who" has been used to emphasize that the decision maker is normally a complex of individual psychological and social forces rather than one person.

Just as in the case of the client, the questions regarding the decision maker pose strategic problems for those who wish to control the system. The system may be conceived very broadly or quite narrowly, and depending on the choice, the nature of the decision maker and the system boundaries change. We say that the components of a social system are capable of being changed by the decision maker, while everything that lies beyond the system boundaries cannot be changed by him, although the world outside the boundaries may influence what happens.

Consider, for example, a large computer installation. From a narrow point of view, one might assume that the decision maker consists of those persons who can directly interface with the computer plus their immediate supervisors. The components might then be regarded as configurations of people and hardware, plus their related software packages. The system boundaries would be defined by the area and personnel of the computer department. Top management policy, the budget, and demand for computer services might then lie outside the system boundaries, the decision makers being unable to change any of these. We note that the process of control is directed toward the decision maker, because if changes are to be made in the light of past events, he is the one to make them.

But one might set the boundaries of the computer installation in a quite different fashion, by assuming that the system also includes all potential users. Now the decision maker, components, and boundaries are all radically different, because the controller assumes, for example, that he can influence the behavior of the users, change management policy, or modify the budget.

It is important to emphasize that the strategic judgments about the client and the decision maker are never obvious, though frequently they appear to be so because the organization may have strong consensus on such matters. To repeat, the controller should never take consensus as a safe basis for his actions; too often whole peoples have strongly agreed on policies that lead to their doom.

The components of a system are essentially ways of looking at the system from the point of view of planning and control. If human powers of reasoning and observation were strong enough and refined enough, we probably would not need to think about social systems in component terms. Ideally, each component has its own measure of performance which the controller can watch. Here again there tends to be the fallacy of using component *activity* as a surrogate measure (e.g., number of houses built or number of criminals apprehended in an urban system). The point is that the component measure of performance must be so related to the system measure of performance that the controller can judge what a change in the component measure will mean to the whole system. One of the simplest ways of representing components occurs in linear programming, where the system measure is a linear function of component measures, subject to certain (linear) constraints. Here the component measure is often represented as the amount of activity multiplied by a "relative value" coefficient: the more important the activity is for the whole system, the higher its coefficient.

It is important to note that all such linear representations of components are partially unrealistic, because they assume that the components are "separable," meaning that any increase in one component's measure implies a system improvement, if all other components remain the same. The last two decades have shown that the major components of sociotechnical systems are highly "coupled": it is quite likely that "bettering" the performance of a transportation component will have unsatisfactory side effects in other components, e.g., produce air pollution, increase traffic hazards, and so forth. This is one reason why programs that attempt to alleviate the great social problems of today may be ill-conceived, since they tend to decouple poverty, education, health, environment, and population, when in fact these problems are all strongly coupled.

To say that a linear representation of a system is unrealistic is not to say that it is useless, because all representatives of social systems are unrealistic. This is the major reason for control: we are undoubtedly wrong in serious ways when we plan and act on our representations of social systems, no matter who we are—VIP, top manager, bottom manager, individual—and no matter how well motivated we are to serve the real client. Control is our saving move, because through it we can record our mistakes and hopefully change for the better. We should also note that considerations of convenience and time often lead to adopting partially unrealistic representations.

In recent years it has become fashionable to treat components of sociotechnical systems as "black boxes," where one tries to identify the inputs to the box and the consequent outputs. (The phrase "black box" is used to convey the idea that no internal description of the system is needed.) Thus a manager might despair of trying to understand how a research laboratory actually works in detail. But he can understand one input, namely money, and he can understand one output, namely, useful results. His question may then be phrased, What do I get as output for an increase of one unit of input? Again the representation is probably unrealistic, but it may help to gain a fairly convenient grasp of some of the reality of the system.

The user of black box thinking needs to be very wary of its basic problem, however, which ancient logicians labeled *post hoc, ergo propter hoc,* meaning "after this, therefore because of this," or the fallacy of inferring that if one thing follows another in time, it is also caused by that other. In modern times, researchers often correlate events by means of regression analysis or other techniques. For example, they correlate inputs at time t_i with outputs at t_{i+1}, and then argue that the inputs caused the outputs.

A little reflection on management practices shows how very risky this analysis may be, simply because management tends to put its money where the results look good. Thus if a research laboratory seems to be doing remarkably well, management will naturally increase its budget: that is, the output at time t_i causes the input at t_{i+1}! Now correlations made over periods of time do not by themselves tell us whether, when X and Y are highly correlated, X causes Y or Y causes X. Other systemic judgments need to be made to establish the way the causal chain operates; in many cases it appears more reasonable to assume that outputs cause inputs rather than the reverse.

The last two questions about sociotechnical systems have really been the basis of the whole discussion: (1) *What is the planner of the system?* (2) *What is the controller of the system?*

Here again the neuter form, "What," is intended to reflect the complexity of both tasks, the planning and controlling of the system. Planning means deliberating about alternative decisions in terms of their outcomes before the actual decision itself. Many decisions are not planned, or little planned, e.g., routine performances like running a machine or responding to requests for service, or emergency actions.

Planning, in this general sense, involves almost every responsible decision maker in an organization and does not reside in a so-called planning department alone. All managers do some deliberating about alternatives, e.g., whether to retain or fire, lease or buy. It is to be noted that not all planning produces actions, as most planners know.

Controlling is the correlative of planning. If we have deliberated about a course of action and explicitly settled on one, then we have in effect "written a scroll," and in control we "copy it"; i.e., we look at what we had deliberately planned to do and see whether our perception of reality is producing a satisfactory replication.

Both planning and controlling require fairly explicit judgments about the nature of the social system, its decision maker, client, components, and boundaries. Most important, the judgments need to specify the value basis of the system, i.e., the most important goals the system should strive for. The German word *Weltanschauung* or "world perception" captures this idea very well. It means, in German philosophy, the framework through which data are filtered to provide us with meaningful information. Sociotechnical systems in national defense provide an excellent example. A technical advance in biochemical weapons is a "datum." If our *Weltanschauung* tells us that survival of the USA is the highest value, then the datum becomes evidence that we should develop the weapon. On the other hand, if the *Weltanschauung* says that man's total survival is the highest value, then the datum tells all nations not to develop the weapon.

Today we are witnessing radically different worldviews of

sociotechnical systems. They have raised many questions. What should be our attitude toward genetic engineering, for example? Should we develop the technology with the aim of creating a race of highly intelligent and healthy men and women? But then, what about individual freedom to have the children that our love creates? And what about the goal of clean air and water that robs man of the opportunity to use that air and water to produce income and to provide recreation?

But there is another fundamental aspect of the *Weltanschauung* that both planning and control need to consider. The very concept of control is an admission that our plans, no matter how thoroughly deliberated, may very well be wrong: the future will not copy the scroll. Furthermore, if we find to our satisfaction, based on our *Weltanschauung*, that the plan was wrong, then we should have the opportunity to correct our error. But what does "correct" mean in this context?

In today's enthusiasm over spectacular developments in sociotechnical systems, we are apt to ignore the implicit grounds of our enthusiasm. To be sure, after some effort we may be able to correct a serious flaw in a moon exploration system, a highway construction design, or a weapons system. These corrections enable the system to work better with respect to such goals as a moon landing, traffic through-put, or defense. But note that if these goals are wrong in the sense that they do not serve society's aims, then a correction is hardly a correction. If I have lost my way in the forest and in eagerly following the wrong trial I make sure that I keep finding my way back to it when I stray, I cannot say that I am controlling my behavior.

In the very broadest sense, every sociotechnical system contains the strong possibility of its own destruction, as well as the destruction of other social systems. Any adequate system of control, therefore, requires a theory or *Weltanschauung* which, if valid, provides grounds for guaranteeing the system's survival.

It seems appropriate to label this aspect of control theory the "theology" of control, because it tries to develop the basis on which the systems designer can believe that the systems he designs will improve in a real sense. The basis can legitimately be called "God," and the belief a "faith." Of course, today's engineer tends to shun such obscure issues, because it is impossible to formulate them in precise terms. For example, one cannot state in clear and unambiguous terms what "survival" and "improvement" mean, nor can one find data to substantiate one's faith. But problems are realities that do not disappear just because one does not think about them.

In a recent book J. Forrester proposes to use his theory of dynamics to design urban communities; in effect he regards cities as sociotechnical systems.[2] Even if one is impressed by Forrester's simulation methods, the wary reader cannot help but ask whether some of his suggestions, e.g., with respect to housing, might not set off the detonator that blows up the whole system.

Note that one need not accept a pessimistic philosophy with respect to system survival guarantees, for the pessimist has his own faith which is no better substantiated than the optimist's. Jacques Ellul tells us that man has become overwhelmed by "la technique," which dictates his life and robs him of his freedom.[3] Technology for him leads to the destruction of human values. But Ellul's *Weltanschauung*, which is the opposite of Forrester's, is also a faith, a faith that God is the Devil, i.e., that the basis of system change is a force which we can no longer change and which is evil. Those who devote a portion of their lives to systems control have the moral responsibility to enunciate their faith in the nature of the guarantor, be it good or evil, Christian or Hindu, white or black, radical or conservative. No word so adequately captures the differences in faith as does "change," which means so many things to today's planners.

But I do not mean to imply that faith is altogether personal, and that there is no real basis for it. The personal aspect of faith must confront the social aspect: faith is man's most gigantic inquiry into his origin and destiny, a collective as well as a personal experience.

From this lofty pinnacle of systems control, suppose we descend to the plain and point out that even in the more constrained environment where specific goals have been set for the system designer, it is often impossible to tell whether a design is operating correctly or not. The reason for this is that the controller needs to make a strong causal inference, namely, that the design *causes* the changes that improve the system. For example, the technique PERT, for controlling large sociotechnological projects, is often credited with improving system performance by cutting down on unnecessary delays. Its critics, on the other hand, can frequently create counter-worldviews which argue forcibly that the PERT technique had little or nothing to do with better system performance and that the project succeeded despite the need to maintain a PERT chart. Thus, even at a specific level, the controller needs to make very general systemic judgments to enable him to infer how his actions relate to the whole system.

From this account of systems and their controls, it is rather obvious that scientific control in one old-fashioned sense is not possible. If "scientific" means the employment of objective evidence unbiased by prejudgments of any kind, then all system management is unscientific. But it seems wiser to say that such a meaning of science is far too restrictive; in a broader meaning of science which includes intuition and faith, the manager-controller does know some important things about his system. This knowledge is always a combination of his own intuitive insights, what his senses tell him and his own reasoning ability. No manager should ever feel embarrassed about telling the story of his system as he intuits and sees it.

BOUNDED VERSUS OPEN CONTROL

With this background on the nature of sociotechnical systems, we can make an important distinction between two kinds of control, bounded and open. Bounded control is a set of procedures for controlling a system when one or more of the salient features of the system are given by some authority outside the control subsystem. In one of its most restricted senses, bounded control occurs when the goals have been clearly specified, the decision maker is clearly delineated, and the available resources (budget) is given. For example, the NASA Apollo program had these characteristics: the goal of landing man on the moon was specified, the Apollo management was clearly recognizable, and the budget-manpower constraints were known.

In open control, on the other hand, the control subsystem does not recognize any outside authority except the vaguely stated values of the client. The process of deciding that the USA should try to get the first man on the moon, and that the budget should be so many billions of dollars, was an open process. Even the decision-making body was vaguely defined, for it consisted of NASA management, the executive branch (specifically the Bureau of the Budget), Congress, the scientific community, industrial firms, the press, and, vaguest of all, the public. Note how, when the process passes from open to bounded control, the decision-making body is carved from the amorphous mass to become a fairly well-specified group of individuals, with the rest of society acting as critics or pressure groups.

TECHNIQUES OF BOUNDED CONTROL

It would be incorrect to infer from its definition that bounded control is cut and dried. A good deal of creativity is required to steer a system toward a specified goal, even when the resources are plentiful, as the soul of the captain of the *Titanic* can attest. A set of mission specifications does not necessarily yield the correct measure of performance the controller needs, nor does it necessarily tell him how to subdivide the project into programs, nor how to set time schedules and resource allocations. Finally, and perhaps most important, the usual specifications of a mission do not tell the manager how he is to get people to work together as a team, to feel highly motivated, to understand what they should be doing, and so on.

Bounded control involves at its best the right mixture of technique and creativity. No technique by itself should ever take on the role of leading the project. Consider, for example, statistical quality control,[4] a technique developed by W. Shewhart in the 1930s primarily to aid manufacturing systems, which are among the most important sociotechnical systems. Statistical quality control is ideally suited for bounded control because the quality of the product can be measured along certain physical dimensions: length, weight, hardness, and so forth. The technique recognizes that no manufacturing system can produce items that are precisely the same in these dimensions of quality. The controller makes the systemic judgment that the system is "in control," meaning that the variation between items can be accurately described by some statistical laws, e.g., by the behavior of a random variable subject to a probability distribution. The technique consists of a continuous check on this assumption. The controller must decide the risk he is willing to take of making two kinds of errors: (1) allowing the system to continue when it is no longer in control, i.e., when the controller's assumption is no longer valid; and (2) changing the system when it is actually in control. These are, indeed, the fundamental and inevitable errors of all control systems and neither can in principle be avoided with certainty.[5] (To avoid the first error one should not run the system at all; and to avoid the second error, one should run it but never change it—both of which are probably absurdities.) Once the risks are specified, the technique can be employed, e.g., in a continuous manufacturing process.

The technique even in more or less standard manufacturing conditions should not, however, be allowed to dominate. If the system is judged to be out of control, it is by no means obvious what should be done about it. The controller must make some strong systemic judgments about the nature of the imputed lack of control, including the judgment that no change should be made. To permit automatic response patterns to the information is in effect to lose managerial control.

This point is often ignored in another control technique, accounting control. Although this is a somewhat cruder technique than statistical quality control, in that the limits of variation are set by more or less arbitrary judgment, the basic logic is the same. The controller identifies cost centers that are responsible for some segment of the system. The cost centers are given a set of standard costs for their operation, e.g., purchasing, manufacturing, and so forth. If there is a significant variance from the standard, a report is filed explaining the variance. It does not take much imagination to see that such an automatic reporting system will generate a great deal of useless and even mythical information. The fault does not lie with the control system, but rather in the blind application of one specific form of response, namely, filing reports.

The final section of this chapter contains references to other techniques of bounded control. Essentially these techniques aid the controller in one or more of the following tasks: (1) determining when to intervene and change the course of the system (as in the two examples just cited); (2) designing information sources and channels, e.g., feedback systems; (3) allocation of funds, time, and manpower to components; (4) developing policies that fit the capabilities and needs of people; (5) coping with system size.

A METHOD OF OPEN CONTROL: DIALECTICS

In open control there are no "givens," no ultimate authority which tells us what is right. To be sure, there is a decision maker, but no one can claim to know what the decision-making force should be. Not even consensus or majority can be regarded as the ultimate authority of right and wrong, since consensus often arises from collective deception.

The naive and unreflective often hasten to adopt a strong personal relativism when faced with the more ultimate questions of open control. "No one can tell what's right and wrong in any final sense," they say; "it's entirely up to each person to decide for himself and to try to convince other people that he's right." A little reflection shows us why this kind of response is so superficial. To be sure, no one can tell us the answers to questions of ultimate value, of the right client and decision maker, of the right allocation of resources. But it by no means follows that "it's up to each person to decide." In no phase of life, including science, are we ever able to reach final answers to our questions, but we may adopt the position that there are better and worse responses. The good responses are the results of good judgments, just as in the courts where no one can really be sure the right verdict and sentence have been imposed. We see again that the attitude toward questions in open control is based on systemic assumptions: to adopt a personal relativism is to assume that the larger system cannot be known even approximately in an objective sense, which is far from being obvious. In a chapter devoted to the concept of control, we need to explore the assumption that open control is possible in a non-relativistic sense.

In the courts, good judgment is reached in the context of a debate between opposing positions, where in principle the judge and jury at the outset are under no strong influences one way or the other. It is appropriate to generalize this model of decision making to all decisions in open control. In this connection it is interesting to note that the word "decision" up to the middle of the nineteenth century meant a judgment reached in the context of a dispute between two parties. Its more subjective, "I decide alone" meaning is a relatively modern invention that works if at all in bounded control.

The methodology of dialectics is the process of confronting at least two plausible views of how the system should work and what its values should be. Its prescription is very simple, though often terribly difficult to follow: whenever you really think you understand the system, then create a plausible counter theory which says that you are wrong and that a plan other than the one you propose should be followed.

For example, if you think it is the function of a university to transmit knowledge, and that the need is to train better teachers and provide more classrooms, then try to develop a counter worldview of the university in which its function is to develop each individual's style of inquiry. In the latter case, better trained teachers and more classrooms may be the wrong policy altogether. Note that in two opposing views of the university, the client and the decision maker shift. In the first view—the information-transmittal picture—the client is that group of persons who wish to acquire knowledge, and the decision maker is the faculty-administration who are experts in transmitting knowledge. In the second view—the style-of-inquiry picture—the client is anyone who needs to develop his (unique) style, including so-called faculty, black or white, poorly or richly educated; and the decision maker is any group of persons who can help an individual to develop his style.

It is to be emphasized that no set of data by itself can prove that a particular world image is right or wrong, as all of us are realizing in connection with one of the biggest sociotechnical systems, the military. No data, secret or public, can destroy the dove's or the hawk's conviction, because all data can be accounted for within the story each one tells. The data are a trick, misrepresented, irrelevant, and so on. The role of sound judgment is to assess the worth of each side's worldview: How direct and realistic does it sound? How frequently does it undergo basic changes in the light of new information? How much does it serve the interests of one side or the other?

It is to be noted in this connection that simulation or experimentation, though highly useful in open control, never settle the matter in the way they may do in bounded control. If it is given that we should move commuters faster during rush hours, then we can experiment with traffic lights, parking laws, and average speed. But if this objective is not a given, a higher speed will not prove that a particular strategy is correct, because opponents may show that it increases risk or inconvenience. Experiments, however, do help to determine the sensitive points of each side in open control, so that judgment becomes more refined. But judgment does not have to adopt either side, especially if it can find a synthesis that is richer in meaning than both opponents.

CONTROL AND PROGRESS

In the nineteenth century, many thinkers, admiring science, believed that they could see the dawn of an age of knowledge in which technology would aid man in the conquest of nature. For Kant[6] it was the convergence of morality and happiness; for Jeremy Bentham[7] the development of legislation based on the measure of performance of all society, the greatest utility for the greatest number; for Hegel[8] it was "Absolute Mind"; for Marx[9] it was the victory of the proletariat and, as Lenin put it, the withering away of the state; for the evolutionists like Herbert Spencer[10] it was the evolution of a higher species, or as Nietzsche[11] would have it, a revolution to a higher form of morality. These were grand schemes of sociotechnical systems, and men like E. A. Singer, Jr.[12] suggested systematic ways in which we might measure man's progress. But Singer, who straddled the nineteenth and the twentieth centuries, realized that progress does not come in a smooth pattern of development, but rather involves deep despair and uncertainty.

In the latter part of the twentieth century we have forgotten all these high-sounding worldviews of our grandfathers, and instead we tend to look at the world's problems in very specific terms, breaking the whole down into poverty, or war, or pollution, or education. Some planners, like D. Braybrooke and C. E. Lindblom,[13] recommend the incrementalist approach of taking small but realistic steps to overcome system deficiencies. In a way our age represents a paradox in its thinking. No other age has ever been so conscious of the complex interrelationships between all facets of the social system, nor has any other age been so anxious to try to solve the problems of proverty, pollution, and population. Yet we are a piecemeal age, without any viable concept of why our sociotechnical system exists and where it should go; at best we see its deficiencies, not its values.

This paradox of the control of sociotechnical systems may account for one of the major crises of management today: the action-revolution movement that wants to end the talk and make change by disruption. Managers and planners who have a narrow vision and concentrate on deficiencies tend to view their chief role as one of survival—for themselves and their institutions. But every great scheme of progress in the nineteenth century included the necessity for the destruction of outmoded institutions, as well as the creation of new ones. It is as though today's managers were blocked off from one vital area of control, the dissolution of institutions. Clearly no one knows how to overcome this serious lack of control, but our basic resource as planners is awareness. Everyone concerned with control should become aware of what D. N. Michaels[14] (p. 93) calls the "psychological" base for resisting threats to the institutional status quo: "there is the strong disinclination to jeopardize a satisfying self-image . . . that sustains those who would have to take the risks to self and organization inherent in changing both."

CONTROL: A DIRTY WORD

One final word is needed about the concept of control. At the very broad level, control can be regarded as man's basic method of changing social systems so that they improve in the service of humanity. But control can also be regarded as an immoral instrument whereby one group of people force everyone else to comply with their own concept of right and wrong. The so-called control of drugs is an example of such an attempt; with all the best will in the world, legislators attempt to stop people from using drugs by threatening them with imprisonment. Even granted that the use of drugs is very harmful, one can still argue plausibly that such a method of control is immoral, as anyone who lived through Prohibition (1919-33) can attest. Real control becomes minimal when it is based solely on rules and laws rather than on education and mutual consent.

There can be no question that control is a dirty word in the minds of many people who are oppressed by the rules of organizations and government. They appreciate the irony of the etymology control: they are the scrolls that are being copied from the script in the heads of the controllers. The problem is not solved by dropping the word and substituting another. For those who believe that man can improve his sociotechnical systems through reason, the task is to free himself from the narrow techniques of control and become aware of the broader moral implications inherent in the concept.[15]

Fiscal and Management Dilemmas in Science Administration

ELMER B. STAATS
Comptroller General of the
 United States
Washington, D.C.

and

WILLIAM D. CAREY
Vice President
Arthur D. Little, Inc.
Washington, D.C.[1]

Twenty years of vigorous public financing of the nation's research and development (R & D) have not erased troubling questions of fiscal and management standards. Taken together, budgeting, appropriating, and controlling amount to a process; yet few are satisfied with it. When cornered, sponsors, performers, and decision makers alike will agree that the processes are chancy, discontinuous, and inherently unstable. Well-publicized analytic techniques which seem to work passably well in other areas of public action appear somehow incompatible with the drives and dynamics that go with advanced research.

A natural tension exists between the doers of research and the managers who must find reasons for supporting them. The researcher expects independence to be creative, along with stable flows of funds. The public manager also wants scientific creativity but is bound by rubrics that were devised for practical pursuits.

These tensions come into critical conjunction under the rationing conditions that prevail today. Budgetary constraints, competition for scarce dollars, and the pressures of scientific and technological opportunities combine to produce acute dilemmas of judgment. Rationing, for its part, implies choices based on equity. It is a balancing exercise conditioned by insufficiency of resources, and at its best it decides outcomes according to preestablished criteria. If criteria are lacking, rationing resembles the game of pinning a tail on a hyperthyroid donkey.

Foreign observers, enchanted by the virility of American science and technology and bent on learning the managerial system associated with it, are tireless in inquiring into our decision methods and our criteria for resolving problems of choice in R & D. They make the habitual mistake of supposing that our public investments in R & D are planned in a total analytic framework which relates scientific and technological opportunities to national objectives, while employing rational criteria to assist the rationing procedure. In reality, nothing like this exists.

R & D are not programmed or budgeted as a homogeneous category of discretionary public investment across the federal government. What emerges as R & D is in reality pieced together in a decentralized setting by the numerous independent administrative communities constituting the arms of the executive branch. Within broad missions and objectives of separate departments and agencies, R & D becomes a means to achieve larger ends and as such it competes with other strategies for the departmental dollar. Its utilities are evaluated, if at all, in the same contexts.

Linear decision making is not a feature of the supervision R & D. Monitoring organizations like the Office of Management and Budget (OMB) and the Office of Science and Technology are unfortunately not equipped to do much more than make running judgments as to levels of effort, and their most valuable impact is upon "go" or "no-go" questions involving conspicuous opportunities and costs. Indeed, the final aggregate outcomes of the budgeting process for R & D—the total "funds for research and development"—for any fiscal year are derived numbers which often as not come as a mild surprise to the budgeteers when the book is in page proof.

ANALYTIC METHODOLOGY

It is understandable that decision makers here and abroad should assume increasing rationality in dealing with R & D as the new analytic tools of management are understood and applied to problems of choice. The Planning, Programming, and Budgeting System (PPBS) with its cost-benefit, systems-analysis, and cost-effectiveness concepts and techniques, looked, at a distance, like salvation for the baffled decision maker. Quantification of costs, benefits, and uncertainty is what we all want in comparing alternative paths in science and technology.

PPBS did in fact add an important and helpful dimension to planning and budgeting, though not as much as its founding fathers envisioned. In the few cases where agency heads elected to manage with the aid of PPBS, the quality of program and budget analysis was upgraded. The reclassification of budget outlays into program categories and the emphasis placed upon clarifying objectives and outputs have begun to make the budget intelligible and almost readable. But these structural gains were not matched by analysis of high quality, particularly in posing and examining real alternatives in the program memoranda and special studies which each year the OMB wistfully called for in the short heyday of PPBS. But it should be said that PPBS was not a simple reform, nor is it one to be enacted between breakfast and lunch. In all likelihood it would take 10 years to reach the level of expectations claimed for PPBS when it was initiated. Like Christianity, it should be admired for its potential and not judged harshly on its performance to date.

Sophisticated management techniques and approaches like PPBS, although saluted ritually in all departments, are practiced principally in the Department of Defense. Even there they have not always saved managers from miscalculation and mistakes of judgment, and this is in itself confirmation of the rule that analytic methods will help in choosing paths to take but cannot eliminate risk from decision making.

PPBS has helped to temper hunch and impulse as factors in deciding what to do next, and it has furnished effective drag on the military's tendency to want and get all that can be produced regardless of relative cost and effectiveness. For this we rightly offer up thanks. But in the civilian departments and agencies it would be quite difficult to unearth examples of decisions made wholly or even largely as the result of systematic analysis of alternatives. The most we can say of PPBS is that it has paid off in causing program planners to think of cities, education, health, and transportation as system problems rather than as straight-line expenditure targets.

But PPBS and its allied methodologies have yet to prove their worth in the management of R & D. The most diligent ransacking of the executive branch fails to bring to light analytic cases where cost-benefit techniques have been used successfully in selecting R & D alternatives. At the development end of the spectrum where hardware choices are involved, cost effectiveness analysis has been helpful; otherwise we meet only frustration. The government is still groping without much hope for the insights, institutions, and methods for selecting certain R & D paths while rejecting others. Criteria of choice have not been devised even though the recent dearth of funds has produced the classic outlines of a rationing situation. This is not to say that, at the stage of *administering* a research appropriation, choices are not made in terms of scientific merit ascertained by peer judgment procedures. But, at the critical stage of budgeting, the absence of criteria for establishing priorities leaves a disquieting managerial gap.

Uncertainty is the bane of even the best intentioned applications of formal analysis to alternative investment choices in R & D. This is illustrated by the report *Energy, R & D and National Progress* issued in 1964 by the Office of Science and Technology.[2] This was an attempt to scrutinize a wide range of energy R & D strategies in cost-benefit terms as well as from the view of scientific merit and technical feasibility. But, wherever cost-benefit approaches were used, it became necessary to qualify the results with language such as this:

> In any field, the planning of optimal R & D programs is imperfectly understood, and we can neither predict the probability of success nor specify the time lag between initiation of a research effort and its payoff. Planning is immeasurably more difficult in a complex field like the energy sector which involves the simultaneous interactions of natural resources, science, technology, economics, sociology, politics, and other factors—none of which is static. All this means, for instance, is that we cannot predicate a plan on the adequacy of a particular energy resource, for the status of the resource may change with time, with technological advances, with consumer preference, or with any of a host of direct or indirect influences. In the circumstances, it is understandable that policies for energy R & D cannot be neatly blueprinted according to a scientific formula, *but judicious study can elevate such policy making from a gamble to an act.* [Emphasis added.]

Thus, notwithstanding the hopeful sequels and gasps heard from the parlors of management science, public decision making in R & D remains all too conventional. Nevertheless, decisions do get made, and choices are somehow reached. There are pragmatic and intuitive criteria buried in the plumbing of public decision making, and diligent flushing would discover them to resemble, more or less, the following:

(1) *The Quality of the R & D.* This is the test of scientific merit and the perceived skills of the performers.

(2) *The Nature of the Opportunity.* International cooperation opportunities may indicate priority for U.S. participation in a worldwide multidisciplinary study of the Year of the Quiet Sun or, alternatively, a World Weather Watch. Advanced biomedical engineering may call for intensive clinical R & D in organ transplants.

(3) *The Need to Create a Research Base.* In the absence of an adequate research base, the government may feel compelled to create one, as in the case of urban and housing problems, regional education laboratories, or experimental preschool programs.

(4) *The Level of Ongoing Budget Support.* Where heavy public investment in R & D is already a reality, as in space and medical research, competition for funds from "deprived" sectors of research or from nonscience claimants may necessitate a reassessment of growth rates and financing levels.

(5) *Preserving an Ongoing Research Facility.* When there is heightened competition for R & D funds, government may have to give first consideration to preventing the erosion of first-rate research establishments which were set up with heavy investment costs and could not be duplicated.

(6) *Costs, Current and Projected.* A decision to stake out a position of U.S. leadership in high-energy physics and to maintain it against Soviet competition may involve modest start-up funds but massive sequential capital and operating costs. In contrast, a decision to go the route in molecular biology might be a low-budget and high-payoff investment.

(7) *Social Pressures.* Public demand may generate irresistible pressures for investment in heart, cancer, stroke, and infant mortality R & D, or in intensive behavioral studies of crime and drug abuse.

(8) *Externalities.* The dictates of foreign policy may lead to bilateral undertakings as illustrated by the United States-Japan joint research program. Intelligence estimates on Soviet or Chinese thermonuclear weapon capabilities might result in escalating United States R & D.

(9) *Momentum of "State of the Art."* Here we confront the dynamics of R & D—the ability and know-how to advance scientific or technical thresholds by more than marginal degrees. Opportunities foregone or postponed may be opportunities lost or seriously compromised. An example might be the question of exploiting nuclear propulsion technology for large manned-space vehicles in the post-Apollo period. Whether to opt for unmanned-space exploration and allow the technology-intensive industrial base to

suffer attrition or to give priority to manned-space research over underfunded domestic social programs presents investment alternatives of the most acute sort.

(10) *Social Change.* Although federal support of medical research grew at astronomic rates in the postwar years, by the late 1960s the government faced problems in the organization and delivery of health services which argued for allocating a higher percentage of the federal health dollar to services than to research, given the presence of rationing requirements.

(11) *Technology Assessment.* Decisions to proceed with advanced technology are to a growing extent subject to the test of social cost and benefit. R & D on nuclear power plants raise questions of environmental pollution and safety. Development of high-speed, long-range aircraft may be delayed until noise and sonic damage are brought under reasonable control.

This is the broad framework within which the government struggles toward choices. Yet these imputed criteria, although they are perhaps better than none at all, do not measure up to an adequately refined or agreed-upon structure of decision criteria for reviewing alternative R & D investments. If we are to believe that the days are past when science provides its own justification for growth budgets, it follows that the demand for accountability necessitates better standard for analyzing the social merit of discretionary R & D.

As perplexing as are the problems of choice within a single field of R & D, they escalate by an order of magnitude when we try to trade off opportunities and costs *across* fields. This raises the issue of commensurability—the budgeteer's old and familiar dilemma of apples versus oranges. If rationing decrees that funds are available for a major move in marine science, *or* for a maximum R & D effort to develop an artificial heart, by what process besides prayer and astrology does the unhappy decision maker reach a choice?

The problems of choice are made more difficult by the fact that many areas of research have their own clientele or special interest support; the result is that some fields are less adequately funded than others. Every year the budget seems to be a little tighter than the previous year. In a nation where wants understandably outrun available resources, the persuasiveness of a particular researcher or a group of researchers may be able to shift research from one area to another—areas which at the moment at least are less new or glamorous or are represented by less vigorous advocates. This is in the nature of the way forces work in a democratic society. We see no formula approach in the offing which would change this basic condition.

As matters stand, not only are there no answers, but the question itself offends many as savoring of heresy. We either fall back upon conventional habits of intuition and bargaining or begin to seriously think about the need to devise indicators of relative social merit against which to test the options. If we face the truth, public policy decisions *are* taken on the basis of intuitive judgments about social utility even though the reasoning process leaves no visible tracks. The step of displaying a social merit matrix with weighted criteria may seem a short and obvious one, but it is another matter viewed politically. Perhaps we are also deterred by a disconcerting suspicion of arrogance associated with the act of even tentatively positing social values—yet this is where we must start in constructing a matrix of social value as a guide to public spending strategies. The question is troublesome; yet, if we really *want* reasons for our priorities, together with clear policy audit trails, it is very hard to see how we can for long evade the necessity for a framework which will throw light on the relative social uses of R & D alternatives.

One of the authors of this chapter achieved passing notoriety a few years ago when he was caught out with his social merit matrix showing. His objective, may it be said by way of extenuation, was solely to provoke constructive discussion and argument about the usefulness of these concepts in allocating funds for R & D. This particular formulation consisted of three broad categories of social values: economic, cultural, and political. They were subcategorized as follows:

Economic values

(1) advancement of health and welfare; (2) technological gain, business expansion, and job creation; (c) conservation of resources, both physical and human; and (4) return on investment.

Cultural values

(1) exploration of the unknown; (2) understanding of man's environment; (3) enrichment of education; and (4) improvement of human relationships.

Political values

(1) national prestige; (2) international understanding; (3) solution of problems of have-not nations; and (4) cold war advantage.

It is possible to apply some or all of such value-related factors to alternative major investments in science and technology to ascertain first-instance relevance. The next step, and a most difficult one, is to contrive a weighting system and to distribute the weights to categories and subcategories. It can be done, but the resulting weighted matrix will be biased by the attitudes and perceptions of the designer. In an open and diverse society, consensus in such matters comes hard, and the motives of the matrix maker become suspect regardless of how faithfully he may think he has aggregated the prevailing social predilections. What he has not bargained with is the fact that social inertia produces a surface pattern of assumed values while below the surface exists an unsuspected turbulence of suppressed preferences which defy quantification. Most sensible men therefore take evasive action; only the battered budgeteer with his idealism ambles forth in the cross fire.

But, for all the difficulties and conceptual "hangups," the question of social merit in scientific choice, first raised by Alvin Weinberg, demands a response. A society which is waking from its romantic trance with science and technology will, in time, see the need to order its values and test its public expenditure options against criteria of social responsibility.

In a setting where it is difficult to assign research values, we should make the most of the arrangements permitting us to view research in identical or closely related fields that cross agency jurisdictional lines. It is not that we favor duplication for this purpose; but program-related research cannot be fully organized in one or in some cases in even a few agencies. Research in the marine science is a case in point; health research, another; and pollution control, still another. Given the need for locating research effort with program-oriented agencies, we should take maximum advantage of the opportunity to evaluate different approaches, the selection of research centers, the development of research findings, and the ability to translate research findings into actionable program choices.

RESEARCH AND/OR DEVELOPMENT?

Budgeting for research *and* development as a combined aggregate of public investment raises painful problems. The distinction between *research* and *development* has always been cloudy. Government has found it awkward to budget large amounts for abstract research and embarrassing to be obliged to explain esoteric research meanderings whose project titles seem out of touch with primary social concerns. Thus, while a good intellectual case exists for classifying basic research separately from development, another instinct warns that research might fare badly. The unhappy reality may be that research, standing by itself, is not yet strong enough or tough enough to survive the rigors of the market place.

Indeed, we come increasingly to the view that new and more descriptive terms are needed if basic research is to hold its own in a rationing situation. Perhaps we need a classification called *associated basic research,* that is, research which is directly or indirectly supportive of applied research and, ultimately, of technology. Most if not all research in the life sciences could be considered "associated" with the pursuit of applied solutions to health and medical problems. For that matter, much social science research can be shown to have strong connectives to applied social strategies. The problem has been that too little effort has been made to mark the trails leading from general research to usable knowledge.

It can also be argued that, with vigorous advocacy, research might be placed within a protective financial shelter. In a very thoughtful presidential essay, Caryl Haskins speculates[3] that we would be better off if we fussed less over setting ceilings on research spending and, instead, concentrated on setting *assured floors* in the interest of injecting more stability and capacity for longer-range research planning. Haskins suggests that the findings of Derek Price, distinguished historian of science, have relevance to this policy approach, since Price has found that the figure of .07 percent of gross national product (GNP) for the support of research runs fairly consistently among nations making significant inputs to science, and he suggests that this may provide an acceptable criterion for establishing an annual support floor for the government's funding of science.

Since technology is quite able to look out for its interests, this route may indeed provide public policy a handle to determine the point below which public support should not fall. It would not tell us how much we ought to budget for science nor how to spread the research dollar, yet it would give us a standard by which the science budget would move as GNP moves, as a constant percentage, and it could be a standard that would appeal to reasonable men. The risk, to be sure, is that, in time, the number might lose its original meaning and the floor become a ceiling. But some risks must be borne cheerfully and there is enough solid merit to the concept to justify its trial.

BUDGET EXPECTATIONS

It is a poor public policy that will not tell science what it may reasonably expect in the way of social investment through time. Science has its own standards of productivity and, though they may be fragile in comparison with the standards of other human endeavors, they still have relevance and are observable to the trained eye. Productivity in science, as elsewhere, is affected by the conditions that are set up for it. Normal administrative routines—time-and-effort accounting, and erratic budgeting patterns—all work against research productivity, while year-to-year swings from feast to famine make a shambles of an enterprise that depends upon organization, motivation, and proximate financial stability.

Science does not have to enjoy prosperity, but it does require steady work. Once research is begun with public funds, its performers should be able to count on up to three years of stipulated support for an approved research plan. Anything less is likely to yield less on the investment than would the same dollars spent on nonresearch activities. Recent and unfortunate experience on this score argues powerfully, though probably vainly, for taking general-purpose research out of the annual budget and appropriations cycle in favor of three-year lump-sum endowments, however modest and below full research cost, to minimize uncertainty and enable managers to program research within known financial ranges. Even limited certainty is more attractive than chronic gambling on better luck next time.

In reasoning that science should be granted a degree of confidence as to prospective budget expectations, we are in no way proposing a guaranteed annual income. Nor do we favor banishing *all* uncertainty. Looking around, the public law is replete with multiyear appropriation authorizations; for education, for housing, for highways, for urban renewal, and so on. This process does not ensure automatic appropriations up to the level of authorizations, but it does establish a range of expectations which constitutes settled public policy. At the same time, it provides a rough yardstick with which to gauge the performance of the resource allocation system in terms of deviation from the standard, and a first stage from which to plan future levels of investment. If R & D as a government responsibility are ever to be liberated from hitchhiking on national defense and other vehicles of public convenience, a place to begin is with a legislative authorization which legitimizes the independence of research in the family of public policies.

THE POLICY PROCESS

In broad terms, we surely have come far enough to accept certain propositions:

(1) that the government's majority role in science and technology carries with it a responsibility to formulate and declare goals and strategies for periods up to 10 years;

(2) that government ought to make up its mind and then disclose its planned levels of public investment for at least five years into the future;

(3) that public policy relating to investment choices should be formulated in the open and in a pluralistic setting involving not only administrators and scientists but others as well, including social scientists whose perceptions of needs and priorities deserve consideration; and

(4) that R & D decision makers adopt the economists' approach of ignoring "sunk" R & D costs in making decisions about the future. For example, it should not matter that we have built a manned-space flight or a new weapon system R & D facility if we decide that our priorities in that decision were wrong or are not in line with the needs of the decade ahead, politically difficult though such a decision may be.

If these propositions hold water, the critical next question is whether government has the policy machinery to carry them out. It would be a hard case to make. However adequate present arrangements may be for making particular incremental choices in R & D, they are limited in their capability to assess R & D in comprehensive and anticipatory terms for goal-setting purposes. Neither the National Science Foundation nor the Executive Office has been able to do very much under statutory assignments to formulate national science policy; hence we have no policy with enough specificity to fulfill these conditions. The Office of Science and Technology serves well as a provider of staff advice to the President, a sometime advocate of science in the corridors of power, and a communications link with the academic scientists. And it has vastly improved consideration of science and technology programs that cross agency boundaries. But this office is too limited in resources and driven by day-to-day pressures to address itself to shaping national policy.

The point is not that the federal government should get into the business of programming science for the nation from "aeronomy" to zoology. But the point is that perspectives on science as a major force in the growth and quality of society are needed badly. What government should begin to do is to make a start on the kind of policy analysis that will provide for flows and perspectives—an arrangement in which R & D are not just a diffusion of puddles on the landscape but more nearly a system in which currents of creativity flow, meet, and diverge, enriching one another as well as the social soil they traverse.

The present pluralistic administration of R & D does not fit these objectives. If we were to continue for a hundred years on our present course, we would not end up much better off because the institutional process simply cannot be responsive to tests of overall balance, goals, and priorities. Since it was not a system in the first place, it should not be expected to function as one. Something different is called for, and there is no assurance that an ivory tower for science could command a listening audience. There is, however, an increasingly persuasive case—one which did not exist during the bonanza years—for a Department of Science and Technology. It need not be an overstuffed catchall for missionrealted R & D swept in from all over the government, using some administrative litmus test for detecting R & D wherever they are carried on. But a few substantial building blocks could produce a strong new department, oriented to both high technology and advanced science, which would provide ministerial stature and a setting for building a center for R & D policy analysis. The roles of such a center could be these:

- to examine the interaction of science with higher education, social change, international cooperation, technological development, and economic growth;
- to assess the mix of the nation's investment in R & D, its quality, and its social returns;
- to identify emerging unmet opportunities for investment;
- to formulate and experiment with models for R & D investment which reckon with society's new problems and needs; and
- to prepare public reports outlining alternative goals and priorities as a basis for policy formulation and long-range budgeting.

These are implicit elements in any serious attempt to formulate national policy, or to begin to apply measures of social accountability to science and technology. The fickle fortunes of R & D may soon be less the function of budgetary quandaries than of social criticism directed against the brutality of technology as it abrades the tissues of civilized life. The terms on which social assent to vigorous R & D is obtained may turn on the degree to which society is provided assurances of social accountability—environmental benefits and costs, additions or depletions of resources, effects on rates of social change, and gains or losses in the arithmetic of national power.

THE PROBLEM OF "HOT PURSUIT"

Among the thorniest of decision dilemmas are those relating to crossing the threshold from advanced research into application. They can be exquisitely painful when public policy is under great pressure for humanitarian reasons to invest heavily in biomedical engineering. Usually, public funds have already been spent heavily on fundamental research, and the demand for hot pursuit of ripe research into the development stage is stimulated by both scientific merit and technical feasibility.

The nature of biomedical research also gives rise to ethical and moral problems, as well as cost-benefit issues, and the inability of our decision making process to cope with such questions. Here we see a striking illustration of the principle of social responsibility in reaching decisions where science and technology impact on public philosophy. In this situation, with technological opportunity constrained by moral and political attitudes toward human experimentation, the budget maker is only one of many actors and by no means the most important. Yet the public investment question eventually must be faced in the context of a "go" or "no-go" decision, and in dealing with problems of choice in the commitment of major outlays for biomedical applications one is obliged to confront four different kinds of questions:

(1) Has uncertainty been minimized? The element of technological gamble has lower appeal in biomedical science than it would have in other R & D ventures, regardless of the potential payoff. Judgments about its progress assume critical importance in evaluating the degree of risk. Where uncertainty cannot be reduced to low limits, our social philosophy leads us to choose more research rather than to force development.

(2) Will health and medical services be adequate to supply the new market demand resulting from a successful breakthrough? It is of little use to bring in a new surgical procedure or a complex treatment regime if it requires such a concentration of manpower, funds, and facilities that only a small fraction of demand can be satisfied. In the absence of an assured delivery capability, the government should be guided by conservative development criteria, giving sufficient weight to structural and cost considerations as well as to technical factors impinging on development possibilities.

(3) What is the calculus of benefits to be derived? The decision to invest in biomedical engineering will be affected by expectations relating to its relative impact on morbidity, discomfort, pain, disablement, and mortality.

(4) Have total costs, immediate and consequential, of a decision to develop and deliver a new medical procedure been factored out? It would be myopic to focus narrowly on the first costs of demonstrating feasibility to the exclusion of follow-through costs to create a new supply of manpower and facilities to satisfy the market demand. A biomedical breakthrough might be proved out for one million dollars but might involve hundreds of millions to bring within reach of the people who need it. Nothing could be worse public policy than to bring a major health benefit within reach only to have to put it on the shelf for lack of economic resources to deliver it.

Opportunity costs enter in, as well, especially if the indicated total investment to benefit a limited category of individuals would preempt resources that would otherwise have been available for such alternatives as increasing medical research on a broad spectrum, improving the general health profile of the poor, or attacking infant mortality with an effective level of effort.

In the end, social policy may lead to a decision in favor of hot pursuit; but it will be a better decision if we have taken fully into account all the benefits and consequences.

GOVERNMENT, RESEARCH, AND CAMPUS

The ideas of independence and accountability in the government's relationships with nonprofit organizations have increasingly come under scrutiny, notably by the Carnegie Corporation, but they remain dusty. University research investigators have been vociferous in criticizing "green eyeshade" administrative burdens imposed by the federal government for time and effort reporting and for cost-sharing, while important sectors of the Congress have stepped up countercriticism of recipients of research grants and contracts on grounds of excessive overhead charges and trivial research. For the most part, the government continues to finance nonprofit research by way of project support, although a growing body of opinion holds that broad institutional grants are all that can save universities from becoming Balkanized by the national government. This love-hate relationship in the research area contributes little to the reputation of either side and exerts a corrosive influence on what began and for a time flourished as a creative partnership between public policy and higher education.

The probability is that neither independence nor accountability can be completely achieved except at a prohibitive price. Both ideas are limited by the realities of the respective environments. For its part, the government can concede independence in the conceptualizing and design of university research strategies, and it can move by gradual stages toward adopting formulas for sustaining grants, but it cannot abstain from asking that the institutions show evidence of qualitative objectives leading to social returns. For their part, the institutions can properly press for removal of meaningless administrative routines while accepting the correctness of the government's need for reasonable evidence of responsibility in the management and employment of public resources.

But this level of generalization leaves many gaps. As far as accountability is concerned, the government's legitimate needs run to assurances of quality in supported research, together with safeguards against the evaporation of research funds into general operating costs of universities. The goal of quality can be reached in part by long-standing peer-group procedures and in part by standards of merit applied to the output of published reports. The problem of evaporation is more difficult, but the proposal of the National Science Board for separate funding of research and associated expense offers a solution which deserves to be tested with a group of institutions and agencies. It has much more in its favor than the device of a statutory limitation on overhead or a statutory formula for cost sharing which makes no allowance for the varying needs and circumstances of different institutions and the differing accounting systems employed.

At best, however, the government-university relationship is unlikely to regain its original felicity. Too many disturbing forces have emerged, the latest being campus reaction against federally financed campus research. University research directors in a number of instances have taken the initiative to terminate ongoing research support, particularly that which is classified, because facilities and records cannot be adequately guarded against seizure and destruction. Strikes in some academic communities against government R & D provide a further measure of the deterioration in the government-university partnership. Government itself is awakening to the realization that it has pursued a misguided policy in establishing major centers for defense-related R & D in the university environment.

One has to begin to think of alternative institutions for performing much of the R & D which until now has been the university's role. Two possible innovations come to mind. One is the "Government Institute" suggested in 1962 in the Bureau of the Budget's report on contracting for R & D (the "Bell Report"). The report said:

> Such an Institute would provide a means for reproducing within the Government structure some of the more positive attributes of the nonprofit corporation. Each Institute would be created pursuant to authority granted by the Congress and be subject to the supervision of a Cabinet officer or agency head. It would, however, as a separate corporate entity directly managed by its own Board of Regents, enjoy a considerable degree of independence in the conduct of its internal affairs. . . . The objective of establishing such an instrumentality would be to achieve in the administration of certain research and development programs the kind of flexibility which has been obtained by the Government corporations while retaining, as was done with the Government corporations, effective public accountability and control.[4]

This proposal, which has never been pursued or even seriously considered by either the Bureau of the Budget or the Congress, was put forward by Harold Seidman as a possible solution to the public policy problems created by massive delegations of responsibility for complex R & D systems to private profit making and not-for-profit enterprises. In the spring of 1969, the General Accounting Office, in its report on the use of management fees, took occasion to sharply remind the executive branch that it had failed to follow up on its own proposal.[5]

A second innovation worth considering is one which David Beckler of the Office of Science and Technology has informally put forward. It stems from rising concern over the disruptive consequences of federal R & D within universities. The essence of the idea is to create a new type of nonprofit research institute between the government and the universities to act as a performer of research. As Beckler views it, this would be a "bridging institution" which could involve academic scientists on an elective basis in conducting research apart from the graduate institutions and without formal involvement of the universities. Unlike the "Government Institute," this entity would operate outside the framework of federal control but possibly under federal charter and with federal funds for research. One of the most appealing features of this proposal is that it would go far to stem the trend toward turning institutions of higher education into programmatic extensions of federal agencies—the incipient innovation in the organization of federal field services.

SOCIAL COSTS

As we survey the government's organization means for making choices in R & D, it becomes apparent that an important missing element is a process for assessing the social costs of technological investment. The government does fairly well in spotting technological opportunities but has not begun to create a methodology for forecasting and analyzing their direct and indirect effects on man and society. As stupefying as may be the investment outlays to develop a supersonic plane, or competitive nuclear power reactors, these direct outlays may turn out to be just a small part of the whole bill, with the greater part attributable to social costs.

We are a people with a strong drive for advanced technology, and on the whole this helps to explain the growth of our national power. But it has also created major liabilities which at some point become payable. In time, the exploitation of forests and river basins for profit led to a social corrective in the shape of conservation organizations which can bring power to bear on decisions. In the same way, the exploitation of man and society by technology, including that portion spurred by public investment and risk assumption, requires machinery to provide early warning of adverse consequences and social costs. This is just as much an element of budgeting and accounting as is the scrutiny of inputs to technological achievement.

Admittedly, technology assessment is difficult to structure and set in motion. Endless arguments will surround the question of where such a function should be lodged in the framework of government: in the executive branch or the legislative branch, or independent of both? If we opt for the executive, would we make technology assessment a responsibility of the very agencies that are hot for technological change, or would we prefer that it be a presidential-level function? We can conceive that assessment ought to be built into the regulatory sector, yet we know that in a market economy the regulatory process is already too repressive and unimaginative a weight on change. Strong objections might be made against a bureaucratization of assessment, yet one finds much in the performance of the Food and Drug Administration to admire.

The dilemmas are therefore many. But it is necessary that we match the dynamics of technology with effective institutional processes to guard the public interest. Trial and error is at least as legitimate in creating effective public institutions and methodologies as we concede it to be in R & D itself, and we should not be embarrassed by it. In late September 1972, Congress passed legislation establishing a Joint Committee on Technology Assessment with a full-time staff director and an advisory council that includes the Comptroller General and the Director of the Congressional Research Service.[6] Although again we could find many things to criticize in this solution, standing alone, the merit in it is that it offers a beginning, a first step in what could become a system linking the Congress, the executive branch, and nongovernmental institutions as a network of social criticism leading to a responsible and accountable technology. Lacking an adequate assessment process, society is likely to pay twice for technological change—once in its initial investment, and again to correct for the unforeseen costs arising from the adoption of the changed technology. By any standard, that is very bad budgeting and social accounting.

EVALUATION IN RESEARCH

One of the real predicaments facing the government, as it launches large-scale social experimentation in the field of human resources, is the infirmity of its resources for critical evaluation of the effectiveness of its strategies relative to costs and expectations.

The Economic Opportunity Act Amendments of 1967 charged the General Accounting Office (GAO) to determine

"(1) The efficiency of the administration of such programs and activities by the Office of Economic Opportunity and by local and private agencies carrying out such programs and activities; and

"(2) The extent to which such programs and activities achieve the objectives set forth. . . ."

In attempting evaluation of the war on poverty, GAO came up squarely against state-of-the-art problems. The issues surrounding the study were critical ones, involving sociological and economic strategies in a context of quasi-revolution and changing values. Matters were not helped by the fact that GAO began its study under a Democratic administration and finished it after a Republican administration had assumed power.

In essence, GAO was expected to determine whether the war on poverty was getting anywhere, and whether it justified its cost to the public—a fair enough pair of questions to be addressed to most public expenditure programs but exceedingly difficult to address to an enterprise that is by nature experimental, research intensive, and long term in payoff. Adding to the hazards of evaluation was the existence of widespread attitudinal biases growing out of the war on poverty's implicit role in challenging customs, institutions, and embedded social practices. GAO indeed had a bear by the tail.

In quantitative terms, GAO could see, as well as anyone who cared to look, that the numbers of people included within the government's definition of the "poor" had declined almost unbelievably since the initiation of the war on poverty. By that single standard, the ranks of the poor had thinned by several millions. What the cold statistics could not prove was a cause-and-effect connection between the programs of the Office of Economic Opportunity (OEO) and the decline of poor families as a percentage of population. For that matter, the statistics revealed nothing of a qualitative nature concerning the real economic and social conditions in which the new nonpoor found themselves. Perhaps nothing more could be said than that the war on poverty had not obstructed the aisles leading to exit from deprivation.

Plainly, the GAO had no objective criteria by which to quantitatively evaluate the Community Action, Head Start, or Legal Services programs or the Job Corps. The question really was whether such programs were effective, *compared with what*? Moreover, even the Community Action Program, despite its name, was anything but a homogeneous entity: there were literally about a thousand variations of community action represented by that many communities with their own social dynamics. In the case of Head Start, a skilled evaluator could extract a few preliminary objective measures of short-run effectiveness but could only speculate concerning the program's lasting benefits. In the case of the Job Corps, evaluation had to rest on disputed meanings of reading scores, post-training job opportunities, and dismaying dropout rates.

For its part, OEO had for years lavishly financed evaluative studies across the spectrum of its activities. In a sense, OEO was creating a new industry by providing a market for program evaluation, and perhaps this should be listed as one of the tangible benefits of the war on poverty. As the GAO struggled, using its own staff and a field of consultants to try to find answers, OEO itself was absorbing a large portion of the country's limited capacities for program assessment. Yet the Congress and the public saw very little of the product, partly for the good reason that OEO's programs had not had sufficient longevity or stability to yield dependable evidence of their merits.

When its work was done and the time came to submit its report, the GAO took pains to point out that

> This task is an extremely complex and difficult one. The methods of evaluating social programs such as these and the

indicators of progress or accomplishment are not well developed or understood. We recognize that, as the scope of governmental activity broadens and as the complexity of governmental programs increases, the Congress is recurrently confronted with the necessity of appraising accomplishments that cannot be measured in terms of dollars expended or in terms of such tangible yardsticks as the number of miles of road built or pieces of mail delivered. We recognize that it is essential that efforts be made to develop new yardsticks of effectiveness, to meet the needs of the Congress.[7]

All of this points up the problem of the feasibility of program evaluation in the field of social R & D. The pervasiveness of uncertainties and risk is, if anything, greater than we encounter in the physical sciences. We are dealing with social investments, and we cannot control the laboratory conditions for research. Moreover, the nature of social investment in human resources is comparable with private entrepreneurial investment in the sense that we are putting resources to work with risk through time; we are not, or should not be, seeking speculative returns before lunch. Education, health, and economic opportunity have their cycles of payoff and they are of a duration that will not speed up to match our impatience, our sense of injustice, or even our anger.

Recognizing that evaluation of social programs cannot be made on a strictly empirical basis, there remains a question of whether it is possible to discipline judgments with respect to their value in something other than strictly political-type debate. Such a debate recently took place on the merits of the President's proposal to close down certain Job Corps Centers on grounds of marginal effectiveness, and resulted in reduction of number of centers and consolidation of others. The uncertain variables relate to the value of such centers in areas such as health, discipline, effect on juvenile delinquency, and many other imponderables.

This is by all odds a major field for intensive research on research, hopefully in university centers concerned with the impact of R & D upon society. There is encouraging evidence that scholars are in fact tackling the decision-making dilemmas. We note that in 1965, Frederic M. Scherer[8] of Princeton University advanced the idea of using panels of experts to choose among R & D opportunities by supplementing cost-effectiveness findings with their own rankings, using paired-comparison techniques. These rankings would then be aggregated by scaling factors into a group consensus ranking. While Professor Scherer's approach seems to be oriented to the type of R & D to which cost-effectiveness methods can be applied, it is worth considering the use of panels of experts in the "softer" areas of evaluation relating to social R & D.

But Scherer has put his finger squarely on the basic problem when he observed that "the whole concept of net benefits and values from programs with essentially political goals is fraught with hazards." As he wryly notes, "Uncertainty is an inescapable water-muddier."

Be that as it may, the pressure to assign values to government programs seems inexorable, and we cannot afford not to experiment with any approaches which may serve the cause of more rational choices. The political arena would still be the point of resolution, but the program evaluator has an obligation to provide the legislator with the best his profession can produce. Again, needs are infinite; resources are finite.

Massive social investments await federal funding after Vietnam. Most of them will involve large-scale experimentation in areas of human interaction with institutional changes, and there is no guarantee of effectiveness for the money and energy that will be spent. We have learned, too, that public opinion is slower to forgive the government's social mistakes than it is to overlook even more costly malfunctions in fields of R & D that are touched by mystery. The conclusion is plain that the government must continue to help create the quality and quantity of competence in program evaluation which it will need desperately before long. It can do this by increasing investment in social science research, and it can justify the cost in terms of its managerial needs and even "fiscal responsibility." But this will not come to pass unless the Congress realizes how improverished we really are in the skills of evaluation and writes into new social legislation a requirement that not less than a designated percentage of program funds be earmarked for program evaluation.

In approaching the evaluation of R & D in the social area it is tempting to borrow some of the methodology applied to other kinds of R & D—such as military and other hardware-oriented programs. Yet, caution is in order. What may be applicable to the evaluation of low-income housing may not help at all in appraising an income maintenance strategy. The differences turn partly on the ability to define objectives and to quantify end results. Objectives, for example, may have to be defined in terms both of a time frame and an expected payoff but with less rigor in the social sector where variables abound.

Obviously, everyone is searching for measurement methods of evaluating effectiveness in meeting social problems. The first barrier is agreement on goals.

Even when we can agree among ourselves as to our goals, we may still find ourselves uncertain of premises, standards, and assumptions leading to the achievement of those goals. Consequently, as a people we find ourselves uncertain about the quality of our measures.

A major influence affecting the quality of our benefit measures—especially those of social programs—is the availability of data from which measures may be constructed. This is intimately related to the problem of uncertain premises, standards, and assumptions. Though we may be uncertain about some of our standards, the necessities of day-to-day performance require that we set such standards, either explicitly or implicitly. Having set them, we try to accomulate data on program activities so that our performance can be measured against our standards. We like to think that the data that we gather, and the measures that we construct from them, are relevant to these standards. We like to think that our data banks, our information systems, are created in response to—and follow from—our standards. By letter of August 11, 1972, the Comptroller General addressed all chairmen of congressional legislative committees suggesting that program requirements be established in legislation to include "in the authorizing legislation specific statutory requirements for a systematic evaluation by the department or agency involved of the results of programs in operation."[9]

But this is often not the case. Information systems tend to become inflexible over time. They may become ends in themselves to those concerned with their operation. This is a subject on which much could be said, but it is very important to recognize that our measures of performance and of benefit, may sometimes simply be creatures of the available data, and the available data may not be the most relevant to the standards against which we would like to measure.

The recent efforts of the President's Panel on Social Indicators are likely to provide a focus that will clarify our present circumstances and move us in the direction of doing better those things which are possible with the measurement of social program benefits. While fundamental questions such as hereditary and environmental influences in education are unsettled—and they may remain unsettled for as long in the future as they have been in the past—many of the measures which we may apply to the benefits of social programs are likely to lack a sound basis, but there is no doubt that we will continue to apply them.

Our social realities demand measurement; measured they will be; and if our measures are not as good as they should be, we will have to continue to use them for now—and push the state of the art to higher ground.

CONCLUSION

The present trials of science administration in the public sector are symptoms of the general search for new meanings and directions for our public policies. Underlying that search is dissatisfaction with the ordering of priorities and values. If the scientific community attributes its recent frustrations to either the accidents of politics or a temporary budgetary crunch, it will miss the point. The great thrusts of R & D in the last decade were generated by external fears and forces. The present evidence is that our society will be less impressed and intimidated by such forces in the coming years. The motivations for vigor, adventure, and creativity in publicly orientated R & D will stem from internalized goals and values.

We are entering an era of humanism concurrently with the massing of an economic, military, and technological abundance that spells new strains and dilemmas for men and society. In this context, the uses of power become our first concern. Whether the values of science and technology to a civilized and purposeful society bent on humanism can be perceived and integrated into the tissues of public policy is the urgent question.

Task setting and Goal Achievement in Technoscientific Missions

C. WEST CHURCHMAN
Professor and Research Philosopher
Space Sciences Laboratory
University of California
Berkeley

INTRODUCTION

In this chapter I am concerned with an organizational role which is easy to describe denotatively, but extremely difficult to describe connotatively. Denotatively, it is the role of the division chief in research organizations and of the dean in universities. It is a position at least one step "down" from top management, with its concerns with overall strategies and policies, long-range plans, and the like. It is at least two steps "above" actual operations, that is, the workforce (researcher or teacher).

If we were to proceed in a somewhat extroverted way, we could easily list some fifty functions which this intermediate role could play, including personnel hiring, recommending promotions or firings, morale boosting, setting schedules, technical advising, entertaining visitors, sitting on advisory committees, and so on. It would be difficult to improve on Hugh Dryden's (1950) description of the responsibilities of the research director,[1] which he broke down into technical and administrative responsibilities, and personal development and leadership. Dryden describes very well the "four-way relationship" of the director, vertically within the organization, and horizontally inside and outside.

But emphasis here is on a "systems approach" to the role, that is, to try to understand what the research director *should* be trying to do and the resources he *should* use to do it. The systems approach is philosophical in that it attempts to provide a conceptual basis for the "should." I am not, therefore, directly concerned with the behavioral science approach (although I shall cite some of the relevant literature) but rather with the more basic values that are involved in the elusive role of the research director.

Part of the elusiveness originates from ignorance about Dryden's "vertical" relationship, or the concept of hierarchy.[2] For the division chief is the essence of the hierarchical structure of the organization. If we ask why such a role is needed at all, the obvious answer is size. There are too many projects or curricula to report to top management, and so we design organizations with intermediate roles to cut down on the span of control. But this obvious answer does not help us understand how the role really works in successful organizations.

In this chapter, we shall develop a somewhat radical theory about the underlying value system of the division chief with respect to his role. The theory, in brief, says that a division chief needs to be "sanely schizophrenic," by holding at the same time two partially conflicting value systems and their associated views of the organization.

The first view of the organization is the one held by top management that the organization has certain overall goals which it seeks to attain and a certain amount of resources to attain them. Specific projects are a means of attaining these goals and should be dropped if their contribution to the goals is not enough or strengthened if their net contribution could be ever greater. Since survival is important, the resources need to be budgeted, and control exerted wherever there is a serious threat to survival. It should be noted that this view is also shared by the planner, who in effect is top management's reflective mind.

The second view of the organization is the one held by the workforce, in our case the researcher or teacher.[3] This view says that the organization is a set of tasks that are to be performed to the satisfaction of the individual who performs them and who in large part decides what the performance is to be. For example, a research chemist identifies an exciting problem and sets forth the details of his investigation, or a professor with some graduate students thinks of a seminar topic and designs a course around it. According to this view, top management is a means of obtaining resources to permit the tasks to be performed. Top management becomes weak when the individuals in the workforce are prevented by management from deciding how their tasks are to be done or fail to attain true satisfaction in their performance. At such times, a change of management is called for.

In the industrial sector, the second viewpoint was that of the artisan in a guild. Of course, the industrial revolution of the worker changed the perspective. But in research organizations and colleges, the second world view of the organization still holds. We can dramatize this view by pointing out that professors are ambivalent about the direction of the organizational hierarchy. On occasion, they will admit that the dean and president are "over" them, but in the main they tend to regard administration as a second-rate university job (for those who could not keep up with the pace): the dean and president are "under" them. This helps to illustrate why "hierarchy" is such an elusive concept.

Now an astute top manager may be pleased that his researchers believe they are the top dogs, because this keeps up their morale, and high morale may make them more productive.[4] However, such reasoning fits into the first (top management) view of the organization and not the second. We see that this morale-building strategy views the researchers as workers—views them with much the same perspective as machines; the better oiled they are, the better they run. From the second point of view of the organization the problem is not morale but rather morality. It is the moral conviction that the researcher (or teacher) ought to determine how the task is to be done and that this is the main reason for the existence of the organization. It is a moral conviction based on Immanuel Kant's (1785) conviction that no person ought to be treated as a means only, but rather as an end. Kant, with a deep perception of things to come, saw the eternal clash between this moral prescription and the concept of maximizing happiness, or welfare, or profit. If society strives to provide the greatest good for the greatest number, it must inevitably treat some people as means only to the attainment of societal goals and not as ends in themselves. Even a "benevolent" society will, for Kant, act immorally.[5]

The division chief (or dean), according to the theory, ought to recognize this clash of value systems and in some sense recognize that no compromise is possible. If he takes on top management's viewpoint only, he is acting as a surrogate for top management's functions and fails to understand the real problems of the researchers (or teachers). On the other hand, if he acts to serve the researcher's ends as ends in themselves, he fails to accomplish the organizational objectives at the very point where service is most needed.

Perhaps the fundamental idea behind the second viewpoint can be clarified if we compare it with McGregor's famous "Theory X" and "Theory Y" (1960).[6] In Theory X, management does not trust his personnel to accomplish their assigned tasks and uses an information system to control their behavior. In Theory Y, management tries to create an environment of mutual trust. But both Theory X and Theory Y are means to management's ends, that is, both treat personnel as means. "Theory Z," on the other hand, states that the personnel's goals are the dominating ones in the organization.

Thus the division manager fully accepts both Theory Z, as well as top management's view of the world. In the end I shall have more to say about the idea of holding conflicting view of the world simultaneously, which I take to be a mark of the mature mind. For the present, it will suffice to say that "holding" conflicting viewpoints means that the mind is willing and open to listening and responding to the debate between them, without feeling the need to "resolve" the conflict once and for all. Primarily because the debate is proceeding in a healthy and virulent fashion, the mind of the division chief is constantly seeking innovative changes that will raise the issue above a somewhat niggardly clash between administrators and intellectuals, to a mode of living in which the conflict of ideas and policies becomes a vital organizational force.

First, we need to elaborate on the two partially conflicting views of the world of the research organization (or college) and the manner in which the division manager (dean) may adapt his role to them. I shall concentrate on the division chief, rather than the dean, reserving for the end some remarks on the similarities and differences of these two roles.

Before describing the two world views of the division manager, it is important to explain the basic orientation of this chapter. I am not concerned about the techniques available to the manager to perform some of his duties, but rather with the basic philosophy which justifies a specific technique. Thus, as we shall see, there are a number of techniques for evaluating research projects; the basic question the division manager needs to answer is how to evaluate one technique against another, or whether a "technique" is appropriate at all. My basic reference point is research and development (R & D) in the public sector, although I shall use the private frequently to illustrate a point, since many techniques of managing research have been developed in private industry.

Now a very useful philosophy of top management is contained in the planner's approach, because the planner tries to conceptualize as clearly as possible what the managers are trying to accomplish and the possible means for reaching their ends.

In the terms of the planner, the world of the top manager is goal-oriented, and the attainment of the goal is supposed to satisfy some group of "clients" of the system. It is essentially a world of opportunities which can be translated into tasks or activities, and the dominating concept of decision making is based on trade-offs between alternative opportunities. The top manager steers his ship in those directions which hopefully produce maximum pay-offs.[7]

This résumé of the top manager's world can now be used to describe the division manager's role in it in some detail. But first we need to distinguish between the *structure* of the system and its *dynamics*. The structure is essentially the elements that make up the system at any moment of time, while the dynamics describes how the structure changes over time and what the managers do about these changes.

To provide a map for the coming exploration, the following list of essential considerations will be discussed.

STRUCTURAL CONSIDERATIONS

1. Ascertain the goals of top management and their relative weights.
2. Define the area where the specific tasks of the division manager lie in the total system.
3. Invent new tasks.
4. Evaluate the list to select projects.
5. Design the research task.
6. Assess the environment.
7. Provide top management with guides for budgeting the division.

DYNAMIC CONSIDERATIONS

1. Detect changes in top management's goal structure with a consequent redoing of items 2–5 if changes occur.
2. Exert internal control through:
   a. personnel hiring and firing
   b. project control techniques
   c. termination, initiation, or changes in funding.

In addition to these considerations, we need to say something about what the manager can expect in the way of supports from various people both inside and outside the organization. As we shall see, the general theme is the use of good judgment in accomplishing the aims of the division manager; in no case can he reasonably expect to find a solid, irrefutable base for his decisions. In each case, however, we will consider what information can assist him and what techniques are helpful.

TOP MANAGEMENT'S GOALS

Basic to all social systems is a set of interests that the system is supposed to serve. I shall call that set "the client," though it is rare that only one person is involved. In the private sector, the client may be the stockholders, possibly the customers, or possibly the managers themselves. In the public sector, it is probably the public, but may also be the administrator or politician. Top managers do not seem too concerned about identifying the client precisely. They recognize that the ultimate client consists of those people who can judge their decisions and, if their judgment is favorable, increase the managers' resources, or if unfavorable, fire the managers.

The planner, on the other hand, tries to be more specific. He attempts to identify the client's long-range interests and then to break them down into short-range goals and their associated programs. Hopefully, the long-range objectives resolve the conflicts between short-range goals.

In the private sector, the long-range objective is often specified as "return on investment" or "discounted net return," subject to certain legal, moral, and stylistic constraints.[8] There are some serious difficulties in making either of these concepts operationally clear, but they are being used more and more frequently in corporate planning. The difficulties largely arise because it is hard to specify what a "return" means to an organization whose lifetime is indefinite. If one knew that the corporation would cease to be at some prescribed point in history, then it might be possible to generate an unambiguous meaning of "return" in terms, say, of the net worth of the company. Consider, for example, a research project that is terminated. What is the "return?" If the project is now in the developmental stage, the return is highly ambiguous, especially if the development is tied into other activities of the firm.

Similarly, in the public sector there is bound to be considerable confusion about the meaning of the long-range objective.[9] The nearest analogy to return on investment is the gross national product, but this figure scarcely encompasses all that is meant by the "public interest."

Despite an inevitable confusion about what top management is really trying to accomplish, the planner firmly believes that a set of specific long-range goals does exist which in principle determines how decisions ought to be made. The goals, at any point in time, have different weights which represent their relative importance. These weights are rarely if ever known with precision, but partial ignorance is never an excuse for failing to estimate. That top managers do make decisions which they consider to be rational is the evidence the planner uses to establish the existence of these weights. Such a set of decisions on policy is often used as evidence of the implicit weights the managers do use, whether they admit it or not.[10] For political reasons, many top administrators of the federal government might be very hesitant to say whether a dollar spent in medical research is more important than a dollar spent in educational research, but a decision at the level of the Bureau of the Budget may reveal the implicit weights.

This point is a very important one in our understanding of the role of the division manager, because basically he must be making estimates of these goal weights of top management in setting the tasks of his division, or else there is no rational basis of his own decisions. Of course the manager may be very hesitant to have the weights revealed.

But where do the weights come from? The only conceivable answer is that, if they are rationally derived, they come from top management's conception of the long-range future of the organization and its proper role in serving the client. Otherwise, the weights are arbitrary, and the whole enterprise becomes the farce of the conventional or random. It is the planner's basic philosophy that conflicts between goals are inevitably resolved by establishing weights in terms of a broader perspective of the system, either in time or in the level in the organizational hierarchy.

Since there are bound to be uncertainties on the part of even the most astute top managers regarding these weights and the associated real long-range objectives, the weights are quite likely to change over time; this is part of the problem of the dynamics of the system which will be discussed after we have reviewed the structure.

The division manager's task is to assist in transforming the long-range values of the top managers into short-range tasks.[11] This is what "task setting" essentially means in the world of the top manager. The basic idea is to determine those tasks which will best serve the long-range objectives. Since the real meaning of long-range objectives is never clear and certain, the division manager's job is inevitably a confusing one. Ideally, he might like to think of the long-range objective in terms of a measure of performance of the whole system. Then he could think of this measure as being some function of a set of tasks and the level at which each is performed (including a zero level for tasks that are rejected). His job would then be one of determining at what levels the various tasks should be carried on.

Even though the planner's idealized version of task setting is rarely achievable in research organizations, it does help to elucidate what the manager is trying to do in principle. Among other things, it shows us that the manager can control the level of certain activities, that is, manage his resources. Essentially, he does this in two ways—by allocating funds and manpower to a task and by trying to improve the task itself.

DEFINITION OF THE TASK AREA

But first of all, the manager needs to know what set of tasks he is supposed to control. In most research organizations, this is done by using the names of the disciplines as guidelines: chemistry, electronics, and so on. The difficulty appears when he tries to understand all the possibilities that lie in any given domain of research. In the private sector, this can sometimes be accomplished in terms of conceivable product lines. In the public sector, the director of a laboratory will often map out his domain in terms of research that is needed in the public interest but is not being done by private laboratories or universities because of a lack of profit or pure intellectual interest.

Despite many attempts to classify the sciences, it is safe to say that we still lack any definitive map of an area of research, which would guide the division manager in his attempt to understand the scope of his responsibilities.

INVENTING NEW TASKS

Since precisely defined maps are not available, the division manager often needs to rely on invention to create new tasks. The planner's model described above assumes that such a list is available and that the job is to set the levels within each task. But how is the list created in the first place? And once a list is made available—for example, by consultation with advisors, staff, and researchers (subordinates)[12] how does the manager build an environment for the invention of new ideas?

Several answers to these questions come readily to mind. One is to follow the leader, that is, watch your most prosperous competitor and try to match his best efforts. Another is to hire people with innovative ideas. A third is to play it safe and consider those tasks which appear to make the most sense to the researchers and other interested persons in the organization. It should be pointed out that a division manager who spends a great deal of his time trying to hire the best people may be wasting his time in a futile task and creating bad morale in the ranks. There may be neglected talents in those he considers to be mediocre. That is why some apparently startling degrees of success have been attained through brainstorming.[13] There is also something to be said for attempting to understand how ideas propagate and survive in research organizations.[14]

What is really needed, but will be some time in coming, is an information system which aids the manager in formulating his problems. Most management information systems today are designed to assist in solving a problem once you know what it is. From the manager's point of view, the far more significant issue is to select the right problem. Solving problems is essentially a task that operates with well-defined descriptors and classes; problem formulation essentially operates with "fuzzy" classes.[15]

EVALUATING PROJECTS

A number of techniques for allocating funds to projects are available in the literature.[16] Essentially the idea is to forecast the project output and compare this with cost, to obtain a net value. Uncertainties are handled by judgment and probability theory.

The division manager is apt to find the formulas for evaluating projects confusing and unconvincing, even in the private sector where long-range return and market opportunity can be quantified.[17] For one thing, there is a strong tendency to use ratios, for example, the ratio of some measure of total return to the total cost of the research and development project. Such a ratio might be adequate if the total cost of a project were some fixed number, arrived at independently of the costs of other projects. But one of the division manager's main concerns is to allocate the optimal resources to all potential projects. In these terms, the cost of a project robs other projects of additional resources.

For example, suppose Project A receives evaluation score of 30 percent, while Project B receives a score of 25 percent and Project C a score of 20 percent. Suppose all three projects are initially costed at the same amount, but there are only funds for two. An innocent manager might then infer that A and B should be selected over C. But it might happen that if all the funds were put in C, the "return" score would be higher than for the combination A-and-B. The point is that the ratios should be regarded as at best suggestive, never as decisive. Of course, this criticism is overcome in the global theoretical models, but not in the practical "scoring systems" as described, say, by Dean,[18] which are applied to individual research proposals.

DESIGNING THE RESEARCH TASK

If we turn now to the improvement of the internal design of a task, we see that the division manager or dean is really at a serious disadvantage compared to his colleagues in other organizations, because he knows so little about what his workers are doing. Now of course there is the question of the extent to which the division manager should be responsible for the internal design of the project, since presumably this is the primary task of the project leader. But a higher level manager should in principle be in a position to understand how a lower level under him operates. Otherwise his judgment that "X is doing a good job" has no basis. Some help is available in development, where techniques like PERT or CPM[19] lay out the overall plan of the project, its phases, and its rate of progress. But even in development, it is very difficult to determine whether the work habits are anywhere near optimal. Both PERT and CPM are based on judgments about the length of time it will take to do specific subtasks. But these judgments are based in part on past experience, which may be far from optimal. Some studies have been made to determine how researchers may spend their time,[20] and it is clear that the majority of it is spent in communication (mostly talking). But whether this mode of operation is correct has not been ascertained. Division managers tend to take output at some quality level as a sufficient guide for evaluating performance on tasks, without worrying too much about improving the performance by rearranging time or by technological innovations. The design of inquiring systems is still largely a mystery[21] as any reader on "scientific method" quickly sees. We are told that researchers test hypotheses by means of well-designed experiments, but we are not told how they create the hypotheses they test (the main point of their endeavor) nor are we told about the many discussions they engage in which somehow seem to influence their research efforts so significantly.

The one obvious way in which the division chief does manage the internal affairs of the research project is in hiring (or firing). In most scientific disciplines, reputation becomes a fairly refined judgment of the research community. Unfortunately, from the manager's point of view, a good reputation does not necessarily mean a highly productive researcher, since his reputation may be based on results which are not relevant to the organization's goals.[22] As I pointed out above, we find many articles urging research managers to hire the very best people, on the basis that excellence of personnel is the only way to succeed. In a way, such advice makes no sense. If about 5 percent of the active researchers in a given field are excellent (and this may be too high an estimate), then it is absurd to expect that every organization will be able to hire people with the highest reputation. It is probably much more sensible for the division manager to think in terms of leadership at the project level, that is, in terms of those people who know how to get a team to work, how to meet a deadline, how to write a report, and so on, even though they may not have a high reputation in their field. In this regard, we may note a real distinction between division chiefs and deans of universities; the latter are usually forced to rely on reputation for research or teaching.

Discussing the role of the division chief in the internal design of a project naturally raises the question of his own required technical and scientific background. It seems more or less obvious that the project leader needs to have a level of sophistication in his discipline on a par with the researchers themselves, just as a professor does with thesis candidates, but does this obvious principle apply equally well to all higher levels in the organization? We must recall the split personality view of the division chief. We are asking him simultaneously to be a good manager from top management's point of view, as well as a good ally of the researcher. To do a good job of task setting from top management's viewpoint, he has to take on a perspective that is not directly the knowledge of his scientific specialty. He has to learn about a new field quite different from his professional training. Furthermore, he must devote considerable time to the managerial area. The question of technical competence of the division chief, then, is one of balance between the conflicting objectives of his acting as a surrogate for top management and as an intellectual advisor or controller of the research project. I am tempted to say that the balance is largely one of style, since some division managers will tend to spend most of their time and energy on their administration role, while others will tend to emphasize their role in bolstering the quality of research projects. There is clear evidence that a wide variety of styles does occur in practice.[23] Evidently, it becomes the personnel task of the next higher level of management to select division chiefs whose style is most appropriate to the organization. If, for example, the research teams are very strong in their technical and scientific backgrounds, but tend to run off into areas with low payoff, then the division chief should be someone whose style of leadership introduces more of top management's concern into the research process. In such cases, it might happen that very little technical or scientific competence is required.

Finally, we should note that there is also a group style, which Thomas Kuhn calls the "paradigm" of a discipline.[24] The paradigm partially determines the value systems of the researchers (the projects, as well as the method of research, they think are most important). When the paradigm is very strong, the division manager may find that his latitude in changing the internal design of a project is very restricted. In such an event, the two world views may tend to clash in a very severe manner, because the "professionalism" of the researchers may tend to work in an opposite direction to the interests of top management. The division manager will then have to be someone who thrives on controversy, because he is not apt to find a satisfactory, permanent resolution.

ASSESSING THE ENVIRONMENT

So far we have depicted the job of setting tasks as one of designing levels of performance to maximize the division's contribution to the overall objectives of the organization. We have been mainly concerned with those aspects of the organization which the division chief can change. But of course many things he cannot control influence the way in which his division performs, and he needs to have information about them. The class of all such external influences can be called the *environment* of the manager. The environment includes government funding policies, attitudes of the public and its representatives, weather changes, top management policies, and more. *Resources,* then, are those relevant aspects that the division manager can control, while the environment includes those relevant aspects he cannot control. But the important point about the distinction is that it is based on the division chief's own decision, which itself is based on his view of his world. He may decide, for example, that a governmental or managerial policy is wrong. He then has to decide what he should do about it. If he decides that realistically he can do nothing, then he regards the policy as residing in the environment. If he decides he has a chance of changing it favorably, he regards it to be partially a resource he can manipulate to serve his purposes. The alert manager is one who never takes for granted that constraints on his decision making are beyond his control; the question is always an open one.

In the idealized model of task setting, the environment becomes a set of constraint equations, which limit total manpower and total budget, as well as various specific activities. Associated with each constraint is a cost, namely, the cost of not being able to go beyond the constraint in the various tasks. It is this cost which in principle guides the manager in deciding whether the constraint can be lived with.[25]

PROVIDING TOP MANAGEMENT WITH BUDGETARY GUIDES

We can illustrate the problem of deciding what is a resource and what is environment in terms of the overall budget of the division. Of course, no division manager believes that the overall budget is entirely in the environment and that he can do nothing about the decision. But division managers do differ in their ideas about how to present their case to the next level of management. Some would argue in terms of their own division's work and the need to sustain or increase its level of activity. They assume that if each division chief makes his case as strongly as possible, the next level manager will have the best basis for his own decision and that basis is entirely up to him. In other words, the decision manager has neither the responsibility nor the authority to decide on his overall budget, but he does have both the responsibility and authority to state his case in his own terms.

There is a growing tendency to suspect that this rather superficial view of the division chief's responsibilities may be inadequate. The point can be illustrated by a meeting I attended of the visiting committee of the National Bureau of Standards (NBS). NBS conducts a wide variety of basic research projects in both the physical and the social sciences. These are conducted in divisions which are defined in both disciplinary terms and application terms, depending on their main purpose. Each division chief has an advisory panel. The visiting committee sits above all the panels and advises the Secretary of Commerce on matters dealing with NBS as a whole.

The meeting was a discussion between the chairmen of the advisory panels and the visiting committee about congressional cuts in funds for basic research. Each chairman in turn explained what the cut would mean in his division, that is, the way it threatened this or that piece of "very important" research. A natural question from any observer might be how the visiting committee is supposed to decide what to advise the secretary. Lacking any other guides than their own scientific backgrounds and interests, they will advise in terms of their own biases. Change the visiting committee membership, and you get another kind of advice. Of course a wise visiting committee avoids the issue if it can, by simply advising the secretary or Congress to try to restore the cut, leaving the issue unresolved at a still higher level.

The counter philosophy is that the manager at one level is responsible for providing the next higher level with information that enables it to decide on budgetary allocations. Through a combination of judgment and evidence the division tries to estimate the gross benefits of its programs, say, in dollar terms. One possible scale in the public domain, which is by no means universally applicable, is the "income stream" that a given educational or research program will produce for a certain group of the public. The division also attempts to estimate the cost of the program, again in dollars. But the cost may not be in terms of actual dollars to be spent, but rather in terms of lost opportunities, that is, the benefits that might have been attained had personnel been occupied with some other task. This estimate must be made in terms of other possible tasks of the personnel *throughout the whole organization*. The division, therefore, needs some feedback from top management to determine whether its opportunity cost estimates are correct.[26] The general usefulness of this type of management information has not yet been adequately tested, but it should be emphasized that when a division manager presents a budget to top management and argues his case, he is implicitly assuming a benefit-minus-cost approach.

To summarize the job of task setting examined so far, we see that it consists of identifying the long-range goals that reflect the client's interest, so that research and other technical tasks can be judged for their relevance in deciding how resources can be deployed and the proper design of their deployment, subject to the constraints imposed by the environment.

DETECTING CHANGES IN THE ORGANIZATIONAL GOALS AND OBJECTIVES

This account, however, leaves out one very important consideration, namely, that the job of managing takes place over time. Given perfect forecasting abilities, managers might feel confident that a proposed way of structuring tasks would be sure to work out satisfactorily. But in general, all the relevant information is never available, and the next phases of a plan may reveal some critical factors which require modification or even abandonment of certain aspects of the plan.[27]

One important aspect of change for the division manager is the changing value structure of top management. This most frequently occurs when there is a change in organization, for example, in the structure of the organization, the personnel of top management, or the ownership of a private firm. But other types of change, which may be less abrupt, are apt to catch the division chief unaware. One type might be called "managerial fads," because it represents more or less a style of managing which may sweep through the whole culture. In recent years, we have seen a change from the "strong-and-forceful leadership" style of managing[28] to what might be called the inquisitive style, where the top manager asks searching questions of his subordinates about the policies of the whole organization.[29] Not that this style precludes forceful leadership, but its impact is more subtle, and the subordinate suddenly realizes that he'd better have some sensible answers to give about matters that are not his direct concern.

Another managerial fad is the adoption of new technologies. In recent years, we have witnessed this fad in the acquisition of computers, systems science, program planning and budgeting, and long-range forecasting and planning. It is perhaps unfair to call these "fads," but it must be conceded that they are often adopted without any extensive analysis and largely because the other fellow is doing it or (as in the case of program budgeting) a blanket executive order comes through. The best advice to the division manager is to become a good reader of management literature, so that he understands the terminology of new managerial technology, knows something of the pitfalls, and can be prepared when a directive arrives or a top management question is asked.

CONTROL

Control is essentially an information feedback device, in which the consequences of taking action are revealed and appropriate measures are taken to steer the ship on its proper course.[30]

The idea can be illustrated in many contexts. Consider, for example, the obvious need to control expenditures, which every division manager faces. His original plan, as we have seen, consists of allocations of expenditures to various projects. But unforeseen events may occur: the need for new equipment, the addition of a higher priced person on a project, resignations, the need to accelerate or decelerate a project, and so on. It is usually impossible for the division manager to follow all the impacts of events on his original plan and to calculate how much his expenditures have deviated from the budget.

But it is a relatively simple matter in many research organizations to project a line of monthly cumulative expenditures based on the yearly plan and to check actual versus projected. Naturally, there is some fuzziness in this simple feedback information system, because "actual" expenditures are often projections themselves (such as vacation pay or travel advances). But there is a fuzziness in all control procedures, so that the manager is always faced with two types of error: (1) changing the plan when no change is really necessary, and (2) not changing the plan when a change is necessary. Students of production control or of hypothesis testing will recognize these as the type I and II errors of statistical theory.[31] In statistical theory, one attempts to assign probabilities, determined by a specific control plan, to these two errors. That is, there are alternative ways of reacting to feedback information, and from each control plan one can infer the probabilities of the two types of error. In managerial practice, however, it may not be possible to be so precise, and the manager needs to use his own intuition to decide when and when not to react.

Also, we still live in the primitive age of budgeting, where nearly everything is budgeted on a yearly basis, no matter how inappropriate this may be. Consequently, the division manager is held responsible for coming under, but just under, the budgetary limit at the end of the year and usually has broad discretionary powers within the year. This means that his control plan will change during the annual period. During the first months he realizes that errors, even large errors, can be compensated later on, because there is time enough. In the middle period, if he is running short, an anxiety sets in and he may tend to react very frequently. On the other hand, if he is running long, then there is much of a scurry to spend the funds before the end of the fiscal year. So the probability of the type II error (not changing when change is called for) is high at the year's end.

This is probably not an optimal control procedure, and undoubtedly large amounts of resources are wasted by the arbitrary annual budgeting procedure, which, it should be pointed out, is a crude information feedback system used by top management. It seems to be well embedded in the environment of both top and middle management, since neither seems capable of changing it one bit.

The information feedback system says that the manager should react, but it does not normally say how. But the How is as important as the When, and both depend on the Why. The Why gives the manager an explanation of the breakdown of his plan, providing a basis for organizational learning. It is really astonishing how slowly organizations learn from their mistakes. This seems to be especially true of research organizations and marks a distinction between research and development. If development means the process of taking an idea and transforming it into a usable product, then it is often possible to learn from experience how to improve plans and estimate times to completion.[32] But there seems to be something frustratingly elusive about the research process which does not permit a conscious use of last year's failures in setting this year's plans. Of course, some specific guides can be generated. For example, if the manager believes that the explanation for failure is the behavior of certain individuals, he may improve his plan by eliminating them. Perhaps more significant is learning about the "blind alleys" of research. For example, at one stage in the research in computer sciences, most people thought we were on the verge of automated translation of one common language (for example, Russian) into another (English, say). The research community was probably unduly slow in realizing that the available basic theory of linguistics was not sufficiently strong for the job. But even this kind of learning is a bit tenuous, since the division manager can never be sure that a blind alley is blind, considering how many such alleys have proved to be illuminating in the history of science.

Nevertheless, even though no completely formal method of organizational learning is available for research organizations, the division manager and his staff obviously do learn, since we usually give some credit to an applicant if he has had extensive experience. What he has learned, essentially, is the art of reacting to both positive and negative change. I have already discussed some of the more obvious methods which can be formalized by information feedback systems. On the informal side, his art must consist of recognition of the personal qualifications of his subordinates but above all a sensitivity to the positive as well as the negative, to real innovation as well as compliance with set standards of performance and conduct.

These remarks suggest a rather radical idea about one side of the manager's role. We can say that the recognized standards of his tasks, such as budgets, completion times, and quality of the finished job, take place in the context of the *well-formulated* problem. The division manager knows what he has to do in a reasonably adequate way, and also knows reasonably well how he should react when the evidence shows that there is a marked deviation from the plan. But most division managers also function in the context of ill-formulated problems, where the nature of the task is not recognized nor structured in terms of standards and steps. These ill-formulated problems reveal themselves in various ways: discontent with the general level of research activity, the feeling that the division should be more innovative, a lack of good morale, and so on. But the feelings of discontent are not translatable into specific tasks, because no one is able to formulate the problem well enough so that the manager can see that a solution to the problem would resolve some or all of the basis of discontent.

In the case of ill-formulated problems it is not possible to use the idealized model of task setting in terms of long-range goals, because not enough is known about the nature of the real problem. Notions like cost and benefit are not used. The situation is much like that of a traveler who does not know exactly what kind of a place he is seeking and so the signposts do not give him enough information. What is needed are some intuitive "surrogate standards" which act in place of the missing standards (guideposts) of the well-formulated problem. The two I would like to suggest are *surprise* and *irrelevance*.

The notion here is that in the context of the ill-structured problem, the manager's role is one of exploration. If nothing surprises him, he is probably not exploring, because, consciously or unconsciously, he has already made up his mind. "Surprise" is an interesting word in its etymology, since it combines "sur," meaning "beyond," with "prise," which comes from the French "prendre," meaning "to take by force" or "seize." To feel surprise, then, means that one is taken by force beyond himself, which I interpret as being forceably taken beyond one's preconceptions. The surprised manager is one who is seized by an idea that he had never been aware of before, which in part transforms his view of the world and in particular his idea of what the problem is.

The other aspect of exploration is irrelevance. Here again the etymology helps explain the idea. The etymological background of relevance is the French "relever," meaning to "relieve" in the military sense of relieving a siege on a fortress, and so meaning to "assist" the beleaguered. The manager who realizes he had some serious problems is beleaguered, but he must be very careful in choosing his allies. Some information will be highly relevant, in the sense that it narrows the area of confusion and brings him closer to problem formulation. But if all information is relevant, then he has probably made up his mind what the problem really is, whether he realizes it or not. One sign that he is still open is that some, or a lot, of information is irrelevant, meaning that it does not relieve the siege or that it is frustrating. Irrelevance is analogous to "noise" in information theory, though the reason for "noise" is not necessarily the reason for irrelevance.

The thesis is that a manager needs to experience surprise and irrelevance as critical aspects of his problem formulation. Of course, the thesis does not imply that he should be in a continuous state of surprise or find everything very irrelevant. Both surprise and irrelevance tend to take him farther away from problem formulation, and so have a negative as well as a positive value. Nor is it possible to indicate how much surprise and irrelevance are appropriate. The most we can say is that a manager who finds his days filled with highly relevant, unsurprising events is probably in a rut that is deepening to the point where he may become stuck for life. The manager's problem is easy enough to state: how to create an innovative environment without ruining the stable environment. But at the present time, there is no adequate way to formulate this problem in terms of specific policies.

SUPPORTS OF THE DIVISION MANAGER

We have been describing the division manager's job from the viewpoint of top management, the things he needs to get done, and the information he needs to do them. But there is one other aspect of this role that needs to be discussed, namely, the "people" resources available to help the manager. Part of these resources are in the more or less hidden power politics of organizations, part in external aids, and part in staff and committee activities. Not much can be said of the first, except that it is undoubtedly an important aspect of the manager's life. The manner in which he builds up support and friendship in other divisions, in top management, and within his own division, may very well determine the success or failure of his enterprise. With respect to the second, the manager clearly needs to know much about the efforts of other managers at his level, especially since R & D feed into these efforts.

The external supports of the manager's activities links his system with other systems. The major aspect of this support is in terms of funding projects. A large amount of the manager's time must be spent talking to people from organizations that do or may support the research work. The general policy is often one of talking to any person who is even remotely connected with possible funding sources, a policy that is certainly suspect but hard to change.

A similar problem arises in connection with proposal writing. A decision must be reached as to how much time personnel should spend on this important activity; the decision is especially difficult in that the best proposal writers are probably the best researchers. The problem is closely related to the problem of free time for an individual's own research, which, from top management's point of view, represents "seed" money for future contracts or grants. The best technique for handling this bundle of problems seems to be some sort of cost information system, in which the time of the manager, staff, and researchers is translated into dollar figures. This includes time spent in talking to potential or actual clients, proposal preparation, preparatory research, and so on. If feasible, costs should be "opportunity" costs, that is, they should reflect the loss incurred in other profitable activities as a result of time spent in "advertising" research. The opportunity cost may be zero, or much higher than the individual's salary, depending on whether no alternative opportunity is present or an extremely lucrative one is being neglected.

Since in this chapter I am concerned with the division manager, I have not addressed myself to the problem of gearing up to a very large contract. But something needs to be said about the opposite problem, the small contract, which characterizes a great deal of R & D in the public, nonmilitary, nonspace domain. Many large research organizations are poorly organized to go after this type of contract, because the effort required tends to increase overhead and to be far less profitable than the large contract. Consequently, government administrators should recognize that their policies are forcing many of the larger research organizations to keep within the defense-space-energy area and should consider whether this is a wise national policy. It can certainly be pointed out that the small amounts of funds spent for research contracts on extremely complex urban problems is an inadequate policy. If we can learn anything significant through research about how to better the city of New York in a significant way, the price tag must be at least a billion dollars per annum.

Finally, we need to examine the aids within his division which the division manager can draw upon. Some of these have already been mentioned in such terms as the information system appropriate to his role, project evaluation and control, and expenditure control. The division manager can also expect assistance in arriving at a choice among alternative strategies and tactics. This assistance may be informal advice from others in his organization, including members of his staff and researchers. Indeed, there is considerable evidence in the organization theory literature that seeking advice is important for morale; the quiet manager generates loud and violent rumors.

But the more critical point is the extent to which division managers should rely on more formal advice. This usually takes place in two ways, via committees and via research. An anthropologist from another culture might find in the Washington scene a rather fascinating ritual, consisting of the convening of advisory panels who are briefed on various research projects, compliment the research staff and division manager with perhaps a suggestion here and there, and take off for home where they forget about the matter until the next ritual. I have already mentioned the NBS, with its three institutes with several divisions. The divisions all have advisory panels; each institute has an advisory panel; the bureau itself has a visiting committee, the Assistant Secretary of Commerce for Science and Technology has advisory panels for the various research units of the Commerce Department, including NBS; and a President's Scientific Advisory Committee sits on top of all these.

One might defend this large amount of advice giving by arguing that it provides a way for the scientific community to upgrade the level of research conducted within government organizations, but experience and common sense show that this is rare. Rather, the advisory committees, especially in recent times, have become agents for securing more funding, suggesting personnel, and lending an aura of respectability. I am not necessarily arguing that the advisory panel system is wrong, but it is certainly misnamed. The division manager who expects to obtain really significant advice for decision making from such panels is apt to be very naive. The main source of advice comes from his project leaders and staff, plus any consultants he may hire to study his problems in depth.

But the real question is whether the advice of people who do know the problem of the division manager in depth is worthwhile, especially when such advice is generated in committees. It should be recognized that committee-generated advice is a method of inquiry and must be judged by comparison with other methods. The general theory which seems to be used in defense of committee advice is that one or more of a group of experienced persons may have encountered the same or a like problem before and may have been able to test the efficacy of a possible solution. Or, one or more persons may have developed organizational policies which imply specific solutions. The fact that the group, using independent judgments, arrives at a consensus lends a great deal of credence to their advice.

However, there is a strong case to be made against the use of committee advice as a partial determinant of decision making. First of all, it can seriously be questioned whether two or more persons are really in agreement on a complicated organizational issue. If the matter under discussion were a technical one, then independently formed opinion may be valid. But trying to decide whether to go into a new area of research or continue an old one which has not fulfilled its promise presents so many facets that overt agreement may be quite deceptive. What typically happens in my experience is that A and B will agree on some point which favors some specific policy; their very agreement on the point carries them over to agreement on the policy. For example, a committee is discussing the advisability of continuing research on computer-aided instruction (CAI). A member points out that CAI costs four dollars per student per hour, whereas ordinary instruction costs, say, four dollars per student per week or month. Another member agrees strongly with the price difference. At this point, the two of them form a coalition based on the conviction that research on CAI is of questionable value relative to the national economy. The many other facets of the problem—such as techniques for cutting costs or applications in special areas—are no longer discussed.

Agreement is a very tricky mood which often leads us down the wrong pathways. Only a very few mavericks feel inclined to stand up against an emerging agreement in a group, as psychologists have revealed. When a group of subjects is shown lines of differing length and all the stooges agree that a given line is the longest, even the independent subject will tend to go along with the rest, despite what his eyesight tells him. This kind of reinforcement must operate strongly in the context of fuzzy problems, especially when the committee member knows that he will not be held accountable for errors.

As is true throughout this chapter, I am not trying to state universally valid rules. Many individuals are superb committee members, who do not buckle even when the group is unanimously opposed. Much can be done by a committee chairman who makes an effort to learn about the members, and who, upon sensing an impending agreement, intentionally calls on members who may have some good reasons to oppose it. He is especially alert to keep the talkers from carrying the day by the well-known technique of boredom. He is also alert for the trickster who twists a meaning and appeals to those around the table with the question, "Does anyone here honestly believe so-and-so?" The adept chairman should step in and twist the meaning back again by saying, "I do, because what so-and-so really meant was thus-and-so."

Back of these remarks on the design of advisory committees is a conviction that the strength of the committee methodology lies in disagreement, not agreement. To explain this remark, we should take another look at the world of the division manager. We have been considering his division as a component of a larger system constituting the whole organization, which itself is a component of some still larger system. We could also regard his division as a component of the research community, which itself is a part of the whole of society. Now the characteristics of these larger systems are at best known only approximately and usually not at all. Yet the nature of the larger system is quite important in judging the performance of or planning for the division. What normally occurs is some judgment, implicit or explicit, about the larger world of the division.[33] "Judgment" is a conclusion arrived at in the context of debate, as in judgments in courts of law. The decision maker needs to review the arguments, pro and con, relating to the kind of world he lives in.

There are several techniques for creating debate in planning. One may simply ask the staff to prepare two opposing cases to be argued before the advisory committee. This "adversary" method has the advantage of creating a competitive environment in which opposing teams try to persuade committee members to judge in their favor. But it may create an artificial atmosphere. Another method is to predesign a balanced debate. A very striking example of this technique consists of building up the pro and con from exactly the same data base.[34]

It should be emphasized that the main point of the debate is not to decide which is right, the pro or the con, since both may be wrong. The idea is to create a healthy doubt in the mind of the listener that his own assumptions are correct; a doubt is "healthy" if it leads not to frustration but to a well-considered judgment based on intuition and experience.

We have now explored the role of the division manager with respect to the aims of top management. We have seen that he has the responsibility of producing activities in a series of tasks which have a high potential of serving the goals of top management. If the real client of top management is the public, then the division manager indirectly is responsible to the public, and his performance in principle is gauged in terms of how well the tasks of his division serve the public's interests.

THE VIEW FROM THE BOTTOM[35]

But as I indicated at the beginning, the division manager has another group of clients and a concomitant responsibility to them. These are the researchers (or professors).

First of all we need to describe a philosophy of individualism. I'll begin by a description in its simplest and most direct form, which is not the form the researchers themselves use. The idea is that each individual, to use Immanuel Kant's phrase, is an end in himself and must never be used as a means.[36] Each individual is unique and therefore not to be classified with other individuals. This is an extremely important aspect of individualistic philosophy, because it contradicts a very basic tenet of top management's philosophy. Management believes in policies, and its policies apply to classes of people, *not* to individuals. So management frequently treats people as means to its ends; it sends out directives to the effect that "all persons satisfying such-and-such properties will be promoted, or fired, or retired, or whatever." But for the pure individualist, such pronouncements are wrong and perhaps immoral, because each person is unique.

Now the only prescription which makes any sense in a pure individualistic philosophy is Polonius's "to thine own self be true," that is, "be what you truly are" or "become what you truly are." Hypocrisy means lying to yourself, not really understanding what it is that makes you unique, trying to hide from yourself your true nature, say, to be socially respectable.[37]

As applied to the present domain of interest, individualism recognizes that each person is a researcher, a special kind of researcher, just as each is a special kind of artist, or teacher, or student. Each individual by his very nature is continuously trying to understand the world he lives in. Some do it by going to school in cloistered halls, some by going to school in embattled halls. The point is that no one is a better or worse researcher than another provided that he is true to himself, that is, his research behavior truly reflects what he is.

One can illustrate the individualist point of view in another context: the so-called merit system. In our society, men are "qualified" by various tests to attain positions in law, medicine, teaching, and so on. In a society dedicated to pure individualism, the merit system would not exist. Instead, each would practice those things which best fit his nature, and no one or group would impose its judgment of qualification on any person who did not approve.

It must seem a blessing to those well entrenched in the modern paradigm of administration that nothing so chaotic as individualism is likely to occur, because in the world view of the pure individualist, there are no "trade-offs"—no idea that one sacrifices some of X's benefit to better Y. It is a philosophy antithetical to one still prevalent view of management, so aptly described by Hower and Orth:

> It assumes that employees (including scientists) are essentially passive instruments, responding to direction and control but generally incapable of initiating action or even of maintaining it long without close oversight. It assumes that people will generally do what they are told to do; it is management's function to assign them tasks and see that they carry out instructions.[38]

The individualist philosophy I have been describing does not merely modify this "classical" view of management, for example, by suggesting that people can have initiative if motivated well enough or if given the opportunity. Instead, the philosophy stresses that organizations exist to enable people to realize themselves, and whenever anyone is treated as a means *only* to another's realization, the act is immoral.

But this simplistic philosophy is not the one which the scientific community has adopted, although the scientists' philosophy bears considerable resemblance to it. It is the discipline[39] rather than the individual which becomes the focal point. The discipline is a collection of researchers who understand each other's research and methods and who set the standards of excellence and acceptability. The discipline designs the curricula which qualify the young to enter the research community, decides what research project deserves funding by judging the method and content, decides what research output should be published or awarded honors. One discipline does not officially pass judgment of merit about another, although, of course, persons in one discipline may be derogatory of work in another. There is no "merit system" among disciplines.

The name of the game is "creating knowledge," and scientists can wax quite poetic about the ultimate value of discovering a truth that was unknown before. The point they make is that managers and administrators *should* not use their managerial ends to judge the ultimate scientific worth of a project; when they do, and when they use basic science as a means only, then they are "immoral." The real "value" of the task lies in its scientific worth, and this is up to the researchers to judge.

Now the research community is not entirely esoteric, nor is it entirely consistent in its philosophy. Despite its claim that basic knowledge is a value in itself, it badly needs application to keep its discipline from becoming more or less meaningless play. Engineering is an essential part of the enterprise of the physical sciences, because it so clearly demonstrates in its technology that the basic physicists are not making up their own rules without any outside reference.

But here we sense a weakness in the scientist's philosophy. On the one hand he wants to keep management out of the decision-making process in judging the scientific merits of research; but on the other hand he recognizes the importance to his own basic work of the applications which management directs. The amphibology is well illustrated in the remark of Gauss, to the effect that it was a blessing that he could not see the application of his abstract ideas. It was a blessing, because he was then intellectually freed to invent a mathematics which later had many applications. In other words, Gauss's failure to see any use of his ideas was a very useful failure!

One quickly sees the difficulties of the scientist's philosophy; they occur at the interface of his discipline with other social institutions, including other disciplines. He is not clear about how the total budget of his discipline should be set, for example, and he is not clear about how important the application of his findings really is. Normally, he assumes that management, for example, the Bureau of the Budget and Congress, must set the total budget. Having conceded this much, he is very uneasy if some bureau begins introducing ideas of "program relevance" to modify the judgment of merit of a project. Of course, if he goes to work for a private company or for the Defense Department, he realizes that he must yield to management, but he is certainly not happy about doing so if he is a believer in the philosophy of basic research.

In any event, the scientist's philosophy makes most of organization theory irrelevant. For him, the most important organization with respect to science is a scientific community, which is essentially nonhierarchical. There may be distinguished men in it, of course, but they have neither the authority nor the responsibility to tell anyone what he should do; they may play a role in judging another's work, but no one person by himself is the ultimate court of appeals.[40] Consequently, in his conscious life the scientist is fundamentally opposed to hierarchy. If he were forced to state who was really "in charge" or "on top," he might well choose himself rather than the manager.

But I am mainly interested in the moral background of the scientists' position, namely, that scientists ought not to be used as instruments of management only. The immorality becomes patent when scientists are used to create destruction either for defense or aggression. Although less dangerous, immorality is there whenever managerial goals dominate basic research to the detriment of research goals.

The division manager needs to be a moral man as well as a management man. Although morality is admittedly elusive, the scientist's moral prescription is clear enough, namely, that he shall not be used as a means only. To this prescription, the division manager is committed as firmly as he is to serving the organizational goals. But the two commitments in today's society often clash. If the basic research reveals a beautiful piece of knowledge but apparently has no application, what then? More to the point, microbiology may find the way to clone humans (make replicate organisms from the cell of the original organism). Should the frightening prospect stop basic research?

There is no adequate answer to this question. Anyone who uses a full-fledged "systems approach" will inevitably have to become immoral, by using people as means only. Anyone who doggedly follows the moral law will interfere with other people's happiness. Since social welfare and morality are both ideals of the human race, both must be sustained. It is people like the division chief,[41] who so vividly see the clash, who must learn that greatest hallmark of the mature mind: a persistent unwillingness to give in completely to either ideal, merely because such a concession would make life peaceful.

Developments in Government Policies toward Science and Technology

HAROLD ORLANS
Senior Fellow
The Brookings Institution
Washington, D.C.

If, as George Bernard Shaw said, love is the illusion that one woman is different from another, "policy" is the illusion that intelligence can reduce the confusion of events and guide us toward desirably, timely, and orderly objectives. To speak of "policy" can be to dignify government unduly, to mistake congressmen and cabinet members for intellectuals and intellectuals for seers. For as anyone who knows Washington must acknowledge, government is a creature of circumstance as well as plan, practical reality as well as general principle, administration as well as law, accident as well as design, events as well as ideas; in brief, one can find as much inconsistency and pragmatism as conscious, consistent purpose in government. Whether consistency be the vice of small or great minds, it is one from which neither politicians nor government officials suffer unduly, and if intellectuals want to understand government and not just spin theories about it, that is a good point of departure. Government "policy" is often merely the rationalization of self-interest, an intellectual gloss on political decision. *Good* policy should introduce a tolerable (not absolute) correspondence between the immediate interests of program beneficiaries and the larger interests of society, between the stated goals of programs and their actual consequences. Illusory goals may make good ideology, but those who prefer reality to illusion must label them bad public policy.

ACADEMIC SCIENCE

Unfortunately, government policies toward academic science, that simulacrum of rationality, have been guided by ideological—that is, irrational—as well as rational considerations.

Three fundamental assumptions have underlain this policy for many years: (1) that expenditures for basic research should increase markedly, (2) that the output of Ph.D.'s should also be greatly increased, and (3) that, whenever possible government-sponsored basic research should be conducted on campus because of the mutually beneficial relationship between research and education.

Perpetual increase in research expenditures

That academic research expenditures should constantly increase and that attempts to restrain them represent an anti-intellectualism which endangers the health of the economy and the welfare of the nation are recurrent themes in the lamentations of scientists, especially during lulls in their seemingly perpetual ascent of budgetary peaks. Federal budgetary restraints, the New York Academy of Sciences warns, will "seriously undermine the potential benefits of science to the economy and human health of the nation and ... the world,"[1] while, with a perfectly straight face, Jerome Wiesner forecasts that if current budgetary trends continue, the United States will be "a very sick country technologically" in five to ten years.[2] Harvey Brooks, for his part, perceives not merely a "new disenchantment with science and technology" but "a deep hostility toward science and scientists" and "an apparent revulsion against science by the whole society" which he (like many other scientists who contrast the purity of their purpose with the villainies of industry) attributes largely to the public's confusion of science with technology.[3] It is a strange revulsion to which the government continues to obligate $17 billion a year. And it is strange logic which holds that science is good in itself (for "how can truth be anything but good?" thinks the scientist who lacks Oppenheimer's sense of guilt and forgets the punishment meted out in Genesis not for man's technology but for his knowledge of good and evil) and ultimately responsible for what is good in industry (such as economic growth)—but not, of course, for what is bad (such as atomic bombs, anti-ballistic missiles, noise, pollution, traffic jams, and many other things that threaten and annoy people).

Though scientists were not wont to protest the extravagance of the 25 percent annual growth in federal expenditures for academic research which prevailed from 1957-63, the lower subsequent growth (often erroneously called decreases) educed the doctrine that, as our agriculture flourishes on an annual rainfall of 42 inches, so our science will flourish only on a budget compounded 15 percent annually (and in physics, I am told, a "budget cut" is now defined as any increase of less than 15 percent).

The first cogent public formulation of this doctrine was by Harvey Brooks, in March 1965, in response to the following question put to the National Academy of Sciences by the House Committee on Science and Astronautics:

> What level of Federal support is needed to maintain for the United States a position of leadership through basic research in the advancement of science and technology and their economic, cultural, and military applications?[4]

Brooks's answer was that "on the basis of educational requirements alone, it appears that a minimum annual rate of increase for university research support of 13-15 percent will be required for the next decade if the United States is to meet its announced goals for graduate education." That represented the sum of two separate projections: (1) "the cost of research per man-year of research effort will increase at an annual rate of 5 percent in constant dollars"—a figure specifically excluding inflation of the dollar and confined solely to the so-called "sophisitication" factor or the increased cost of equipment and the higher standard of scientific living; and (2) an annual increase in the number of graduate science students which had been about 9 percent the preceding two years and was then estimated at from 5 to 10 percent for future years.[5]

Brooks's 15 percent proposal (which was actually closer to 20 percent, allowing for inflation) was accepted as the Johnson Administration's official target for fiscal years 1966 and 1967. However, under the mounting demands of our two-front war in Vietnam and urban America, HEW Secretary John Gardner challenged the wisdom of that policy in the summer of 1966[6] and the following spring even the President's science advisor Donald Hornig was admonishing his fellow scientists that though "we [that is, the administration] accept . . . that America must be second to none in most of the significant fields of science [which he carefully did not enumerate]. . . . what is *not* accepted is the notion that every part of science should grow at some automatic and predetermined rate, 15% per year or any other number. . . ."[7]

For about fifteen years—roughly, from 1949, when GI enrollments had fallen off, until 1965, when the Office of Education became the predominant source of federal aid to higher education—research programs were the main channel by which federal funds flowed to higher educational institutions; and one important reason for this was because they were widely recognized as a politically convenient means of aiding graduate schools when no broader formula for aiding all institutions could be agreed upon. Today, however, many other programs offer viable alternatives; in 1968, some $3.2 billion in federal money was spent on such programs of grants and loans to institutions and students, as compared to $1.5 billion for on-campus research.[8] Accordingly, research can no longer (or, at any rate, less readily) be justified as a form of indirect aid to higher education; it must be justified in its own right, in terms of the benefits society derives from it as compared to the benefits of alternative programs.

Ph.D.'s in science

As it happens, instead of rising, graduate enrollments have lately been declining. In engineering, mathematics, chemistry, physics, and psychology, first-year male enrollments were down slightly in 1968 from their 1967 levels.[9]

Therefore, it takes no special talent to question the 15 percent policy today. The wish of tenured professors for additional security is understandable but insufficient to warrant such a permanent tax on our future; a government which thus mortgaged its budget to every reasonable claimant might just as well go out of business. The most chauvinistic scientists recognize the ultimate mathematical confrontation between a 15 percent growth rate in any sector and a 4 or 5 percent growth of the economy, but they relegate it to an undefined "near future" or, as Lee DuBridge put it, to "the next few years"[10]—a period as ample as "tomorrow."

But tomorrow is already here. Not long ago, the academy may have provided a limited sanctuary from the harsher conflicts of society, but who can believe that today, when it is more peaceful in Washington than at Cambridge or Morningside Heights, and more fires burn on campus than at the Pentagon? The students' cry of "relevance" may often be ill-defined and short-sighted, mistaking journalism for scholarship, politics for morality, protest for politics, and change for progress; but in their heartfelt search for significant truths, they are closer to the call of the true intellectual than are many scientists. Distance has lent academic research a certain enchantment in Washington, so that both natural and social scientists have successfully persuaded both their government and themselves of the larger national significance of insignificant research. Evidently they have been less successful persuading the students in their midst. It remains to be seen whether the student rebels will win more allies among faculty (as at Harvard) and together wring concessions from academic administrators, or among administrators (as at Cornell) and exact from the faculty a greater measure of institutional and social responsibility (and, perhaps, classroom attendance). Should events take the latter course, Mario Savio may yet accomplish more good than he intended.

Whether graduate enrollments rise or fall, to my mind, it makes little sense to gear total governmental expenditures for academic research to the number of graduate students who, as research assistants, receive only a small fraction of the project funds going to principal investigators. Stipends awarded directly to graduate students would support their research more effectively and more cheaply, and would distribute funds in closer correspondence to the actual number of students enrolled at different institutions.

But the more important question is whether graduate science enrollments *should* expand as rapidly in the future as during the last two decades. Though I believe the answer should be "no," public policy should be founded upon the careful and objective assessment of all the relevant facts, rather than mere opinion. Unfortunately, the agencies largely responsible for this assessment—the Office of Science and Technology and the National Science Foundation—have disregarded inconvenient facts and acted more as protagonists of graduate research than of the public interest.

Thus, the National Science Foundation was embarrassed by, and did its best to forget, a 1957 study by David Blank and George Stigler that the foundation had itself financed, which concluded that "up to at least 1955 there had been no shortage—in fact an increasingly ample supply—of engineers," that there was "no reason" to anticipate a shortage of doctorates in mathematics and physics, and that "on the contrary, it is other fields, such as the humanities, that have reason for concern."[11] NSF preferred, instead, to rely upon Nicholas DeWitt's study of *Soviet Professional Manpower* which found that the USSR "has reached a position of close equivalence with or even slight numerical supremacy over the United States as far as the supply of trained manpower in specialized professional fields is concerned. . . . Our own policies . . . in regard to specialized manpower resources will decide whether within the next decade or so the scales will be tipped off balance."[12] This impressed Congress at the time and still more after *sputnik*, when both NSF and Office of Education science education and fellowship programs were greatly expanded. Subsequently, a supposed decline in the proportion of academic faculty with Ph.D.'s noted in National Education Association surveys during the 1950s and '60s lent credence to assumptions of a Ph.D. shortage; and the same assumptions were perpetuated by reports of the President's Science Advisory Committee in 1962[13] and the National Academy of Sciences in 1964 (though the latter was tempered by the fact that defense cutbacks had then produced some unemployment among scientists and engineers).[14]

Contrary evidence advanced by Bernard Berelson in 1960, being uncongenial, was disregarded. Berelson discounted the NEA statistics and disputed the prevalent forecast that the proportion of faculty with doctorates might decline from 40 percent in the 1960s to as low as 20 percent by 1970, insisting that enough doctorates would be forthcoming "to *raise* the proportion of doctorates. . . ."[15] His judgment has since been vindicated by Allan Cartter of the American Council on Education and John Folger of the Commission on Human Resources and Advanced Education. Writing in 1965, Cartter discredited the NEA findings, pointing out that the percentage of teaching faculty with the doctorate had not, in fact, declined but had *risen* since 1955, "and has improved within each major category of institutions (for example, public, private, two-year college, four-year college, and university.[16] One Office of Education study showed that, in 1962-63, 51 percent of faculty in four-year institutions had Ph.D.s.[17] In 1967, Folger foresaw a serious problem of research employment for science doctorates after 1975, if prevailing trends continued.[18]

In view of this history, the National Science Board's March 1969 pronouncement that "it is not possible to produce too many highly educated people in the United States as long as appropriate educational standards are not sacrificed"[19] must be deemed either innocent or irresponsible—either the ignorant or the informed assault of a special interest upon the public purse. "A foreseeable consequence of *apparent* overproduction of graduate school-trained scientists and engineers," the board argued, "would be the upgrading of the teaching staffs of the Nation's secondary school system, an event which could only be deemed desirable in itself."[20]

Is the diet of the poor, then, best upgraded with cake? Will students in high schools be the next who must educate themselves while their teachers sift the dross of nature for particles of silver? At a time of turmoil and distress, when trust has diminished between students and teachers, whites and blacks, citizens and police, civilians and military, can we do nothing better with our money than spend $50,000 training a high school teacher when $10,000 will do?

That statement of the National Science Board is only one indication—unfortunately, there are others—of the poverty of thought among too many of the men responsible for the nation's science affairs. "By and large," Daniel Greenberg observes, "the statesmen of science are still telling Congress what they told it nearly a quarter of a century ago."[21] Indeed they are, and it is time for a change; but there are few signs of fresh thinking in the stale councils of government science affairs.[22]

The Seaborg credo

Perhaps the most outmoded element in our academic science policy prescribes that, wherever possible, research, and especially basic research, should be conducted on campus or in close association with a university, because of the natural and mutually beneficial alliance of research and higher education. This credo was well expressed in the 1960 Seaborg report, which stressed that "when it can be managed, basic research should be done in, or at least in association with, universities."[23] In his introductory statement, President Eisenhower called "particular attention" to the importance of uniting basic research and graduate education" if the nation is to produce the research results . . . that will maintain the leadership of American science" and concluded, "in this great endeavor, the partnership between the Federal Government and the nation's universities will assume growing importance in the future."[24] The report directed its recommendation not only to small projects but explicitly to "big science" installations:

> We specifically reject the view that such large operations as those of the Ames Laboratory of the Iowa State University are inevitably alien to the university. We believe that great fields of research like nuclear physics simply must not be cut off from universities just because they now require very large instruments and correspondingly large staffs of specialists and technicians. The very difficulties of such large laboratories, in our view, are an argument for strengthening their connection to the universities.[25]

There is a great deal in the foregoing with which no one would quarrel: the Ph.D. has traditionally been a research degree and for those graduate students who will continue to do research, graduate school is the natural place to learn to do it. And surely the support of good, as distinct from mediocre, research at universities has been firmly established as a legitimate and significant function for both government and private agencies.

However, these valid points of policy conceal less valid points which the well-written and well-thought Seaborg report left unsaid in the fervor of its effort to plight the troth between government and the universities (an effort so fervid that, for a time, doubt existed if Eisenhower would sign the report before leaving office). There are, of course, Ph.D.'s (for example, in teaching, administration, and clinical psychology) and larger numbers of M.A.'s who neither do nor wish to do research, as well as those who should be discouraged from doing, and particularly from publishing, any. Let us grant, nonetheless, that good research generally remains necessary to good graduate education. But now, years after the Berkeley uprisings, years of increasing disruption and unrest, can we any longer say that the increasing level of academic research, which has put many of the best faculty out of touch with undergraduates except via microphones and closed-circuit television, has also been good for undergraduate education and for the general sense of community and *esprit de corps* on campus? Government is not all powerful and is commonly blamed for too many things; I do not want to add to its grievous responsibilities for peace, war, and taxes the primary responsibility for what is now happening on campus. But, insofar as the government is *in part* responsible, its relationship to the university bears an uncomfortable resemblance to the farmer's relationship to the unhappy goose that laid the golden eggs.

The "union of research and education" cannot be assessed, as a public policy, solely in terms of its good and bad consequences on campus, or as a defense of the university's role in big as well as little science. In public policy, we must ask not only if an idea is good and sound but why, among a multitude of good and sound ideas one is singled out for special attention. In Washington, at any rate, that choice often has something to do with money; and it may accurately be said that, regardless of its educational and scientific merit, the Seaborg policy had a certain usefulness in directing toward universities men and money that might otherwise have gone to government agencies, independent research organizations, and even, upon occasion, private industry.

The Wooldridge committee report on the National Institutes of

Health is an excellent example. Normally, an important function of private scientific advisers is said to be maintaining professional standards of quality against political pressures in R & D awards. Yet in this case, the distinguished private scientists assigned to evaluate the quality of NIH research gave first priority to the political interests of academic scientists. Though government salaries "are likely to be lower than those available in universities and medical schools" and regulations more troublesome, the committee found that "the average quality of individual research conducted intramurally by NIH is in every way equal to that conducted extramurally." Hence, the government was getting more good research for its salary dollar intramurally than extramurally. Nevertheless, the committee expressed "serious concern" about the size of the intramural program. "The value to the nation of the intermingling of basic research and higher education is such as to bias us strongly in its favor," the committee declared honestly enough; and, since the NIH campus at Bethesda was not a second-rate degree-granting institution but merely a first-rate research institution, the committee "inclined to the opinion that . . . some decrease in the present proportion of intramural research" was desirable.[26]

Now, the appropriate size of intramural government R & D expenditures has long been of concern to private industry as well as universities, and this is not the place to review every swing of the pendulum between the governmental and private sectors in the Army and the Air Force, on the Hill and in the White House, in the September 1959 directive of the Budget Director Maurice Stans and the April 1962 report of Budget Director David Bell, and on many other occasions.[27] According to some accounts, recent criticism of cost escalation in defense R & D contracts may lead Defense Secretary Melvin Laird to strengthen military laboratories in the hope that they will then be better able to monitor the work of industry.

But governmental laboratories are not the most natural competitors for much of the research that has been done on campus; in this respect, the NIH labs are unusual as government laboratories go. (How many others house a Nobel laureate?) The universities' most likely competitors for government research funds are rather a variety of independent research institutions—those which conduct research for industry as well as the government, including both nonprofit laboratories like Battelle and profit-making ones like Arthur D. Little and a host of smaller enterprises spawned by faculty entrepreneurs; endowed research institutions like the Carnegie Institution of Washington and the Sloan-Kettering

Institute; so-called government research centers operated under contract by universities and other private organizations, like the MIT Lincoln Laboratory, Brookhaven, RAND, and Battelle at Hanford; and a growing crop of institutes once, or still nominally, affiliated with universities, which have been, or may soon be, set adrift from the sponsoring university once deemed so indispensable to their success, such as the Institute for Defense Analyses, the Cornell Aeronautical Laboratory, the Center for Naval Analyses, the Human Resources Research Office, the Center for Research in Social Systems, the Stanford Research Institute—and who knows which will be next?

How long can government policy remain oblivious of what every newspaper reader knows: that military-sponsored research is increasingly unwelcome on many campuses—unwelcome to faculty and administrators as well as to student demonstrators?

Let me state my own opinion clearly: Military and intelligence agencies must inevitably maintain close ties to universities not only in this capitalist democracy but in communist and socialist nations as well, because military power and national intelligence dare not for long be separated from the best scientists, engineers, social scientists, and humanists, many of whom will always be found in university laboratories and library stalls. If the Department of Defense is forced to break its formal ties with these men via grants and contracts to their universities, it will only have to reestablish them in other ways via consultantships; grants and contracts with neighboring, nonacademic organizations; and other formal and informal, public and private arrangements.

Nonetheless, the first task of rational policy is to face reality frankly; and it is a simple fact that military, and especially classified, research has been, or is being, expelled from many campuses. According to one story that is probably not apocryphal, when Roger Kyes was Under Secretary of Defense, a group of university presidents complained to him about the volume of DOD applied research on campus; but when he offered to withdraw that research, the presidents protested more loudly than before. Today, many presidents would heave a sign of relief at that prospect, hoping to avoid a "confrontation" on their campus by retreating faster than student militants advance. From the standpoint of the Defense Department, an honorable withdrawal from campus may soon be as welcome as one from Vietnam; and, as the domestic withdrawal does not wait upon Paris negotiations, it would not be surprising if some such directives were forthcoming. Already, there has been a significant reduction in the volume of classified research on campus[28]; the Senate has exerted pressure to reduce the volume of defense expenditures on foreign area research and on the work of DOD research centers; and an address by Stephen Tonsor recommending the removal of most defense research from universities has received President Nixon's general endorsement.[29]

To summarize, I have tried to show how far government policy toward academic research has been outdistanced by events, concentrating on three of the most basic elements of that policy: that academic research expenditures should increase by at least 15 percent a year; that we cannot produce too many science Ph.D.'s; and that, wherever possible, government-sponsored research, and especially basic research, should be closely associated with higher education.

Though I have not attempted to spell out in detail an alternative set of policies, their general outline seems clear:

1. Since the relative stabilization of academic research budgets helps to direct more attention to undergraduate education and to the practical needs of society, it should be continued, to borrow DuBridge's phrase, "for the next few years."
2. The infinite expansion of Ph.D. production should be replaced with more modest and more selective goals.
3. At least until peace is restored on campus, or the academy and the government fight again as allies instead of foes, much military research, as well as certain other kinds of government-sponsored research (including some large-scale basic research and that applied research for which results must be delivered on schedule or to meet necessary specifications) should be withdrawn from universities and undertaken by research institutions.

CIVILIAN TECHNOLOGY

If science represents what we know about nature, technology represents the practical use that we make of some things that we know. While scientific knowledge is never complete (although in designated fields it can be, if not completed, at least exhausted for periods of time) it is, in principle, constantly being purified and refined of error. One can imagine a time when, after centuries of diligent effort, all erroneous and irrelevant information will be winnowed away and the particles of pure scientific knowledge will stand—like what? a mountain, or an ocean, of granulated sugar? the gargantuan storehouse of a cosmic apothecary? a vast bank of computer tapes and programs? of Jorge Borges's *Library of*

Babel?[30] By contrast, technology is unlikely to be "pure" or "perfect," though it may be "honest," "simple," "elegant," "cheap," or "durable." Because much of the knowledge that is utilized in technology is not "scientific" but pragmatic. Something works and therefore is made and used, though *why* it works is not understood by those who make or use it and perhaps not by anyone (as fire, light, air, electricity, or gravity have been used for centuries without being understood as well, or as poorly, as they are today). Many aspects of technology are governed not by knowledge but by custom and economics.

That technology expresses the values, standards, and fashions, as well as the knowledge, of a people is evident not only in our diet, clothing, furniture, and architecture but also in the number, character, and design of our homes, cars, farms, cities, airports, battleships, schools, and coffins. That technology also reflects the social and economic structure of a society—its allocation of power and rewards—can be seen by examining the quality and distribution of common and precious goods, as an archeologist can discern the structure of a dead society by examining and mapping its remains. And, unlike science, which has a more contemporaneous quality, technology also reflects the (vanishing and surviving) heritage of the past, since no nation can daily replace its inventory of dams and roads, buildings and tools, mines and towns.

The transmogrification of technology

All of this may be obvious, but it is worth noting because of the follies that abound in discussions of technology. "Nothing can be so absurd but it has been said by some philosopher," Cicero remarked long before the advent of social science. Somehow, technology is conceived as a product of machines rather than men, not as good or bad things that are made well or poorly by good or bad men but as an independent historical force or even (since social scientists often view society as part of nature) as a force of nature. This common transmogrification of technology from the fallible product of fallible men into a demonic power for good or evil constitutes a suitable basis for a theology of science, the free enterprise system, or "scientific" socialism but not for intelligent analysis or practical action. The anthropological expression "material culture" is in many ways preferable to "technology," lacking the dangerous "ology" and conveying the intimate and generally quite pedestrian relationship between a people's way of life or "culture" and the artifacts and machines with which they surround themselves.

It is harder, even for a philosopher, to make a myth of "material culture."

What the philosophers and intellectuals have in mind when they glorify or, more often, excoriate "modern technology" are not the humdrum things we take for granted (though they were wonders in their day—wheels, glass, paper, books, planks, beds, matches, streets, sewers, cattle, wheat) but simply what is, or appears to be, new (the product of what is sometimes called "science" or "knowledge-based" industry—as if all industry were not based on science *and* history, knowledge *and* custom, what is mechanically and economically practical *and* what is culturally and politically acceptable).

The statistics are all against them, showing the heavy concentration of R & D expenditures in a few industries; common experience is against them, demonstrating that little or no "R" or "D" is necessary for the economic manufacture and distribution of many staples of life (salt, bread, milk, cutlery, clothing); and a closer inspection of R & D activities is against them, indicating how many are redundant, trivial, unproductive (serving to increase costs without improving quality), or unsuccessful on any reasonable and objective test of success. Two examples only need be cited of fruitless and wasteful R & D expenditures in "science-intensive" industries—airplanes and pharmaceuticals.

Before becoming party to such waste himself as Department of Defense comptroller, Charles Hitch observed: "It has been estimated that half the aircraft developed in the United States since [1945]—military and civilian—have been, in the vernacular of the industry, 'dogs'—not merely inferior to some other aircraft, but wrongly conceived, technically unsatisfactory, failures."[31] And after leaving office as commissioner of the Food and Drug Administration, James Goddard castigated the drug industry for such duplicative and "phony" R & D practices as "molecular manipulation" that "makes no contribution to medical science at all" but serves to circumvent competitors' patents, and animal "testing," the results of which "can be predicted in advance" and which "merely . . . flesh out the supporting bibliography that the law states must accompany any promotional or advertising literature in which therapeutic claims are made for [a] drug."[32]

Nonetheless, the ideologists of technology see both our doom and our salvation in ever more R & D, directed either away from or toward their hearts' desire: away from bombs (that is, war), supersonic planes (noise), and large automobiles (traffic jams); toward world peace, long life, pleasant work, good commuting, clean air, safe streets, and cool summers. Following the completion of Athelstan Spilhaus's experimental city in Minnesota, a climatic experiment will doubtless be undertaken to develop an American Garden of Eden. Indeed, I understand that a pilot project has already been initiated secretly by a great industrial laboratory in collaboration with the Livermore laboratory and the Hudson Institute. The water is carbonated; the vegetation, synthetic; the grass, genuine Bigelow; the insects, glass; the tree, photographically lifelike plastic walnut with steroid leaves rustling convincingly in the fan-blown, air-conditioned breeze. The serpent (to be banished from the domestic market but included in exports to communist countries) is beyond doubt the treasure of the piece. It moves exactly like a serpent and talks through a small battery-powered speaker, and its artificial fangs emit a poison deadlier than any known to snakes. Eve is a *Playboy* playmate and though, when merchandized, each man will be his own Adam, it is said that, during the developmental stages, Edward Teller and Herman Kahn themselves will play the part.

Why does an artificial Eden seem somehow macabre? Not because of any special technical difficulty of manufacture or any shortage of prospective Eves and Adams; periodically, zoos receive offers from persons, probably no madder than many of us, who would exhibit themselves; no fewer would sojourn in a prefabricated Eden, and price would be an incentive, not an obstacle, at Nieman-Marcus or Abercrombie and Fitch. Only if secrecy were obligatory or the purchaser were obliged to remain in Eden permanently would sales be affected. For what authentic American would want to be stuck forever in an old-fashioned Eden?

If there is any feature that has seemed fundamental to American society during these decades of our technological triumph, it has been technological change. Yet as any observer of women's skirts and automobile headlights knows, much technical change is stylistic rather than substantive. There is no ready way to estimate how much of our vast national expenditures on R & D goes for essentially stylistic aspects of science and engineering, but plainly a substantial amount does. It is safer to make minor changes to stimulate the seasonal turnover to which we have grown accustomed than to hazard substantial sums on radically new products.

Probably the largest volume of technical change, in the military and space industries, involves little financial risk because the cost of development is borne by the government, which provides an assured market for the final product. These truly research-intensive industries are economically aberrant islands of socialism in a sea of free enterprise; and though their scale renders them important to the national economy, their high-technology products have less obvious effect on our daily lives than newspapers or razor blades.

The technology of daily life

If we discount unsuccessful or redundant R & D, military and space R & D, and merely stylistic R & D as having little fundamental influence on our way of life, what kind of R & D, then, has such an influence? A reasonable answer is: that which improves the quality or durability or lowers the cost of products or services used and needed by many people—food, clothing, housing, transportation, communications, and medical services are among the most important; educational, sanitary, and police services, and recreational and cultural facilities may also be added, as well as any technical changes that affect the quality of our environment at home, at work, or in the local or national community.

It is difficult to find a satisfactory objective measure of "the quality of our environment" or even of the goods in daily use at home or work. According to one test suggested by an economist, a panel given two Sears Roebuck catalogs for, let us say, 1925 and 1965, and asked from which they would prefer to equip their house with a given sum such as $1,000 (making no allowance for inflation) invariably prefers the more recent catalog, thus "proving" what we are in any case disposed to believe—that dollar for dollar the quality of consumer goods has been improving. There are numerous other indications of technological improvements that affect our daily lives, such as the number and quality of telephones, radios, airplanes, automobiles, roads, eyeglasses, hospitals, and toilets—the favorite items of *World Almanac* international comparisons. And, insofar as statistics of the average standard of living, income, national product, or wealth are related to the average "quality of life" or, at least, the quality of that technology which is commonly available to the ordinary citizen, we might almost accept the common opinion that in the "low" technology of daily life as well as the "high" technology of war and space, most technical change has been for the better.

Almost—but not quite.

That the quality of many common goods and services has improved may be accepted, although it is not difficult to cite examples of those which appear to have deteriorated. Some maintain that the art of repair and maintenance is dying on the altar of mass production industries that find replacement more profitable. And a recent

Wall Street Journal article, "Caveat Emptor—Many People Complain the Quality of Products is Deteriorating Rapidly," began:

> Roofs leak. Shirts shrink. Toys maim. Toasters don't toast. Mowers don't mow. Kites don't fly. Radios emit no sounds, and television sets and cameras yield no pictures.
> Isn't *anything* well made these days?
> Yes, some things are. A man at Consumers Union, the publisher of Consumer Reports magazine, says that refrigerators are better than ever, for instance, and that wringer washing machines are becoming much safer. But he agrees that shoddy goods abound, and Wall Street Journal reporters' talks with Americans from coast to coast indicate that quality of merchandise is worse than ever.[33]

But let us forget the difficulty and expense of getting good car repairs and shirt ironing, the decline of skilled crafts, the unreliability of home deliveries, the carelessness of plumbers, electricians, waiters, and garbagemen. Let us allow that the quality of most common merchandise has improved, if not from year to year then from generation to generation: that automobiles and tractors are better than horses, refrigerators than ice boxes, electric lights than gas lights, central heat than coal stoves, indoor plumbing than outdoor privies, and penicillin than prayer.

Let us also disregard the problem of statistical averages that can conceal some of our most distressing domestic problems, because our average standard of living, of education, and of community amenities can rise nationally while falling in the central city.

Grave doubts must still persist about the quality of our technical progress and its social consequences.

One set of doubts is aroused by portentous technologies such as thermonuclear weapons and doomsday machines; uniquely powerful computers which can remember what everyone has done, operate factories, or gain fractional advantages in stock market or other critical affairs; instruments of genetic, biological, or mental manipulation; and other horrific products that could enslave men. Hydrogen bombs are assuredly with us, and more economic weapons of comparable deadliness will doubtless be developed. Each man has his own nightmares, and it is as hard for mere facts to erase unfounded fears as to instill those which do not register. However, the fears of a computer-controlled society with mass unemployment, enforced leisure, and key public decisions in the hands of an elite are premature, and those of mad geneticists are even more fanciful.[34]

Fortunately, truly portentous technologies are rarer in life than in science fiction, although even one, such as the technology of nuclear weaponry, can pose vast, intractable problems. Yet some lessons, if little comfort, can be derived from the largely unsuccessful history of international efforts to control nuclear weapons. It has proven easier, but not easy, to control the testing and proliferation of weapons than their laboratory development. The same may prove true of many potentially dangerous or noxious domestic technologies; and, of course, we should expect more success with controls that the government can impose than with those requiring the agreement of hostile powers.

Most of our technical problems arise less from a few isolated technologies than from the cacophonous assemblage of the whole. Individually, our automobiles, roads, skyscrapers, telephones, and power stations may be the best in the world; but in the center of the average city they conspire to make an awful mess. Each tailpipe, chimney, garbage pail, and dump may be the most convenient and economic way to dispose of the exhaust of a car, factory, household, and town, but all together can make life highly unpleasant in metropolitan areas. Open-pit mining, open-forest stripping, open-sea fishing, dumping sewage in open rivers, and running telephone and power lines through open country may each be the cheapest method of its kind, but the economies of this generation can impose onerous expenses on the next.

Although we recognize the systemic nature of our technological problems, their technical and human sources are so complex and our knowledge and foresight so inadequate that we have been unable to deal with them comprehensively. Our technological policies have, accordingly, been determined mainly on an *ad hoc* basis[35] and have been focused on immediate, not future, choices. And, despite valiant efforts which deserve further encouragement and may achieve modest success, that will long be true. Congress's constituency is alive today, not in the year 2000. The technical problems thrust upon government for decision are sufficiently numerous and troublesome without searching for others that lie patiently in the background. Should oil drilling be resumed off Santa Barbara and nuclear testing near Las Vegas or Amchitka? Should chemical mace be used on rioters? Should the laws on marihuana be relaxed while those on other drugs are tightened? What should be done about the supersonic plane, manned planetary exploration, breeder reactors, urban transportation, interstate highways, airport congestion, air pollution, garbage disposal, tobacco subsidies, multiphasic health screening, educational TV, venereal disease, birth control, and gun control? Federal, state, and local agencies are called upon frequently, if not constantly, for decisions on these and countless other issues of technological policy.

The power and the will

Through the powers of taxation, regulation, and licensure, if not of direct purchase or subsidy, government agencies can exercise as much or as little control as they wish over the development and deployment of new and old products and services. The government has ample power to control technology in the public interest. What is lacking is not the power but the will and/or the knowledge of what is indeed in the public interest. It is also likely that a government which in both its executive and legislative branches is organized to represent and serve special interests lacks a central machinery adequate to identify and serve the large common interest.

That the political will is often lacking to regulate industry, to set minimum product standards, or to stimulate the development and production of new products better suited to current needs can hardly be disputed. This is the argument for the solution of our technological problems often advanced by consumer representatives. It concentrates on technological problems for which technical solutions or improvements are known but not widely available, often because there appears to be no special profit, goad, or other incentive for industry to adopt the improvements. Ralph Nader has offered many examples in his criticism of industry's failure to produce a safer car and *Consumer Reports* provides innumerable other examples of the failure of industry to manufacture (and of the failure of government regulatory agencies to require the manufacture of) appliances as durable, safe, effective, or cheap as would be possible if all models incorporated the better features of some. While it is unrealistic to expect any automobile, washing machine, or refrigerator to contain the best of all possible features, it is more reasonable to expect a higher general standard of safety *or* durability *or* economy, to describe these performance standards honestly, and to offer the consumer an informed and meaningful product choice.

If an industry's profitability is due to its heaping upon taxpayers, consumers, and insurance companies the costs of repairing or enduring its damages (such as automobile defects, lung cancer, and soot-soiled clothes) it is reasonable for the government to redistribute these costs more equitably. An already profitable industry can thus be taxed, regulated, embarrassed, and cajoled into improving its products. Insofar as the harmful effects of a new product can be anticipated, industry can be required to correct them from the outset. But, of course, the inability to anticipate these effects is a root cause of our technological troubles.

Nicholas Golovin of the Office of Science and Technology has suggested that the shoe be put on the other foot: that instead of the government having to demonstrate adverse effects before regulating a new technology, industry has to demonstrate that the technology does *not* have harmful effects before widespread marketing is permitted. Thus, manufacturers of a supersonic plane would have to show that it would *not* lead to unacceptable noise levels before the plane would be licensed, as manufacturers already have to demonstrate that the location and design of a nuclear power reactor meets minimum safety standards before the Atomic Energy Commission will license its construction. Such control over the proliferation of new technology is needed, Golovin argues, because, due to the increasing rate of technological change and the speed with which a new product can now be introduced, "the number and variety of ways in which new technology can damage the environment and harm the population is also growing explosively."[36] The difficulty of demonstrating what a technology will *not* do is apparent. True, Golovin would require this demonstration only if "technically plausible arguments" have been made "that the mass introduction of a new product or process will tend to degrade environmental characteristics important to physical and psychological well-being;"[37] but the problem of accurately defining all such characteristics, let alone of showing that a new technology would not "degrade" them, alone or in conjunction with other technologies, would remain. The net effect (and, presumably, the basic objective) would probably be to inhibit the introduction of new technology, but that would depend on how the government was organized to review technological proposals, for experience has shown that regulatory agencies can be as sympathetic to industry as promotional ones.

Central government organization

Which brings us again to the matter of government organization and, more particularly, central government organization, since if the separate executive departments and agencies represent and serve special constituencies, who but the executive Office of the President and the Congress as a body can speak for the nation as a whole? Occasionally, this principle may have to be modified;

if presidential and congressional staff do not always speak for "the nation," they are at least in a position to advocate different policies than those of the executive agencies and to subject agency proposals to fresh critical scrutiny. Thus, the Office of Science and Technology and the President's Science Advisory Committee have been consistently partisan to basic research and academic science; but they have dealt more critically with many proposals for the development of new technology emerging from the Defense Department, the Atomic Energy Commission, and other agencies. Mere location in the executive Office of the President is no guarantee of wisdom; time may prove the decisions made there either more right or more wrong than those advocated by a "parochial" agency. But if the White House staff do their job well, their decisions should reflect a broader range of factors than those of agencies with narrower responsibilities, and the net outcome should be more in the public interest.

That, in any event, is the thinking behind a multitude of proposals to establish in the executive Office of the President one or more bodies to evaluate new technologies, to set policies and coordinate programs in various fields of technology (national security, space, oceanography, environmental quality, and urban affairs already have their own presidential- or cabinet-level councils), to formulate national goals (a White House staff on national goals is being formed), to assess the status of the nation's science and technology (the National Science Board has already initiated an annual report on the former), and to evaluate the social state of the nation. In some versions, responsibility would be assigned to an existent body, but the proposals all reflect dissatisfaction with the way in which the executive office, and especially the Office of Science and Technology, has performed some part of its job. (Nothing is less noteworthy than for the Congress to solve governmental problems by reorganizing the executive, while White House staff would solve them by reorganizing the Congress).

It is a mistake to believe that government reorganization by itself solves any problem; the substantive technological problems and their social and economic repercussions remain, regardless of how federal or local authorities are organized to deal with them. The fight for a place at the summit of government is, in part, a fight to direct public and congressional attention to designated issues. In part, it is a fight for a second chance to influence policy. Those who are satisfied with departmental policies are decidedly cool to their reexamination by the White House. And Democratic congressional committees with strong ties to established bureaus may suddenly discover that their (and, in their view, the public's) interests are better served by expansive bureau proposals than by those of an economy-minded Republican White House staff. Finally, it is an effort to introduce a greater degree of consistency and rationality (or, as the charter of the House Committee on Government Operations puts it, "effectiveness and efficiency") into the discordant, overlapping government programs. Thus, some of the same congressmen who have urged the establishment of new evaluation of policy machinery in the executive office have also sought greater utilization of the social sciences in the evaluation and the formulation of governmental technical and social policies.

The attention-getting and second-chance functions of an executive office agency organized by statute and responsible for reporting to the public and the Congress are indicated by Senator Walter Mondale's dissatisfaction with President Nixon's recent announcement about the formation of a National Goals Research Staff. Though the functions of forecasting social trends and preparing an annual social report that this staff has been assigned are similar to those that Mondale has advocated for a Council of Social Advisers, he has criticized the move as an "inhouse effort" lacking the visibility of a council and a counterpart congressional committee which would be set up, under his proposal, to hold hearings on council reports.[38]

Technology assessment board[39]

Representative Emilio Daddario's suggestion that an independent Technology Assessment Board of five members be appointed by the President with the consent of the Senate, with a General Advisory Council also appointed by the President, is bound to receive further attention when the two experimental technology assessment reports commissioned by his Science and Astronautics Committee from the National Academies of Science and Engineering are published. The functions of the board would be to "(1) make a continuing assessment of applied research and technology, current and potential; (2) identify areas or aspects of applied research and technology which may be or may become detrimental to the social, economic, international, and other interests of the United States; and (3) determine and recommend how such detriments might be avoided and inform the public accordingly."[40]

Plainly, these functions are too broad to be realized and, in practice, the board would have to concentrate attention on a few selected technologies. If these are too important, the board would risk major political confrontations that could damage its reputation for political independence; if they are too unimportant, it could quickly achieve a reputation for inconsequentiality. Technologies of middle-range importance, or of larger potential importance but with weak proponents, would offer a good compromise.

As with Golovin's proposal, a too-negative outlook presents another danger. Daddario has recognized that assessment "could easily become a stifling influence on progress if the dangers are emphasized rather than the potentials for good."[41] But emphasis upon "the potentials for good" is a promotional function. How can an independent review board respond to serious hazards, to which countermeasures are not apparent, but by calling for additional R & D to overcome them? The fear that overly critical assessment by an overly powerful agency might lead to the unwarranted suppression of new technology has been expressed by Philip Handler:

> Years of caution, the unpleasant consequences of error—such as approval of a drug which later proves to have serious, but unforeseen, consequences—have engendered within the [Food and Drug Administration] the most cautionary of attitudes. The hero of the Administration almost necessarily now, is he who has prevented the introduction into society, as a drug or food additive, [of] some material which would have had untoward consequences. . . . Were aspirin or beer unknown and invented tomorrow . . . , I doubt that either could find approval in the Food and Drug Administration.[42]

It is interesting to note that, while speculating about aspirin and beer, Handler says of thalidomide only that it "could not have been anticipated and no stepped up biological requirement would have detected the problem which finally emerged." It is also interesting to note that the day after resigning his post, HEW Assistant Secretary for Health and Scientific Affairs Philip Lee charged Handler with "at least a possible conflict of interest" because, as president-elect of the National Academy of Sciences, he was also a director of the Squibb, Beechnut drug firm.[42] Shortly thereafter, former FDA Commissioner Goddard criticized the academy's Drug Research Board as being "composed of the same individuals who work elsewhere in the marketplace. The Board represents . . . a limited forum in which consensus is developed for the [drug] Establishment. . . ."[43] I note these charges not to take either side in the dispute but to indicate that absolute political independence is a dream, not a reality, either in or out of the government. The academy, the nation's most august and influential scientific body, is supposed to provide the government with "independent" technical advice, and Daddario has periodically called upon it for such advice. But here are government officials charging that the academy is in league with the drug industry, whereas they, in turn, are charged with frustrating that industry's innovative efforts. No mortal men can escape one or the other charge of being either sympathetic, or hostile, to the industry being assessed.

Countering the danger of suppressing useful innovation is the practical reality that an assessment board must rely in good measure upon data supplied by the developers of a new technology. The Daddario bill would give the board power to subpoena witnesses, records, and documents on penalty of contempt; to hold hearings under oath; and to publish "technological and other information."[45] But developers can hardly be expected to furnish as complete documentation of the drawbacks as of the advantages of their technology, or to reveal proprietary details which might be useful to competitors. Accordingly, the board would either have to base its analysis largely upon information selected by advocates, or invest substantial sums in obtaining its own data (as, for example, the large sums spent by the Food and Drug Administration and the Consumers' Union in their own testing laboratories). Where very large sums have already been invested in a development on the scale of a supersonic plane, a new type of power plant, or a high-speed railroad, there seems little alternative to inspection of the developer's own facility and/or the data yielded by it.

Technology assessment and related efforts to protect the welfare of crowded populations dependent upon interlinked, vulnerable services represent the emergence of a more critical attitude to the virtues of technological innovation comparable to that which has been increasingly directed at the virtues of basic scientific research. And it is no coincidence that this attitude has arisen at a time when government expenditures for both development and research have been leveling off, for the practical function of such criticism is to help in the stricter review of proposed expenditures that must now take place.

Excessive faith

But it is as wrong to infer from this attitude any Luddite hostility to new technology as for scientists to see know-nothing anti-intellectualism in appropriations that rise by 5 instead of 15 percent a year. On the contrary, the nation continues to display an excessive faith in the power of science, reason, and rational technology to solve national problems. Evidence of this can be found on every hand: in the yearning for technologies to transform urban life, glowing hopes for "systems" solutions to complicated technical as well as social problems, mounting efforts to forecast the future, the upsurge of interest in the social sciences, and the attempt to introduce more systematic procedures into the choice, evaluation, and budgeting of governmental programs. Science has become a powerful element of American ideology, and new technology remains as gratifying to adults as new toys are gratifying to their children.

The faith is excessive not because the achievements of science and technology have been inconsiderable but because technical disciplines can solve only technical problems, whereas our persistent national problems are palpably more human than technical. Machines are as innocent as ideas: it all depends on how they are used. I favor both gun controls and safer cars. Nonetheless, there is truth in the gun dealers' slogan that "guns don't kill—people do," and in auto manufacturers' claim that defective driving causes more accidents than defective cars.

If our most important problems are social and political, not technological, then, with due deference to Alvin Weinberg's insights about "technological fixes" to social problems,[46] they will be alleviated or aggravated mainly by social and economic, not technical, measures. The excessive importance widely assigned to technology is a reflection of the excessive importance Americans attach to material things and of a hope to avoid the sacrifices and dislocations that would be entailed by more direct social action. The implicit hope is that "new technology" can preserve the status quo—that cheap housing can keep the poor content, clean air can keep cities viable, and educational gadgets can keep our schools functioning without major increases in taxes on the well-to-do or major shifts in the political power of whites and blacks, producers and consumers, urban and rural areas. I believe that hope is futile—either we must deal more directly with our social problems or we will continue to live with them. In public affairs, as in the private market, it is still roughly true that you get what you pay for.

Conclusion

Briefly, to evaluate government policies toward the development of new technology is almost impossible. The subject is too vast and the degree of governmental responsibility for various technological sectors too varied to permit a concise and meaningful discussion of policy alternatives comparable to those that readily arise in government policy toward academic research. Virtually all academic research is conducted by a hundred institutions and half by twenty; and all would like to receive more money from the government, with fewer strings attached. By contrast, industry is not merely divided but utterly fractionated in its attitudes toward government R & D programs. The aerospace and munitions industries are heavily dependent upon government both for R & D funds and for their market. The agricultural, medical, and nuclear power industries are heavily dependent upon government for R & D but not for a market. Much of the rest of American industry has traditionally received—and wanted—little R & D money from the government, because such money does not come as a free gift. It opens company books to government auditors and company performance to governmental and congressional scrutiny. And, as R & D findings belong to the government and, via the government, to the public, they may also (subject to agency patent and information policies) become available to competing companies. The government does not simply supply money for any R & D a firm may like to do; it has its own idea, or its own preference among the ideas offered to it, about the kind that should be conducted.

In short, government R & D programs violate the traditional rules of a free private marketplace. Inherently, such programs are a reflection on the ability of the free enterprise system to meet all the needs of the American people. As Congressman Daddario observed in arguing for a mechanism to assess the value of new technology by standards other than its immediate profitability, "the marketplace does not take into account all the important values to society as a whole."[47] And there are enough alumni of the free enterprise school to contest governmental intervention in civilian technology as un-American, socialist, or worse. It is instructive to recall that the modest program of R & D aid to textile and construction technologies proposed by the Department of Commerce in 1962 was rejected by Congress and by many representatives of the very industries it was designed to aid. One industrialist castigated the proposal as "a threat to our American way of life,"[48] and the Construction and Community Development Committee of the U.S. Chamber of Commerce declared:

> The construction industry leaders of business firms and associations have not been asked if they want a centralization of responsibility for research and development vested in the federal government. . . . [The proposal] makes no contribution to the private enterprise system. . . . [It] adds more government intervention and more government spending at a time when less government intervention and lower levels of federal spending are most needed by the construction industry.[49]

Proposed R & D programs in housing and urban technology, similarly, were repeatedly defeated before Congress approved a modest program for 1968.[50]

The social scientist is supposed to be able to help the public to understand any social problem (especially ideological ones) and the policy analyst to come up with clear recommendations on any issue, including the future of mankind or, at least, of American civilization. Therefore, to discharge my responsibilities, I should express my unhesitant conclusions about the course that government policy should take toward civilian technology; but to remain honest, I must insist that these are only opinions.

The failures of our civilian technology cluster in unprofitable or unforeseen tailings and interstices of industry and particularly in the technical structure of underfunded public services. They represent failures of the private enterprise system; failures of the private citizenry to uphold communal rather than personal values, goods, and services; and failures of political leadership at all levels to demand and obtain from private interests the powers and resources necessary to defend the larger public interest. Detroit produces only cars; the traffic jams are produced by taxpayers who will not allocate sufficient funds for efficient public transportation, and by governments too timid to tax, regulate, and police traffic so as to prevent them. Housing R & D will never lead to free housing, nor can public or private construction await any particular advance in the perpetual evolution of technology. Just as the military must always be prepared to fight with existing weapons while attempting to develop better ones, so the nation must make intelligent use of existing technology while attempting to improve it. The development of new technology should not substitute for needed public works and social action.

However, more R & D will also be needed to improve the quality of technology in the public sector and in those private sectors that befoul the public scene. As a practical matter, public funds will be needed to stimulate that R & D in both sectors, but particularly in the former. Stricter standards will also be necessary, their strictness being proportionate to the hazards and the costs they impose upon the public.

A technology assessment board should help to render noxious technologies more fragrant and raw technologies more mellow, but too much should not be expected of it, for, to be effective, such a board must also be highly selective. The Office of Science and Technology should also be strengthened, and it should more frequently take the initiative to weld concerted policies out of scattered public and private efforts to improve the urban environment.

These and other measures will help but, in a larger perspective, they are palliatives rather than solutions. If a nation's technology represents the material expression of its social and economic values, then the excesses of technology can only be subdued together with the excesses of society. Insofar as our technological problems stem from our rampantly expanding population, economy, and industries, which have previously known few frontiers and brooked few restraints, their more lasting resolution may require that we foresake some of our most characteristically American habits and philosophy for those of the more stable European populations we have long spurned. As our own population grows more crowded and eventually stabilizes, the notion of limited frontiers and resources may grow more acceptable, and with it the notion of human limitations, of ecological and human balance, of restraint on the size of cities, families, and automobiles, even of restraint in production, advertising, ambition, and change for the sake of change.

This is, to be sure, an idyllic—some will say, an idle—fancy, and one man's idyll can be another's hell. But I would like at least to imagine (if I cannot quite believe) that one day our restless, raucous, rambunctious people will live in greater harmony, that our technologies will be more happily and willingly orchestrated, and that we will live at peace with ourselves in a natural, not artificial, Eden.

Reflections on Public Science Policy and Administration in a Troubled Milieu

DWIGHT WALDO
Albert Schweitzer Professor in
   Humanities
Program in Public Administration
Syracuse University

   For America the sixties was a decade of rising social turbulence. The well-informed and the ill-informed, Left, Right, and Center, generally unite in the expectation that the seventies will bring more, and perhaps increasing, turbulence. This essay seeks the implications of such a milieu for making and administering policy for technoscience.
   As shown by the several references to campus turmoil, the preceding authors are aware of the changing environment of technoscience, and often seek the implications of various manifestations of turbulence for the topics they discuss. Harold Orlans is especially aware of rapid and radical change as he discusses government policy development. But I shall reverse the perspective: Given the turbulent environment, what then follows? I shall say some trite things, because they are important; and some foolish things, because in predicting the future this is inescapable. But I shall hope nevertheless to open to further inquiry some matters of crucial importance to technoscience and its direction.

The argument I shall be making is to these propositions, though not with the rigidity they suggest:

> That the causes of increasing turbulence are real, consisting of a tangled skein of facts, dangers, and problems and that turbulence will increase, not decrease, in the future
>
> That technoscience is deeply implicated *as the cause* of present and anticipated perils and problems and is also *perceived* as the cause, which is itself a form of reality
>
> That technoscience is also related and perceived as related, positively or negatively, to the reduction of perils and the resolution of problems
>
> That given the real and/or perceived relationship of technoscience to the perils and problems to which increasing turbulence is a response, the milieu of technoscience policy and administration will become increasingly unstable, problematic, contentious, and politicized
>
> That functions and roles in technoscience policy making and administration will need substantial redefinition and change
>
> That the direction of redefinition and change must be the addition of knowledge, attributes, and skills
>
> That what is now needed is nothing less than knowledge of how to survive and be creative, wise, and effective in a turbulent milieu

The use of "technoscience" in title and text is deliberate. I am aware of the distinctions made between, and the arguments concerning the relationships of, science and technology or pure science and applied science. But for the most part these distinctions will not be relevant to my argument.

AN ENVIRONMENT OF CRITICAL PROBLEMS, QUICKENING CHANGE, AND INCREASING TURBULENCE

It is hardly news that we live in an environment that is problem ridden, disturbed, and disturbing. We need, however, to take note of its main features and dimensions as a necessary prelude to understanding the present and future guidance of technoscience. Staats and Carey's statement, "if the scientific community attributes its recent frustrations to either the accidents of politics or a temporary budget crunch, it will miss the point," indicates that there is indeed much missing-of-the-point. A rough and incomplete catalog of threats and/or problems follows.

At the global level

> A threat of violent encounter of a type which would annihilate a sizable part of humanity immediately and much (some say all) of humanity ultimately, certainly destroying "civilization as we know it"
>
> A population explosion threatening at best misery, and at worst extinction, for hundreds of millions of human beings
>
> The depletion, or depletion relative to expectations or needs, of the earth's unrenewable resources
>
> The contamination and degradation of the biosphere, making life increasingly unpleasant, danger-filled, and short
>
> A revolution of rising expectations by reason of hundreds of millions of people on all continents expecting to have more of the material goods of life—a new and yeasty ingredient in world history
>
> A division of the world into more than sixscore nation-states, each nominally an independent decision-making and administering unit; superimposed upon these numerous nation-states is a *de facto* division of much world power and influence between competing and more or less hostile "super-states" and their ideologies and systems because no effective *world* political-economic-social system now exists

At the national level

> A racial-ethnic problem that centers upon the status and ambitions of blacks but reaches out in concentric circles of involvement, action, interaction, and reaction
>
> The decay of the central city and beyond it, urban blight and suburban sprawl: the problem of finding a design, technical and human, to provide for increasing, and increasingly large, agglomerations of people
>
> The generation gap, presenting in this era a chronic problem in social mechanics, dealing with the "continuous barbarian invasion" of the young, which has assumed acute proportions

with profound implications for all primary and secondary societal institutions

The proper scope and direction of official force, centrally the military and the police, seen by some as a problem of the military-industrial complex and by others as a problem of the nonmilitary-industrial complex

Constantly accelerating technoscientific change, with resultant disorientation, even anomie, and what could be called "future shock"

An interrelated crisis in values and crisis of authority

The delivery of promised and expected social services for more social equity

Maintaining order and/or relevance and effectiveness in educational institutions

Patently, the list of serious problems could be extended indefinitely: escalating crime and lawlessness, actual and potential destruction of privacy, an information explosion and communications overload, drug use and narcotics addiction, unemployment and inflation, transportation inadequacies and crises, sexual inequalities, refuse disposal and/or resource recycling. And other serious problems are rapidly approaching, including weather modification and genetic engineering. The listing is simply a sampling; my categories are open to challenge, real distinctions between world and national problems are impossible, and many of these problems interrelate and intertwine. Problems in a large and complex civilization parallel its size and complexity, or pessimistically, progressively exceed them.

My purpose in this recitation of problems which are well known by all literate persons is to make it unmistakably clear that the conditions under which technoscientific enterprises operate are certain to become more turbulent, with resulting implications for making and administering technoscientific policies. The causes of turbulence are *there*; and it is not simply that there is a tangle of interrelated critical problems: an adequate institutional, emotional-intellectual apparatus does not exist for their definition, much less their solution. In addition, what is one person's solution is often another person's problem, and vice versa. Thus USSR solutions are USA problems, and the reverse is also true. Thus the Catholic Church has its solutions to problems of birth control, but to others the Church is a part of the problem. Thus an antiballistic safeguard system solves a grave security problem for some, but creates a grave security problem for others. Thus to some, hippies are drop-outs from the desperately earnest task of making a civilization work, but to others they are the hope of the future.

Technoscientific factors, far from being peripheral or incidental, are at the *center* of these problems because they are deeply involved as the cause and are centrally at issue in proposed remedies. There are of course many analysts who see the technoscientific as *the* cause of social change, but for this discussion, it is enough to recognize that technoscience is involved as a complex cause-effect-solution and is widely so perceived. The worldwide revolution of rising expectations, for example, is unthinkable without its technoscientific causes. Now there is also a growing counterrevolution of declining expectations—a phrase to designate the movement to save the environment, with all it implies for reducing material consumption and changing life-styles. This counterrevolution is a response to technoscientific factors and in them finds its solutions. Clearly, in the confrontation of the two revolutions we cannot escape turbulence, and we shall be lucky to avoid chaos.

AN ENVIRONMENT OF INTELLECTUAL-SOCIAL CHANGE

I wish to discuss now factors in intellectual-social change that stand between the turbulent environment resulting from the above problems and technoscientific enterprises. These factors relate in a complex way to both, and again I must risk belaboring the obvious and oversimplifying the complex to reveal important emerging considerations for the direction of technoscience.

A new romanticism

There is presently under way a change in mood, thought, and life-style similar in many ways to the romantic reaction of the late eighteenth and early nineteenth centuries. Romanticism as a reaction to the classicism and rationalism of the eighteenth century exalted feeling above reason, the senses above the mind, and individual spontaneity, creativity, and self-fulfillment above convention and rules. The romantics saw man as inherently good but corrupted by bad institutions, natural man as better than civilized man, simple man as superior to sophisticated man. They often sought fulfillment in new forms of community and sometimes in revolutionary activity in an attempt to break away from traditions and start anew on sounder foundations.

The parallels to contemporary developments are many and striking. It is beyond my purpose to dwell on them at length, but in the West and especially in the United States parallels exist: in music, in art, in literature, in drama, in philosophy, in manners and morals, and in social and political movements. Of course, one risks sounding foolish in pushing the analogies too far since it is possible that another, and more pessimistic, comparison would be the contemporary United States with second- and third-century Rome. But in what follows I shall assume the existence of a movement akin in its nature and import to that of the romantic era.

The import is clear: resistance to and trouble for scientific-technological enterprises since science emphasizes rationality and discipline, mind as opposed to emotion. It is, or is perceived as, demanding, impersonal, and abstract. Its spawn and ally is technology: cold, impersonal, artificial, meretricious, dehumanized, and dehumanizing. Both science and technology, in a creator-and-created relationship, are a part of the establishment. And the establishment is the enemy. It causes wars, supports brutalizing tyrannies, destroys and pollutes the earth, permits needless deprivation and suffering, squeezes out the joy of living in a mad, senseless scramble for power, wealth, and material goods—and at the same time it professes noble ideals and even claims divine sanction. It is instructive to remember that Lavoisier got the guillotine: "The Revolution has no need of scientists."

Of course, I oversimplify and perhaps exaggerate. But 400,000 young people did *not* gather at Oak Ridge to celebrate science, nor at Cape Kennedy to celebrate technology, nor in Washington to celebrate American policies and power, nor on Madison Avenue to celebrate the American standard of living. They gathered in a cow pasture to celebrate individual and collective release from or opposition to the establishment. My reading is that the overwhelming majority at Woodstock thought the moon landing was not a triumph of science, technology, and the human spirit, but at best senseless gadgeteering, at worst criminal folly. Some observers thought they saw at Woodstock the lineaments of a future America or—in the assertions by participants and their spiritual fellow travelers—of a "Woodstock Nation."

A few years ago, impressed with the growing importance and scope of science in American life, I predicted half-seriously that by the 1980s we would elect a scientist-turned-politician as President. But in a time in which a Norman Mailer, not an Isidor I. Rabi, seeks the mayoralty of New York City, I withdraw the prediction.

An antiorganizational revolution

In 1953 Kenneth Boulding published *The Organizational Revolution*. At base, his argument was that we live in a period of greatly increased "organizationness"; that for a number of historical socioeconomic reasons we are experiencing an increase in the number of organizations, the size of organizations, and the intensity of organizational phenomena. I suggest that an appropriate and needed book at the present time is one entitled: *The Antiorganizational Revolution,* arguing that we have entered a period in which the factors of erosion and decay in organizational life are in ascendancy.

An abundant and complex organizational growth depends on support and encouragement from the socioeconomic substructure and because such support and encouragement existed, there was an efflorescence of organizational life, which reached a climax in mid-century. Recently, however, the basic social institutions are changing toward a less supportive direction, and various forces in our national life are either indifferent or hostile toward organizational phenomena.

Much of the work of Max Weber was concerned with tracing the supportive structure for the bureaucratic mode of organization, which he regarded as the most rational and efficient way for human being to relate to accomplish specific goals. As he viewed it, bureaucratic organization rose and flourished only in a complex social milieu, with relatively advanced religious, economic, educational, and legal institutions. Bureaucracy assumed and needed a certain type of personality structure. To function optimally in a bureaucratic organization, members must have the ability to accept and impose discipline and an orientation toward punctuality, efficiency, productivity, and "bureaucratic virtues" generally. Such qualities, while they may be reinforced in a bureaucratic organization, are basically the products of society—first of all of the basic societal unity, the family.

Some argue persuasively that other types of organization are more appropriate to and more efficient for other social arrangements, life-styles, and personality structures. Perhaps this is true, and perhaps we are moving, and should move, away from bureaucratic modes of organization. But for the present purposes the argument is simply that if there are currently significant changes in the societal substructure for our predominantly bureaucratic organizations, then these organizations are experiencing, and will further experience, stress and change.

It is clear that many of the currents and events that constitute the new romanticism are a part of, and further, an antiorganizational revolution. Organization is the establishment and the establishment is organization. Specific organizations are instruments of evil: they invent fiendish devices for killing, force young people into the dangerous and obscene business of war, plunder and destroy the natural world, threaten to destroy all life—and educate for and justify all this. More, the very "organizationness" of our society, apart from the evils of specific organizations, narrows and cripples, takes away our freedom and spontaneity, squeezes life dry. So "drop out," destroy the establishment, or at least *reform* the establishment. However, these three alternatives are not necessarily mutually exclusive, and probably the majority of college-educated youths are adopting a pattern of life that in part reflects a combination of all three.

A change in values and interests

The new romanticism implies significant shifts in values and interests in many disciplines, in philosophy, and in the enterprises of science and technology. There is a shift *away from* "scientism," positivism, and neutrality of or indifference to values and *toward* "policy," humanism, and concern for and orientation to values; in still broader if more uncertain and arguable terms, the shift is from the abstract and rational toward the concrete and affectual.

These trends are unmistakable in political science and public administration—the academic-professional field in which I am a card-carrying member. In both fields youth and New Left movements have been directed against an establishment in the professional organizations considered part of the larger establishment, with all that is thereby implied. There is an accompanying revolt against positivism and "scientism" (though most would probably still deny that it is against science), and a cry for personal sensitivity, human concern, social reform—and perhaps, political activism. These movements have not succeeded in formally capturing the professional organizations, nor are they likely to. But formal capture is unnecessary and irrelevant; more gradual, subtle, social-organizational processes are operating to effect a shift in the direction of these new forces.

Somewhat similar movements are in progress, as I understand it, in anthropology, sociology, and even economics. They also exist in psychology and social psychology, where there is a vogue, especially among the young, for the personal-affective and the "humanist" psychologies. The professional schools are similarly affected—and not just social welfare and public health, but engineering, architecture, law, and even medicine.

In philosophy the various varieties of positivism, while they have scarcely disappeared, have become more refined and more defensive, and are increasingly perceived as arid or irrelevant; and phenomenology, existentialism, and still newer schools and trends have moved toward the center of the stage. Philosophy of science is of central relevance. Here, as I read the situation, there is less dogmatism and more flexibility than a generation ago; most important, the conception of natural science as a value-free activity is now suspect or openly challenged. The doubt and ferment spill over into—and even flow from—the very centers of hard scientific activity; such publications as *Science* and the *Bulletin of the Atomic Scientists* show much new concern for the social relevance of science and technology. Indeed, they show more concern with social problems generally than many journals of social science. The end of innocence which atomic physicists experienced with Hiroshima is now a widely-felt phenomenon, as evidenced by the call from Massachusetts Institute of Technology for a national "day of reflection" for all scientific researchers.

These matters I have discussed relative to an environment of social-intellectual change are of course interrelated with the causes and manifestations of problems previously inventoried. They are also interrelated with the complex of technoscientific enterprises for which they form the immediate intellectual, social, and institutional matrix.

PREDICTIONS AND SPECULATIONS

What are the implications of the increasingly turbulent milieu for making and administering technoscience policy and administration? Can one do more than admit the fact of change and uncertainty? I think so. That the turbulence does exist and that it has certain known qualities make some predictions possible, with a large measure of confidence. Prediction soon must give way to speculation; but speculation, too, has its uses in preparing for a problematic future. In presenting my thoughts on the future I intend, for the most part, to predict. But at times this is a literary convenience because the points at which predictions become speculations are often not clear even to myself.

Pro- and anti-technoscience contention

In the period ahead there will be increasing contention between pro- and anti-technoscience forces. Concluding a long, secular buildup of science and technology, the last generation has seen its sharp upward spurt, some claimed its logarithmic progression. Recall the much-quoted, portentous statement of a decade ago: ninety percent of the scientists who ever lived are living *now*. But presently there is a vigorous counterrevolution to the scientist's image, ranging from neo-Luddite let's-go-dirty-and-let-our-hair-grow movements to sophisticated arguments that we should now put more resources into social equity, the arts, and the humanities and/or that science and technology should be basically reoriented to work on new problems—reoriented perhaps from national defense to the inner city. NASA's "post-Apollo problem" is symbol and harbinger.

Our society which is historically oriented toward science and technology is now experiencing a revolt against both. Harold Orlans is correct in saying that as a nation we still display "excessive faith in the power of science, reason, and rational technology"; but Elmer Staats and William Carey are also correct in saying that we are "a society which is waking from its romantic trance with science and technology." In short we are, at this juncture, collectively confused, even schizoid.

A general movement against technoscience

A *general* movement against technoscience will arise in the period ahead, insured by the variety and strength of ideas and causes moving in this direction. The popular media often present an anti-technoscientific message, and it is a leitmotif in the counterculture and/or the youth culture. Technoscience is seen by many people today as an accomplice if not a cause of most of the perils and problems discussed at the beginning of this article.

But while general, this movement against technoscience will be diffuse, divided, and also opposed since the issues involved, from the level of high philosophy to simple social mechanics, are too complex and divisive to permit a society-wide Luddite movement. As a practical matter, technoscience is too fundamentally a part of contemporary society to be simply repealed; and after all, many reformist-Leftist causes require more, or different, technoscience, not its abolition. But nevertheless, generalized repugnance and hostility toward it will be an important force with real consequences, from national decisions on budgetary allocations to corporate decisions on product development.

Related to anti-technoscientific sentiment is the belief that the production of material goods has grown to monstrous, indefensible proportions and should be reduced, accompanied by a rise in the delivery of social services, the provision of amenities, or the enjoyment of leisure. Although the arguments of this persuasion are varied and complex in themselves, and by no means equate precisely with a general opposition to technology or science, it is indisputable that there is some mutual reinforcement between the two currents of thought.

Single-issue movements against technoscience

Single-issue movements against or concerning some aspect of technoscience will increase in number and intensity. The reference here is to such matters as space exploration, the use of complex and long-lived pesticides and herbicides, the manufacture of internal-combustion automobiles, the basing of defense-related or industry-supported research in universities, and the modification of weather. Often the argument will not be directed against technoscience as such, but against its abuse or even directed toward technoscientific alternatives. But such campaigns will become so widespread and heated that they will tend to merge into and reinforce the general anti-technoscientific mood, and certainly *they* will be reinforced *by* this mood.

We are increasingly experiencing such single-issue movements and countermovements—"disturbances." They are already a part of our political life in a way that would have been inconceivable in our fairly recent past. If one takes seriously the introductory inventory of perils and problems, he can only conclude that they will increase in number, complexity, and intensity; and in every one, technoscience is clearly involved.

Politicization of technoscience policy and administration

Technoscience policy making and administration will become increasingly contentious, public, and thereby politicized. The political, according to the most widely quoted definition, concerns the "authoritative allocation of values." Clearly, what has taken place in the last few decades is the creation of a new dimension of the political with technoscience as it has become larger and more centrally involved in our lives. It is difficult if not impossible to find a significant area of public policy in which the issues—economic, ethical, or legal—are not intimately joined with technoscientific issues. For all that is important for contemporary man, decisions about the authoritative allocation of values are decisions about technoscience.

Changes within technoscience

As technoscience becomes increasingly politicized and more drawn into the center of social turbulence, the "cultures" of technology and science will change. "Culture" is used here as a shorthand designation for such matters as orienting beliefs, institutional arrangements, and procedures for getting work done. In general, these cultural changes will be toward making technology and science less autonomous.

Technology and science always exist in a social context and relate to it in an intricate and significant way. In our history this paradoxical situation has existed: (1) Both science and technology have had a high degree of autonomy and an accompanying pervasive belief that it was desirable; but (2) science and technology, far from being autonomous with respect to their *effects*, were often prime movers in the political-social realm. This imbalance is ending. Given problems now perceived and forces now in motion, it is certain that there will be more political-social control of technology, resulting from movements dealing with specific causes such as automobile safety, drug regulation, and crime control; from attempts to deal more effectively with the larger problems of national security, urban reconstruction, and environmental control; and from problems now certainly emerging, such as weather modification, and likely to emerge, such as genetic engineering. Whether technological research and development take place in private corporation, government bureau, independent institute, or university, the trend is toward less autonomy.

Science, though separable from technology, will experience a similar invasion and constriction of autonomy which will of course touch the most sensitive feelings and imperil many values, specifically, the values and beliefs that are deftly sketched in West Churchman's essays: knowledge is a good, a value, in itself; important problems for a science are generated internally by that science; and judgment on a scientific product can only be rendered by scientific peers. But we can already see the process of limiting autonomy under way; it should not be regarded as simply a threat to a unified scientific community with a single, coherent set of beliefs; the scientific community—if indeed the term is a meaningful one— is itself in ferment since the issues that make for turbulence in our society touch this community directly, and some may be bred there.

Distinctions between science and technology, or between pure and applied research, are for some purposes real and useful but for other purposes unclear, unrealistic, and impractical. As change approaches, we may expect much rehearsal of old arguments and the development of new ones to defend institutional arrangements and intellectual climates. We may expect controversies over technology's uses and alternatives to carry over into what is regarded as pure science, with resulting heat and confusion. Massive politically-mandated research in new areas—e.g., education, crime control, and urban reconstruction—will cause dislocation, turmoil, and perhaps rebellion. Newly mandated research and development requiring a new or closer joining of the biophysical sciences with the social sciences will become increasingly common and will be a fertile source of misunderstanding, confusion, and controversy. Controversies about the institutional base and/or geographical locale of research will also be intensified. (The disturbed university is already becoming a less useful and less used habitat.)

Crisis in institutional development

We are entering a crisis period in adjusting political-governmental theories and institutions to those of technoscience. Centuries after the birth of modern science and generations after the rise of a new, massive, science-related technology, we lack ideas and institutions to help the two work together. Short of total societal reconstruction—following cataclysm or long evolution toward utopia—there probably is no grand and final solution to the present tangle of problems since two worlds *do* exist: one oriented toward knowledge, the other toward action; one toward certainty of fact, the other toward workability; one toward an unending pursuit of truth, the other toward seeking practical solutions and operating in the present. In spite of these opposing orientations, ideas and institutions must be devised for compromise, cooperation, and coexistence between these two worlds.

Until recently, we have not done badly in devising such new governmental functions to coordinate science and technology, as

Don K. Price and James McCamy, among others, have made clear; and paradoxically our present problems arise in part from certain past successes. But with a new order of magnitude of problems, we cannot continue with the haphazardly developed, complicated structure of regulatory agencies, research bureaus, congressional committees, advisory committees, institutes, research contracts, and so forth, which collectively now attempt to link politics and technoscience. While the entire structure must be revised, one new direction is clear: increased political control of the applications of technoscience. Many interrelated movements and problems make it inevitable, some of which have been indicated: a general shift in mood away from fascination with technology, the environmental crisis, the campaign against the military-industrial complex, and compaigns for such specific reforms as safety of automobiles and food additives.

Other developments, related to the preceding in complex ways, also reflect the move toward more control of technology. One is the growing interest in technology assessment and technology transfers, attempts to establish how the second- and third-level effects of technology can be determined so that choices can be made with knowledge of consequences. Another is interest in social reporting, the movement to broaden society-wide reporting to include all significant social phenomena to obtain an adequate base of knowledge for making decisions on public policy which consider not only the technological but also its ramifications. Another development is the recent growth of studies of the future: the establishment of programs to project trends ("computerized crystal balls"), estimate probabilities, and hypothesize results of alternative courses of action.

Two aspects of the inevitable drive to gain more societal control of technology's applications deserve special note. One is glaringly obvious: the constriction of the present private, largely corporate, sphere of private decision making about technology will on the whole be vigorously resisted with the inevitable resulting conflict. The other is not immediately obvious: the social sciences, and the "soft sciences" generally, will be deeply involved in the making and executing of decisions and will have a buffering role between the technoscientific and the political. That the social sciences will function imperfectly in this role needs no argument, much less one as sharp and negative as that in Moynihan's *Maximum Feasible Misunderstanding*; but without their participation in the process of inventing and administering new policies, the changes for their success sink to near zero. Since in any case they will be there, they must be considered as a factor as early as possible.

Increasing decentralization

The traditional tug-of-war between geographical localism and centralism, or between functional (largely economic) autonomy and governmental control, is entering a new phase for technoscience. The arguments for decentralization that have recently been discussed are diverse but collectively impressive. They include scientifically based theories that decentralized organization results in better decisions and more efficient execution of them, as well as ethical and philosophical arguments for personal freedom from organizational coercion. The arguments appear in a wide variety of programs and causes, from corporate reorganization to university reform and from neighborhood control of schools to "intentional communities."

In general, these newer forces toward decentralization spring from or become identified with liberals or the political Left. In the days of the New Deal, liberals favored centralization. Many still do, but there has been a falling away from it, especially among the young. Meanwhile advocates of older trends toward decentralization have never been converted to centralization, nor have the older trends weakened or disappeared. Business does not like to be regulated, suburbs resist incorporation into metropolitan governments, white-controlled schools block integration, states seek to defend themselves against federal pressures. The upshot is that Left, Right, and Center, while in contest and even sometimes in violent conflict, often seem, ironically, in agreement on the nature of the solution: return the power to the people.

Allied with and nourishing the impetus toward decentralization are the ideas and sentiments that form the antiorganizational revolution, discussed previously; there is a general resistance to organizational procedures and disciplines, a revulsion from the inherent complexities and time-consuming organizational solutions to pressing problems. Moreover there is a specific resistance to governmental organization and a more specific resistance to federal organization. From student anarchism to Peter Drucker's analysis of "The Sickness of Government," the tide of antiorganizational and antigovernmental sentiment is awesome—heartening, frightening, or perhaps both, depending on the point of view of the observer.

These forces toward decentralization *exist* and must be reckoned with; there is much substance and persuasiveness in the arguments made on its behalf, and it is beyond question that the solution to some of our problems will come from more decentralized methods of policy making and administration. But on the other hand it is clear that decentralization will not solve all problems and that some centralized organization and even certain centralized coercive control will be necessary. If one runs through the inventory of vexing and urgent problems, it is obvious that they are so large in both spatial and social dimensions that they *cannot* be dealt with on a local, uncoordinated basis. Many of them, in fact—certainly controlling violence and rescuing the biosphere—run far beyond the national boundaries, and history up to this point has provided us with only moderately effective methods for making and administering policy *within* national boundaries.

POLICY MAKING AND ADMINISTRATION

In attempting to discern the characteristics of our mounting social turmoil, I have suggested some implications for technoscience policy and administration that I wish now to take up directly, both reemphasizing and drawing further implications.

Major problems

We are entering a period of unprecedented stress in coordinating the political and the technoscientific at the national level, and at least four types of problems involved.

1. Policies regarding support for t technoscientific research. Policies that originated after World War II are no longer adequate. Allocation of research monies is already politicized and will inevitably become more so; the camouflage of political questions by the elaborate devices of "government by contract" is ending.
2. National policies on overriding issues, preeminently the control of violence, both external and internal; the salvation of the environment; and the attaining of more social and racial equity.
3. Sectoral and partial policies, within larger national issues and apart from them. This list is long, and their contemplation disturbing. Few of them are local, although they are more specific than the larger issues; many of them, such as marine exploitation have worldwide implications.
4. The uses of technoscience in the making and administration of policies. At a new level of urgency and complexity old issues (e.g., expert versus amateur and the relationship between facts and values) must be reargued; old accommoda-

tions and solutions (e.g., the independent regulatory commission and the independent institute) reexamined; and new theories and technologies (e.g., computer science and social reporting) must be adapted for use.

Changes in administration

The "culture" of administration of course must change as do the "cultures" of science and technology. The changes in each are interrelated to changes in the others; and the changes in all are related to the social milieus. There are two important areas of change, one in which the direction of evolution is clear and one in which the outcome is quite problematic.

The direction of change is clear in attempts to bridge the gap between politics and policy making on one hand and technoscience and its effects on the other. I have in mind developments, now in effect or proposed, indicated by such labels as PPBS (Planning, Programming, Budgeting System), systems analysis, organizational development, policy planning, social indicators, technology evaluation, computer technology, managerial science, studies of the future—and still others. Such developments reflect a response of the social sciences to a perceived gap between the social, political, and institutional and technoscience and its effects. They attempt to combine the concern of the social sciences for values with technoscientific theory. The promise of such efforts and their success or failure where now in operation are crucially important, but beyond the scope of this article. The present point is only that they exist and that these efforts to reconcile science and politics will not only continue but will expand and that they will profoundly affect methods of policy making and administration.

The area of the administration in which I would not make any prediction, beyond the prediction that confusion and controversy will intensify, concerns the conflicting currents of centralization and decentralization discussed above. Here the variables are unknown and too numerous for a direction of change to be apparent. If we survey administrative theory, we find a great deal indeed to suggest that for a generation if not longer the trend has been toward decentralization: toward functionalism, delegation, participation, and democracy. The point is well demonstrated by Rensis Likert's argument in this volume: "System 4" is superior and evolution moves in this direction. Indeed, it can be persuasively argued that the direction of this evolution is in response to the needs and results of technoscience and hence represents what the future will be.

While not hostile to such theories and sentiments, I am not certain of the universal applicability and inevitable triumph of decentralization. As I have indicated, I think that the inherent complexities and large scope of the many problems we face will impose inevitable barriers to a general triumph of decentralized organization. It is perhaps significant that the advocates of decentralization have been on the whole students of private rather than public administration. There is no need to question their conclusions, based on study of R & D establishments, banking offices, insurance firms, retail chains, and manufacturing plants. However, there *is* reason to question some of their generalized prescriptions—putatively for a whole society—which are loosely extrapolated and currently fashionable. Legal norms, societal control, formal organization, hierarchy—such are not about to disappear, however nice it would be if they did. In fact, they are as likely to become more prominent in the period ahead.

THE TECHNOSCIENCE ADMINISTRATOR

I conclude with some summary observations on the roles and functions of the technoscience administrator, especially one in a public context. I have tried to analyze an emerging reality, but the future is always reached from the present, and even in a revolutionary period, much of the present and the past is carried forward. The present state of the art or science of administration is relevant to any future one. Now, and in any foreseeable future, budgets must still be made and executed; people must still be hired and paid; supplies and equipment must still be ordered; and space and transportation must still be provided. The developments predicted in this article will change the conditions of performance, but administrators will always be needed for these matters that are literally the *sina quo non* of technoscience within organizations, which is substantially all technoscience now existing or likely to exist.

But the administrator with any significant general or program responsibility cannot be simply an administrative technician, however competent. It is of course already well recognized that if the program administrator is trained in some field of technoscience he must learn about administration; and that if he is trained in administration, he must understand at least that branch of technoscience with which he is concerned. But if I am even partially correct in my reading of the future much more will be necessary. In terms of Lynton Keith Caldwell's analysis, the "latent" function of the administrator will be greatly expanded in its importance. The technoscience administrator will be at the very center of things political; he cannot, if he would, escape participation in the "authoritative allocation of values." He will have to direct and channel conflicting pressures that arise from a society heatedly contesting matters of life and death. He will have multiple roles: technician, interpreter, counselor, analyst, policy maker, advocate, therapist, leader, negotiator. What he will need, in addition to rare native endowment, will draw not just upon administrative techniques and upon technoscience, but upon the whole range of knowledge represented by the humanities and the social sciences. We will need at least a fair number of wise men and statesmen. This is, to be sure, an idealized portrait, an impossible set of "specs." But even to muddle through, we will need to achieve very nearly the impossible.

References and Notes

CHAPTER 1

1. *United States Constitution,* article I, section 8.
2. The National Academy of Science was established by act of Congress, approved by President Abraham Lincoln on March 3, 1863.
3. Daniel S. Greenberg, *The Politics of Pure Science* (New York: New American Library, 1967), p. 65; see also Hunter A. Dupree, *Science in the Federal Government* (Cambridge, Mass.: Harvard University Press, 1957).
4. Vannevar Bush, *Science, the Endless Frontier* (1945; reprint ed., Washington, D.C.: National Science Foundation, 1960). Bush was then director of the Office of Scientific Research and Development.
5. Bush, *Science, the Endless Frontier,* p. 4.
6. National Science Foundation Act of 1950 (Public Law 507, 81st Cong., 64 Stat. 149, 42 U.S.C., 1861).
7. National Sea Grant College and Program Act of 1966 (Public Law 688, 89th Cong., 80 Stat. 998, 33 U.S.C., 1122); and Title IX, National Defense Education Act, 1958 (Public Law 864, 85th Cong., 42 U.S.C., 1876).
8. U.S. Congress, Senate, S. 32, 92d Cong., 2d Sess., August 9, 1972. See also "Jobless Engineers Would Tackle Urban Problems and New Programs," *ENR* (McGraw-Hill's Construction Weekly, August 24, 1972), p. 12.
9. U.S. Congress, Senate, Preface to S. 32, 92d Cong., 2d Sess., August 9, 1972.
10. The President's Message to the Congress, March 16, 1972, *Science and Technology,* Weekly Compilation of Presidential Documents (March 20, 1972), p. 1. (Hereafter cited as President's Message.)
11. President's Message, p. 2.
12. President's Message, p. 10.
13. Cf. *U.S. Government Organization Manual,* 1971-72 (Washington, D.C.: Office of the Register, 1971), pp. 73, 74.
14. Daniel S. Greenberg, "David and Indifference," *Saturday Review* (October 1972), pp. 41-43.
15. *Public Technology: A Tool for Solving National Problems,* Report of the Committee on Intergovernmental Science Relations to the Federal Council for Science and Technology (Washington, D.C.: U.S. Government Printing Office, May 1972).
16. *Power to the States: Mobilizing Public Technology,* published by the Council of State Governments, May 1972, 111 pp.; also, *Public Technology,* p. 27.
17. *Public Technology,* pp. 24-25.
18. Michael D. Reagan, *Science and the Federal Patron* (New York: Oxford University Press, 1969), p. 9.
19. Don K. Price, *Government and Science* (New York: New York University Press, 1954).

20. Greenberg, *Politics of Pure Science;* and William R. Nelson, ed., *The Politics of Science* (New York: Oxford University Press, 1968).

21. Nelson, *Politics of Science*, p. vii.

22. Ibid.

23. Ibid.

24. Everett C. Ladd, Jr., and Seymour M. Lipset, "Politics of Academic Natural Scientists and Engineers," *Science*, vol. 176, no. 4039 (June 9, 1972), p. 1099.

25. Harvey Brooks, *Basic Research and National Goals*, p. 87, cited by Greenberg, *Politics of Pure Science*, p. 35.

26. *Research Addressed to the Nation's Needs: Guidelines for Proposal Preparation* (Washington, D.C.: National Science Foundation, 1971).

27. James A. Bayton and Richard Chapman, *Transformation of Scientists and Engineers into Managers,* NASA SP-291 (Washington, D.C.: National Aeronautics and Space Administration, 1972).

28. The author served from 1951 to 1964 as an HEW regional director.

29. Thomas A. Cohan, "Paradoxes of Science Administration," *Science*, vol. 177, no. 4053 (September 15, 1972), p. 964.

30. G. W. F. Hegel, *The Phenomenology of Mind*, trans. J. B. Baillie (New York: Harper and Row, 1931), p. 239.

31. Donald C. Pelz and F. M. Andrews, *Scientists in Organizations: Productive Climates for Research and Development* (New York: Wiley, 1966).

32. *Science Resources Studies Highlights*, National Science Foundation, NSF 72-305 (April 25, 1972), page 1; "Federal R & D Funding Shows Upward Trend," *Science Resources Studies Highlights*, National Science Foundation, NSF 71-24 (September 7, 1971); *National Patterns of R & D Resources, Funds and Manpower in the U.S., 1953-1972,* National Science Foundation, NSF-72-300 (December 1971).

33. *National Patterns of R & D, 1953-1972.*

34. *The Washington Post,* December 3, 1970, p. A-6.

35. Claude E. Barfield, "Scientists Report Money Shortage Forces New Look at Federal Science Policy," *National Journal,* August 22, 1970, p. 1797. See also, "Cuts in Budget Will Close Research Units," *Albuquerque Tribune,* September 16, 1969, p. B-5.

36. Philip Handler, testimony before the Subcommittee on Science, Research and Development of the Committee on Science and Astronautics of the House of Representatives, April 7, 1971.

37. U.S. Congress, House, Technology Assessment Act of 1972, Conference Report, 92d Cong., 2d Sess., H. R. 92-1436, September 25, 1972; also William M. Magruder, "Technology and the Professional Societies," *Mechanical Engineering* (September 1972), pp. 9-15.

38. Hubert H. Humphrey, "The Need for a Department of Science," *Annals of the American Academy of Political and Social Science* (January 1960), p. 30.

39. Reagan, *Science and the Federal Patron,* p. 263.

40. Hunter A. Dupree, testimony before the Senate Committee on Government Operations, 2d Sess., 1958, part 2, pp. 306-7.

41. Wallace Sayre, "Scientists and American Science Policy," ed. R. Gilpin and C. Wright, *Scientists and National Policy Making* (New York: Columbia University Press, 1964), p. 105.

42. William D. McElroy, Director, National Science Foundation, testimony before the Subcommittee on Science, Research and Development of the Committee on Science and Astronautics of the House of Representatives, July 29, 1970.

NOTES: CHAPTER 1

43. Ibid.
44. Barry Commoner, *Science and Survival* (New York: Viking Press, 1966), p. 3.
45. Ibid., p. 132.
46. Peter Schrag, "The Road to Yakima," *Saturday Review* (August 26, 1972), pp. 5, 12.
47. McElroy, testimony before House Subcommittee.
48. Ibid.
49. President's Message.
50. Handler, testimony before House Subcommittee.
51. U.S. Congress, House, Report of the Subcommittee on Science, Research and Development of the Committee on Science and Astronautics, 91st Cong., 1st Sess., July 1969, p. 4.
52. Cf. Theodor D. Sterling, "Scientific Data: Public or Private?" Letter in *Science*, vol. 177, no. 4050 (August 25, 1972), p. 651.
53. Cf. *Program for Advanced Study in Public Science Policy and Administration*, Division of Public Administration, University of New Mexico, 1971, p. 6.
54. *Annual Report* (Boulder, Colo.: University Corporation for Atmospheric Research, 1971), pp. 39-45; and *Annual Report* (Boulder, Colo.: National Center for Atmospheric Research, 1971), pp. v and vi.
55. John V. Tunney and Meldon E. Levine, "Genetic Engineering," *Saturday Review* (August 5, 1972), pp. 23-28. See also Daniel Lang, "Ex-Oracles—On the New Unpopularity of Scientists," *Harpers* (December 1972), pp. 34-43.
56. Peter F. Drucker, "Saving the Crusade," *Harpers* (January 1972), p. 66. For a questioning view of the objectivity of technology assessment when performed by grant recipients, see Daniel S. Greenberg, "Don't Ask the Barber Whether You Need a Haircut," *Saturday Review* (November 25, 1972), pp. 58-59.

CHAPTER 2

1. This thesis has been persuasively stated by Harlan Cleveland in "Dinosaurs and Personal Freedom," *Saturday Review* (February 28, 1959), pp. 12-14, 38.
2. Contrary to popular belief, the public administrator may in some respects enjoy greater freedom of choice and action than many business executives. For an analysis of organizational goals and choices, see Herbert A. Simon, "On the Concept of Organizational Goal," *Administrative Science Quarterly*, vol. 9 (June 1964), pp. 1-22; and Richard M. Cyert and James G. March, *A Behavioral Theory of the Firm* (Englewood Cliffs, N.J.: Prentice-Hall, 1963).
3. The influence of public agencies and administrators in the public policy process has been demonstrated in studies of the origins and histories of legislation in the United States: e.g., Malcom E. Jewell and Samuel E. Patterson, *The Legislative Process in the United States* (New York: Random House, 1966). The influence of the administrator in corporate business decisions is generally conceded and has been demonstrated in numerous studies of business administration: e.g., Robert A. Gordon, *Business Leadership in the Large Corporation* (Washington, D.C.: Brookings Institution, 1945). The extreme view of administrative dominance in policy making may

be found in James Burnham, *The Managerial Revolution* (New York: John Day, 1941). A more moderate description of the merging of managerial and technological expertise in policy making is provided by Bertrand de Jouvenel, "The Technocratic Age," *Bulletin of the Atomic Scientists,* vol. 20 (October 1964), pp. 27-29.

4. The literature is too large to permit citation to more than a few representative examples. A list of 141 items, articles, books, and government documents may be found in Lynton K. Caldwell and William B. DeVille, "Topic 18, The Man-Machine Interface," *Science, Technology and Public Policy: A Syllabus for Advanced Study,* vol. II (Bloomington: Indiana University, Department of Government, 1968-69). Among writings of direct relevance to technology as a parameter of administrative behavior are: James D. Thompson and Frederick L. Bates, "Technology, Organization and Administration," *Administrative Science Quarterly,* vol. 2 (December 1957), pp. 325-43; P. T. Veillette, "The Impact of Mechanization on Administration," *Public Administration Review,* vol. 17 (autumn 1957), pp. 231-37; Joan Woodward, *Management and Technology: Problems of Progress in Modern Industry,* no. 3 (London: HMSO, 1958-60), especially pp. 16-21; and Fremont Kast and James E. Rosenzweig, eds., *Science, Technology and Management* (New York: McGraw-Hill, 1963).

5. Fred E. Emery and Eric L. Trist, "The Causal Texture of Organizational Environments," *Human Organization,* vol. 18 (February 1965), pp. 21-32.

6. Peter F. Drucker, "Management Science and the Manager," *Management Science,* vol. 1 (January 1955), pp. 115-26; and Paul J. Gordon, "Administrative Strategy for a Graduate School of Administration," *Academy of Management Journal,* vol. 10 (December 1967), pp. 351-64.

7. Hans B. Thorelli, "Organization Theory: An Ecological View," *Academy of Management Proceedings,* 27th Annual Meeting (December 27-29, 1967), pp. 66-84; and Fred Warren Riggs, *The Ecology of Public Administration* (New York: Asia Publishing House, 1961).

8. U.S. Congress, House, Special Subcommittee to Investigate Power Failures, Committee on Interstate and Foreign Commerce, *Northeast Power Failure—November 9, 10, 1965,* 89th Cong., 1st and 2d sess., 1966.

9. Theodore N. Ferdinand, "On the Obsolescence of Scientists and Engineers," *American Scientist,* vol. 54 (March 1966), pp. 46-56.

10. William V. Shannon, "Supersonic Question Mark," *Commonweal,* vol. 82 (July 23, 1965), p. 513. Note especially testimony of Stuart G. Tipton, President of the Air Transport Association of America, U.S. Congress, House, Special Investigating Subcommittee, Committee on Science and Astronautics, *Supersonic Air Transports,* 86th Cong., 1st sess., May 19, 1960, p. 69.

11. Among the more articulate critics are Robert Boguslow in *Utopians: A Study of Systems Design and Social Change* (Englewood Cliffs, N.J.: Prentice-Hall, 1965); Jacques Ellul in *The Technological Society* (New York: Alfred A. Knopf, 1964); Siegfried Giedion in *Mechanization Takes Command* (New York: Oxford Press, 1948); Frederick Juenger in *The Failure of Technology* (Chicago: Regnery, 1957); and Lewis Mumford in numerous articles and books. For a specific criticism of the dominance of techniques in public administration, see Wallace S. Sayre, "The Triumph of Techniques over Purpose," *Public Administration Review,* vol. 8 (spring 1948), pp. 134-37.

12. Aaron Katz, "Toward High Information Level Culture," *Cybernetica,* vol. 7, no. 3 (1964), pp. 203-45.

13. Many of the often-criticized techniques of public personnel administration and labor relations management are intended to force administrative procedures to be impersonal and to prevent any discrimination for or against any special ethnic or economic group. Where discrimination is favored, as for veterans, techniques are invoked to make the discriminatory advantage operate in an accountable and automatic manner, e.g., extra points added to civil service examinations.

14. Robert S. Brumbaugh, *Ancient Greek Gadgets and Machines* (New York: Crowell, 1966), pp. 59-68.

15. Herbert A. Simon, *The New Science of Management Decision* (New York: Harper & Row, 1960).

16. Two well-known, useful, and influential studies of what administrators do are Chester Barnard, *The Functions of the Executive* (Cambridge, Mass.: Harvard University Press, 1947); and Herbert A. Simon, *Administrative Behavior: A Study of Decision-Making Process in Administrative Organizations*, 2d ed. (New York: Macmillan Co., 1957). Eric Ashby describes the kind of administrator with which we are concerned "as a machine which integrates and transforms into simple decisions two-way messages between science and society, and which can estimate probabilities in areas of ignorance." "The Administrator: Bottleneck or Pump," *Daedalus* (Proceedings of the American Academy of Arts and Sciences), vol. 91 (spring 1962), pp. 264-78.

17. "People and Systems," in Richard A. Johnson, Fremont E. Kast, and James E. Rosenzweig, *The Theory and Management of Systems*, 2d ed. (New York: McGraw-Hill, 1967), pp. 365-89.

18. For a similar analysis of social circumstances, technological influences, and administrative needs, see M. Zvegintzov, "Management in a Modern Scientific and Technological Age," *Impact of Science on Society*, vol. 11, no. 1 (1961), pp. 53-73.

19. Robert C. Albrook, "How to Spot Executives Early," *Fortune*, vol. 78 (July 1968), pp. 106-11. Reporting on a survey for *Fortune* magazine, the author writes: "Some psychologists question whether any test for executive potential yet developed can measure the potential for managerial effectiveness in any pure or fundamental way" (p. 111).

20. Adherents to the "muddling through" philosophy of administration no doubt would question the relevance of these criteria to administrative success. See Charles E. Lindblom, "The Science of 'Muddling Through,'" *Public Administration Review*, vol. 19 (spring 1959), pp. 79-88; but also see Yehezkel Dror, "Muddling Through—Science or Inertia," *Public Administration Review*, vol. 24 (September 1964), pp. 153-57. My argument does not pertain to administrative behavior that has been good enough to "get by" until now; it is directed to the quality of administration that we must somehow develop if we are serious about survival into the twenty-first century.

21. An argument supporting this conclusion may be found in J. Herbert Hollomon, "Modern Engineering and Society—The Marriage Between Technical Ability and Social Need," *Chemical and Engineering News*, vol. 42 (June 29, 1964), pp. 66-71; see also Ferdinand, "On the Obsolescence of Scientists and Engineers."

22. For a description of these programs, see *A Study of the Career Education Awards Program of the National Institute of Public Affairs* (Washington, D.C.: U.S. Civil Service Commission, Bureau of Training, 1967); and *University Offerings on the Career Education Awards Program, 1969-1970* (Washington, D.C.: National Institute of Public Affairs, 1968).

23. An extensive survey reported by C. Wilson Randle in "Problems of R & D Management," *Harvard Business Review*, vol. 37 (January-February

1959), pp. 128-36, indicated that a large minority of research workers wanted to move to laboratory administrative positions.

24. R. M. Hower and C. D. Orth, *Managers and Scientists* (Boston: Harvard Graduate School of Business Administration, 1963). See also Renato Tagiuri, "Value Orientations and the Relationship of Managers and Scientists," *Administrative Science Quarterly*, vol. 10 (June 1965), pp. 39-51; and Warren O. Hagstrom, "Traditional and Modern Forms of Scientific Teamwork," *Administrative Science Quarterly*, vol. 9 (December 1964), pp. 242-63.

25. Robert Best, "The Scientific Mind vs. the Management Mind," *Industrial Research*, vol. 5 (October 1963), pp. 50-52.

26. E.g., Theodore Zaner, "Action Research in Management Development," *Training and Development Journal*, vol. 22 (June 1968), pp. 28-33. This journal is a continuing source of information on administrative development programs and methods.

27. Marshall E. Demick, "The Administrative Staff College: Executive Development in Government and Industry," *The American Political Science Review*, vol. 50 (March 1956), pp. 166-76.

28. Ashby, "The Administrator: Bottleneck or Pump," p. 273. Ashby does, in fact, provide "a skeleton of a syllabus" for the study of science and administration, p. 277.

29. See Zbigniew Brzezinski, *America in the Technetronic Age* (New York: Columbia University, School of International Affairs, 1967), p. 9.

30. The need for education to strengthen human capabilities for value discrimination to match capabilities for technological implementations has been stated well by John McHale in various publications, e.g., "Education for Real," *Newsletter of the World Academy of Art and Science* (June 1966). For additional insight into the relationships between science, administration, and social responsibility, see the following articles: Lynton K. Caldwell, "Managing the Scientific Super-Culture: The Task of Educational Preparation," *Public Administration Review*, vol. 27 (June 1967), pp. 128-33; Alexander King, "Management as a Technology," *Impact of Science on Society*, vol. 8, no. 2 (1957), pp. 65-85; J. A. H. Gifford (Earl of Halsbury), "Management, Group Conflict and the Sciences," *Impact of Science on Society*, vol. 8, no. 3 (1957), pp. 121-40; Sven Lundstedt, "Administrative Leadership and the Use of Social Power," *Public Administration Review*, vol. 25 (June 1965), pp. 156-60; and J. A. Stratton, "Science and the Process of Management," *Research Management*, vol. 7 (March 1964), pp. 79-90.

31. An organization consisting initially of past presidents of the American Society for Public Administration with annually elected additions of notable persons in public administration. Its purpose is to provide advice and assistance to public agencies on administrative matters. Headquarters are shared with ASPA in Washington, D.C.

32. See also *Science and Public Policy in the American University*, papers delivered at a conference sponsored by Indiana University and Purdue University (Bloomington: Indiana University, Department of Government, 1969).

33. John Kenneth Galbraith and M. S. Randhawa, *The New Industrial State* (Boston: Houghton Mifflin Co., 1967).

34. Thomas S. Kuhn, *The Structure of Scientific Revolutions* (Chicago: University of Chicago Press, 1962).

CHAPTER 3

1. Nicholas J. Oganovic is a former Executive Director of the U.S. Civil Service Commission, Washington, D.C.
2. *Scientists and Engineers in the Federal Government*, Personnel Bibliography, series no. 30 (Washington, D.C.: U.S. Civil Service Commission Library, January 1970).
3. Jacques Richardson and Ford Park, "Why Europe Lags Behind," *Science and Technology*, no. 77 (May 1968), pp. 20-29; and J.-J. Servan-Schreiber, *The American Challenge* (New York: Atheneum House, Inc., 1968).
4. J. S. Webb, "Can Technical People Fill the Management Gap?" *Engineering Opportunities*, vol. 5, no. 3 (March 1967), p. 60; and Chauncey Starr, "The Engineer-Manager, a New Professional Challenge," *Proceedings, National Conference on Engineering Brainpower for the Aerospace Industry* (Washington, D.C.: National Association of Professional Engineers, October 1963, p. 84.
5. Edwin L. Miller, "Identifying High Potential Managerial Personnel," *Michigan Business Review* (Ann Arbor: University of Michigan, November 1968), p. 12.
6. Donald M. MacArthur, "Personnel Management for R & D," *Personnel Administration*, vol. 31, no. 5 (September-October 1968), p. 28.
7. Donald F. Hornig, "Charles Lathrop Parsons Award Address," *Chemical and Engineering News*, vol. 46, no. 1 (January 1, 1968), p. 52.
8. Data provided by National Science Foundation, February 1969.
9. Starr, "Engineer-Manager," p. 85.
10. C. W. Churchman, C. E. Kruytbosch, and P. Ratoosh, *The Role of the Research Administrator* (Berkeley: Space Sciences Laboratory, Social Sciences Project, University of California, October 1965), appendix.
11. Julian S. Frank, "A Short Course in Psychology for Engineer-Managers," *Training and Development Journal*, vol. 22, no. 10 (October 1968), pp. 8-16.
12. J. R. Glennon, W. D. Buel, and Lewis E. Albright, "Making the Best Use of R & D Manpower," *Business Horizons* (Bloomington: Indiana University, April 1968), pp. 63-68.
13. Harriet Bruce Moore and Sidney J. Levy, "Artful Contrivers: A Study of Engineers," *Personnel*, vol. 28, no. 2 (September 1951), pp. 148-53.
14. Webb, "Management Gap," pp. 64, 68; and Starr, "Engineer-Manager," p. 87.
15. Starr, "Engineer-Manager," p. 87; and Arnie Solem, "How Effective Are Management Development Programs?" *Proceedings, Conference on Increasing the Effectiveness of Scientists & Engineers* (Kansas City, Missouri: University of Kansas City, April 1959), p. 70.
16. David E. Lilienthal, "Society and Its Leaders in Transition," speech to American Management Association (New York, September 26, 1968).
17. V. Wayne Cobb, "The Mid-Career and Senior Federal Research & Development Employee," *Science Administration, Education, and Career Mobility* (Bloomington: Institute of Public Administration, Indiana University, 1966), p. 67.
18. Melvin W. Wachs, "The Federal Laboratory, Scientific, and Technical Director," *Science Administration, Education, and Career Mobility* (Bloomington: Indiana University, 1966), p. 79.
19. Starr, "Engineer-Manager," p. 86; Solem, "Management Development Programs," p. 71; Lewis C. Mainzer, "The Scientist as Public

Administrator," *Western Political Quarterly*, vol. 16 (1963), pp. 814-29; Daniel D. Roman, *Research and Development Management: The Economics and Administration of Research* (New York: Appleton-Century-Crofts, 1968), pp. 137-38; and John J. McNab, "Preparing Scientists for Management," *The Bridge Between Science and Management, Proceedings of the 19th International Management Conference* (New York: Society for Advancement of Management, October 1964), pp. 105-13.

20. Albert F. Siepert, "Creating the Management Climate for Effective Research in Government Laboratories," *The Management of Scientists*, Karl Hill, ed. (Boston: Beacon Press, 1964), p. 91.

21. *The Environment for Quality* (Washington, D.C.: Committee on Scientific Personnel, Federal Council for Science and Technology, November 1965), pp. 10, 12.

22. James L. McCamy, *Science and Public Administration* (University: University of Alabama Press, 1960), p. 115.

23. William D. Carey, *Public Administration Review*, vol. 9, no. 1 (winter 1949), pp. 53-63.

24. *The Environment of the Federal Laboratory, Proceedings*, Third Symposium (Washington, D.C.: Federal Council for Science and Technology and U.S. Civil Service Commission, December 1964), p. 93. Dr. J. Herbert Holloman, then Assistant Secretary of Commerce for Science and Technology, was the proponent of the generalist manager.

25. Don K. Price, *Government and Science* (New York: New York University Press, 1954), pp. 185-86.

26. McCamy, *Science and Public Administration*, p. 115.

27. Don K. Price, "Educating for the Scientific Age," *Bulletin of the Atomic Scientists*, vol. 24, no. 8 (October 1968), p. 29.

28. *The Civil Service*, vol. 1 (5 vols.), Report of the Committee, 1966-68, Chairman: Lord Fulton (London: HMSO, 1968), pp. 11, 12.

29. Ibid., vol. 2, p. 59.

30. Thomas Moranian, *The Research and Development Engineer as Manager* (New York: Holt, Rinehart and Winston, 1963), p. 132.

31. John J. Dougherty, "Joel Nordica Turns Administrator," *Professional Engineer*, vol. 38, no. 10 (October 1968), pp. 46-50.

32. H. W. Case, W. K. Le Bold, and W. D. Diemer, as quoted in *Scientific, Engineering, Technical Manpower Comments*, vol. 5, no. 11 (December 1968), p. 18.

33. *Science Administration, Education, and Career Mobility* (Bloomington: Indiana University, 1966), p. 21.

34. McNab, "Preparing Scientists," p. 107.

35. Robert M. Page, "Motivation of Scientists and Engineers," *Personnel Administration*, vol. 21, no. 5 (September-October 1958), pp. 30, 31.

36. Solem, "Management Development Programs"; McNab, "Preparing Scientists"; George L. Royer, "Salary Administration of Research Personnel," *Research Management*, vol. 1, no. 2 (summer 1958), p. 120; Herbert A. Shepard, "The Dual Hierarchy in Research," *Research Management*, vol. 1, no. 3 (autumn 1958), pp. 177-87; William Kornhauser, *Scientists in Industry* (Berkeley and Los Angeles: University of California Press, 1962), p. 141; *Research and Development Management*, Society for Advancement of Management Bulletin, R & D 001 (March 1966), p. 20; Delmar W. Karger and Robert G. Murdick, *Managing Engineering and Research* (New York: The Industrial Press, 1963), p. 168; Thomas A. Natiello, "Motivation for Work Preference," *MSU Business Topics*, vol. 16, no. 2 (East Lansing: Michigan State University, spring 1968), pp. 59-60; Simon Marcson, *The Scientist in American Industry* (Princeton, N.J.: Princeton University Press, 1960), p.

30; and Spencer Klaw, "The Industrial Labyrinth," *Science and Technology*, no. 86 (February 1969), p. 43.

37. Kornhauser, *Scientists in Industry*, p. 141.

38. *Research Grade-Evaluation Guide* (Washington, D.C.: Standards Division, U.S. Civil Service Commission, June 1964), pp. 9, 10.

39. *Research Scientist Evaluation Plan* (Washington, D.C.: U.S. Department of Agriculture, Agricultural Research Service, May 1965), pp. 2, 3.

40. C. Wilson Randle, "Problems of R & D Management," *Harvard Business Review*, vol. 37, no. 1 (January-February 1959), p. 135.

41. Howard M. Vollmer, *A Preliminary Investigation and Analysis of the Role of Scientists in Research Organizations* (Menlo Park, Calif.: Stanford Research Institute, for Air Force Office of Scientific Research, 1962), pp. 49, 53.

42. Shepard, "Dual Hierarchy," pp. 177-87.

43. Kornhauser, *Scientists in Industry*, p. 147.

44. Natiello, "Motivation for Work Preference," pp. 59-60.

45. Lee E. Danielson, "Characteristics of Engineers in Industry," *Management and the Engineer in Industry, Proceedings of Third Annual Conference of Professional Engineers in Industry* (Washington, D.C.: National Society of Professional Engineers, October 1965), p. 20.

46. Marcson, *Scientist in American Industry*, p. 30.

47. *Executive Manpower in the Federal Service* (Washington, D.C.: U.S. Civil Service Commission, Bureau of Executive Manpower, January 1972), p. 6.

48. Klaw, "Industrial Labyrinth," p. 43.

49. Shepard, "Dual Hierarchy," p. 186.

50. Frank D. Leamer, "Professional & Administrative Ladders—The Advantages of Broad Job Classification in a Research Organization," *Research Management*, vol. 2, no. 1 (spring 1959), pp. 53-62.

51. "The White Collar Worker," *American Labor*, vol. 1, no. 6 (October 1968), pp. 41-47.

52. Abraham K. Korman, "The Prediction of Managerial Performance: A Review," *Personnel Psychology*, vol. 21 (1968), pp. 295-322.

53. McNab, "Preparing Scientists," p. 36; and Society for Advancement of Management Bulletin, *Research and Development Management*.

54. *Civil Service Handbook X-118*, Qualification Standard, Supervisory Positions in General Schedule Occupations, T.S. 120 (Washington, D.C.: Standards Division, U.S. Civil Service Commission, November 1968), p. 3.

55. Robert E. Bailey and Barry T. Jensen, "The Troublesome Transition from Scientist to Manager," *Personnel*, vol. 42, no. 5 (September-October 1965), p. 53.

56. McNab, "Preparing Scientists," p. 108.

57. *Toward Better Utilization of Scientific and Engineering Talent* (Washington, D.C.: Committee on Utilization of Scientific and Engineering Manpower, National Academy of Sciences, 1964), p. 25.

58. J. E. Walters, *Research Management: Principles and Practices* (Washington, D.C.: Spartan Books, 1965), pp. 150-57; George S. Odiorne, "Making Managers out of Engineers," *Personnel*, vol. 33, no. 3 (November 1956), p. 266; and Burt K. Scanlan, "A Commonsense Approach to Making Good Managers of Good Technical Men," *Training in Business and Industry*, vol. 1, no. 2 (November-December 1964), pp. 40, 41.

59. Odiorne, "Making Managers," p. 266.

60. *Federal Personnel Manual*, chapter 335 (Washington, D.C.: U.S. Civil Service Commission, 1968), pp. 16, 17.

61. Announcement of course *Introduction to Supervision* (Washington, D.C.: Bureau of Training, U.S. Civil Service Commission, October 1968).
62. Webb, "Management Gap," pp. 64, 68; and Starr, "Engineer-Manager," p. 85.
63. McNab, "Preparing Scientists," p. 108.
64. Announcement of course *Supervisory Scientists and Engineers* (Washington, D.C.: Bureau of Training, U.S. Civil Service Commission, March 1972).
65. Announcement of course *Executive Institute on Management of Scientific & Engineering Organizations* (Washington, D.C.: Bureau of Training, U.S. Civil Service Commission, April 1972).
66. Announcement of course *Science and Government* (Washington, D.C.: Bureau of Training, U.S. Civil Service Commission, February 1969).
67. *Off-Campus Study Centers for Federal Employees* (Washington, D.C.: Bureau of Training, U.S. Civil Service Commission, FY 1971).
68. Ibid.
69. Eugene A. Confrey, "Science Administration: NIH Training for a Young Profession," *Civil Service Journal*, vol. 9, no. 1 (July-September 1968), pp. 8-11.
70. John Wall and Reuben Pomerantz, "A Science and Technology Fellowship Program," *Civil Service Journal*, vol. 5, no. 3 (January-March 1965), p. 20.
71. Roman, *Research and Development Management*, p. 141; Siepert, "Creating Management Climate," p. 92; *Science Administration, Education, and Career Mobility*, p. 20; Karger and Murdick, *Managing Engineering and Research*, pp. 650-56; and Howard Reiss, "The Organization of Science in a Technology-Oriented Organization," *The Fundamental Research Activity in a Technology-Dependent Organization* (Washington, D.C.: Air Force Office of Scientific Research, 1965), p. 43.
72. Churchman, Kruytbosch, and Ratoosh, *Research Administrator*, Table I.
73. Leamer, "Professional and Administrative Ladders," p. 59.
74. *Environment of Federal Laboratory*, p. 94.
75. Moranian, *Engineer as Manager*, p. 134.
76. Roman, *Research and Development Management*, p. 134; Harold Mosher, "Motivating Your Engineers for Greater Creativity and Productive Effort," *Management and the Engineer in Industry* (Washington, D.C.: National Society of Professional Engineers, October 1965), pp. 85-91; and M. J. Bevans, "Technical Personnel: Managing this 'Elite' Corps," *Administrative Management*, vol. 39, no. 11 (November 1968), pp. 20, 21.
77. Walters, *Research Management*, p. 7.
78. Mosher, "Motivating Engineers," p. 90.
79. Roman, *Research and Development Management*, p. 134.
80. *Environment of Federal Laboratory*, pp. 14-33.
81. *Scientists and Engineers in the Federal Personnel System* (Washington, D.C.: Bureau of Policies and Standards, U.S. Civil Service Commission, December 1971).
82. MacArthur, "Personnel Management for R & D," p. 28.
83. Allen V. Astin, chairman, Committee on Federal Laboratories, Federal Council for Science and Technology, testifying before the Subcommittee on Science, Research and Development of the House Committee on Science and Astronautics, March 27, 1968.
84. *Better Utilization of Talent*, p. 47.
85. Ibid., p. 84. (Arthur M. Ross article.)
86. Ibid., p. 111. (Allen O. Gamble article.)

87. *Functional Classification System for Scientists and Engineers* (Washington, D.C.: Standards Division, U.S. Civil Service Commission, June 1966), p. 5.

CHAPTER 4

1. Wesley L. Hjornevik served as Associate Director of the Manned Spacecraft Center, NASA, Houston, Texas, from 1968 to 1969.
2. Robert L. Rosholt, *An Administrative History of NASA, 1958-63*, NASA SP-4101 (Washington, D.C.: U.S. Government Printing Office, 1966), p. 48.
3. Ibid., p. 178.
4. Loyd S. Swenson, Jr., James M. Grimwood, and Charles C. Alexander, *This New Ocean*, NASA SP-4201 (Washington, D.C.: U.S. Government Printing Office, 1966), p. 508.
5. William Kornhauser, *Scientists in Industry: Conflict and Accommodation* (Berkeley and Los Angeles: University of California Press, 1962).
6. Ibid., pp. 195-96.
7. Ibid., p. 16.
8. Ibid., p. 197.
9. Mark Abrahamson, *The Professional in the Organization* (Chicago: Rand McNally & Company, 1967), p. 133.
10. Donald C. Pelz and Frank M. Andrews, *Scientists in Organizations* (New York: John Wiley & Sons, Inc., 1966).
11. Kornhauser, *Scientists in Industry*, p. 200.
12. Peter F. Drucker, "The Executive's Job in Its Three Dimensions," *The Commercial Letter*, a magazine published by the Canadian Imperial Bank of Commerce, Toronto, Canada (n.d.), p. 2.
13. Simon Marcson, *The Scientist in American Industry* (New York: Harper and Brothers, 1960); Kornhauser, *Scientists in Industry*; Abrahamson, *The Professional in the Organization*; and Pelz and Andrews, *Scientists in Organizations*.
14. Pelz and Andrews, *Scientists in Organizations*, pp. 310-25.
15. Donald C. Pelz, "Some Factors Related to Performance in a Research Organization," *Administrative Science Quarterly*, vol. 1 (1956-57), pp. 310-25.
16. Federal Council for Science and Technology, *Proceedings of the 3rd Symposium, Environment of the Federal Laboratory*, December 7-8, 1964 (Washington, D.C.: U.S. Government Printing Office, 1965), p. 47.
17. Richard A. Hamilton, *A Comparative Analysis of the Professional's Occupational Environment at the Manned Spacecraft Center*, MSC-BM-MR-69-2 (Houston: Manned Spacecraft Center, January 1969).

CHAPTER 5

1. D. C. Pelz and F. M. Andrews, *Scientists in Organizations: Productive Climates for Research and Development* (New York: Wiley, 1966).
2. D. C. Pelz, "Creative Tensions in the Research and Development Climate," *Science*, vol. 157, no. 3785 (July 14, 1967), pp. 160-65.

3. Ibid.

4. W. Weaver, editorial, *Science*, vol. 130 (1959), p. 301.

5. W. Evan, "Conflict and Performance in R & D Organizations: Some Preliminary Findings," *Industrial Management Review*, vol. 7, no. 37 (1965), p. 46.

6. R. Richard Ritti, "Engineers and the Industrial Corporation" (New York: Columbia University Press, 1970).

7. T. Burns and G. M. Stalker, *The Management of Innovation* (London: Tavistock, 1961); and W. H. Gruber and D. G. Marquis, eds., *Factors in the Transfer of Technology* (Cambridge, Mass.: Massachusetts Institute of Technology Press, 1969).

8. K. K. White, *Understanding the Company Organization Chart* (New York: American Management Association, 1963), pp. 36-41.

9. See, for example, H. Stieglitz, *Organizational Planning* (New York: National Industrial Conference Board, 1962), p. 14.

10. B. C. Ames, "Payoff from Product Management," *Harvard Business Review*, vol. 41, no. 6 (1963), pp. 141-52.

11. D. G. Bowers, ed., *Applying Modern Management Principles to Sales Organizations* (Ann Arbor, Mich.: Foundation for Research on Human Behavior, 1963); D. G. Bowers, "Organizational Control in an Insurance Company," *Sociometry*, vol. 27, no. 2 (1964), pp. 230-44; D. G. Bowers and S. E. Seashore, "Predicting Organizational Effectiveness with a Four-Factor Theory of Leadership," *Administrative Science Quarterly*, vol. 11, no. 2 (1966), pp. 238-63; Basil S. Georgopoulos and F. C. Mann, *The Community General Hospital* (New York: Macmillan Co., 1962); R. L. Kahn, "Human Relations on the Shop Floor," *Human Relations and Modern Management*, ed. E. M. Hugh-Jones (Amsterdam: North Holland Publishing Co., 1958), pp. 43-74; R. L. Kahn et al., *Organizational Stress: Studies in Role Conflict and Ambiguity* (New York: Wiley, 1964); D. Katz and R. L. Kahn, "Some Recent Findings in Human Relations Research," *Readings in Social Psychology*, eds. E. Swanson, T. Newcomb, and E. Hartley (New York: Holt, 1952), pp. 650-55; D. Katz and R. L. Kahn, *The Social Psychology of Organizations* (New York: Wiley, 1966); Rensis Likert, *New Patterns of Management* (New York: McGraw-Hill, 1961); F. C. Mann and H. J. Baumgartel, *The Supervisor's Concern with Costs in an Electric Power Company* (Ann Arbor, Mich.: Institute for Social Research, 1953); F. C. Mann and J. Dent, *Appraisals of Supervisors and Attitudes of Their Employees in an Electric Power Company* (Ann Arbor, Mich.: Institute for Social Research, 1954); F. C. Mann and L. R. Hoffman, *Automation and the Worker: A Study of Social Change in Power Plants* (New York: Holt, Rinehart and Winston, 1960); F. C. Mann, B. P. Indik, and V. H. Vroom, *The Productivity of Work Groups* (Ann Arbor, Mich.: Institute for Social Research, 1963); F. C. Mann, H. Metzner, and H. Baumgartel, "The Supervisor and Absence Rates," *Supervisory Management*, vol. 2, no. 7 (1957), pp. 7-14; Paul E. Mott et al., *Shift Work: The Social, Psychological, and Physical Consequences* (Ann Arbor, Mich.: University of Michigan Press, 1965); Pelz and Andrews, *Scientists in Organizations*; S. E. Seashore, *Group Cohesiveness in the Industrial Work Group* (Ann Arbor, Mich.: Institute for Social Research, 1954); S. E. Seashore and D. G. Bowers, *Changing the Structure and Functioning of an Organization* (Ann Arbor, Mich.: Institute for Social Research, 1963); and Arnold S. Tannenbaum, *Control in Organizations* (New York: McGraw-Hill, 1968).

12. Likert, *New Patterns of Management*; and *The Human Organization: Its Management and Value* (New York: McGraw-Hill, 1967).

13. Likert, *New Patterns of Management*, p. 103.

14. Ibid., p. 99.

15. Likert, *The Human Organization*, App. II.
16. Likert, *The Human Organization*; Rensis Likert and D. G. Bowers, "Organizational Theory and Human Resource Accounting," *American Psychologist*, vol. 24, no. 6 (June 1969), pp. 585-92; Alfred J. Marrow, D. G. Bowers, and S. E. Seashore, *Management by Participation: Creating a Climate for Personal and Organizational Development* (New York: Harper & Row, 1967); and Tannenbaum, *Control in Organization*.
17. See, for example, Likert, *The Human Organization*, Chapter 6; and Likert and Bowers, "Organization Theory."
18. Likert, *The Human Organization*, App. II.
19. See, for example, Karlene Roberts, Raymond E. Miles, and L. Vaughn Blankenship, "Organizational Leadership Satisfaction and Productivity: A Comparative Analysis," *Academy of Management* (December 1968), pp. 401-14; and references cited in footnotes 11 and 16.
20. From *The Human Organization* by Rensis Likert. Copyright 1967 by McGraw-Hill, Inc. (Used with permission of McGraw-Hill Book Company, New York.)
21. Ibid., Chapter 10.

CHAPTER 6

1. Norbert Wiener, *Cybernetics: Or Control and Communication in the Animal and the Machine*, 2d ed. (New York: John Wiley & Sons, 1961).
2. J. Forrester, *Urban Dynamics* (Cambridge, Mass.: M.I.T. Press, 1969).
3. Jacques Ellul, *The Technological Society* (New York: Alfred A. Knopf, 1964).
4. Walter A. Shewart, *Statistical Method from the Viewpoint of Quality Control* (Washington, D.C.: Graduate School Press, U.S. Department of Agriculture, 1939).
5. S. B. Littauer et al., *Introduction to Statistical Method* (New York: McGraw-Hill, 1964).
6. Immanuel Kant, *Fundamental Principles of the Metaphysics of Morals* [1785].
7. Jeremy Bentham, *Introduction to Principles of Morals and Legislation* [1789] (Hafner Library of Classics, 1948).
8. Georg Hegel, *Phenomenology of Spirit* [1807].
9. Karl Marx, *Das Kapital* [1867].
10. Herbert Spencer, *First Principles* [1862].
11. Friedrich Nietzsche, *Thus Spake Zarathustra* [1883].
12. E. A. Singer, Jr., *On the Contented Life* (New York: Henry Holt & Co., 1936).
13. D. Braybrook and C. E. Lindblom, *A Strategy of Decision: Policy Evaluation as a Social Process* (Glencoe, N.Y.: Free Press, 1963).
14. D. N. Michael, *The Unprepared Society* (New York: Basic Books, 1968).
15. The literature on control is voluminous and sprawls across many disciplines. It also reaches far back into history, as some of the following citations indicate. And they are merely a sampling to guide the interested reader to other sources in the books cited. (For full references, consult the Bibliography.)

F. Emery (1969) provides a broad spectrum of readings on systems. Geoffrey Vickers (1967) defines management as a form of social regulation, and has many wise things to say about control, as does Beer (1966). Ackoff (1970, pp. 112 ff.) describes the "four steps" of control, predicting the outcomes of decisions, collecting information on performance, comparing predicted and actual outcomes, correcting for deficiencies. Jenkins and Youle (1968) discuss methods of "studying a firm in its totality." Johnson et al. (1964) discuss the application of general systems theory to management. Anthony et al. (1965) provide a set of readings on management control systems. Strong and Smith (1968) rely heavily on "information" as a basis of control. Bonini et al. (1964) emphasize budgets and other accounting devices in control. Vollmer (1967) writes about organizational design and its relation to control.

De Greene (1970) is a recent work which cites many references on the psychology and sociology of system management, an important subject virtually untouched in this chapter.

Sackman (1967) provides one of the most comprehensive books on systems and computers. Koelle and Vos (1965) provide sources on the design of large space programs. See Webb (1969) for a broad perspective of this problem from the point of view of NASA's former administrator.

Abt (1970) discusses the use of simulation games in management control.

Bernstein and Cerron (1969) discuss one of many techniques of "telling the future," one very popular idea about long-range control.

CHAPTER 7

1. William D. Carey is the former Assistant Director of the Bureau of the Budget from 1966 to 1969.

2. *Energy R & D and National Progress,* a report prepared for the Interdepartmental Energy Study under the direction of Ali Bulent Cambel (Washington, D.C.: U.S. Government Printing Office, 1964).

3. *Report of the President* (Washington, D.C.: Carnegie Institution of Washington, 1967-68).

4. *Report to the President on Government Contracting for Research and Development* (Washington, D.C.: Bureau of the Budget, 1962).

5. Elmer B. Staats, *Need for Improved Guidelines in Contracting for Research with Government-Sponsored Nonprofit Contractors,* Report to the Congress by the Comptroller General of the United States (February 10, 1969).

6. U.S. Congress, House, Technology Assessment Act of 1972, Conference Report to Accompany H.R. 10243, 92d Cong., 2d Sess., H.R. 92-1436, September 25, 1972.

7. Elmer B. Staats, *Review of Economic Opportunity Programs,* Report to the Congress by the Comptroller General of the United States (March 1969).

8. Frederic M. Scherer, "Government Research and Development Programs," *Measuring Benefits of Government Investments,* ed. Robert Dorfman (Washington, D.C.: Brookings Institution, 1965).

9. Letter from Elmer B. Staats, Comptroller General of the United States, to all Congressional Committee Chairmen, August 11, 1972, Comptroller General Letter No. B-161740, p. 2.

CHAPTER 8

1. See also D. Cartwright, "The Economics of Deaning," *Western Economic Journal* (spring 1965); Norman Kaplan, "The Role of the Research Administrator," *Administrative Science Quarterly*, vol. 4 (June 1959); and H. L. Dryden, "Responsibilities of the Research Director," *Scientific Research: Its Administration and Organization*, G. P. Bush and L. H. Hattery (Washington, D.C.: American University Press, 1950).

2. See, for example, L. R. Sayles and George Strauss, *Human Behavior in Organizations* (Englewood Cliffs, N.J.: Prentice-Hall, 1966), p. 347.

3. For further discussion of researcher's goals, see Renato Tagiuri, "Value Orientations and the Relationship of Managers and Scientists," *Administrative Science Quarterly* (1965), pp. 39-51; and Herbert A. Shepard, "Nine Dilemmas in Industrial Research," *Administrative Science Quarterly*, vol. 1, no. 3 (December 1956), pp. 295-305.

4. Among behavioral scientists, there is no consensus on the productivity of morals per se. See S. Katz and R. L. Kahn, "Leadership Practices in Relation to Productivity and Morale," *Group Dynamics: Research and Theory*, eds. Cartwright and Zander (Evanston, Ill.: Row Peterson, 1953, 1st ed.; 1956, 2d printing, pp. 612-27 (1st ed.), pp. 559-70 (2d ed.); Robert L. Kahn, "Productivity and Job Satisfaction," *Personnel Psychology*, vol. 13, no. 3 (fall 1960), pp. 257-87; Donald C. Pelz and Frank M. Andrews, *Scientists in Organizations* (New York: Wiley, 1966), p. 112; and Raymond Miles, "Human Relations or Human Resources?" *Harvard Business Review*, vol. 43, no. 4 (July 1965), pp. 148-63. But morale combined, say, with participation, is taken to be an important element of productivity.

5. I. Kant, *Fundamental Principles of the Metaphysic of Morals* [1785].

6. D. McGregor, *The Human Side of Enterprise* (New York: McGraw-Hill, 1960). McGregor argues that "the assumptions of Theory Y imply that unless integration is achieved *the organization will suffer*" (italics his). Thus management becomes committed to Theory Y to serve its own organizational ends.

7. For further elaboration of this point, see C. West Churchman, *Challenge to Reason* (New York: McGraw-Hill, 1968) and the reading suggestions at the end of that book.

8. For a further discussion of these constraints, see A. Papandreou, "Some Basic Problems in the Theory of the Firm," *A Survey of Contemporary Economics*, ed. B. F. Haley, vol. 2 (Homewood, Ill.: Irwin, 1952), pp. 183-222.

9. For empirical evidence of a public's attitute toward research and its importance, see H. Krauch and K. Schreiber, "Forschung und technischer Fortschritt im Bewusstein der Offenlishkeit—Ergebnisse einer Repräsentativbefragung," in *Soziale Welt*, Jahrg, 17 (1966), Heft 4, S. 289-315.

10. See C. West Churchman, *Prediction and Optimal Decision* (Englewood Cliffs, N.J.: Prentice-Hall, 1961), chapter 9 and its references.

11. A "classic" description of this process is given by Herbert A. Simon, *Administrative Behavior* (New York: The Free Press, 1965), p. 5.

12. See, for example, Miles, "Human Relations or Human Resources?"; Rensis Likert, *The Human Organization* (New York: McGraw-Hill, 1967); and Robert Tannenbaum and Fred Massarik, "Participation by Subordinates in the Managerial Decision-Making Process," *The Canadian Journal of Economics and Political Science*, vol. 16 (August 1950), pp. 408-18.

13. See, for example, W. J. J. Gordon, *Synectics* (New York: Harper & Row, 1961).

14. See J. Seligman, N. R. Baker, and A. H. Rubenstein, *Control Mechanisms in the Idea Flow Process: Model and Behavioral Study* (Evanston, Ill.: The Technological Institute, Northwestern University, June 1966).

15. See L. A. Zadeh, "Fuzzy Algorithms," *Information and Control,* vol. 12 (1968), pp. 94-102.

16. See Merrill M. Flood, "Research Project Evaluation," *Proceedings of the Fifth Annual Conference on Industrial Research,* ed. A. Rubenstein (New York: King's Crown Press, 1955), p. 28; James B. Quinn, "How to Evaluate Research Output," *Harvard Business Review,* vol. 38, no. 2 (March 1960), pp. 69-80; E. Mansfield, "Ratio of Return for Industrial R & D," *American Economic Review,* vol. 55, no. 2 (1965), p. 310; E. Mansfield and R. Brandenburg, "The Allocation, Characteristics and Outcome of the Firm's R & D Portfolio," *Journal of Business,* vol. 39 (1966), p. 447; Burton V. Dean, *Application of Operations Research to R & D* (New York: Wiley, 1963); and Burton V. Dean, *Evaluating, Selecting and Controlling R & D Projects* (New York: American Management Association, 1968).

17. See, for example, E. Duer Reeves, *Management of Industrial Research* (New York: Reinhold Publishing Corp., 1967), pp. 17-28; and Peter C. Sandretto, *The Economic Management of Research and Engineering* (New York: Wiley, 1968).

18. Dean, *Evaluating, Selecting and Controlling R & D Projects,* pp. 62-63.

19. Ibid., chapter 6.

20. See R. L. Ackoff and M. Martin, "The Dissemination and Use of Recorded Scientific Information," *Management Science* (1963), pp. 322-26; and H. Krauch, "Strukturwandel der Forschung," in *Strukturwandel der Wirtschaft im Gefolge der Computer* (Hrsg. F. Scharpenack), Verlag, J. C. B. Mohr (Paul Siebeck), Tubingen, Germany (1966).

21. See C. West Churchman, "The Design of Inquiring Systems," Internal Working Paper No. 107 (Berkeley: Space Sciences Laboratory, University of California, September 1969).

22. Edgar Schein et al., "Career Orientations and Perceptions of Rewarded Activity in Research Organizations," *Administrative Science Quarterly,* vol. 9, no. 4 (March 1965), pp. 333-49.

23. C. West Churchman, P. Ratoosh, and C. Kruytbosch, "The Role of the Research Administrator," *Research Program Effectiveness,* eds. M. C. Yovits et al. (New York: Gordon & Breach, 1966).

24. See T. S. Kuhn, *The Structure of Scientific Revolutions* (Chicago: University of Chicago Press, 1962).

25. For the theory of these costs, see, for example, R. L. Ackoff and M. Sasieni, *Fundamentals of Operations Research* (New York: Wiley, 1968).

26. What is being described in a simplified form is a version of the "decomposition algorithm." See G. B. Dantzig and Philip Wolfe, "The Decomposition Principle for Linear Programs," *Operations Research Journal,* vol. 8, no. 1 (January-February 1960).

27. For the dynamics of this process, see T. Marschak and J. Yahow, "The Sequential Selection of Approaches to a Task," *Management Science,* vol. 12, no. 9 (1966), p. 627.

28. As advocated, say, by Frederick J. Taylor, *Principles of Scientific Management* (New York: W. W. Norton & Co., 1967).

29. See Miles, "Human Relations or Human Resources?" or Likert, *The Human Organization.*

30. The engineering term is "cybernetics." See S. Beer, *Decision and Control* (New York: Wiley, 1966).

31. First introduced in this manner by J. Neyman and E. Pearson, "Contributions to the Theory of Testing Statistical Hypotheses," *Statistical Research Memoirs*, vol. 1 (1936). See also Paul Hoel, *Introduction to Mathematics & Statistics* (New York: Wiley, 1966), p. 48.

32. For example, the use of learning curves in the aircraft industry.

33. For further details of this argument, see C. West Churchman, *The Systems Approach* (New York: Delacorte Press, 1968).

34. See Richard O. Mason, *Dialectics in Decision Making: A Study in the Use of Counterplanning and Structural Debate in Management Information Systems*, Internal Working Paper No. 87, Social Sciences Project (Berkeley: Space Sciences Laboratory, University of California, June 1968).

35. A somewhat different but related view can be found in R. G. Siu, *The Tao of Science* (New York: The Technology Press, Massachusetts Institute of Technology and Wiley, 1957).

36. Kant, *Fundamental Principles of Metaphysic of Morals*.

37. Carl G. Jung states the idea quite well in *Two Essays on Analytical Psychology*, Bollinger Series XX (New York: Pantheon Books, 1953), pp. 223-24.

38. See R. M. Hower and C. D. Orth, *Managers and Scientists: Some Human Problems in Industrial Research Organizations* (Boston: Graduate School of Business Administration, Harvard University, 1963).

39. A "discipline," as I use the term, may in fact be only part of a larger discipline like physics, chemistry, and so on. It is essentially the leaders and followers of one area of intellectual interest, and, of course, may grow or decline, or even disappear altogether.

40. There is, of course, the old Germanic idea of a professor and his flock of student followers, and the professor often did dominate. No doubt some of this concept of the research community does occur today, but few researchers would like to admit it if it does.

41. Or dean. The distinction between the research director and the dean seems to be mainly a matter of emphasis. A college dean of a science department is emphatically committed to the scientist's philosophy, and his problem is how to be a good administrator at the same time; a research director may be more emphatically committed to management's goals, and his problem is how to serve the scientists as well.

CHAPTER 9

1. Ad Hoc Committee for Evaluation of Federal Support of Science, *The Crisis Facing American Science* (New York: New York Academy of Sciences, 1968), Foreword.

2. Quoted by Gene Bylinsky in "U.S. Science Enters a Not-So-Golden Era," *Fortune* (November 1968), p. 197. Bylinsky adds correctly that "this is a view widely shared by other leaders of science."

3. Harvey Brooks, "Physics and the Polity," *Science* (April 26, 1968), pp. 396-400.

4. *Basic Research and National Goals*, a report to the Committee on Science and Astronautics, U.S. Congress, House (Washington, D.C.: National Academy of Sciences, March 1965), p. 1.

5. Harvey Brooks, "Future Needs for the Support of Basic Research," *Basic Research and National Goals*, pp. 77-110, especially pp. 94 and 98.

6. "Much speculation has been directed to the identification of the necessary rate of growth of graduate research and education. Some say that a rate of 15 per cent per year is the necessary minimum increase in level of support. But I have not yet encountered the thorough economic analysis that one might expect to lie behind such a widely quoted figure," Gardner told a meeting of consultants at the National Institutes of Health, August 23, 1966.

7. From an address by Donald Hornig to the American Physical Society (Washington, D.C., April 26, 1967).

8. Clark Kerr, "New Challenges to the College and University," *Agenda for the Nation*, Kermit Gordon, ed. (Washington, D.C.: Brookings Institution, 1968), pp. 258-63.

9. "Private Enrollment Drops; Graduate Totals Fall Short," *Chronicle of Higher Education* (March 24, 1969), p. 1.

10. When interviewed by the *New York Times* shortly after his designation as President-elect Nixon's science adviser, DuBridge stated: "If the basic research budget of this country were right last year, it would not be right this year or next year unless there was built into it something like a 10 per cent a year increase.

"Now, obviously, a 10 per cent increase can't go on for a hundred years, or it would exceed the total Federal budget. But in the next few years, at least something on the order of 10 per cent, maybe it is 12 or 19 per cent, is a built-in increase factor in the state and private university budgets, and the Government must recognize this." DuBridge to Seek Closer Ties of Government with Scientists," *New York Times* (December 17, 1969), p. 30.

11. David M. Blank and George J. Stigler, *The Demand and Supply of Scientific Personnel* (New York: National Bureau of Economic Research, 1957), pp. 29, 105.

12. Nicholas DeWitt, *Soviet Professional Manpower* (Washington, D.C.: National Science Foundation, 1955), pp. 256-57.

13. *Meeting Manpower Needs in Science and Technology* (Washington, D.C.: The White House, December 12, 1962). The report declared, "Impending shortages of talented, highly trained scientists and engineers threaten the successful fulfillment of vital national commitments. Unless remedial action is taken promptly, future needs for superior engineers, mathematicians, and physical scientists will seriously outstrip the supply." The report recommended raising the proportion of college students who go on to graduate school and increasing the number of Ph.D.'s awarded each year in engineering, mathematics, and the physical sciences from 2,000 in 1950 and 3,000 in 1960 to 7,500 by 1970. In 1965, 5,635 Ph.D.'s and in 1967, 6,785 Ph.D.'s were awarded in these fields.

14. The report stated, "In the years ahead, the nation's needs for scientists and engineers unquestionably will increase, and probably at a faster rate than they have in the past. Although the supply of this manpower also will increase, it may not keep pace with all the possible needs to which domestic and international influences will give rise." On the other hand, the report noted, "At present, there are both unfilled positions and unemployed scientists and engineers.... there are identifiable surpluses resulting, for example, from industries changing from older to newer technologies.... Currently, changes in the programs of the Department of Defense are resulting in cutbacks in certain types of employment. A number of engineers face problems of adapting themselves to more advanced

technologies as their older skills become obsolete. Thus, the employment situation remains mixed." See also *Toward Better Utilization of Scientific and Engineering Talent, A Program for Action,* report of the Committee on Utilization of Scientific and Engineering Manpower (Washington, D.C.: National Academy of Sciences, 1964), pp. 1-2.

15. Bernard Berelson, *Graduate Education in the United States* (New York: McGraw-Hill, 1960), pp. 76-77 and 79 (his italics). Deficiencies in the NEA statistics were also noted in Harold Orlans, *The Effects of Federal Programs on Higher Education* (Washington, D.C.: Brookings Institution, 1962), pp. 13-14.

16. Allan Cartter and Robert Farrell, "Higher Education in the Last Third of the Century," *The Educational Record* (spring 1965), p. 125.

17. Ibid., note 5.

18. John Folger, "The Balance Between Supply and Demand for College Graduates," *The Journal of Human Resources* (spring 1967), p. 167.

19. *Toward a Public Policy for Graduate Education in the Sciences* (Washington, D.C.: National Science Board, 1969), p. 11.

20. Ibid., pp. 10-11.

21. Daniel S. Greenberg, *The Politics of Pure Science* (New York: New American Library, 1967), p. 291.

22. One is the National Science Board's proposal for a basic shift to departmental grants in the government's funding of academic science. (See *Toward a Public Policy for Graduate Education in the Sciences,* 1969).

23. *Scientific Progress, the Universities and the Federal Government,* statement by the President's Science Advisory Committee (Washington, D.C.: The White House, November 15, 1960), p. 20.

24. Ibid., p. v.

25. Ibid., p. 21.

26. *Biomedical Science and Its Administration, A Study of the National Institutes of Health* (Washington, D.C.: The White House, February 1965), pp. 36-37.

27. The Stans memorandum of September 21, 1959, "Commercial-industrial Activities of the Government Providing Products or Services for Governmental Use," is reprinted in *The Future Role of the Atomic Energy Commission Laboratories* (Washington, D.C.: Joint Committee on Atomic Energy, October 1960), pp. 274-77; the Bell Report to the President *Government Contracting for Research and Development* (Washington, D.C.: Bureau of the Budget, April 30, 1962).

28. In testimony on May 1, 1969, Science Adviser Lee DuBridge stated, "Just in the last couple of years the number of classified research agreements which DOD has with universities has been cut in half. Only about 4 percent of all the research agreements which DOD has with universities now are in the classified area, and these are still being further reduced by mutual agreement." U.S. Congress, Senate, Committee on Government Operations, Subcommittee on Government Research, *Federal Support of Project Grants: Indirect Costs and Cost Sharing,* 91st Cong., 1st sess., April 22, 23, and May 1, 1969, part 1, p. 93.

29. In the course of an April 1, 1969, address to a conference of the National Association of Manufacturers in Washington, D.C., Tonsor stated, "In order to ensure circumstances in which teaching rather than research or community service [is] the primary objective of the university, government at all levels must forego the temptation of easy recourse to the enormous resources of the university.... both the government and the university would be better served, under most circumstances, were both basic and applied research in the national defense area done in antonomous research

institutes." The address was distributed by President Nixon to his principal staff and officials concerned with government policy toward higher education with the note that "this happens to be my view.... I want everyone who has anything to do with education to read this speech carefully and to follow this line in their public announcements." (See *Higher Education and National Affairs*, April 25, 1969, pp. 1ff. and *Chronicle of Higher Education*, May 5, 1969, p. 3). To be sure, the President can hardly be said to have committed himself to every sentence in Tonsor's address, and his advisers would be in sharp disagreement about the desirability of reducing military research on campus.

30. Borges's library contained error as well as truth; however, one may wonder if a library of the *whole* truth, every last speck of it in the universe, would be of any greater help to man who could wander forever in the catalogs and stacks, unable to find, absorb, and use precisely those truths that he needs each moment of his life. Jorge Luis Borges, "The Library of Babel," *Labyrinths* (Norfold, Conn.: New Directions, 1962), pp. 51-58.

31. Charles J. Hitch and Roland N. McKean, *The Economics of Defense in the Nuclear Age* (Cambridge, Mass.: Harvard University Press, 1960), p. 262.

32. James L. Goddard, "The Drug Establishment," *Esquire* (March 1969), reprinted in *Congressional Record*, daily ed. (March 4, 1969), pp. S 2310-13.

33. *Wall Street Journal* (June 26, 1969), reprinted in *Congressional Record*, daily ed. (July 7, 1969), p. E 5630.

34. See, for example, Donald Michael: "In twenty years, other things being equal [just which "other things"?], most of the routine blue-collar and white-collar tasks that can be done by cybernation will be.... Most of our citizens will be unable to understand the cybernated world in which they live.... There will be a small, almost separate society of people in rapport with the advanced computers." *Cybernation: The Silent Conquest* (Santa Barbara, Calif.: Center for Study of Democratic Institutions, 1962), p. 44.

35. In his historical review, "Technology and Public Policy," Morgan Sherwood reaches the same conclusion. "With rare exceptions, the government, throughout American history, has approached technological issues pragmatically, one at a time...." Eds. Melvin Kranzberg and Carroll Pursell, Jr., *Technology in Western Civilization*, vol. 2 (New York: Oxford University Press, 1967), p. 497.

36. Ibid.

37. Golovin's full proposal is as follows: "In the presence of technically plausible arguments that the mass introduction of a new product or process will tend to degrade environmental characteristics important to physical and psychological well-being, such introduction will be controlled by industry and the local, state and federal governments so as to insure that mass public exposure is minimized or does not occur until adequate evidence has been accumulated of the absence of significantly deleterious or publicly undesirable consequences." Nicholas E. Golovin, "The Public and National Noise Standards," presented at the symposium *Where Do We Stand on Standards for Noise?* (Cleveland: 76th Meeting of the Acoustical Society of America, November 19-22, 1968); see also "Golovin's Law," *New Scientist* (November 28, 1968), p. 478.

38. See "President Establishes Social Research Staff," *The Washington Report* (August-September 1969), sec. A, p. 12.

39. The author's discussion of a technology assessment board was written some months before the establishment by Congress in 1972 of the

NOTES: CHAPTER 9

Joint Committee on Technology Assessment, shortly before this volume went to press.—Editor's note.

40. U.S. Congress, House, Committee on Science and Astronautics, Report of the Subcommittee on Science, Research, and Development, *Science, Technology and Public Policy During the Ninetieth Congress*, 91st Cong., 1st sess. (July 1969), p. 106.

41. U.S. Congress, House, Committee on Science and Astronautics, Proceedings before the Subcommittee on Science, Research, and Development, *Technology Assessment* (see statement of Emilio Q. Daddario, chairman), 90th Cong., 1st sess. (1967), p. 4.

42. U.S. Congress, House, Committee on Science and Astronautics, Report of the Subcommittee on Science, Research, and Development, *Technology Assessment Seminar*, 90th Cong., 1st sess. (September 21 and 22, 1967), p. 152.

43. Morton Mintz, "Lee Questions Fitness of Next NAS Chief," *Washington Post* (February 17, 1969), sec. A., p. 12.

44. Goddard, "The Drug Establishment."

45. U.S. Congress, House, H.R. 6698, 90th Cong., 1st sess. (March 7, 1967), sec. 7.

46. See Alvin Weinberg, "Social Problems and National Socio-Technical Institutes" (and the other papers by Weinberg cited in footnote 1 of that paper), *Applied Science and Technological Progress*, a report to the Committee on Science and Astronautics, U.S. Congress, House (Washington, D.C.: National Academy of Sciences, 1967), p. 415. A similar argument is developed by Amitai Etzioni, "'Shortcuts' to Social Change?" *The Public Interest* (summer 1968), pp. 40-51.

47. Statement of Emilio Q. Daddario, p. 8; for complete reference, see n40.

48. Remarks of J. William Zabor, Vice President for Industrial Chemicals Research, Wyandotte Chemicals Corporation, at the October 1964 meeting of the Industrial Research Institute, in *Research Management* (March 1965), p. 114.

49. Cited by James D. Carroll in "Science and the City: The Question of Authority," *Science* (February 28, 1969), p. 908.

50. Ibid., p. 905.

Bibliography

BOOKS

Abrahamson, Mark. *The Professional in the Organization.* Chicago: Rand McNally & Co. (1967).

Abt, Clark. *Serious Games.* New York: Viking Press (1970).

Ackoff, R. L. *A Concept of Corporate Planning.* New York: John Wiley & Sons (1970).

———, and Sasieni, M. *Fundamentals of Operations Research.* New York: John Wiley & Sons (1968).

Anthony, Robert N. "Characteristics of Management Control Systems." In *Management Control Systems,* edited by Robert N. Anthony et al. Homewood, Ill.: Richard D. Irwin (1965).

Barnard, Chester. *The Functions of the Executive.* Harvard University Press (1947).

Beckner, Lloyd. *Scientific Age—Impact of Science on Society.* New Haven, Conn.: Yale University Press (1964).

Beer, Stafford. *Decision and Control, The Meaning of Operational Research and Management Cybernetics.* London: John Wiley & Sons (1966).

Bentham, Jeremy. *Introduction to Principles of Morals and Legislation* [1789]. Hafner Library of Classics (1948).

Berelson, Bernard. *Graduate Education in the United States.* New York: McGraw-Hill (1960).

Blank, David M., and Stigler, George J. *The Demand and Supply of Scientific Personnel.* New York: National Bureau of Economic Research (1957).

Boguslow, Robert. *Utopians: A Study of Systems Design and Social Change.* Englewood Cliffs, N.J.: Prentice-Hall (1965).

Bonini, C., Jaedicke, R., and Wagner, H. *Management Controls: New Directions in Basic Research.* New York: McGraw-Hill (1964).

Borges, Jorge Luis. "The Library of Babel." In *Labyrinths.* Norfolk, Conn.: New Directions (1962).

Bowen, Howard R. *Toward Social Economy.* New York: Rinehart (1948).

Bowers, D. G., ed. *Applying Modern Management Principles to Sales Organization.* Ann Arbor, Mich.: Foundations for Research on Human Behavior (1963).

Braybrooke, D., and Lindblom, C. E. *A Strategy of Decision: Policy Evaluation as a Social Process.* Glencoe, N.Y.: Free Press (1963).

Brooks, Harvey. *The Government of Science.* Cambridge, Mass.: M.I.T. Press (1968).

Brumbaugh, Robert S. *Ancient Greek Gadgets and Machines.* New York: Crowell-Collier Publishing Co. (1966).

Brzezinski, Zbigniew. *American in the Technetronic Age.* New York: Columbia University, School of International Affairs (1967).

Burkhead, Jesse. *Government Budgeting.* New York: John Wiley & Sons (1956).

Burnham, James. *The Managerial Revolution.* New York: John Day Co. (1941).

Burns, T., and Stalher, G. M. *The Management of Innovation.* London: Travistock Publications (1961).

Bush, George P., and Hattery, Lowell H. *Scientific Research: Its Administration and Organization.* Washington, D.C.: University Press of Washington (1950).

Bush, Vannevar. *Science: The Endless Frontier.* Washington, D.C.: U.S. Government Printing Office (1945).

Caldwell, Lynton K., and DeVille, William B. *Science, Technology, and Public Policy: A Syllabus for Advanced Study,* vols. 1 and 2. Bloomington: Indiana University, Department of Government (1968-69).

Carey, William D. "Equipping Congress to Deal with Science." In *Science Policy and the University.* Washington, D.C.: Brookings Institution (1968).

———. "Research, Development, and the Federal Budget." In *Science and Society,* ed. N. Kaplan. New York: Rand McNally (1965).

———. "Science Policy Making in the United States." In *Decision Making in National Science Policy,* ed. A. de Reuck, M. Goldsmith, and J. Knight. London: J. A. Churchill, Ltd. (1968).

———. "The Support of Scientific Research." In *The Politics of American Science,* ed. J. Penick. New York: Rand McNally (1965).

Churchman, C. West. *Challenge to Reason.* New York: McGraw-Hill (1968).

———. *Design of Inquiring Systems,* Internal Working Papers no. 28, 29, 31, 31b, 45, 46, 49, Social Sciences Project. Berkeley: Space Sciences Laboratory, University of California.

———. *Prediction and Optimal Decision.* Englewood Cliffs, N.J.: Prentice-Hall (1961).

———. *The Systems Approach.* New York: Delacorte Press (1968).

———. Kruytbosch, C. E., and Ratoosh, P. *The Role of the Research Administrator,* Social Sciences Project. Berkeley: Space Sciences Laboratory, University of California (October 1965); see also *Research Program Effectiveness,* ed. M. C. Yovits et al. New York: Gordon & Breach (1966).

Cobb, V. Wayne. "The Mid-Career and Senior Federal Research & Development Employee." In *Science Administration, Education, and Career Mobility.* Bloomington: Institute of Public Administration, Indiana University (1966).

Colm, Gerhard. *Essays in Public Finance and Fiscal Policy.* New York: Oxford University Press (1955).

"Commercial-Industrial Activities of the Government Providing Products or Services for Governmental Use." In *The Future Role of the Atomic Energy Commission Laboratories.* Washington, D.C.: Joint Committee on Atomic Energy (October 1960).

Commoner, Barry. *Science and Survival.* New York: Viking Press (1966).

Cyert, Richard M., and March, James G. *A Behavioral Theory of the Firm.* Englewood Cliffs, N J.: Prentice-Hall (1963).

Danhof, Clarence. *Government Contracting and Technological Change.* Washington, D.C : Brookings Institution (1968).

Danielson, Lee E. "Characteristics of Engineers in Industry." In *Management and the Engineer in Industry,* Proceedings of the Third Annual Conference of Professional Engineers in Industry. Washington, D C.: National Society of Professional Engineers (October 1965).

Dean, Burton V. *Application of Operations Research to R & D*. New York: John Wiley & Sons (1963).
———. *Evaluating, Selecting and Controlling R & D Projects*. American Management Association (1968).
De Greene, K. D., ed. *Systems Psychology*. New York: McGraw-Hill (1970).
DeWitt, Nicholas. *Soviet Professional Manpower*. Washington, D.C.: National Science Foundation (1955).
Dorfman, Robert, ed. *Measuring Benefits of Government Investments*. Washington, D.C.: Brookings Institution (1965).
Drucker, Peter F. *The Age of Discontinuity: Guidelines to Our Changing Society*. New York: Harper & Row, Publishers (1968).
Dryden, H. L. "Responsibilities of the Research Director." In *Scientific Research: Its Administration and Organization*, ed. G. P. Bush and L. H. Hattery. Washington, D.C.: University Press of Washington (1950).
Dupree, A. Hunter. *Science in the Federal Government*. Cambridge, Mass.: Harvard University Press, Belknap Press (1957).
Ellul, Jacques. *The Technological Society*. New York: Alfred A. Knopf (1964).
Emery, F. E., ed. *Systems Thinking*. Harmondsworth, England: Penguin Books (1969).
Etzioni, Amitai. *Modern Organizations*. Englewood Cliffs, N.J.: Prentice-Hall (1964).
Flood, Merrill M. "Research Project Evaluation." *Proceedings of the Fifth Annual Conference on Industrial Research*, ed. A. Rubenstein. New York: King's Crown Press (1955).
Forrester, J. *Urban Dynamics*. Cambridge, Mass.: M.I.T. Press (1969).
Galbraith, John Kenneth, and Randhawa, M. S. *The New Industrial State*. Boston: Houghton Mifflin Co. (1967).
Georgopoulos, Basil S., and Mann, F. C. *The Community General Hospital*. New York: Macmillan Co. (1962).
Giedion, Siegfried. *Mechanization Takes Command*. New York: Oxford University Press (1948).
Gilpin, Robert, and Wright, Christopher. *Scientists and National Policy Making*. New York: Columbia University Press (1964).
Ginzberg, Eli, ed. *Technology and Social Change*. New York: Columbia University Press (1964).
Glaser, Barney G. *Organizational Scientists: Their Professional Careers*. New York: Bobbs-Merrill Co. (1964).
Goodman, Richard A., and Abernathy, William J. *Summary of a Workshop on Dimensional Analysis for Design, Development, and Research Executives*. Washington, D.C.: Office of Naval Research and NASA (October 1971).
Gordon, Robert A. *Business Leadership in the Large Corporation*. Washington, D.C.: Brookings Institution (1945).
Gordon, W. J. J. *Synectics*. New York: Harper & Row (1961).
Greenberg, Daniel S. *The Politics of Pure Science*. New York: New American Library (1967).
Gruber, W. H., and Marquis, D. G., eds. *Factors in the Transfer of Technology*. Cambridge, Mass.: M.I.T. Press (1969).
Haley, B. F., ed. *A Survey of Contemporary Economics*, 2 vols. Homewood, Ill.: Richard D. Irwin (1952).
Hamilton, Richard A. *A Comparative Analysis of the Professional's Occupational Environment at the Manned Spacecraft Center*, MSC-BM-MR-69-2. Houston, Texas: Manned Spacecraft Center (January 1969).
Hegel, Georg. *Phenomenology of Spirit* [1807].

Hill, Karl B., ed. *The Management of Scientists.* Boston: Beacon Press (1964).
Hitch, Charles J., and McKean, Roland N. *The Economics of Defense in the Nuclear Age.* Cambridge, Mass.: Harvard University Press (1960).
Hoel, Paul. *Introduction to Mathematics & Statistics.* New York: John Wiley & Sons (1966).
Hower, R. M., and Orth, C. D. *Managers and Scientists: Some Human Problems in Industrial Research Organizations.* Cambridge, Mass.: Graduate School of Business Administration, Harvard University (1963).
Hugh-Jones, E. M., ed. *Human Relations and Modern Management.* Amsterdam: North Holland Publishing Co. (1958).
Jewell, Malcom E., and Patterson, Samuel E. *The Legislative Process in the United States.* New York: Random House (1966).
Johnson, Richard A., Kast, Fremont E., and Rosenzweig, James E. *The Theory and Management of Systems,* 2d ed. New York: McGraw-Hill (1967).
Juenger, Frederick. *The Failure of Technology.* Chicago: Henry Regnery Co. (1957).
Jung, Carl G. *Two Essays on Analytical Psychology,* Bollinger Series, no. 20. New York: Pantheon Books (1953).
Kahn, R. L. "Human Relations on the Shop Floor." In *Human Relations and Modern Management,* ed. E. M. Hugh-Jones. Amsterdam: North Holland Publishing Co. (1958).
Kahn, R. L., et al. *Organizational Stress: Studies in Role Conflict and Ambiguity.* New York: John Wiley & Sons (1964).
Kant, Immanuel. *Fundamental Principles of the Metaphysics of Morals* [1785].
Karger, Delmar W., and Murdick, Robert G. *Managing Engineering and Research.* New York: Industrial Press (1963).
Kast, Fremont, and Rosenzweig, James E., eds. *Science, Technology and Management.* New York: McGraw-Hill (1963).
Katz, Daniel, and Kahn, Robert L. *The Social Psychology of Organizations.* New York: John Wiley & Sons (1966).
———. "Some Recent Findings in Human Relations Research." In *Readings in Social Psychology,* ed. E. Swanson, T. Newcomb, and E. Hartley. New York: Henry Holt & Co. (1952).
Katz, S., and Kahn, R. L. "Leadership Practices in Relation to Productivity and Morale." In *Group Dynamics: Research and Theory,* 3d ed., ed. Dorwin Cartwright and A. Zander. New York: Harper & Row, Publishers (1968).
Kerr, Clark. "New Challenges to the College and University." In *Agenda for the Nation,* ed. Kermit Gordon. Washington, D.C.: Brookings Institution (1968).
Kilpatrick, F. P., Cummings, M. C., and Jennings, M. K. *The Image of the Federal Service.* Washington, D.C.: Brookings Institution (1964).
Kidd, Charles V. *American Universities and Federal Research.* Cambridge, Mass.: Harvard University Press (1959).
Koelle, H. H., and Vos, R. G., eds. *A Procedure to Analyze and Evaluate Alternative Space Program Plans,* NASA N65-19694 (March 1965).
Kornhauser, William. *Scientists in Industry: Conflict and Accommodation.* Berkeley and Los Angeles: University of California Press (1962).
Kranzberg, Melvin, and Pursell, Carroll, Jr., eds. *Technology in Western Civilization,* vol 2. New York: Oxford University Press (1967).

Krauch, H. "Strukturwandel der Forschung," *Strukturwandel der Wirtschaft im Gefolge der Computer* (Hrsg. F. Scharpenack). Tubingen, Germany: Verlag, J. C. B. Mohr (Paul Siebeck, 1966).

Kuhn, Thomas S. *The Structure of Scientific Revolutions.* Chicago: University of Chicago Press (1962).

Likert, Rensis. *The Human Organization: Its Management and Value.* New York: McGraw-Hill (1967).

——. *New Patterns of Management.* New York: McGraw-Hill (1961).

Lindblom, C. E. *The Policy Making Process.* Englewood Cliffs, N.J.: Prentice-Hall (1968).

Littauer, S. B., et al. *Introduction to Statistical Method.* New York: McGraw-Hill (1964).

Mann, F. C., and Baumbartel, H. J. *The Supervisor's Concern with Costs in an Electric Power Company.* Ann Arbor, Mich.: Institute for Social Research (1953).

——, and Dent, J. *Appraisals of Supervisors and Attitudes of Their Employees in an Electric Power Company.* Ann Arbor, Mich.: Institute for Social Research (1954).

——, and Hoffman, L. R. *Automation and the Worker: A Study of Social Change in Power Plants.* New York: Holt, Rinehart and Winston (1960).

——, Indik, B. P., and Vroom, V. H. *The Productivity of Work Groups.* Ann Arbor, Mich.: Institute for Social Research (1963).

Marcson, Simon. *The Scientist in American Industry.* New York: Harper & Row, Publishers (1960).

Marrow, Alfred J., Bowers, D. G., and Seashore, S. E., *Management by Participation: Creating a Climate for Personal and Organizational Development.* New York: Harper & Row, Publishers (1967).

Marx, Karl. *Das Kapital* [1867].

Mason, Richard O. *Dialectics in Decision Making: A Study in the Use of Counterplanning and Structural Debate in Management Information Systems,* Internal Working Paper No. 87, Social Sciences Project. Berkeley: Space Sciences Laboratory, University of California (June 1968).

McCamy, James L. *Science and Public Administration.* University, Ala.: University of Alabama Press (1960).

McGregor, Douglas. *The Human Side of Enterprise.* New York: McGraw-Hill (1960).

McNab, John J. "Preparing Scientists for Management." In *The Bridge Between Science and Management.* Proceedings of the 19th International Management Conference. New York (October 1964), pp. 105-13.

Michael, D. N. *Cybernation: The Silent Conquest.* Santa Barbara, Calif.: Center for Study of Democratic Institutions (1962).

——. *The Unprepared Society.* New York: Basic Books (1968).

Moranian, Thomas. *The Research and Development Engineer as Manager.* New York: Holt, Rinehart and Winston (1963).

Mosher, Harold. "Motivating Your Engineers for Greater Creativity and Productive Effort." In *Management and the Engineer in Industry.* Washington, D.C.: National Society of Professional Engineers (October 1965).

Mott, Paul E., et al. *Shift Work: The Social, Psychological, and Physical Consequences.* Ann Arbor, Mich.: University of Michigan Press (1965).

Musgrave, Richard A. *The Theory of Public Finance: A Study in Public Finance: A Study in Public Economy.* New York: McGraw-Hill (1959).

National Institute of Public Affairs. *University Offerings on the Career Education Awards Program, 1969-1970.* Washington, D.C.: (1968).

Nelson, William. *The Politics of Science.* New York: Oxford Univeristy Press (1968).

Nietzsche, Friedrich. *Thus Spake Zarathustra* [1883].

Orlans, Harold. *The Effects of Federal Programs on Higher Education.* Washington, D.C.: Brookings Institution (1962).

———, ed. *Science Policy and the University: A Symposium.* Washington, D.C.: Brookings Institution (1968).

Papandreou, A. "Some Basic Problems in the Theory of the Firm." In *A Survey of Contemporary Economics,* vol. II, ed. B. F. Haley. Homewood, Ill.: Richard D. Irwin (1952).

Pelz, Donald C., and Andrews, F. M. *Scientists in Organizations: Productive Climates for Research and Development.* New York: John Wiley & Sons (1966).

Predicting Managerial Success. Ann Arbor, Mich.: Foundation for Research on Human Behavior (1968).

Price, Derek J. *Little Science, Big Science.* New York: Columbia University Press (1963).

Price, Don K. *Government and Science.* New York: New York University Press (1954).

———. *The Scientific Estate.* Cambridge, Mass.: Harvard University Press (1965).

Randall, Raymond L., and Simpson, Dick W., eds. *Science Administration, Education and Career Mobility: Summary of the Proceedings and Working Papers of the University-Federal Agency Conference Sponsored by Purdue and Indiana Universities for the United States Civil Service Commission, November 7-9, 1965.* Bloomington, Indiana: Indiana University, Institute of Public Administration (1966).

Reagan, Michael D. *Science and the Federal Patron.* New York: Oxford University Press (1969).

Reeves, E. Duer. *Management of Industrial Research.* New York: Reinhold Publishing Corp. (1967).

Reiss, Howard. "The Organization of Science in a Technology-Oriented Organization." In *The Fundamental Research Activity in a Technology-Dependent Organization.* Washington, D.C.: Air Force Office of Scientific Research (1965).

Riggs, Fred Warren. *The Ecology of Public Administration.* New York: Asia Publishing House (1961).

Ritterbush, Philip C., ed. *Scientific Institutions of the Future.* Washington, D.C.: Acropolis (1972).

Ritti, R. Richard. *Engineers and the Industrial Corporation.* New York: Columbia University Press (1970).

Roman, Daniel D. *Research and Development Management: The Economics and Administration of Research.* New York: Appleton-Century-Crofts (1968).

Rosenthal, Albert H. *An Evaluation of the Management Intern Program.* Houston, Texas: Manned Spacecraft Center, NASA (1967).

Roshold, Robert L. *An Administrative History of NASA, 1958-63,* NASA SP-4101. Washington, D.C.: U.S. Government Printing Office (1966).

Roudsepp, Eugene. *Managing Creative Scientist and Engineers.* London and New York: Collier-Macmillan (1963).

Sackman, Harold. *Computers, Systems Science, and Evolving Society: The Challenge of Man-Machine Digital Systems.* New York: John Wiley & Sons (1967).

Samuelson, Paul. *Economics: An Introductory Analysis.* New York: McGraw-Hill (1964).
Sandretto, Peter C. *The Economic Management of Research and Engineering.* New York: John Wiley & Sons (1968).
Sayles, Lenonard R. *Managerial Behavior.* New York: McGraw-Hill (1964).
———, and Strauss, George. *Human Behavior in Organizations.* Englewood Cliffs, N.J.: Prentice-Hall (1966).
Scherer, Frederic M. "Government Research and Development Programs." In *Measuring Benefits of Government Investments,* ed. Robert Dorfman. Washington, D.C.: Brookings Institution (1965).
Schooler, Dean, Jr. *Science, Scientists and Public Policy.* Glencoe, N.Y.: Free Press (1971).
Schultze, Charles L., et al. *Setting National Priorities: The 1973 Budget.* Washington, D.C.: Brookings Institution (1972).
Science and Public Policy in the American University, papers delivered at a conference sponsored by Indiana University and Purdue University. Bloomington: Indiana University, Department of Government (1969).
Seashore, S. E. *Group Cohesiveness in the Industrial Work Group.* Ann Arbor, Mich.: Institute for Social Research (1954).
———, and Bowers, D. G. *Changing the Structure and Functioning of an Organization.* Ann Arbor, Mich.: Institute for Social Research (1963).
Seligman, J., Baker, N. R., and Rubenstein, A. H. *Control Mechanisms in the Idea Flow Process: Model and Behavioral Study.* Evanston, Ill.: The Technological Institute, Northwestern University (June 1966).
Servan-Schreiber, J.-J. *The American Challenge.* New York: Atheneum Publishers (1968).
Sherwood, Morgan. "Technology and Public Policy." In *Technology in Western Civilization,* vol. 2, ed. Melvin Kranzberg and Carroll Pursell, Jr., New York: Oxford University Press (1967).
Shewart, Walter A. *Statistical Method from the Viewpoint of Quality Control.* Washington, D.C.: Graduate School Press, U.S. Department of Agriculture (1939).
Siepert, Albert F. "Creating the Management Climate for Effective Research in Government Laboratories." In *The Management of Scientists,* Karl Hill. Boston: Beacon Press (1964).
Simon, Herbert A. *Administrative Behavior.* New York: Free Press (1965).
———. *Administrative Behavior: A Study of Decision-Making Process in Administrative Organization,* 2nd ed. New York: Macmillan Co. (1957).
———. *The New Science of Management Decision.* New York: Harper & Row (1960).
Singer, E. A., Jr. *On the Contented Life.* New York: Henry Holt & Co. (1936).
Siu, R. G. H. *The Tao of Science.* New York: Technology Press, M.I.T. and John Wiley & Sons (1957).
Snow, C. P. *Two Cultures: And a Second Look.* Cambridge: Cambridge University Press (1964).
Solem, Arnie. "How Effective Are Management Development Programs?" In *Proceedings of the Conference on Increasing the Effectiveness of Scientists & Engineers.* Kansas City, Mo. (April 1959), p. 70.
Spencer, Herbert. *First Principles* [1862].
Stanley, David. *The Higher Federal Service.* Washington, D.C.: Brookings Institution (1964).
Starr, Chauncey. "The Engineer-Manager, a New Professional Challenge." *Proceedings of the National Conference on Engineering Brainpower for the Aerospace Industry.* Washington, D.C.: National Association of Professional Engineers (October 1963), p. 84.

Stieglitz, H. *Organizational Planning.* New York: National Industrial Conference Board (1962).
Strong, Earl P., and Smith, Robert D. *Management Control Models.* New York: Holt, Rinehart and Winston (1968).
A Study of the Career Education Awards Program of the National Institute of Public Affairs. Washington, D.C.: U.S. Civil Service Commission, Bureau of Training (1967).
Swanson, E., Newcomb, T., and Hartley, E., eds. *Readings in Social Psychology.* New York: Holt, Rinehart and Winston (1952).
Swenson, Loyd S., Jr., Grimwood, James M., and Alexander, Charles C. *This New Ocean,* NASA SP-4201. Washington, D.C.: U.S. Government Printing Office (1966).
Szilard, Leo. *The Voice of the Dolphins.* New York: Simon & Schuster (1961).
Tannenbaum, Arnold S. *Control in Organizations.* New York: McGraw-Hill (1968).
Taylor, Calvin W., and Barron, Frank, eds. *Scientific Creativity: Its Recognition and Development.* New York: John Wiley & Sons (1963).
Taylor, Frederick J. *Principles of Scientific Management.* New York: W. W. Norton & Co. (1967).
Teich, Albert H., ed. *Technology and Man's Future.* New York: St. Martin's Press (1972).
Thayer, Lee O. *Administrative Communication.* Homewood, Ill.: Richard D. Irwin (1961).
Thorelli, Hans B. "Organization Theory: An Ecological View." *Academy of Management Proceedings.* 27th Annual Meeting (December 27-29, 1967), pp. 66-84.
Vickers, Geoffrey. *Towards a Sociology of Management.* New York: Basic Books (1967).
Vollmer, Howard M. *A Preliminary Investigation and Analysis of The Role of Scientists in Research Organizations.* Menlo Park, Calif.: Stanford Research Institute (for Air Force Office of Scientific Research, 1962).
Wachs, Melvin W. "The Federal Laboratory, Scientific, and Technical Director." In *Science Administration, Education, and Career Mobility.* Bloomington: Indiana University (1966).
Waldo, Dwight C. *Comments on "Research on Government, Politics and Administration".* Washington, D.C.: Brookings Institution (1961).
Walters, J. E. *Research Management: Principles and Practices.* Washington, D.C.: Spartan Books (1965).
Webb, James. *Space Age Management.* New York: McGraw-Hill (1969).
Weidenbaum, Murray. *The Modern Public Sector.* New York: Basic Books (1969).
Weinberg, Alvin. *Reflections on Big Science.* Cambridge, Mass.: M.I.T. Press (1967).
Weston, Alan F., ed. *Information Technology in a Democracy.* Cambridge, Mass.: Harvard University Press (1972).
White, K. K. *Understanding the Company Organization Chart.* New York: American Management Association (1963).
Wiener, Norbert. *Cybernetics,* 2d ed. New York: John Wiley & Sons (1961).
Woodward, Joan. *Management and Technology: Problems of Progress in Modern Industry,* no. 3. London: Her Majesty's Stationery Office (1958-60).
Ziman, John M. *Public Knowledge: An Essay Concerning the Social Dimension of Science.* Cambridge: Cambridge University Press (1968).

ARTICLES, DOCUMENTS, AND SPEECHES

Abelson, Philip. "Departure of the President's Science Adviser." *Science* Editorial (19 January 1973), p. 233.

Ackoff, R. L., and Martin, M. "The Dissemination and Use of Recorded Scientific Information." *Management Science* (1963), pp. 322-26.

Adams, Walter. "New Industrial State." *American Economic Review*, vol. 58, no. 2 (May 1968), p. 653.

"Aerospace Tries to Pick Up the Pieces." *Business Week*, no. 2154 (12 December 1970), pp. 13, 22.

Albrook, Robert C. "How to Spot Executives Early." *Fortune*, vol. 78 (July 1968), pp. 106-11.

Ames, B. C. "Payoff from Product Management." *Harvard Business Review*, vol. 41, no. 6 (1963), pp. 141-52.

Ashby, Eric. "The Administrator: Bottleneck or Pump." *Daedalus* (Proceedings of the American Academy of Arts and Sciences), vol. 91 (spring 1962), pp. 264-78.

"Aspects of Public Expenditure Theories." *Review of Economics and Statistics* (November 1958), pp. 337-38.

Astin, Allen V., Chairman, Committee on Federal Laboratories, Federal Council for Science and Technology, Testimony before the Subcommittee on Science, Research and Development of the Committee on Science and Astronautics, U.S. Congress, House, 27 March 1968.

Bailey, Robert E., and Jensen, Barry T. "The Troublesome Transition from Scientist to Manager." *Personnel*, vol. 42, no. 5 (September-October 1965).

Barfield, Claude E. "Science Report/Money Shortage Forces New Look at Federal Science Policy." *National Journal* (22 August 1970), pp. 1797-1806.

Bayton, James A., and Chapman, Richard L. *Transformation of Scientists and Engineers into Managers*. Prepared under contract for NASA by the National Academy of Public Administration. Washington, D.C.: National Academy of Public Administration (1972).

Bell, David. *Government Contracting for Research and Development*. Report to the President. (Washington, D.C.: Bureau of the Budget (30 April 1962).

Bernstein, G. B., and Cerron, M. J. "SEER: A Delphic Approach Applied to Information Processing." *Technological Forecasting* (June 1969).

Best, Robert. "The Scientific vs. the Management Mind." *Industrial Research*, vol. 5 (October 1963), pp. 50-52.

Bevans, M. J. "Technical Personnel: Managing This 'Elite' Corps." *Administration Management*, vol. 39, no. 11 (November 1968), pp. 20, 21.

Biomedical Science and Its Administration, A Study of the National Institutes of Health. Washington, D.C.: The White House (February 1965), pp. 36-37.

Boffey, Phillip M. "R & D Funding: Top Treasury Aide Decries Blind Faith Approach." *Science* (30 October 1970), p. 515.

Boulding, Kenneth W. "The End Is in Sight for Galloping Science." *Washington Post* (6 November 1970), p. 81.

Boulgarides, J. D., and San Fillippa, V. C. "The Engineer's Point of View of Continuing Education." Doublas Paper No. 4998, presented to Discussion Meetings on Continuing Education for Engineers, American Association for the Advancement of Science, Huntington Beach, California.

Bowers, D. G. "Organizational Control in an Insurance Company." *Sociometry*, vol. 27, no. 2 (1964), pp. 230-44.

———, and Seashore, S. E. "Predicting Organizational Effectiveness with a Four-Factor Theory of Leadership." *Administrative Science Quarterly*, vo. 11, no. 2 (1966), pp. 238-63.

"Brain Drain: Fewer Scientists Enter U.S., More Seek to Leave." *Science* (7 August 1970), pp. 565-66.

Branscomb, Lewis M. "Taming Technology." *Science* (12 March 1971), pp. 972-77.

Brooks, Harvey. "Future Needs for the Support of Basic Research," *Basic Research and National Goals*. Washington, D.C.: National Academy of Sciences (March 1965), pp. 77-110.

———. "Models for Science Planning." *Public Administration Review*, vol. 3 (May-June 1971), pp. 364-74.

———. "Physics and the Polity." *Science* (26 April 1968), pp. 396-400.

Bylinsky, Gene. "U.S. Science Enters a Not-So-Golden Era." *Fortune* (November 1968), pp. 145, 197.

Caldwell, Lynton K. "Managing the Scientific Super-Culture: The Task of Education Preparation." *Public Administration Review*, vol. 27, (June 1967), pp. 128-33.

"Capital Comment: McElroy Testifies on Technology Assessment." *BioScience*, vol. 20 (15 June 1970), p. 20.

Carey, William D. "Funding and Managing an Accelerated Program of Applied Biomedical Research." *Research in the Service of Man: Biomedical Knowledge, Development, and Use*. Report to the Committee on Government Operations. U.S. Congress, Senate, 1967.

———. "The Need for Priorities," guest editorial. *Science* (January 1968).

———. "Needed: A National R & D Policy." *Astronautics and Aeronautics* (July 1969).

———. "New Ways to Budget for R & D." *Research/Development* (September 1964).

———. *Public Administration Review*, vol. 9, no. 1 (Winter 1949), pp. 53-63.

———. "U.S. Science Policy: After Anxiety, What?" guest editorial. *Science Policy*. London: Science Policy Foundation (1972).

Carnegie Institution of Washington. *Report of the President*. Washington, D.C. (1967-68).

Carpenter, Richard A. "Technology Assessment and Human Possibilities." *Science* (31 October 1969), p. 653.

Carroll, James D. "Science and the City: The Question of Authority." *Science* (28 February 1969), p. 908.

Carter, H. E., Chairman, National Science Board. Statement before the Committee on Science and Astronautics. U.S. Congress, House, 25 February 1971.

Cartter, Allan, and Farrell, Robert. "Higher Education in the Last Third of the Century." *The Educational Record* (spring 1965), p. 125.

Cartwright, D. "The Economics of Deaning." *Western Economic Journal* (spring 1965).

Case, H. W., Le Bold, W. K., and Diemer, W. D., as quoted in *Scientific Engineering Technical Manpower Comments*, vol. 5, no. 11 (December 1968), p. 18.

"Civil Service Reform: Science Agency Heads Balk at Nixon Plan." *Science* (14 Man 1971), pp. 652-53.

Cleveland, Harlan. "Dinosaurs and Personal Freedom." *Saturday Review* (28 February 1959), pp. 12-14.

Coddington, Dean C., and Milliken, J. Gordon. "Future of Federal Contract Research Centers." *Harvard Business Review* (March-April 1970), p. 115.

Comptroller General of the United States. Comptroller General Letter No. B-161740. Letter to all Congressional Committee Chairmen, 11 August 1972.
Confrey, Eugene A. "Science Administration: NIH Training for a Young Profession." *Civil Service Journal*, vol. 9, no. 1(July-September 1968), pp. 8-11.
Council of State Governments. *Power to the States*: *Mobilizing Technology, Report and Summary Analysis.* Lexington, Kentucky (May 1972).
Culliton, Barbara J. "NIH Training Grants: Going, Going, Gone?" *Science* (26 January 1973), pp. 356-60.
Curry, William N. "Can Idle Experts Aid Ecology?" *Washington Post* (19 November 1970), p. K1.
Daddario, Emilio Q. "Technology and the Democratic Process." *Technology Review*, vol. 73 (July-August 1971), pp. 18-24.
Dantzig, G. B., and Wolfe, Philip. "The Decomposition Principle for Linear Programs." *Operations Research Journal*, vol. 8, no. 1 (January-February 1960).
"David, PSAC Exit Predicted." *Science* (12 January 1973), p. 160.
Demick, Marshall E. "The Administrative Staff College: Executive Development in Government and Industry." *The American Political Science Review*, vol. 50 (March 1956), pp. 166-76.
Dougherty, John J. "Joel Nordica Turns Administrator." *Professional Engineer*, vol. 38, no. 10 (October 1968), pp. 46-50.
Dror, Yehezkel. "Muddling Through—Science or Inertia." *Public Administration Review*, vol. 24 (September 1964), pp. 153-57.
Drucker, Peter F. "The Executive's Job in Its Three Dimensions." *The Commercial Letter*. Toronto: Canadian Imperial Bank of Commerce (n.d.).
———. "Management Science and the Manager." *Management Science*, vol. 1 (January 1955), pp. 115-26.
———. "Saving the Crusade; How to Make Technology Serve Man and Nature." *Harper's Magazine* (January 1972), pp. 66-71.
Emerson, Thomas I. "Communication of Expression." *Scientific American* (September 1972), pp. 163-72.
Emery, Fred E., and Trist, Eric L. "The Casual Texture of Organizational Environments." *Human Organization*, vol. 18 (February 1965), pp. 21-32.
Energy, R & D and National Progress. A report prepared for the Interdepartmental Energy Study under the direction of Ali Bulent Cambel. Washington, D.C.: U.S. Government Printing Office (1964).
Etzioni, Amitai. " 'Shortcuts' to Social Change?" *The Public Interest* (summer 1968), pp. 40-51.
Evan, W. "Conflict and Performance in R & D Organizations: Some Preliminary Findings." *Industrial Management Review*, vol. 7, no. 37 (1965), p. 46.
Federal Council for Science and Technology, Committee on Scientific Personnel. *The Environment for Quality*. Washington, D.C.: (November 1965).
———, Executive Office of the President. *Public Technology: A Tool for Solving National Problems*, Report of the Subcommittee on Intergovernmental Science Relations. Washington, D.C.: U.S. Government Printing Office (May 1972).
———. *Proceedings of the 3rd Symposium, The Environment of the Federal Laboratory, December 7-8, 1964.* Washington, D.C.: U.S. Government Printing Office (1965).

"Federal R & D: Domestic Problems Get New Efforts But Little Money." *Science* (19 February 1971), pp. 657-61.

The Federal R & D Programs. Washington, D.C.: U.S. Government Printing Office (1966).

Ferdinand, Theodore N. "On the Obsolescence of Scientists and Engineers." *American Scientist*, vol. 54 (March 1966), pp. 46-56.

Folger, John. "The Balance Between Supply and Demand for College Graduates." *The Journal of Human Resources* (spring 1967), p. 167.

Frank, Julian S. "A Short Course in Psychology for Engineer-Managers." *Training and Development Journal*, vol. 22, no. 10 (October 1968), pp. 8-16.

Giffard, J. A. H. (Earl of Halsbury). "Management, Group Conflict and the the Sciences." *Impact of Science on Society*, vol. 8, no. 3 (1967), pp. 121-40.

Glennon, J. R., Buel, W. D., and Albright, Lewis E. "Making the Best Use of R & D Manpower." *Business Horizons*. Bloomington: Indiana University (April 1968), pp. 63-68.

Goddard, James L. "The Drug Establishment." *Esquire* (March 1969); and *Congressional Record*—Senate, daily ed., 4 March 1969, p. S 2310-13.

Golovin, Nicholas E. "Golovin's Law." *New Scientist* (28 November 1968), p. 478.

———. "The Public and the National Noise Standards." Presented at the symposium *Where Do We Stand on Standards for Noise?* Cleveland: 76th Meeting of the Acoustical Society of America (19-22 November 1968).

Gordon, Paul J. "Administrative Strategy for a Graduate School of Administration." *Academy of Management Journal*, vol. 10 (December 1967) pp. 351-54.

Great Britain. "Report of the Committee, 1966-68," Chairman, Lord Fulton, *The Civil Service*, vol. 1 (1968). London: Her Majesty's Stationery Office (1968), pp. 11-12.

Greenberg, Daniel S. "Don't Ask the Barber Whether You Need a Haircut." *Saturday Review* (November 25, 1972), pp. 58-59.

Hagstrom, Warren O. "Traditional and Modern Forms of Scientific Teamwork." *Administrative Science Quarterly*, vol. 9 (December 1964), pp. 244-63.

Harr, Karl G., Jr. "Technology Trade and Government." *The Wall Street Journal*, 13 January 1972, p. 10.

Holloman, J. Herbert. "Modern Engineering and Society—The Marriage Between Technical Ability and Social Need." *Chemical and Engineering News*, vol. 42 (29 June 1964), pp. 66-71.

Hornig, Donald. Address to the American Physical Society. Washington, D.C. (26 April 1967).

———. "Charles Lathrop Parsons Award Address." *Chemical and Engineering News*, vol. 46, no. 1 (1 January 1968), p. 52.

"House Probes Science." *Government Executive* (August 1970), p. 14.

International City Management Association. "Science-Technology Advice in Local Governments." Vol. 2 (November 1970).

Jenkins, G. M., and Youle, P. V. "A Systems Approach to Management." *Operations Research Quarterly* (April 1968).

Johnson, R., Kast, F., and Rosenzweig, J. "Systems Theory and Management." *Management Science* (January 1964).

Jouvenal, Bertrand de. "The Technocratic Age." *Bulletin of the Atomic Scientist*, vol. 20 (October 1964), pp. 27-29.

Kahn, Robert L. "Productivity and Job Satisfaction." *Personnel Psychology*, vo. 13, no. 3 (fall 1960), pp. 257-87.

Kaplan, Norman. "The Role of the Research Administrator." *Administrative Science Quarterly*. vol. 4 (June 1959).
Katz, Aaron. "Toward High Information Level Culture." *Cybernetica*, vol. 7, no. 3 (1964), pp. 203-45.
King, Alexander. "Management as a Technology." *Impact of Science on Society*, vol. 8, no. 2 (1957), pp. 65-85.
Klaw, Spencer. "The Industrial Labyrinth." *Science and Technology*, no. 86 (February 1969), p. 43.
Korman, Abraham K. "The Prediction of Managerial Performance: A Review." *Personnel Psychology*, vol. 21 (1968), pp. 259-322.
Krauch, H., and Schreiber, K. "Forschung und technischer Fortschritt im Bewusstein der Offenlichkeit-Ergebnisse einer Reprasentativbefragung." *Soziale Welt*, Jahrg, 17 (1966), Heft 4, S. 289-315.
Ladd, Everett Carll, Jr., and Lipset, Seymour Martin. "Politics of Academic Natural Scientists and Engineers." *Science* (9 June 1972), pp. 1091-99.
Lang, Daniel. "Ex-Oracles—On the New Unpopularity of Scientists." *Harpers* (December 1972), pp. 34-43.
La Porte, T. R. "The Context of Technology Assessment." *Public Administration Review*, vol. 31 (January-February 1971), pp. 63-73.
Leach, Gerald. "Why Scientists Are So Out of Touch." *The London Observer*, 7 September 1970, p. 8.
Leamer, Frank D. "Professional & Administrative Ladders—The Advantages of Broad Job Classification in a Research Organization." *Research Management*, vol. 2, no. 1 (spring 1959), pp. 53-62.
Lear, P. "Predicting Consequences of Technology." *Saturday Review* (28 March 1970), pp. 44-46.
Levine, Meldon E., and Tunney, John V. *"Genetic Engineering."* Saturday *Review* (5 August 1972), pp. 23-29.
Likert, Rensis, and Bowers, D. G. "Organizational Theory and Human Resource Accounting." *American Psychologist*, vol. 24, no. 6 (June 1969), pp. 585-92.
Lilienthal, David E. "Society and Its Leaders in Transition." Speech to American Management Association. New York (26 September 1968).
Lindblom, Charles E. "The Science of 'Muddling Through.' " *Public Administration Review*, vol. 19 (spring 1959), pp. 79-88.
Lundstedt, Sven. "Administrative Leadership and the Use of Social Power." *Public Administration Review*, vol. 25 (June 1965), pp. 159-60.
MacArthur, Donald M. "Personnel Management for R & D." *Personnel Administration*, vol. 31, no. 5 (September-October 1968), p. 28.
Mainzer, Lewis C. "The Scientist as Public Administrator." *Western Political Quarterly*, vol. 16 (December 1963), pp. 814-29.
Mann, F. C., Metzner, H., and Baumgartel, H. "The Supervisor and Absence Rates." *Supervisory Management*, vol. 2, no. 7 (1957), pp. 7-14.
Mansfield, E. "Ratio of Return for Industrial R & D." *American Economic Review*, vol. 55, no. 2 (1965), p. 310.
———, and Brandenburg, R. "The Allocation, Characteristics and Outcome of the Firm's R & R Portfolio." *Journal of Business*, vol. 39 (1966), p. 447.
Mansfield, M. "Rechanneling the Public Resources for Basic Science Through the Civilian Agencies: A New Goal for National Science Policy." *Congressional Record*, 116, 21 August 1970, pp. 29696-98.
Marschak, T., and Yahow, J. "The Sequential Selection of Approaches to a Task." *Management Science*, vol. 12, no. 9 (1966), p. 627.
McHale, John. "Education for Real." *Newsletter of the World Academy of Art and Science* (June 1966).

Meeting Manpower Needs in Science and Technology, White House Report. Washington, D.C.: The White House (12 December 1962).
Miles, Raymond. "Human Relations or Human Resources?" *Harvard Business Review* (July 1965).
Miller, Edwin L. "Identifying High Potential Managerial Personnel." *Michigan Business Review.* Ann Arbor: University of Michigan (November 1968), p. 12.
Mintz, Morton. "Lee Questions Fitness of Next NASA Chief." *Washington Post,* 17 February 1969, see A, p. 12.
Monthly Labor Review, vol. 91, no. 11 (November 1968), p. 14.
Moore, Harriet Bruce, and Levy, Sidney J. "Artful Contrivers: A Study of Engineers." *Personnel,* vol. 28, no 2 (September 1951), pp. 148-53.
Morgan, Edward P. "Scientists and the World's War for Survival." *Washington Post,* 29 August 1970, p. A14.
Mosher, C. A. "Counterbudget: A Blueprint for Changing National Priorities 1971-76—Chapter 14—Research and Development." *Congressional Record,* 117, 21 May 1971, pp. E 4874-77.
Murphy, Thomas P. "Congress, PPBS, and Reality." *Polity,* vol. 1 (summer 1969), p. 463.
"NAS Head Deplores Research Cutbacks." *Washington Post,* 11 January 1971, p. K1.
Natiello, Thomas A. "Motivation for Work Preference." *MSU Business Topics.* Lansing: Michigan State University (spring 1968), pp. 59-60.
National Academy of Engineering. *A Study of Technology Assessment.* Report to the Committee on Science and Astronautics. 91st Cong., 1st sess., 1969.
National Academy of Sciences. *Basic Research and National Goals.* Report to the Committee on Science and Astronautics. U.S. Congress, House, March 1965.
———, Committee on Utilization of Scientific and Engineering Manpower. *Toward Better Utilization of Scientific and Engineering Talent.* Washington, D.C. (1964).
National Science Board. *Toward a Public Policy for Graduate Education.* Washington, D.C. (1969).
National Science Foundation. "Federal Funds for Research, Development and Other Scientific Activities." *Surveys of Science Resources Series,* vol. 18, NSF 69031 (FY 1968, 1969, and 1970), pp. 95-96.
———, Office of Intergovernmental Science and Research Utilization. *Intergovernmental Science Programs: Grant Information and Proposal Requirements.* Unpublished report. Washington, D.C. (n.d.).
———. *Research Applied to National Needs (RANN): Interim Description and Guidelines for Proposal Preparation.* Washington, D.C. (September 1971).
———. *National Science Foundation Statutory Authority as Amended through August 14, 1968.* Washington, D.C.: U.S. Government Printing Office (1968).
"New Policy for Government-University Partnership." *Science* (10 July 1970), p. 131.
New York Academy of Sciences, Ad Hoc Committee for Evaluation of Federal Support of Science. Foreword to *The Crisis Facing American Science.* New York (1968).
Neyman, J., and Pearson, E. "Contributions to the Theory of Testing Statistical Hypotheses." *Statistical Research Memoirs,* vol. 1 (1936).
Nichols, Rodney W. "Mission-Oriented R & D." *Science* (2 April 1971), pp. 29-37.

Niemann, Ralph A. "Pitfalls of R & D Management." *Personnel*, vol. 47 (January-February 1970), pp. 46-56.

"Nixon's New Economic Policy: Hints of a Resurgence for R & D." *Science* (27 August 1971), pp. 794-96.

Odiorne, George S. "Making Managers Out of Engineers." *Personnel*, vol. 33, no. 3 (November 1956), p. 266.

Orlans, Harold. "Social Science Research Politics in the U.S." *Minerva*, vol. 9 (January 1971), pp. 7-31.

Page, Robert M. "Motivation of Scientists and Engineers." *Personnel Administration*, vol. 21, no. 5 (September-October), pp. 30-31.

Pelz, Donald C. "Creative Tensions in the Research and Development Climate." *Science*, vol 157, no. 3785 (14 July 1967), pp. 160-65.

———. "Some Factors Related to Performance in a Research Organization." *Administrative Quarterly*, vol. 1 (1956-57), pp. 310-25.

Pitzer, K. S. "Science and Society: Some Policy Changes Are Needed." *Science* (16 April 1971), pp. 223-26.

President's Message to Congress, March 16, 1972. Weekly Compilation of Presidential Documents, *Science and Technology* (20 March 1972).

President's National Goals Research Staff. *Toward Balanced Growth: Quantity with Quality*. Washington, D.C.: U.S. Government Printing Office (4 July 1971).

President's Science Advisory Committee. *Scientific Progress, the Universities, and the Federal Government*. Washington, D.C.: The White House (15 November 1960).

President's Task Force on Science Policy. *Science and Technology Tools for Progress*. Washington, D.C.: U.S. Government Printing Office (April 1970).

Price, Don K. "Educating for the Scientific Age." *Bulletin of the Atomic Scientists*, vol. 24, no. 8 (October 1968), p. 29.

———. "Science at a Policy Crossroads." *Technology Review*, vol. 73 (April 1971), pp. 30-39.

"Private Enrollment Drops; Graduate Totals Fall Short." *Chronicle of Higher Education* (24 March 1969), p. 1.

Quinn, James B. "How to Evaluate Research Output." *Harvard Business Review*, vol. 38, no. 2 (March 1960), pp. 69-80.

Randle, C. Wilson. "Problems of R & D Management." *Harvard Business Review*, vol. 37, no. 1 (January-February 1959), pp. 128-36.

Reagan, Michael. "Congress Meets Science: The Appropriations Process." *Science* (23 May 1969), p. 930.

"Research and Development Management." *Society for Advancement Bulletin* (March 1966), p. 20.

"Research Fund Losses Decried by Scientists." *Washington Post*, 3 December 1970, p. A6.

Reston, James. "Science and Politics." *New York Times*, 7 February 1971, p. 13.

Richardson, Jacques, and Park, Ford. "Why Europe Lags Behind." *Science and Technology*, no. 77 (May 1968), pp. 20-29.

Roback, H. "Do We Need a Department of Science and Technology?" *Science* (4 July 1969), pp. 36-44.

Roberts, Karlene, Mines, Raymond E., and Blankenship, L. Vaughn. "Organizational Leadership Satisfaction and Productivity: A Comparative Analysis." *Academy of Management* (December 1968), pp. 401-14.

Rosenthal, Albert H. "Behavior and Administration." *Public Administration Review*, vol. 19, no. 3 (summer 1959).

———. "Preparing the Science Administrators of Tomorrow." *Public Personnel Reviews* (April 1969), pp. 70-76.

———. "Public Administration in Theory and Practice." *Administration*, vol. 12, no. 4 (Winter 1964), published in Dublin, Ireland.

Royer, George L. "Salary Administration of Research Personnel." *Research Management*, vol. 1, no. 2 (summer 1958), p. 120.

Sayre, Wallace S. "The Triumph of Technique over Purpose." *Public Administration Review*, vol. 8 (spring 1948), pp. 134-37.

Scanlan, Burt K. "A Commonsense Approach to Making Good Managers of Good Technical Men." *Training in Business and Industry*, vol. 1, no. 2 (November-December 1964), pp. 40-41.

Schein, Edgar, et al. "Career, Orientations and Perceptions of Rewarded Activity in Research Organizations." *Administrative Science Quarterly*, vol. 9, no. 4 (March 1965), pp. 333-49.

"Science Committees: NRC Report Asks Better Mix in Advisory Groups." *Science*, (16 June 1972), pp. 1222-24.

"Science Policy: An Insider's View of LBJ, DuBridge and the Budget." *Science* (5 March 1971), pp. 874-77.

Shannon, William V. "Supersonic Question Mark." *Commonweal*, vol. 82 (23 July 1965), p. 513.

Shepard, Herbert A. "The Dual Hierarchy in Research." *Research Management*, vol. 1, no, 3 (autumn 1958), pp. 177-87.

———. "Nine Dilemmas in Industrial Research." *Administrative Science Quarterly*, vol. 1, no. 3 (December 1956), pp. 295-305.

Simon, Herbert A. "On the Concept of Organizational Goal." *Administrative Science Quarterly*, vol. 9 (June 1964), pp. 3-8.

"Social Scientists Still Poor Cousins." *Nature*, vol. 230 (April 1971), pp. 423-24.

Spinrad, Bernard J. "America's Energy Crisis: Reality or Hysteria." *Science and Public Affairs*, vol. 27 (September 1971), pp. 3-8.

Staats, Elmer B. *Need for Improved Guidelines in Contracting for Research with Government-Sponsored Nonprofit Contractors*, Report to the Congress by the Comptroller General of the United States, 10 February 1969).

———. *Review of Economic Opportunity Programs*. Report to the Congress by the Comptroller General of the United States, March 1969.

Starr, Chauncey. "Energy and Power." *Scientific American* (September 1971), pp. 37-49.

Stratton, J. A. "Science and the Process of Management." *Research Management*, vol. 7 (March 1964), pp. 79-90.

Tagiuri, Renato. "Value Orientations and the Relationship of Managers and Scientists." *Administrative Science Quarterly*, vol. 10 (June 1965), pp. 39-51.

Tannenbaum, Robert, and Massarik, Fred. "Participation by Subordinates in the Managerial Decision-Making Process." *The Canadian Journal of Economics and Political Science*, vol. 16 (August 1950).

Tax Foundation. "Nature of Study and Major Findings." *Tax Burdens and Benefits of Government Expenditures by Income Class, 1961 and 1965.* New York (1967), pp. 7-22.

Thompson, James D., and Bates, Frederick L. "Technology, Organization, and Administration." *Administrative Science Quarterly*, vol. 2 (December 1957), pp. 325-43.

"Thorns in the Academy's Flesh." *Nature* (5 November 1971), pp. 7-8.

Tonsor, Stephen. *"Higher Education and National Affairs."* Address to a Conference of the National Association of Manufacturers (April 25, 1969), pp. 1ff; and *Chronicle of Higher Education* (5 May 1969), p. 3.

"Toward Balanced Growth: Quantity with Quality." Press Conference on the Report to the President by the National Goals Research Staff, July 18, 1970. Compilation of Presidential documents. Washington, D.C.: U.S. Government Printing Office (20 July 1971).

"Understanding of Science." *Science* (4 August 1972), p. 301.

United Nations, UNESCO: *Science for Development: An Essay on the Origin and Organization of National Science Policies.* Unpublished report. July 1972.

U.S., Bureau of the Budget. *The Budget of the United States Government, 1970, 1971, 1972, 1973.* Washington, D.C.: U.S. Government Printing Office (1969, 1970, 1971, 1972).

———. *Report to the President on Government Contracting for Research and Development.* Washington, D.C. (1962).

———. *Steps in the Budget Process.* Washington, D.C. (n.d.).

U.S., Civil Service Commission, Bureau of Policies and Standards. *Scientists and Engineers in the Federal Personnel System.* Washington, D.C. (1968).

———, Bureau of Training. "Executive Institute on Management of Scientific and Engineering Organizations." Announcement of course. Washington, D.C. (March 1969).

———, Bureau of Training. "Introduction to Supervision." Announcement of course. Washington, D.C. (October 1968).

———, Bureau of Training. *Off-Campus Study Centers for Federal Employees.* Washington, D.C. (FY 1968).

———, Bureau of Training. "Science and Government." Announcement of course. Washington, D.C. (February 1969).

———, Bureau of Training. "Supervisory Scientists and Engineers." Announcement of course. Washington, D.C. (January 1969).

———. *Federal Personnel Manual.* Washington, D.C. (1968).

———, Standards Division. *Civil Service Handbook X-118.* Washington, D.C. (November 1968).

———, Standards Division. *Functional Classification System for Scientists and Engineers.* Washington, D.C. (June 1966).

———, Standards Division. *Research Grade-Evaluation Guide.* Washington, D.C. (June 1964).

U.S., Congress, House, Committee on Foreign Affairs. *Science, Technology and American Diplomacy: A Selected, Annotated Bibliography of Articles, Books, Documents, Periodicals and Reference Guides.* Prepared for the Subcommittee on National Security Policy and Scientific Developments of the Committee on Foreign Affairs, by the Science Policy Research and Foreign Affairs Divisions, LRS, Library of Congress, as part of an extended study of the interactions of science and technology with U.S foreign policy. Washington, D.C.: U.S. Government Printing Office (March 1970).

———, House, Committee on Foreign Affairs. *Science, Technology and American Diplomacy: Toward a New Diplomacy in a Scientific Age.* Prepared for the Subcommittee on National Security Policy and Scientific Developments of the Committee on Foreign Affairs by the Science Policy Research and Foreign Affairs Divisions, as part of an extended study of the interactions of science and technology with U.S. foreign policy. Washington, D.C.: U.S. Government Printing Office (April 1970).

———, House, Committee on Interstate and Foreign Commerce, Special Subcommittee to Investigate Power Failure. *Northeast Power Failure—November 9, 10, 1965,* 89th Cong., 1st and 2d sess., 1966.

———, House Committee on Science and Astronautics. *Management of Information and Knowledge*. Compilation of papers prepared for the Eleventh Meeting of the Panel on Science and Technology for the Committee on Science and Astronautics. 91st Cong., 2d sess. Washington, D.C.: U.S. Government Printing Office (1970).

———, House, Committee on Science and Astronautics. *The National Institutes of Research and Advanced Studies*. Report of the Subcommittee on Science, Research and Development. 91st Cong., 2d sess., 1970.

———, House, Committee on Science and Astronautics. *Science, Technology, and Public Policy During the Ninetieth Congress*, 1st and 2d Sess., 1967-68. Report of the Subcommittee on Science, Research and Development. 91st Cong., 1st sess., July 1969.

———, House, Committee on Science and Astronautics, Special Investigating Subcommittee. *Supersonic Air Transports*. 86th Cong., 1st sess., 19 May 1960.

———, House, Committee on Science and Astronautics. *Summary of Activities of the Subcommittee on Science, Research and Development, 1963-1970*. Washington, D.C.: U.S. Government Printing Office (1970).

———, House, Committee on Science and Astronautics. *Technology Assessment* (see statement of Emilio Q. Daddario). Report of the Subcommittee on Science, Research and Development. 90th Cong., 1st sess., 1967.

———, House, Committee on Science and Astronautics. *Technology Assessment Seminar*. Proceedings before the Subcommittee on Science, Research and Development. 90th Cong., 1st sess., 21-22 September 1967.

———, House. H.R. 6698. 90th Cong., 1st sess., 7 March 1967, sec. 7.

———, House. *Hearings Before the Committee on Science and Astronautics*. 93rd Cong., 1st sess., February-April 1971.

———, House. *Report No. 92-1436*, Technology Assessment Act of 1972. Conference Report to Accompany H.R. 10243. 92d Cong., 2d sess., 25 September 1972.

———, *Public Law 92-218*, S. 659. 92d Cong., 23 June 1972. To amend the Higher Education Act of 1965, the Vocational Education Act of 1963, the General Education Provisions Act (creating a National Foundation for Postsecondary Education and a National Institute of Education), the Elementary and Secondary Education Act 1965, Public Law 874, Eighty-first Congress and related Acts, and for other purposes.

———, Senate, Committee on Government Operations. *Hearings—Reorganization Plan No. 2 of 1970*. OMB. April, May 1970.

———, Senate, Committee on Government Operations. *PPBS Hearings*, Part 1. "Statement of Charles L. Schultz." 23 August 1967.

———, Senate, Committee on Government Operations. *PPBS Hearings*, Part 3. "Statement of Elmer B. Staats." 26 March 1968.

———, Senate. *An Inventory of Congressional Concern with Research and Development, Ninety-first Congress, 1969-1970*. Bibliography prepared for the Subcommittee on Executive Reorganization and Government Research of the Committee on Government Operations. Washington, D.C.: U.S. Government Printing Office (1971).

———, Senate, Committee on Government Operations, Subcommittee on Government Research. *Federal Support of Project Grants: Indirect Costs and Cost Sharing*, Part 1. 91st Cong., 1st sess., 22-23 April and 1 May 1969.

U.S., Department of Agriculture, Agricultural Research Service. *Research Scientist Evaluation Plan*. Washington, D.C. (May 1965).

Veillette, P. T. "The Impact of Mechanization on Administration." *Public Administration Review*, vol. 17 (autumn 1957), pp. 231-37.

Vollmer, Howard M. "Organizational Design—An Exploratory Study." Stanford Research Institute Project 6329. Stanford (December 1967).

Wade, Nicholas. "Peer Review System: How to Hand Out Money Fairly." *Science* (12 January 1973), pp. 158-61.

Wall, John, and Pomerantz, Reuben. "A Science and Technology Fellowship Program." *Civil Service Journal*, vol. 5, no. 3 (January-March 1965), p. 20.

Weaver, W. Editorial. *Science*, vol. 130 (1959), p. 301.

Webb, J. S. "Can Technical People Fill the Management Gap?" *Engineering Opportunities*, vol. 5, no. 3 (March 1967), p. 60.

Weinberg, Alvin. "Social Problems and National Socio-Technical Institutes" (and other papers by Weinberg cited in footnote 1 of that paper). *Applied Science and Technological Progress.* Report to the Committee on Science and Astronautics, U.S. Congress, House. Washington, D.C.: National Academy of Sciences (1967), p. 415.

Wharton, John F. "The Making of Leaders." *Saturday Review* (13 April 1968), pp. 25-27, 67.

"Where High Technology Can Help the Cities—Public Technology, Inc. Labors to Apply Space Age Techniques to Urban Ills." *Business Week* (5 August 1972), pp. 42-43.

"The White Collar Worker." *American Labor*, vol. 1, no. 6 (October 1968), pp. 41-47.

White, George C. "Energy, the Economy and the Environment," *Technology Review*, vol. 74 (October-November 1971), pp. 18-31.

Wolfe, Dael. "Assessing Technology." *Science* (21 November 1969), p. 951.

Wolff, Harold. "The Impact of Society on Science." *American Behavioral Scientist*, vol. 10 (May 1967), pp. 2-7.

York, Carl M. "Steps Toward a National Policy for Academic Science." *Science* (14 May 1971), pp. 643-48.

Zabor, J. William. Remarks at October 1964 meeting of the Industrial Research Institute. *Research Management* (March 1965), p. 114.

Zadeh, L. A. "Fuzzy Algorithms." *Information and Control*, vol. 12 (1968), pp. 94-102.

Zaner, Theodore. "Action Research in Management Development." *Training and Development Journal*, vol. 22 (June 1968), pp. 28-33.

Zuckerman, H., and Merton, R. K. "Patterns of Evaluation in Science: Institutionalization, Structure and Functions of the Referee System." *Minerva*, vol. 9 (January 1971), pp. 66-100.

Zvegintzov, M. "Management in a Modern Scientific and Technological Age." *Impact of Science on Society*, vol. 11, no. I (1961), pp. 53-73.

Index

Academic research: governmental regulations on, 245-51; governmental support of 228-36 passim; growth ratios of, 229, 230, 232, 249; policies needed for, 228, 229, 233, 234, 235, 236, 237, 243, 244, 250, 251, 252
Accounting control, 172
Ad Hoc Subcommittee on the National Science Foundation (Senate), 9
Administrators in R & D programs, 32, 33, 43, 45, 47; and controls, 39, 40, 41, 44; development of, 34, 36, 42, 46, 47, 51-63, 82, 91-95; future needs for, 32, 33, 47; professional data on, 91-95; qualifications for, 42, 45, 48, 49, 55; self-development among, 46, 48, 50, 51, 52, 54, 55, 59, 60, 78, 85, 87; technical tasks of, 35, 39, 40, 41, 45. *See also* Managers of R & D programs; Manned Space Center
Administrators, recruiting of, 47, 49, 51, 55, 77, 78; among scholars, 50, 53, 60; educational programs for, 53, 54, 55, 56; funding for, 57; mid-career method, 48, 52, 54, 55, 58, 60; planning for, 60-63. *See also* Federal employees
Advisory committees, 212, 220, 221, 222
AEC. *See* Atomic Energy Commission
Aerospace Technologist (AST) Examination, 139, 140
Agricultural research, 2, 250
Agricultural Research Service evaluation guide, 80
Agriculture, Department of, 7, 127; Bureau of Chemistry of, 2
Air Force, Department of, 7, 28, 113, 235
Albuquerque, N. Mex., 28
Allison Commission, 21
ALSEP. *See* Apollo Lunar Surface Experiments Package
American Council on Education, 232
American Garden of Eden, 240
American Labor (magazine), 82

Ames Research (Laboratory) Center, 8, 113, 233
Apollo Lunar Surface Experiments Package (ALSEP), 131-35 passim; departments assisting, 132, 133, 134
Apollo Spacecraft Configuration Control Board, 126, 134, 136
Apollo Spacecraft Program, 29, 112, 118-27, 131, 137, 170
Apollo Spacecraft Program Office, 132, 133, 138, 141
Appropriations Subcommittee on Independent Offices (House), 9
Army, Department of the, 2, 7, 28, 92, 110, 113, 235. *See also* Defense, Department of
Arthur D. Little Laboratory, 235
Astin, Dr. Allen V., 73
Atomic Energy Commission (AEC), 7, 8, 28, 29, 113, 245, 246; administrative qualities listed, 61; Albuquerque Office of, 61
Atmospheric studies, 16, 29, 125, 181
Attorney General, Office of, and research laboratories, 7

Battelle Laboratory, 235, 236
Beckler, David, 192
Bell Telephone Laboratories, 82
"the Bell Report," 192, 235
Bendix Corporation, 133
Bloomington conference, 70, 77-78
Boulding, Kenneth, 260
Bounded control, 170, 171, 172, 174
Bradbury, Norris, 12
Brookhaven National Laboratory, 8, 236
Brookings Institution, 88
Budget, Bureau of the, 192, 206, 225; reports, 192, 235
Bulletin of the Atomic Scientist (magazine), 63, 262
Bureau of. *See* other part of title
Bush, Vannevar, 3-4, 24

315

Carey, William, 17, 255, 263
Carnegie Corporation, 190
Carnegie Institution of Washington, 235
Census, Bureau of the, 2
Center for Naval Analyses, 236
Center for Research in Social Systems, 236
Chamber of Commerce, United States, committee report, 251
Churchman, C. West, 14, 265
Civil Service, British, 75; report of, 75-77
Civil Service Commission, United States, 64, 87, 90, 91; Bureau of Executive Manpower, 67; Career Education Awards Program, 51; functional classification system, 81; job evaluations, 67-69, 73, 79-80, 81, 82-83; statistics, 64, 65, 70, 71, 72; studies by, 12, 13, 70, 73; training courses offered by, 54, 58, 84, 85, 86. *See also* Federal employees
Coast and Geodetic Survey, 2, 9
Commerce, Department of, 7, 251; management programs, 88
Commission on Human Resources and Advanced Education, 232
Committee on Aeronautical and Space Sciences (Senate), 9
Committee on Intergovernmental Science Relations, 8
Committee on Labor and Public Welfare (Senate), 9
Committee on Science and Astronautics (House), 9, 22, 229, 247
Community Action program, 195
Comptroller General of the United States, 194, 198
Computer-aided instruction (CAI), 221
Computers, 164, 165, 214, 242
Conant, James B., 24
Congress, 1, 2, 4, 8, 9, 10, 11, 20; and controls for R & D programs, 5, 8, 19, 29, 235, 245, 246, 247, 252; and funding for R & D programs, 15, 16, 18, 128, 170, 186, 190, 191, 192, 212, 213, 225, 232; and policy decisions on R & D programs, 18, 29, 195, 196, 236. *See also* House of Representatives, Committees of; Senate, Committees of
Construction and Community Development Committee (U.S. Chamber of Commerce), 251
Consumer Protection, 7
Consumer Reports (magazine), 242, 244
Consumers' Union, 242, 249
Control systems, 160-76; bounded, 170, 171, 173, 174; open, 170, 172, 173, 174; techniques of, 160, 164, 165, 169, 170, 171, 172
Cooperative motivation, 149-50; cross-function activity, 156, 157; group decisions, 150, 156, 157, 158, 159; under System 4, 155
Cornell Aeronautical Laboratory, 236
Cosmic Ray Ionization Spectrograph Program (CRISP), 125
Cost-benefit concepts, 164, 179, 180, 189, 190, 194, 196, 197
Council of Social Advisers, 247
Council on Environmental Quality, 6
Creativity development, 79, 80, 89-91
CRISP. *See* Cosmic Ray Ionization Spectrograph Program
Critical Path Method (CPM), 209
Culliton, Barbara, 20
Cytosine arabinoside, 26

Daddario, Emilio, 22; and Technology assessment, 247, 248, 249, 250
"David, PSAC Exit Predicted," 21
Dean of universities. *See* Division chief in R & D programs
Defense, Department of, 124, 225; management policies in, 65, 89, 90, 91, 179; and Mansfield Amendment, 12, 29; research and, 7, 17, 236, 237, 240, 241, 246
Defense for Research and Technology, Department of, 65
Departments. *See* other part of title
"Departure of the President's Science Adviser," 21
Director of the Congressional Research Service, 194
"Dither," 145, 147
Division chief in R & D program, 200-22; budgets and, 212, 213, 214, 215; resources factor and, 210, 211, 218, 219, 220; as task supervisor, 206-13 passim, 217, 222
DOD. *See* Defense, Department of
"Don't Ask the Barber Whether You Need a Haircut," 19
Drucker, Peter, 268
Drug problems, 175, 243, 257, 265
Dual ladder system, 78-82 passim
Dryden, Hugh L., 113

Economic Opportunity Act Amendments of 1967, 194
Economic Opportunity, Office of, 28, 194, 195

INDEX

Education, 230; and degrees, 57, 60, 87, 234; for managers, 52, 70, 71, 72, 74, 78; problems and, 174, 179, 186, 196, 198, 206; specialized, 37, 44, 46, 50, 51. *See also* Training programs
Education, Office of, 230, 232
Eisenhower, Dwight D., 233, 234
Electronic industries, 65, 81
Energy needs, planning for, 12, 24, 180
Engineers in R & D programs, 10, 50, 51, 52, 65, 69, 70, 72, 77; as administrators, 13, 45, 59, 74, 77, 78; classification of, 96; at Manned Space Center, 116, 119, 124, 140; professional advancement and, 85, 86, 87, 88, 89, 95, 97; studies on, 91-95, 144, 147, 159. *See also* Researchers
Environmental factors, and administrators, 35, 36, 37, 119, 141
Environmental Health Services, 7
Environmental problems, 12, 16, 193, 258
Environmental Protection Agency, 7
Environmental Science Services Administration, 7, 88
Esso Research and Engineering Service Commission, 85
the "establishment," 259, 260, 261, 264, 265
Executive Office of the President, 11; Assistants to, 5, 65; and controls on Federal Departments, 21, 235, 245, 246, 247; and support of R & D research, 18, 56, 187, 235, 245, 246, 247
Executives. *See* Administrators in R & D programs; Division chief in R & D programs; Managers of R & D programs; Project managers in R & D programs
Extravehicular activity (EVA), 135

FCST. *See* Federal Council for Science and Technology
Federal civilian laboratory directors, study on, 71-72
Federal civilian scientific directors, study on, 71-72
Federal civilian technical directors, study on, 71-72
Federal Council for Science and Technology (FCST), 6; study by, 8, 73, 91
Federal employees, 12, 13; education of, 70, 71, 72, 86; at Manned Space Center, 113, 117, 139-41; statistics on, 65, 67, 69, 81, 84, 85; and training courses, 86, 87, 88
Federal Personnel Manual, 139
Federal Personnel System, 91
Federal Register of General Services Administration, Office of, 7

Federal research laboratories, 7, 8, 13, 86, 113, 114, 124, 139, 235, 236
Florida State University, 87
"focused basic research," 29
Fogerty, James, 22
Food and Drug Administration, 193, 239, 248, 249
Forest Service, 7
Fulton Committee report, 75-77
Funding of R & D programs, 15, 18, 128, 170, 177-99, 212, 213, 220, 225, 232; evaluations for, 181-82, 183, 184, 185, 191, 194-98; and nonprofit organizations, 190, 191, 192, 235; policies for, 187, 188, 192, 193, 194; and research science, 185, 186, 187, 189

Gauss, Karl Friedrich, 225
Gemini Spacecraft Program, 120
General Accounting Office (GAO), 192, 194, 195
General Advisory Council, 247
Goals: organizational, 34, 36, 37, 40, 41, 201; and priorities, 35, 66, 67; public, 36, 41; sociotechnical systems, 162, 163, 169, 170, 171. *See also* Social R & D programs
Golovin, Nicholas, 245, 248
Government Furnished Equipment (GFE), 133
"Government Institution," 192
Government Operations Committee (House), 9, 247
Government Operations Committee (Senate), 9
Government Organization Manual, 7
Grants, research, 4, 20, 27, 87, 190, 191, 230
Gross national product (GNP), 185, 205

Handler, Philip, 16, 17, 248
HAPPE. *See* High Altitude Particle Physics Experiment
Haskins, Caryl, 185
Head Start program, 195
Health, Education and Welfare, Department of, 7, 13, 248
Health research, 3, 11, 17, 18, 24, 183, 184. *See also* Medical research
Health Services, 7
Henley-on-Thames, Administrative Staff College, 54
HEW. *See* Health, Education and Welfare, Department of
Hierarchical management levels, 155, 201, 202. *See also* Administrators in R & D programs; Division chief in R & D programs; Managers of R & D programs

High Altitude Particle Physics Experiment (HAPPE), 125
Hill, Listor, 22
Hjornevik, Wesley J., 14
House of Representatives, Committees of, 4, 8, 9, 22, 229, 247. *See also* Congress
Human relations in R & D administration, 43, 67, 70, 82, 83, 149-59; communications and, 150-58, 159; work groups and, 156, 157, 158
Human Resources Research Office, 236

Ideas and Authors program in Science and Government, 86
Impact of Science on Society (magazine), 63
Independent Research and Development Agreements, 124
Indiana University, 70
Industry and Technoscience, 5, 15, 65, 81, 113, 119, 219, 235, 245, 248, 249, 250
Institute for Defense Analyses, 236
Institute for Social Research (University of Michigan), 14, 149
Intelligence agencies, 236
Interior, Department of the, 7, 127
Internal Revenue Service, 58

Job Corps Centers, 196
Job Corps program, 195
Johnson, Lyndon Baines, 6
Johnson Administration, and Government support of R & D, 229
Joint Committee on Atomic Energy, 9
Joint Committee on Technology Assessment, 193-94

Kahn, Herman, 240
Kennedy, John F., 115
Kennedy Space Center (KSC), 87, 110; staffing of, 113-14
Killian, James R., Jr., report of, 83, 95, 96
Kyes, Roger, 236

Labor Statistics, Bureau of, 95
Laird, Melvin, 235
Langley Research (Laboratory), 113, 114, 115, 123
Leadership, in R & D programs, 42, 46, 70, 90; functions of 34, 35, 36, 39; responsibilities of, 40, 44, 138-40
Legal Services program, 195
Leich, Harold H., 13
Leukemia, new treatment of, 26
Lewis Research Laboratory, 113
Libby, Dr. Willard, 25
Likert, Rensis, 14, 29, 270

Linear programming, 165, 166
Lincoln Laboratory (MIT), 236
LRL. *See* Lunar Receiving Laboratory
LSPO. *See* Lunar Surface Project Office
Luddite concept, 249, 263
Lunar landings, equipment for, 131-35 passim
Lunar Receiving Laboratory (LRL), 127-31
Lunar Receiving Laboratory Policy Board, 130
Lunar Receiving Laboratory Project Office, 128, 129, 130
Lunar Surface Operations Panel, 133
Lunar Surface Project Office (LSPO), 132, 133

Management and Budget, Office of, 18, 178, 179
Management of Scientific and Engineering Organizations course, 86
Management systems for R & D programs, 143-59; System 1, 151, 154, 159; System 2, 151, 154, 157, 158, 159; System 3, 151, 159; System 4, 151, 154, 156, 157, 158, 159, 270
Managers of R & D programs, 178, 179, 201-7, 210, 214; data on, 66, 68; education of, 70, 71, 72, 74, 78; and personal research 88, 89; and planners, 203, 204, 205, 206, 207, promotional channels for, 77, 78-82 passim; responsibilities of, 65, 66, 67, 68, 69, 70, 73, 74, 85, 88; studies on, 64, 65, 67, 70, 71, 73, 75, 81, 91; training of, 82-85, 86, 87. *See also* Administrators in R & D programs; Federal employees; Manned Spaced Center
Manned Space Center, 112, 113, 127; administrative policies, 110, 113, 114, 116, 119, 120-36 passim, 141-43; professionals responsibilities of, 112, 115, 116, 117, 118, 123, 124, 126, 130, 131, 138, 139; program manager, 121-31 passim, 138, 139, 141, 142; program planning, 118, 136, 137, 138, 140, 141; staffing of, 113, 114, 117, 118, 139-41. *See also* Apollo Spacecraft Program; Lunar Receiving Laboratory
Manned Space Science Coordinating Committee, 131
Mansfield Amendment, 12, 29
Marshall Space Flight Center (MSFC), 110
Massachusetts Institute of Technology, 262
Master of Public Administration, a need for, 60

INDEX

Master of Science in Management, a need for, 87
"Material culture," 238, 239, 240, 241, 253
Maximum Feasible Misunderstanding (Moynihan), 267
Medical research, 18, 26, 206, 248; biomedical, 181, 189, 190
Mental Health Administration, 7
Merchant Marine and Fisheries Committee (House), 9
Mercury Spacecraft Program, 115, 120
Military research. *See* Defense, Department of
Mines, Bureau of, 28
Mondale, Walter, 247
Moon programs. *See* Space Research
Moon rocks. *See* Lunar Receiving Laboratory
MSC. *See* Manned Space Center
MSFC. *See* Marshall Space Flight Center

NACA. *See* National Advisory Committee for Aeronautics
Nader, Ralph, 244
NASA. *See* National Aeronautics and Space Administration
NASA Summer Conference on Lunar Exploration and Science, 131
National Academies of Science and Engineering, 247
National Academy of Engineering, 7, 19
National Academy of Public Administration, 59
National Academy of Sciences, 2, 7, 19, 127, 229; Drug Research Board of, 248; funding for, 16, 17; and Killian report, 82, 95, 96
National Advisory Committee for Aeronautics (NACA), 110, 113
National Aeronautics and Space Administration (NASA), 7, 9, 12, 20, 28, 29, 109, 119, 125, 127, 130, 132, 133; managerial structure, 113, 117, 118; staffing of, 87, 110, 112, 113, 114, 116, 117. *See also* Manned Space Center
National Aeronautics Space Council, 6
National Bureau of Standards, 2, 7, 9; committees of, 212, 220; management programs of, 88, 220
National Center for Atmospheric Research (NCAR), 29, 30
National Council on Marine Resources and Engineering Development, 6
National Defense Education Act of 1958, 4

National Education Association, 232
National Foundation for Administrative Development, 59
National Goals Research Staff, 247
National Institutes of Health, 7, 12, 20, 22; laboratories of, 234, 235; programs of, 9, 11, 87
National Register of Scientific and Technical Personnel, 66
National Research Centers, 23
National Research Council, 2, 7, 19
National Science Board, 4, 191, 233, 246
National Science Foundation, 3, 4, 7, 9, 20, 21, 22, 96, 187, 231, 232; funding for, 15, 17; organizations under, 6, 29; programs, 29; statistics, 66
National Science Foundation Act, and 1968 amendments, 4
National Science Priorities Act, 4
National Sea Grant College and Program Act of 1966, 4
Naval Weapons Center, 87
Navey, Department of the, 2, 7, 28, 110, 113
NBS. *See* National Bureau of Standards
NCAR. *See* National Center for Atmospheric Research
New York Academy of Sciences, 228
NIH. *See* National Institutes of Health
"NIH Training Grants: Going, Going, Gone?" 20
Nixon, Richard Milhous, 6, 237, 247; Message on Science and Technology, 4, 24-25, 26
Nonprofit organizations and R & D programs, 29-30, 190, 235. *See also* Universities, R & D research in
NSF. *See* National Science Foundation

Obsolescence, 39, 242
OECD. *See* Organization for Economic Cooperation and Development
OEO. *See* Economic Opportunity, Office of
Office of. *See* other part of title
Oganovic, Nicholas J., 13
Open control, 170, 172, 173, 174
Oppenheimer, Robert, 12, 228
Organizational Revolution, The (Boulding), 260
Organization for Economic Cooperation and Development, 26
Organization structures, 43, 74, 204; dual ladder, 78-82 passim; at Manned Space Center, 121, 123, 125, 126, 128, 129, 130, 138, 139; pyramid policy, 74, 76, 77

Orlans, Harold, 18, 254, 263
OST. *See* Science and Technology, Office of
Patent Office, 88
"Peer Review System: How to Hand Out Money Fairly," 20
Performance levels in R & D programs, 143-48; data on, 144, 147; lateral coordination, 148, 156, 159; tensions, 144-48; under System 4, 151, 154
PERT. *See* Program Evaluation and Review Technique
"Peter Pan rig," 135
Planning, Programming, and Budgeting System (PPBS), 178, 179, 270
Policy decisions, 5, 33, 34, 39, 40, 42, 43; and the public, 39, 44, 45, 174-76, 183, 190, 222; on R & D programs, 18, 20, 187, 188, 189, 190, 192, 195, 196, 223, 236
Political pressures, and R & D programs, 10, 11, 12, 15, 206, 235, 243, 247, 248, 249, 250
Pollution control, 174, 175, 182, 184, 243
Poverty, and social R & D programs, 174, 175, 194, 195
Powell, John Wesley, 21
PPBS. *See* Planning, Programming, and Budgeting System
Presidential Message on Science and Technology, 4-5, 24-25, 26
President's Advisor in Science, 5, 21
President's Panel on Social Indicators, 198
President's Science Advisory Council (PSAC), 5, 6
President's Scientific Advisory Committee, 220, 232, 246
Price, Derek, 185
Price, Don K., 267
Program Evaluation and Review Technique (PERT), 169, 209
Program for Advanced Study in Public Science Policy and Administration, 13, 25, 28, 92
Program/functional organization, 121-23
Project managers in R & D programs, 148; and organizational objectives, 150, 156, 158; and personnel, 149, 150
Project Mercury, 115, 120
"Project Mohole," 9
PSAC. *See* President's Science Advisory Council
Public Health Service, 127
Public needs, 12, 13, 24, 32, 35, 180, 182, 184, 186; administrators for, 32, 33, 34, 36; changes in, 174, 175. *See also* "Material culture"

Public science. *See* Public needs; Social sciences and technoscience; Space research; R & D peace programs
Public understanding of science, 18, 22-27 passim, 30
Purdue University, 70
Pyramid advancement policy, 74, 76, 77

RAND Corporation, 29, 236
R & D peace programs, 3, 4, 24, 30, 31, 181-86 passim, 194, 195
Recruiting. *See* Administrators, recruiting of
Regional Advisory Committee on Public Science Policy and Administration, 28
Reorganization Plan 2 of 1962, 5
Report to the President, July 1945, 3
Research applied to national needs, 17, 26, 29
Researchers, 201, 202, 209, 210, 223-26. *See also* Engineers; Scientists
"Research Fund Losses Decried by Scientists," 16
Risen, Isadore, study by, 67, 68, 69, 81
Roosevelt, Franklin D., 3
Rosenthal, Albert H., 91

Sandia Laboratories, 8, 13, 29, 92, 93, 95
Savio, Mario, 231
Science (magazine), 20, 21, 262
Science and Applications director (NASA), 134
Science and Technology, Office of, 5, 6, 9, 21, 178, 180, 231, 245, 246, 252
Science Committee (House), 9
Science, Department of, proposed, 21, 188
Science Information Service, 4
Science, the Endless Frontier (Bush), 24
Scientific Research and Development, Office of, 3
Scientist and Citizen (magazine), 63
Scientists, 50, 51, 52, 72, 116, 125, 252; as administrators, 12, 13, 45, 59, 66, 73, 74, 77, 78; classification of, 96; funding for, 11, 30; grants for, 4, 20, 27, 87, 190, 191, 230; as politicians, 10, 11, 12,; and professional advancement, 81, 82, 84, 85, 86, 87, 88, 89, 95, 97-98; studies on, 91-95, 144-48. *See also* Researchers
Seaborg report, 233, 234
Sears Roebuck catalog test, 241
Secretary of Commerce, 212; Assistant Secretary for Science and Technology, 220
Secretary of Defense Office, statement on managers, 89

INDEX

Seidman, Harold, 192
Senate Commerce Committee, 8-9
Senate, Committees of, 8, 9, See also Congress
"The Sickness of Government," 268
Sloan-Kettering Institute, 235-36
Smithsonian Institution, 7, 11
Social organizations: changes in, 254-57; controls for, 264-72; role of administrator in, 271-72; Structures of, 259-65
Social R & D programs, 3, 174, 175, 184, 186, 190, 194-99 passim
Social sciences and technoscience, 254-72. See also Social organizations
Social system: changes sought in, 174, 175, 176, 242, 243, 244, 245, 250, 252; defined, 162; diversity in, 38, 39; forces of, 164; and public policies of, 174-76, 183
Sociotechnical systems: boundaries, 164, 165; components of, 58, 164, 165, 166; controls for, 160-76; goals of, 162, 163, 169, 170, 171, 205, 206; input and output, 166, 167; performance, 163, 164, 165, 170
Space research. See Apollo Spacecraft Program; Lunar Receiving Laboratory; Manned Space Center; National Aeronautics and Space Administration
Space Sciences Laboratory, 66
Space Task Group, 114, 115
Space vehicles, 115 181, 182, 232. See also Apollo Spacecraft Program; Manned Space Center
Special-interest groups and R & D programs, 2, 18, 19, 182, 244, 245, 248, 250
Spilhaus, Athelstan, 240
Sport Fisheries and Wildlife, Bureau of, 28
Sputnik (USSR), 115, 232
Squibb, Beechnut drug firm, 248
Staats, Elmer, 17, 255, 263
Standard of living, 241, 242. See also Social system
Stanford Research Institute, 236
State government and R & D programs, 1, 2, 5, 8, 23, 27
Statistical quality control, 171
Stockberger, Dr. W. W., 78
Student protests, 230, 231, 234, 236, 254, 266
Subcommittee on Intergovernmental Relations (House), 9
Subcommittee on Research and Technical Programs (House), 9
Subcommittee on Science, Research and Development (House), 4, 9, 22

Supervisors. See Technical staff in R & D programs
Supervisory Scientists and Engineers course, 85
Syracuse University, 25

Technical staff in R & D programs, 69, 70, 71, 72, 73, 74, 201, 202; advancement and, 70, 83, 84. See also Training programs
Technology Assessment Board, 247
Technology, assessment of, 193, 194, 228, 237, 238, 242, 243-49, 250, 259; changes in, 240, 241; controls and, 243, 244, 245, 246, 247, 248, 252. See also "Material culture"
Technoscience, 254-72; emerging directions and, 258, 260, 263, 267, 270; policy problems and, 264-72 passim; unrest and, 254-59. See also Social organizations
Teller, Edward, 240
Tensions, creative, 144-48; conflicts, 145, 202, 203; independence, 144; interaction, 144; multiple assignments, 147
Training programs, 45, 54, 55, 56, 59, 89-91, 97, 98
Transportation, Department of, 7

United States-Japan joint research program, 181
Universities: grants to, 20, 190, 191; R & D research in, 17, 29, 228-37 passim, 266; studies on R & D personnel, 13, 25, 28, 45, 54, 55, 56, 59, 67, 68, 81, 91-95; and training administrators for R & D programs, 44-63 passim
University Corporation for Atmospheric Research (UCAR), 29
University of California, study on engineers, 77
University of Michigan, Institute for Social Research, 14, 149
University of New Mexico, studies initiated by, 13, 25, 28, 67, 68, 69, 81
University of Southern California, 87
Urban problems, funding, 16
USSR and research 115, 181, 231, 232

Vietnam War, 197, 229, 236

Wade, Nicholas, 20
Waldo, Dwight, 24, 30
Weapons, thermonuclear, 181, 239, 242, 243
Weather Bureau, 2, 9
Webb, James, 12

Weber, Max, 260
Weinberg, Alvin, 184, 228
Weltanschauung, 167, 168, 169
Western Electric Company, 92
White Sands Missile Range, 92
Wooldridge committee report, 234-35
World Almanac, 241
Worldview, and sociotechnical systems, 167, 168, 174, 202, 203

World War I, 2
World War II, 2, 3, 11; R & D developments after, 18, 29, 269

Youth and technoscience, 256, 258, 259, 261, 262, 263, 268. *See also* Student protests